Georg Alfred Müller, Alexander Glass

Diseases of the dog and their treatment

Vol. 1

Georg Alfred Müller, Alexander Glass

Diseases of the dog and their treatment
Vol. 1

ISBN/EAN: 9783337814885

Printed in Europe, USA, Canada, Australia, Japan

Cover: Foto ©ninafisch / pixelio.de

More available books at **www.hansebooks.com**

DISEASES OF THE DOG

AND THEIR TREATMENT

BY

DR. GEORG MÜLLER

PROFESSOR

DIRECTOR OF THE CLINIC FOR SMALL ANIMALS AT THE VETERINARY HIGH SCHOOL AT DRESDEN

TRANSLATED, REVISED, AND AUGMENTED BY

ALEXANDER GLASS, A.M., V.S.

LECTURER ON CANINE PATHOLOGY AT THE UNIVERSITY OF PENNSYLVANIA

WITH NINETY-THREE ILLUSTRATIONS

PHILADELPHIA
W. HORACE HOSKINS
1897

NOTE.

WHILE lecturing on the diseases of the dog the writer recognized the fact that there was not in existence a work that could really be called a text-book for the student and the practitioner; there were then, and have been issued since, a number of "popular" works that endeavored to fill the dual rôle of text-book for the veterinarian and a "Dog Book" for the layman; these, as a rule, have been inadequate for the former and confusing to the latter. With the purpose of supplying this want the writer, several years ago, began to write a book on the subject, but two years ago read this work by Professor Müller, and instantly recognized its value as a text-book: every detail in the diseases of the dog being carefully considered, and the whole so admirably arranged that the student can readily find and study any subject in a clear and condensed form.

He secured from the author the right of translation, and has made it as exact as possible, perhaps in some parts too literal, but has done so in the endeavor to closely follow the original. He has also added, in the proper places, the results of his own observations, and also everything of value that has been added to veterinary science since the appearance of Dr. Müller's work, thus making a second and much enlarged edition.

The metric system, as in the German work, has been followed, with the hope that its use may be a slight aid to the general adoption of what may be the future international system of measurement.

ALEXANDER GLASS.

PHILADELPHIA, April 11, 1897.

PREFACE.

In writing these pages the author has endeavored to give a short, accurate, and clear definition of the modern knowledge of diseases of the dog, and to adapt his treatise to the requirements of the profession.

Speculations and hypotheses have been studiously avoided, while, on the other hand, plain facts have received careful consideration.

Diagnosis has been given the most prominent place, as it deserves in a work of this kind, and the author has endeavored to establish the symptoms with their relation to the disease and to confine their therapeutic treatment to a knowledge of normal and pathological anatomy and physiology, for he believes that it is on a clear and accurate knowledge of the normal and pathological structure of life the fundamental base of all clinical science lies.

The writer has also included some selected formulæ which he considers of practical value to the reader.

Due consideration has been given to modern literature whenever it appeared consistent, and a glance at the contents will also show that the author has added the results of his own researches and observations. These have been derived from his experience as director of the clinic of small animals in this locality.

His space has been somewhat restricted, and he has had to dispense with the details of the bibliography of our literature, but this is not of much consequence when we have such works as Friedberger and Fröhner's, Hoffmann's, Vogel's, and others at our disposal.

The illustrations in this work are nearly all original. Some, however, have been obtained from other works, principally from Ellenberg and Baum's *Anatomy of the Dog*, edited by Paul Parey, and the author expresses his thanks for their use.

The author would feel gratified if his work be favorably received by those who are interested in the diseases of the dog.

G. MÜLLER.

DRESDEN, October, 1891.

CONTENTS.

	PAGE
General examination	17
the physical condition	17
the skeleton	18
the constitution	19
the mucous membranes and the skin	19
œdema	22
emphysema	22
the temperature	23
increased temperature	23
subnormal temperature	25
local temperature	26
Diseases of the digestive apparatus	27
the examination of the digestive apparatus	27
the condition of the throat and mouth	27
examination of the œsophagus	30
examination of the stomach	31
digestion of the stomach on a meat-diet	34
physical examination of the bowels and peritoneum	37
the feces	38
physical examination of the liver	41
examination of the spleen	42
diseases of the mouth, tongue, and salivary glands	43
inflammation of the mucous membrane of the mouth	43
aphtha	43
parenchymatous inflammation of the tongue	43
ulcerous inflammation of the mouth	44
diseases of the teeth	45
dentition	47
malformations of the cavity of the mouth	47
ranula	48
inflammation of the salivary glands	49
parotitis	49
idiopathic parotitis	49
abscess of the glands	49
inflammation of the mucous membranes of the throat	51

Diseases of the digestive apparatus—*Continued.*

	PAGE
diseases of the œsophagus	53
foreign bodies in the œsophagus	53
œsophagitis	55
stenosis	55
diseases of the stomach	55
acute catarrh of the stomach	55
chronic catarrh of the stomach	57
ulceration of the stomach	58
diseases of the intestines	59
intestinal catarrh	59
toxic inflammation of the stomach and intestines	64
mycotic inflammation of the stomach and intestines	64
hemorrhoids	65
contraction or stenosis of the intestines.	66
chronic constipation	71
prolapsus of the rectum	71
imperforate anus	74
intestinal parasites	74
round worms	74
tapeworms	75
oxyuris vermicularis	81
dochmius	81
other parasites	82
diseases of the peritoneum	83
inflammation of the peritoneum	83
dropsy of the abdomen	86
diseases of the liver	91
catarrhal jaundice	91
hyperæmia of the liver	94
inflammation of the liver	95
acute parenchymatous inflammation of the liver	95
chronic interstitial hepatitis	95
abscess of the liver	96
fatty liver	97
neoformations of the liver and gallstones	97
amyloid liver	97
lardaceous liver	97
poisons	98

Diseases of the respiratory organs 101

the physical examination of the respiratory apparatus	101
examination of the nose	101
physical examination of the larynx and windpipe	102
physical examination of the lungs	103
shape of the cavity of the chest.	106

Diseases of the respiratory organs—*Continued.*

	PAGE
number and character of the respiratory movements	106
percussion of the thorax	109
auscultation of the thorax	110
diseases of the nose	113
nasal catarrh	113
pentastoma tænioides	114
diseases of the larynx	116
acute laryngeal catarrh	116
chronic laryngeal catarrh	118
diseases of the upper air-passages and bronchia	120
catarrh of the windpipe and bronchia	120
acute catarrh of the windpipe and bronchia	120
chronic catarrh of the windpipe and bronchia	121
acute catarrh of the bronchia	121
chronic bronchial catarrh	122
diseases of the lungs	124
catarrhal inflammation of the lungs	124
chronic interstitial inflammation of the lungs	126
chronic induration of the lungs	126
œdema of the lungs	127
croupal inflammation of the lungs	129
anthracosis of the lungs	129
emphysema of the lungs	129
diseases of the pleura	130
pleuritis	130
hydrothorax	134
pneumothorax	135
hæmatothorax	136

Diseases of the circulatory apparatus

Diseases of the circulatory apparatus	137
examination of the circulatory apparatus	137
examination of the heart	137
size and position of the heart	138
character of the heart-pulsations	139
character of the heart-sounds and bruits	139
character of the pulse	141
diseases of the heart	142
valvular defects	142
idiopathic hypertrophy of the heart	146
diseases of the pericardium	147
pericarditis	147
dropsy of the pericardium	148
hemorrhage of the pericardium	148
filaria in the heart	148

	PAGE
Diseases of the urinary and sexual apparatus . . .	152
examination of the urinary apparatus	152
examination of the prepuce and urethra . . .	152
examination of the prostate	154
examination of the bladder	155
examination of the urine	156
amount of urine.	156
color of the urine	156
transparency of the urine	157
the specific gravity of the urine . . .	157
foreign substances in the urine . . .	158
diseases of the kidneys	162
inflammation of the kidneys	162
acute inflammation of the kidneys . . .	162
chronic inflammation of the kidneys . .	165
amyloid kidney	166
abscess of the kidneys	167
inflammation of the pelvis of the kidney .	169
cysts of the kidneys	169
nephritic stones	170
diseases of the bladder	170
catarrh of the bladder	170
debilitated conditions of the bladder . .	173
cystic cramp	175
stone in the bladder	176
urethrotomy	179
diseases of the prostate	181
inflammation of the prostate . . .	181
hypertrophy of the prostate . . .	182
cancer of the prostate	182
diseases of the penis and prepuce . . .	183
phimosis and paraphimosis	183
gonorrhœa	183
specific gonorrhœa	184
neoformations of the glands and prepuce .	184
diseases of the testicle and its coverings . .	184
inflammation of the testicle	184
injuries to the testicle and scrotum . .	184
cuterebro emasculator	185
diseases of the vagina and uterus . . .	185
inflammation of the vagina	185
prolapsus of the vagina	186
inflammation of the uterus	188
catarrhal metritis	188
septic metritis	189
obstetrics and castration in the bitch . .	191

CONTENTS. xi

	PAGE
Diseases of the nervous system	196
examination of the nervous system	196
disturbances of consciousness	196
disturbance of sensitiveness	196
disturbance of motility	197
diseases of the brain and its coverings	202
hyperæmia of the brain	202
anæmia of the brain	204
cerebral hemorrhage	204
inflammation of the brain	206
diseases of the spinal cord and its membranes	209
cerebro-spinal meningitis	209
inflammation of the spinal cord and its membranes	210
epilepsy	214
chorea	217
catalepsy	219
tetanus	219
eclampsia	220
Diseases of true infection	223
distemper	223
infectious bronchial catarrh	234
rabies	236
tuberculosis	249
anthrax	254
Constitutional diseases	255
anæmia	255
leukæmia	256
pseudo-leukæmia	257
diabetes mellitus	258
diabetes insipidus	259
obesity	261
hæmoglobinuria	263
uræmia	264
scurvy	265
Diseases of the bones and articulations	267
rhachitis	267
diseases of the joints	269
inflammation of the joints	269
acute synovial inflammation of the joints	271
chronic synovial inflammation of the joints	272
purulent inflammation of the joints	272
rheumatic inflammation of the joints	273
disease-producing malformation of the joints	274

CONTENTS.

Diseases of the bones and articulations—*Continued.*

	PAGE
injuries to the joints	277
wounds of the joints	277
contusions of the joints	279
distortions of the joints	280
luxation of the joints	280
dislocation of the lower jaw	282
dislocation of the elbow	283
dislocation of the patella	284
diseases of the bursa mucosa	286
muscular rheumatism	287
fractures of bones	290
amputation and exarticulation of bones	297

Wounds and their treatment 300
   wounds 300
   course and healing process in a wound 303
   diseases resulting from septic infection of wounds . . 305
   treatment of wounds 310
   ulcers and ulcerations 315
   contusions 316

Hernia 319
   description of hernia 319
   reducible hernia 320
   irreducible hernia 321
   inguinal hernia 326
   method of castration 326
   sarcocele 327
   hydrocele 328
   umbilical hernia 329
   femoral hernia 330
   perineal hernia 330

Tumors 332
   soft and hard fibroma 332
   lipoma 332
   enchondroma 332
   osteoma 333
   sarcoma 333
   angioma 334
   papilloma 334
      warts 334
      flat condyloma 335
   adenoma 335
      tumors of the anal glands 336
      goitre 337

CONTENTS. xiii

	PAGE
Tumors—*Continued.*	
cysts	340
dermatoid cysts	340
retention cysts	340
extravasation cysts	340
carcinoma	341
squamous cancer	341
cylindrical cell cancer	341
anæsthetics	345
Diseases of the eyes	349
affections of the eyelids	349
closure of the eyelids	349
entropion	349
ectropion	351
diseases of the conjunctiva	352
inflammation of the conjunctiva	352
catarrhal ophthalmia	353
purulent ophthalmia	354
diseases of the sclerotic coat of the eye	357
inflammation of the sclerotic coat	357
keratitis superficialis	358
keratitis profunda or parenchymatosa	358
abscess of the sclerotic membrane	359
ulceration of the sclerotic membrane	360
dermoid of the cornea	363
pterygium	363
injuries to the cornea	363
diseases of the lens, cataract	364
diseases of the sclerotic membrane, of the nervous portion of the eye, and of the vitreous humor	368
inflammation of the iris	369
purulent inflammation of the eye	369
dropsy of the anterior chamber (glaucoma)	370
diseases of the optic nerve and the retina	370
prolapsus of the eyeball	371
Diseases of the ear	374
serous cyst	374
external canker	376
internal canker (otitis)	377
parasitic canker of the ear	380
Diseases of the skin	383
inflammatory conditions of the cutaneous membrane	383
erythema	385

Diseases of the skin—*Continued.*

	PAGE
urticaria	386
eczema	386
burning and freezing	391
gangrene of the skin	392
acne	393
cutaneous diseases due to animal parasites	394
ceratopsyllus canis	395
hæmatopinus piliferus	396
trichodectes latus	396
ixodes ricinus	397
leptus autumnalis	397
sarcoptic mange	398
sarcoptes canis	398
demodex follicularum	401
filaria	403
cutaneous affections caused by vegetable parasites	404
favus	404
herpes tonsurans	405
atropic conditions of the cutaneous membranes	406
alopecia	406

ILLUSTRATIONS.

FIG.		PAGE
1.	Thermometer	23
2.	Temperature-chart	24
3.	Method of holding open the mouth	27
4.	Laryngoscope	28
5.	Mouth-gag	28
6.	Transverse section of the peritoneal cavity	31
7.	Diagram showing the position of the stomach when empty	32
8.	Diagram showing the position of the stomach when full	32
9.	Stomach-pump	33
10.	Contents of the stomach (four hours after eating)	34
11.	Rectal dilators	38
12.	Microscopical appearance of feces	40
13.	Right side, showing the position of the various organs	41
14.	Longitudinal section through a tooth and portion of the jaw	45
15.	Dental forceps	46
16.	Wire écraseur	48
17.	Salivary glands of the head and neck	50
18.	Clyster apparatus	63
19.	Method of stitching the intestine	70
20.	Stitch for prolapse of the rectum	73
21.	Ascarides	74
22.	Magnified section of the tænia cœnurus	76
23.	Tænia serrata	77
24.	Tænia marginata (natural size)	77
25.	Tænia cucumerina (natural size)	78
26.	Tænia cœnurus (natural size)	78
27.	Tænia echinococcus	79
28.	Oxyuris vermicularis (magnified and natural size)	81
29.	Dochmius duodenalis	82
30.	Section through the middle of the intestinal cavity	87
31.	Abdominal trocars	90
32.	Diagram showing the position of the organs on the right side of the body	104
33.	Diagram showing the position of the organs on the left side	105
34.	Pleximeter and percussion hammer	109
35.	Stethoscope	110
36.	Pentastoma tænioides	114

(xv)

FIG.		PAGE
37.	Pentastoma denticulatum	114
38.	Trocar for puncture of the chest	134
39.	Position of the heart	137
40.	Diagram of the circulation	143
41.	Heart containing filaria immitis	150
43.	Catheters for dog and bitch	152
42.	Method of passing the catheter in the dog	153
44.	Position of the bladder and urethra in the bitch	153
45.	Bladder, prostate, and urethra in the floor of the pelvis	154
46.	Urinometer	157
47.	Epithelium found in the urine	159
48.	Cylinders found in the urine	159
49.	Crystals and blood-corpuscles	160
50.	Bathing apparatus	164
51.	Crystals and blood-corpuscles found in the urine	172
52.	Method of irrigation of the bladder	174
53.	Vaginal speculum	186
54.	Diagram of the female genital organs	187
55.	Double catheter	189
56.	Extraction of the fetus by Defay's and Brulet's apparatus	192
57.	Diagram of the brain, showing the various motor centres	198
58.	White blood-corpuscles	259
59.	Spectrum of blood	264
60.	Hæmatin crystals	264
61.	Large hypodermatic syringe	277
62.	Muzzle	284
63.	Bath-tub	291
64.	Method of union in a fracture	294
65.	Plaster-cutting scissors and bone forceps	296
66.	Effects of tight bandaging	297
67.	Different forms of amputation	298
68.	Amputation of the tail	299
69.	Wound-irrigation apparatus	312
70.	Different stitches used in the closing of wounds	314
71.	Nose- and mouth-gag	316
72.	Diagram of the male genital organs	328
73.	Right side of the pelvis	329
74.	Wire écraseur	345
75.	Thermo-cautery (Paquelin)	346
76.	Methods of muzzling	347
77.	Inhalation-mask and apparatus	347
78.	Method for incisions in entropion	352
79.	Eye-cap	363
80.	Instruments used in the cataract operation	367
81.	Method of puncturing the lens	368
82.	Muscles of the eyeball	371

FIG.		PAGE
83.	Ear-cap	376
84.	Dilator for the ear	379
85.	Ear syringe	380
86.	Head of the dog-flea	397
87.	Hæmatopinus piliferus	398
88.	Trichodectes latus	398
89.	Ixodes ricinus	398
90.	Sarcoptes of the dog	399
91.	Acarus folliculorum	402
92.	Bath-tub	404
93.	Favus spores	405

DISEASES OF THE DOG.

GENERAL EXAMINATION.

The examination of the sick dog is divided into a general and special one. The former refers to symptoms which involve the whole organism, the latter considers the single organs of the body, the secretions, and the excretions. We proceed either by beginning at the head and moving gradually backward, or, if our attention is called by some specially striking symptoms, we may examine at once a certain part or organ or group of organs; this is chiefly in surgical diseases, in which we examine first the injured region and afterward direct our attention to the other parts of the body, or to the whole organism, or pass that altogether, according to the general condition of the animal.

In making a general examination the following points have to be observed: 1. The physical condition. 2. The constitution and nutritive condition. 3. The mucous membranes and the skin. 4. The temperature of the body and the extremities, and the pulse.

The physical condition presents more rapid and marked changes in the dog than in any other animal. Even in slight indispositions, such as disturbances of the stomach or digestive apparatus, the animal will be downcast, irritable, or nervous, and often show a disinclination to move, or may constantly change from one place to another. Nervousness, a staring look in the eye, great restlessness, constant barking or howling, point to beginning congestion of the brain; but these symptoms may be found in other diseases—for instance, in cases of pentastomes in the nose or the cavity of the forehead, or in cases of parasites in the intestines, or rabies. Howling is observed in a great many of the various painful diseases. A tendency to biting or destroying may lead to a suspicion of rabies; a hoarse, howling bark, a craving for indigestible objects (wood, coal, bits of cloth) or even gnawing or licking them, with a staggering gait, will change an existing suspicion to a certainty

Further, we have the uncontrollable movements which are caused by changes in the physical condition; they appear in diseases of the cerebellum, and in certain forms of poisoning—for instance, when cocaine is used. Dulness or total indifference to external influences, a staring expression of the eye, a slow, staggering gait, sleepiness or coma (entire unconsciousness) are recognized in the diverse diseases of the brain and its coverings, from injury or shock of the skull, in serious infectious diseases (distemper and septicæmia), also in poisoning by some narcotics, in uræmia, and during the acute period of many diseases. In some instances we see a short attack of unconsciousness, which occurs during great excitement or pain; we may also see an impaired condition of the senses as a secondary complication in diseases of the brain. For further information on this subject, see the article on Examination of the Nervous System. In making an examination of the physical condition we must always take into consideration the fact that symptoms may be very much modified by the presence of strangers or the veterinarian, so as to hide very serious symptoms from the professional man.

Very sick animals will not rise when called by a stranger, or even by the owner if the stranger is present; while a healthy animal will rise or bark or show its presence in various ways. The position of the animal when lying down is, to a certain extent, a diagnostic symptom. Dogs which are affected by lateral or one-sided diseases of the chest (for instance, lateral pneumonia, pleurisy) like to lie on the affected side, but they may also lie on the healthy side; while those cases where there is difficult or labored respiration, as in pleurisy and hydrothorax or double pneumonia, they take a sitting position or lie on the sternum with the legs under the body.

The development of the skeleton may be used as a basis for determining what sort of constitution the animal has; at the same time, taking into consideration the great differences there are in form between the different breeds of dogs, in the strength and shape of the bones, we can frequently obtain some diagnostic information concerning a defective constitution from the following indications of softness of the bones: there are flat, non-arched ribs, a narrow chest, a marked change in the shape of the skeleton, the swelling of the ends of the ribs at the union of the bone to the sternum, by a contortion of the long bones, and a swelling of the joints, as is seen in all rhachitic animals. In very rare instances there is a marked deformity of the spinal column, a lateral contraction of the column, an upper contraction (kyphosis), a side contraction (skoliosis), an upper and side contraction (kypho-skoliosis), and a downward contraction (lordosis).

The general condition of the constitution may depend to a large extent on the age of the animal, how he has been fed, and the amount of exercise he has had; but, as a general rule, if the animal's condition is poor, it is due to some disease being present. The skin is, to a certain extent, a diagnostic guide: if the animal is healthy, it will be loose and pulled easily from different parts of the body; whereas in disease it is tight; the skin loses its softness and smooth feel to the fingers; the eyes are depressed and sunken in their sockets. In very slight cases of emaciation we must depend to a certain extent on the history of the case from the owner. Weighing the animal is also useful to determine whether an animal is gaining or losing during the course of treatment; this is especially valuable where an animal is being reduced, as in cases of plethora, or in convalescence from acute disease the gain shows that the animal is improving, but at the same time the fact must not be lost sight of that we may have increase of weight from œdema or any dropsical condition. A rapid emaciation is seen in diseases of the digestive apparatus, in all acute and chronic feverish affections, in certain cases of poisoning, in rabies, and in that very rare disease in the dog—diabetes. A slight loss of flesh is seen in all internal diseases and following surgical operations.

In making a general examination the first thing to do is to examine the visible mucous membranes to see the color of them, the conjunctiva, and also the mouth and throat. It is best to examine more than one mucous membrane, as the examination of only one may lead to an error in the diagnosis, as the conjunctival tissue is often red and inflamed in some breeds of dogs. Abnormal paleness of the mucous membranes may be caused by a decrease in the amount of blood in the system, as in severe internal or external hemorrhage or in slight but frequent hemorrhages internally; it may be due to decrease in the amount of hæmoglobin in the blood-corpuscles in diseases peculiar to the blood, as in anæmia, chlorosis, leukæmia, pseudo-leukæmia; in all diseases producing great loss of fluids, especially of a chronic nature, such as diseases of the kidneys and bowels, and also slow pus-formations that are accompanied with or without fever; in defective heart-action, as in collapse, where the heart's action is, to a certain extent, paralyzed for the time, as in many acute diseases or violent poisoning from some depressing drugs; also in diseases of the heart and its covering (pericardium). A blue (cyanotic) coloring is sometimes seen in cases where there is defective oxygenation of the blood, and it is loaded with carbon dioxide. This is seen where the blood in the lungs does not come in contact with oxygen, as in some contraction of the trachea or larynx produced by an inflammation or swelling in the parts, foreign bodies, internal or external tumors pressing on the air-passages; also in acute bronchitis; in the various forms of pneumonia; in large pleuritic exudates; in hydrothorax; in severe ascites where the diaphragm is pressed on; in rigidity of the muscles, as in eclampsia in bitches; in strychnine-poisoning, and in some heart-affections; in cases of defective blood-circulation in the capillaries from disease of the heart, especially if there is fatty degeneration; from defective valvular action, from deposits on them, from pericardiac exudates, from the action of a poison acting directly on the heart, or from some injury or pressure on the jugular; in diseases where there is great accumulation of blood in the head, as in acute hyperæmia of the brain and inflammation of the brain; in the latter case the redness of the mucous membrane is lighter in color or more of an arterial tint. A yellow color (icteric) generally denotes some disorder of the liver, such as gastro-duodenal catarrh, causing a swelling and obstruction of the ductus choledochus; occasionally from calcareous deposits in the bile-ducts or the presence of tumors that press on the biliary ducts. This coloring may be due to a decomposition of the blood as a result of certain poisons in the system, such as phosphorus.

It is seen as a result of the effects of certain infectious diseases. The reddening of the mucous membrane may be due in some instances to phosphorus-poisoning (Müller), to true scurvy (Siedamgrotzky, Friedberger and Fröhner), and occasionally in cases of decayed meat poisoning (Müller).

The nasal and buccal discharges are treated fully under the head of Examination of the Digestive and Respiratory Apparatus. We will only consider here such discharges as are seen in very sick animals and are due to acute febrile disturbances. In some cases the pad of fat that fills the posterior part of the orbital cavity is very rapidly absorbed and the eye has a sunken look; the fever may produce an irritation of the mucous glands surrounding the eye and cause the accumulation of a profuse mucous discharge, varying in color from gray to grayish-yellow or yellow. This accumulates about the corners of the eyelids, or may even close and glue up the lids entirely. This is not a symptom of true conjunctivitis, but some acute disorder involving the entire system.

The skin presents a number of conditions which are diagnostic. Of course, there are a number of local diseases of the skin, the symptoms of which must be kept separate from those of a general febrile disturbance. The skin-changes in color are seen mainly on the belly and the inner fascia of the thigh; a reddened or slightly yellow color is to be classed under the same head as if it had been present on the mucous membranes. That is, if the skin is very red, it indicates a high temperature or the commencement of some sympathetic skin eruption; or if it is yellow, it indicates some disturbance of the liver or portal system. In cases of distemper we often see a pustulous rash on the abdomen and inner fascia of the thigh (the exanthema of distemper—dogpox); this is a very prominent diagnostic symptom of the disease. The skin of a very sick dog is dry and hard; it is very hot in cases of intense fever, and cold in animals that are very much debilitated, or after severe external or internal hemorrhage, or in collapse from shock. In fat dogs the skin has a very unpleasant, greasy feel to the touch. Profuse perspiration is rarely seen in dogs except where they may have been badly frightened.

The hair is also a useful guide in diagnosis. In sick, badly fed, or neglected animals, or if they are infested with parasites, it loses its gloss, becomes dry and brittle, breaking easily, and in some cases falls out partially or entirely. As a rule, in all dogs that have undergone a severe illness the hair falls out to a large extent; the odor of the skin is sometimes very offensive, especially in dogs suffering with distemper.

Œdema and emphysema of the skin are very important diagnostic points. By œdema or dropsy of the skin (anasarca) we understand it to be an abnormal accumulation of fluids in the skin and the subcutaneous cellular tissues. This condition is caused by the fluids not being reabsorbed in the same proportion that they come out of the bloodvessels. We recognize œdema by a swollen, bloated, cool condition of the skin, with the obliteration of all wrinkles; if the swelling is pressed with the finger, the indentation remains visible for some time ; this may come from a number of diseased conditions, and it is seen sometimes over the entire body, but chiefly in the lower portion of the body and extremities, testicles, prepuce, abdomen, and chest. It occurs as a complication in diseases of the heart, especially where there is imperfect valvular action, in acute disorders of the kidneys, and in the majority of prolonged acute affections. In rare instances it is caused by true diseases of the blood—anæmia, leukæmia, and pseudo-leukæmia.

The œdema which appears in the locality of an inflammation (collateral œdema) is of special interest to the surgeon, as it is often the only visible symptom of the inflammatory process that is going on under the skin. Œdema may be also seen as a result of the pressure caused by tight or improper bandaging.

Emphysema of the skin is where the skin looks as if there was air under it. As a rule, it is confined to small, circumscribed parts of the body, but it has been observed by the author where the whole body has been involved. There is an intense swelling of the parts, and on pressure with the finger the indentation, unlike œdema, immediately disappears. On rubbing over the parts with the hand a slight crackling sound can be heard ; on pressure the air can be driven from the affected portion into the other tissues beyond the border-line. This condition may be caused by the admission of atmospheric air from the outside into the subcutaneous tissues by means of small wounds in the skin, especially in the neck, wall of the chest, and head, or gas or air from some of the internal organs by a perforation of their walls, such as the larynx, trachea, œsophagus, the bowels, or stomach, in cases where there is perforating wounds of the chest, wounds of the larynx or windpipe, or from fractures of the ribs, with complicated injuries of the lungs. Emphysema may also occur from gas formed by breaking down of the contents of abscesses or hemorrhagic infiltrations.

Temperature. The temperature of the body in dogs is very uniform, being 38.5° Celsius. It may, however, vary from 38° to 39° C. As a rule, younger animals have a slightly higher temperature than older subjects.

The temperature is generally taken by means of what is known as the blood-thermometer (Fig. 1). The thermometer is introduced into the rectum as far up as possible. Hard, dry pieces of excrement or a high inflammatory condition of the bowel may prevent the thermometer giving the exact temperature of the body, and it should be allowed to remain at least four or five minutes, according to the sensitiveness of the instrument. The thermometer can also be introduced into the vagina of the bitch; and from a number of observations made by M. Tempel, of Dresden, the lower bowel-temperature is slightly lower than that of the vagina. It is better, as a rule, in severe cases to take the temperature at least twice daily—in the morning and the early evening (from three to five o'clock, when the temperature is highest in the day); or, if you wish to follow minutely the course of the temperature, it can be taken hourly. [The translator believes that this does more harm than the results gained, as the hourly insertion of the thermometer and the irritation of a very sick animal make it restless and afraid of the attendant.] The temperature should always be kept on a temperature-chart (Fig. 2), and can be watched with much more certainty than trusting to the memory. Any change in the temperature as indicated in the chart, either rise or fall, indicates some change in the animal's condition, and should be considered a symptom.

FIG. 1.

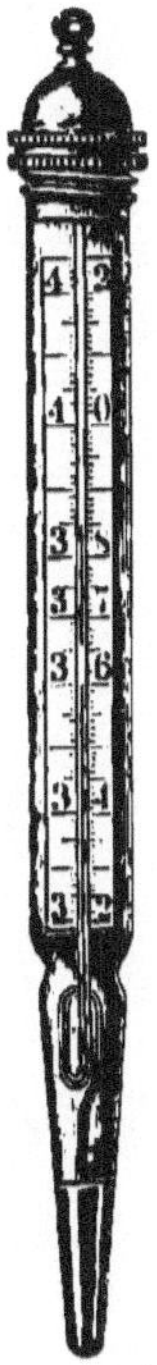

Thermometer.

INCREASED TEMPERATURE OF THE BODY. As soon as we detect an increase of the temperature of the body above the normal that we know is not due to overheating or too great exertion we define it under the name of fever.

The course and severity of a fever are regulated according to the amount and character of the fever-producing substances (pyrogenes) which have penetrated into the blood-circulation. In some cases we may have a rapid increase in the temperature (fever-paroxysm); this is often observed in the early stages of distemper. In other cases when the temperature changes very slightly it is called a constant fever, and if it does not change more than one degree (Celsius) it is known as a remittent fever; but when it is found that it varies greatly, vacillating between a very low normal and very high subnormal temperature, it is called an intermittent fever.

Fig. 2.

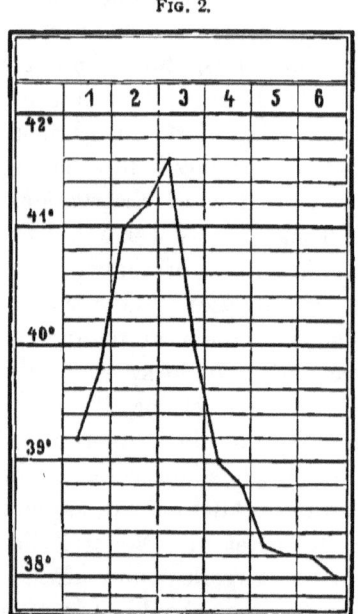

Fever chart, showing rise and fall of temperature.

A constant and prolonged high temperature is very rarely seen in the dog. The temperature, as a rule, in the early stages of all acute diseases rises very quickly, but it generally falls slowly as the disease advances, notwithstanding the complications, and may reach a normal or frequently a subnormal condition. In cases of septicæmia, which is rather a common disease in the dog, we may see an abrupt lowering of the temperature below the normal and continue so, the animal falling into a state of coma and death in a short time.

A fever, as a rule, begins with a chill or a number of them; this is a shivering or quivering of the muscles and skin and finally the entire body. These chills come on at intervals. The rise in the temperature is not always an accompaniment of fever, as has been shown in cases of septicæmia; we must, therefore, always take into consideration the other symptoms of fever. These are: increase in the number of the pulse and respirations; the digestion is immediately impaired and the urine is changed in quantity and composition. All the secretions and excretions are altered from the normal and the nerve-centres show increased irritability. The changes in the pulse and respiration are fully described under the head of Examination of the Circulatory Apparatus. The changes in digestion are seen in the entire loss of appetite, constipation, and increased thirst. The kidneys show the effects of the disturbance by a decrease in the amount of urine secreted, a much higher specific gravity, and a decreased amount of the chlorides in the urine, an increase in the amount of urates, and a high acid reaction. In the nursing-bitch the milk is much lessened in quantity, the skin becomes dry and firm, and the sebaceous glands almost cease secreting. The nerve-centres show the effect by the dulness of the animal and the indifference to surrounding objects or persons; great restlessness and twitching of the muscles. If the temperature is high, the animal becomes weak and falls away in weight very rapidly; the muscles become very tender to the touch and firm; in walking the movements are stiff, inelastic, and with an effort.

A TEMPERATURE BELOW NORMAL (SUBNORMAL) OF THE BODY. A subnormal temperature is often observed in cases where the crisis or highest temperature has passed and the animal is going on toward recovery or convalescence. In the majority of cases as the temperature goes down the pulse lessens, the respirations become even and regular, the appetite begins to return, and the animal shows more interest in its surroundings. In collapse there is a rapid fall of temperature, and the heart's action, as shown by the pulse, becomes weak and fluttering and soon imperceptible; the mucous membranes are pale, and the animal weak or even paralyzed. There is also a subnormal temperature in great hemorrhage, in icterus gravis (acute congestion of the liver, with yellowness of the mucous membranes and dark coloring of the mucous membranes), in all acute diseases of the brain, in various cases of poisoning, in cases of distemper, and in septicæmia.

INCREASE OR DECREASE OF LOCAL TEMPERATURE. Increased heat of a part is generally due to some injury or a surgical disease, and, as a rule, has with it tenderness to the touch and swelling. A local heat can also be felt in all inflammations that are not located too far from the surface of the body.

Coldness of any part indicates an impaired circulation in the part. In all cases of collapse the extremities are the first to become cold, as they are furthest from the heart. In cases of compression of an artery by ligatures, or tumors, or an embolus, or thrombus, the part of the body that is cut off becomes cold from impaired circulation. Paralyzed extremities are always slightly colder to the touch than active parts.

DISEASES OF THE DIGESTIVE APPARATUS.

EXAMINATION OF THE DIGESTIVE APPARATUS.

In making an examination of the digestive apparatus we have to consider, besides the loss of appetite, the following points:

The Condition of the Mouth and Throat. The examination

Fig. 3.

Holding the mouth open with tapes.

of these parts requires a good light, such as daylight, or a clear lamp. This can be accomplished by means of a perforated laryngeal mirror (Fig. 4) or any reflecting mirror.

28 DISEASES OF THE DIGESTIVE APPARATUS.

To obtain a good view of the interior of the mouth it is best to put two strings or tapes around both the lower and upper jaw; lay the dog on his side, or, what is better, directly on his back, and throw the light into the cavity of the mouth (page 27, Fig. 3). The tongue can be pressed down by means of a spatula or the handle of a spoon; the mouth and a large part of the throat can now be easily examined. If the mouth has to be kept open for some time, it is best to use the gag (Fig. 5), which can be placed between the teeth on one side, or by means of a piece of wood.

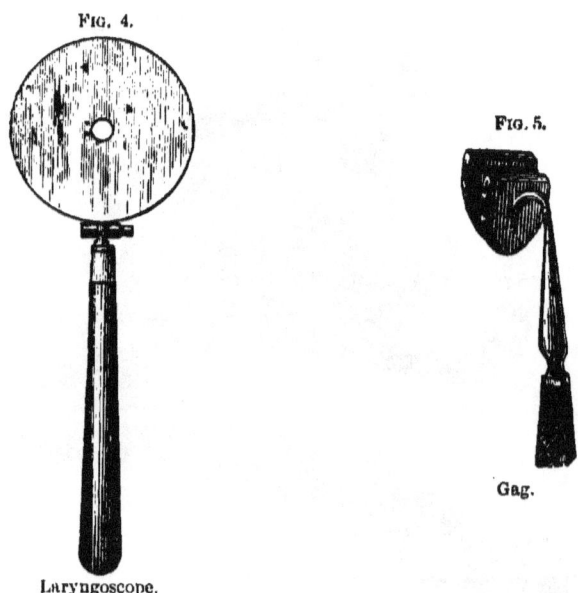

Fig. 4.
Laryngoscope.

Fig. 5.
Gag.

In cases where the mouth remains partially open, the animal being unable to close it, we must examine it carefully, as it may be a symptom of rabies; it may be due to some foreign bodies located between the teeth or to some strain of the articulation of the inferior maxillary. In paralysis of the jaw the mouth can be closed by putting a stick under the jaw and closing it; this cannot be done in cases of luxation of the articulation or where there is some foreign body between the teeth, such as bones or pieces of wood. The mouth cannot be opened in trismus (tetanus) or in inflammation of the articulation, in some cases of toothache, and in injuries to the various masticating muscles.

On opening the mouth there is often a very offensive odor from it. This indicates either an ulceration of the mouth due to ulcerative stomatitis, which has erroneously been called scurvy, or it is seen in any disease of the teeth, in dyspepsia, fetid bronchitis, or in gangrene of the lungs; it is frequently noticed in very sick animals where the mouth is filled with unhealthy mucus or particles of food in the mouth and throat. In cases of poisoning by phosphorus or prussic acid the odor of the drug is frequently detected in the breath. On examining the teeth and gums we may find large ossific deposits or caries of the alveolar process (dental alveolar periostitis), causing separation of the gums and loosening of the teeth. An intensely inflamed state of the gums, bleeding and ulcerated, indicates ulcerative stomatitis or mercurial poisoning; very often tumors (epulides) are found on the inner border of the incisors, and interfere more or less with eating. The cutting of the milk (temporary) teeth and the change of dentition (cutting of the permanent teeth) may cause intense inflammation of the entire mouth. The tongue is now examined; it may be drawn to one side, indicating paralysis, but must not be confounded with a normal "lolling" of the tongue so often seen in pugs and king charles spaniels. A slight enlargement of the tongue may be noticed in all inflammations of the mouth; it may show scars or wounds from an animal biting it while in a spasm. The tongue will be found to be enlarged in all fevers, in most cases dry; and where there is difficult respiration and large quantities of carbon dioxide in the blood this organ is dark blue in color (cyanotic). A slight white coating is seen on the posterior part of the tongue of the majority of healthy animals; if, however, it is very copious and covers the greater part of the organ, it indicates acute or chronic disease of the stomach; a brownish-red coating indicates some grave internal disease, such as an acute case of distemper.

The mucous membranes of the cheeks and inferior surface of the tongue after the administration of violent poisons are found to be gray in color, hanging in shreds, and intensely inflamed, and later on abscesses form on the sloughed parts. Elongated swellings, about the thickness of the finger, are often found on the inferior surface of the tongue, and run parallel with the frenum.

The salivary glands frequently form abscesses, and after inflammation become indurated. The secretion of saliva is sometimes greatly increased, and runs out of the mouth in long, thready strings; this is also seen in all inflammatory conditions of the mouth, or where there is an abscess located in the mouth or throat during teething, in cases of mercurial poisoning, and from the results of some poisons, and after the hypodermic injection of pilocarpine.

The secretion of saliva is lessened during all fevers, and from the effects of some poisons and after the injection of atropia.

The soft palate and pharynx are sometimes the seat of acute or chronic inflammations, and sometimes we find abscesses of these parts from the presence of foreign bodies (needles, splinters of bone or wood). It is well to feel these parts with the finger when making an examination. The tonsils are affected, as a rule, in all cases of pharyngitis. It generally protrudes from the side of the base of the tongue in a dark-red sausage-like formation.

Examination of the Œsophagus.

The œsophagus projects from the pharynx on a level with the first cervical vertebra. The anterior part of it lies between the windpipe and the longus colli in the median line of the neck. It extends from there to the left side of the windpipe and runs into the cavity of the chest behind that organ; from there it again goes to the dorsal surface of the windpipe and passes to the right side of the aortic arch between both membranes of the mediastinum, in the shape of a flat arch, and perforates the diaphragm and reaches the stomach. The width of the œsophagus is not regular in its entire length, being narrower at the region of the pharynx and the heart.

The œsophagus can be examined externally by the hand or internally by the pharyngeal sound or probang. Foreign bodies (pieces of bone, wood, large pieces of food) become lodged in the œsophagus generally just beyond the pharynx in the region of the neck, where they can be readily felt by the hand. The thyroid gland is sometimes enlarged, and care must be taken not to mistake this for a foreign body. Carcinomas or sarcomas are sometimes found along the course of the œsophagus.

Introduction of the Laryngeal Sound (Probang). The best sound is a large, flexible catheter (7 or 14, according to the size of the animal).

EXAMINATION OF THE DIGESTIVE APPARATUS.

The mouth is held open as described on page 28; the head is extended, and, having the sound well lubricated with oil, it is introduced along the upper wall of the throat, keeping it high up, so as to avoid the larynx. The animal will attempt to swallow it, but that will assist the passage of the sound. It will glide along easily until the obstruction is reached. (For further details, see Foreign Bodies in the Œsophagus.)

Examination of the Stomach.

Baum has made a thorough examination of the position of the dog's stomach. When the stomach is filled with food, the form of which can be easily recognized (Fig. 6), it lays in the left side

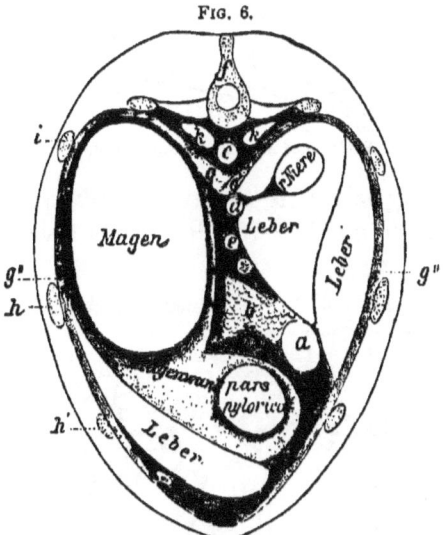

Section through the centre of the abdomen.

of the abdominal cavity, the inferior portion resting on the liver, and the anterior portion against the diaphragm, the left surface going toward the abdominal wall, but between that and the wall lies the left wing of the liver. This left lobe extends as far as the pelvis, coming close to the anterior edge of the left kidney; the larger part of the stomach is inclosed by the liver and the diaphragm coming in contact with the anterior side. The cardiac end of the stomach is directed toward the median line and the pyloric toward the right.

32   DISEASES OF THE DIGESTIVE APPARATUS.

The empty stomach extends anteriorly as far as the left pillar of the diaphragm and toward the chest, as far forward as the tenth

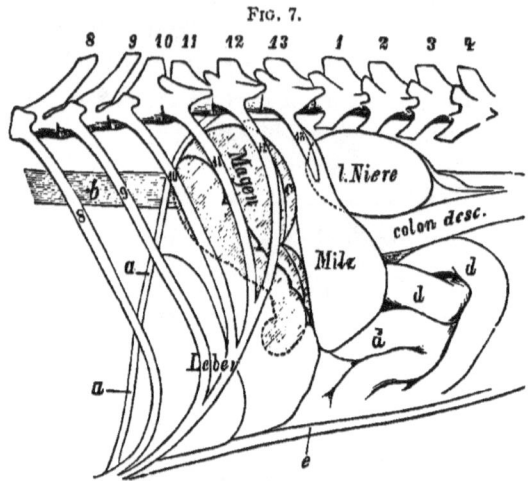

Position of stomach when empty.

rib, and posteriorly as far as the twelfth rib, and is completely covered by the liver on the left side. Only a very small part of

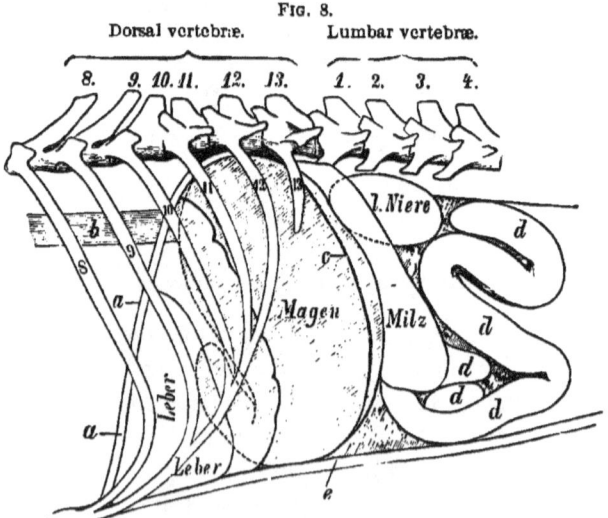

Position of stomach when full.

it comes in contact with the diaphragm. The pyloric opening is directed toward the right (Fig. 7). In a stomach that is very much distended with gas or food the organ comes almost directly in contact with the abdominal walls, and when greatly distended it extends as far as the umbilical region and lies against the ribs and left abdominal wall, the liver being pushed almost entirely away from the surface of the stomach (Fig. 8).

From the above anatomical details it can be readily seen that it is nearly impossible to make a reliable examination of the stomach when it is empty or even when it is fairly well distended. The cardiac and pyloric openings are so deep seated they are extremely hard to examine; it is impossible to make a manual examination from below, as the shovel-like end of the sternum prevents it; the only method of examination is by digital pressure, and that when the stomach is moderately filled by pressing on the left lobe of the liver, push it to one side, and by that means get pressure on the stomach. In cases of poisoning we may get evidences of pain; but it might be some disturbance of the liver, and is not a safe way to get a sure diagnosis. The examination of the contents of the stomach would be advisable in such a case.

We can obtain the contents of the stomach either by the substances which the animal may vomit itself or by means of the stomach-pump. This has been recommended by Frick, and only for therapeutic purposes (Fig. 9).

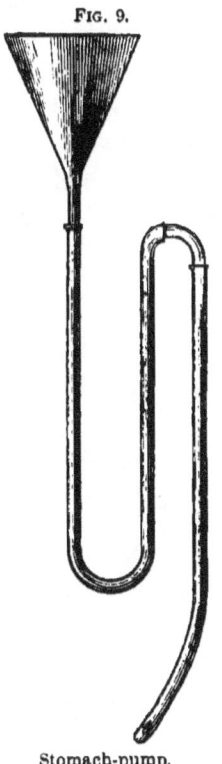

Fig. 9.

Stomach-pump.

The stomach-pump is operated in the following manner: In large dogs an ordinary male horse-catheter, and in small dogs a large male human catheter or a small rubber hose. We pass the catheter as was described in the examination of the œsophagus, and put a small funnel at the end of the tube. Pour a certain amount of water into the stomach through the tube, at the same time holding the tube high; then manipulate the region of the stomach and next depress the tube, and the siphon which has been formed will soon empty the stomach of its contents. This method is to be used in very urgent cases where poison is suspected; but, as a rule, is very hard to do except in very quiet animals and where there is a trained assistant, such as in a hospital; but in private practice the easier way is the best—that is, to administer an emetic. The best means is to give a dose of apomorphia hypodermatically.

  ℞.—Apomorphia hydrochlorate 0.04
  Aqua destil. 4.00
 S.—Ten to twenty drops hypodermatically.

In a few minutes free vomiting occurs and the contents of the stomach can then be examined. Of course, you must take into consideration the time which has elapsed since the animal had taken the food and the character of the alimentary matter. It would be well, therefore, that you know the following facts concerning (Fig. 10) the digestion of the dog's stomach:

Fig. 10.

Contents of the stomach (four hours after eating): Muscular fibre, starch-cells, fat-crystals and cells, round cells, epithelium, vegetable cells, fungus.

Digestion of the Stomach on a Meat-diet. After taking a full meal of meat cut in small pieces the digestion in the stomach is very active and free; it increases until the third hour and slowly decreases until the ninth, and is nearly over at the twelfth hour. After eating a very large meal the digestion is somewhat slower; the different kinds of meat also vary in the time of their digestion. Pork is the hardest to digest, and the others are classified in the following order: Mutton, veal, beef, and lastly the flesh of other animals (Astley Cooper). Skin, sinew, cartilage, and bones are very hard to digest; the latter are digested from their surface, and are reduced as the lime-salts are acted upon and dissolved. Fat meat is harder to digest than lean; fat undergoes no change in the stomach, but passes on and is digested in the intestines. It has never been satisfactorily settled whether raw or cooked meat is easiest to digest.

The Digestion of Milk in the Stomach. Milk is comparatively slow in digestion.

Action of Digestion on Hydrocarbonaceous Food. Five hours after a meal consisting of rice and potatoes the mass was liquefied and softened; the mashed portion of the potatoes had disappeared, but the lumps remained. After a meal of rice the following observations were made: After one hour 10 per cent. was digested; after two hours, 25 per cent.; after three hours, 50 per cent.; after four hours, 82 per cent.; after six hours, 90 per cent.; after eight hours, 99 per cent.; and at the end of ten hours it had entirely disappeared (V. Hofmeister). Both Ellenberger and Hofmeister have come to the conclusion that rice is chiefly digested in the intestines, as there is so much muriatic (hydrochloric) acid in the stomach immediately after eating that saccharation cannot take place; and also that the dog swallows his food with so little mastication that the saliva has not time to make any change in the starch.

The Effect of the Disturbance of Gastric Secretion on Digestion. When from any cause the secretion of gastric juice is lessened or altered the following changes are observed: The digestion of albumin, the antiseptic and antizymotic action of the gastric juice is much lessened, caused by the secretion being much less acid, and with the lessened digestion of albumin fermentation is easily started. When the gastric secretion is subacid it irritates the mucous membranes and lessens the peristaltic action. Subacidity is frequently seen in all anæmic diseases, in fevers, in erosion of the mucous membranes, from the effects of corrosive poisons in cancer of the stomach, and in chronic catarrh of that organ.

The digestion of starch is impaired by an over-secretion of muriatic acid; this condition, according to the researches of Ellenberger and Hofmeister, is not of great importance, although in man it is frequently seen in ulceration and in acute and chronic catarrh of the stomach. "Nervous dyspepsia," so common in man, does not seem to occur in the dog.

In testing the contents of the stomach for free hydrochloric acid the best reagent is tropæolin paper and phloroglucin-vanillin solution. Moisten a small piece of this paper with a few drops of the filtered fluid-contents of the stomach, and it is then placed in a watch-glass and slowly heated; if muriatic acid is present, it will turn lilac; if the acid is in large quantities, the paper will color without heating. In testing with phloroglucin (vanillin) place a few drops of the following solution: Phloroglucin, 3 parts; vanillin, 1 part; alcohol, 30 parts, with an equal quantity of the filtered fluid of the stomach. If there is free hydrochloric acid present, it will produce a dark red precipitate; if it is present in small amount, the precipitate will be bright red; if the acid is not present, the precipitate will be brown or reddish-brown. Unfortunately this test is not reliable with either of the above reagents if albumin or phosphates are present in any quantity.

Testing for lactic acid is much easier and certain. The best method is that of Uffelman: 100 grammes of a 2 per cent. solution of carbolic acid are to be mixed with one drop of chloride of iron solution, which makes the mixture deep blue; if a few drops of the filtered contents of the stomach are added and muriatic acid only is present, it becomes clear as water; if lactic acid is also present, it becomes greenish-yellow in color.

In summing up the preceding investigations it is readily seen that the stomach may not be digesting all that the animal eats, but still the animal be in fairly good health; while, of course, it must be also understood that in fevers or any general disturbance the digestive powers are greatly impaired.

Albumin is almost entirely digested in the intestines, the stomach merely preparing it; fat and starch are digested only in the small intestines; muscular tissue must have a previous preparation in the stomach, or if it reaches the small intestines without becoming saturated with gastric juice it is not digested in the intestines. No digestion whatever takes place in the large intestines.

No animal vomits easier than the dog, and it may be produced from a number of causes, as a reflex irritation of the stomach, viz.:

1. By irritation of the mucous membranes of that organ by emetics, poisons, splinters of bone, or even by overloading. Vomiting frequently is caused by the animal eating grass.

2. By sympathetic irritation from other organs, nephritis,

uræmia, peritonitis, irritation of the intestines, or uterine inflammations.

3. Serious coughing spells will cause it, from laryngitis, bronchitis, or liquids getting into the larynx.

4. In obstruction of the bowels (foreign bodies blocking up the bowel, hernia or twisting of the intestines) excrement is vomited up.

5. Beginning of distemper.

6. From various brain-affections (meningitis, commotio cerebri).

Very often in certain diseases of the pharynx movements of the throat resembling vomiting are frequently noticed.

The vomited matter of an empty stomach in acute or chronic catarrh is a thin, watery mucus; in chronic catarrh, however, the matter is slimy and thick. Coming from an empty stomach it is always slightly green in color, indicating the presence of bile. In cases of repeated vomiting pure greenish bile may be thrown out. Sometimes the vomited matter is tinged with blood, or the blood may be in clots, due to a laceration of the mucous membranes of the stomach, from the swallowing of sharp objects, such as bones, pieces of wood, or the presence of an abscess in the stomach. There may, however, be a hemorrhage of blood that may come from the mouth or the throat. Sometimes an abscess may form in the region of the œsophagus and break into it, and from the vomiting of blood looks as if it was from the stomach.

The vomited matter is generally acid in reaction, and if there is much acid present the smell is sour and penetrating; very offensive when excrement is vomited and putrid when the animal has eaten decayed meat, or a carcinoma or an abscess is present. In cases of poisoning the matter may correspond in odor with the poison itself, as phosphorus, carbolic acid, or hydrocyanic acid.

Physical Examination of the Bowels and Peritoneum.

In making an examination of the abdomen it is best to make the animal stand if possible, and by the pressure in the abdomen we can tell if there is any tenderness present, which will be evinced by the animal trying to escape, or by groans, or even attempting to bite. There is intense pain on pressure in peritonitis or carcinoma of the peritoneum. In enteritis the pain is very severe, especially from the effects of some poisons; also in constipation. In chronic catarrh of the bowels the pain is not very severe on pressure. In twisting of the bowel, foreign bodies, and the presence of tumors, abnormal growths on the intestines or the abdominal walls can be detected either by pain on pressure or also by manipulation of the hand.

The circumference of the abdomen is increased by accumulations of gas in the intestines in fat animals and in bitches in whelp; it is also observed in chronic catarrh of the intestines and all peritoneal inflammations, or, in rare instances, where air has escaped from the intestines or stomach by perforation of abscesses, accumulations of fluids, as in exudative peritonitis or ascites, or by bursting of the bladder, or where the bladder is abnormally distended.

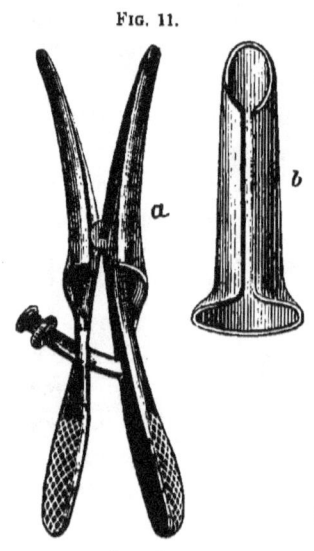

Fig. 11.

Speculums.

The circumference of the abdomen is lessened where the animal has been starved, or in obstinate diarrhœa or dysentery.

The lower bowels can be examined per rectum by means of the finger. This method of examination is used to determine any diseased condition of the bowel and to see the character of the feces or to examine the neighboring organs—prostate gland, vagina, uterus, or the floor of the pelvis. To make this examination the author frequently uses a mirror in conjunction with the apparatus illustrated in Fig. 11. The bowel is first emptied by means of enemas or a glycerin suppository; the apparatus is introduced into the rectum, and then the mirror can be used to throw the light into the cavity. Inflammation of the rectum from any cause, such as hemorrhoids, fistulæ, foreign bodies, or abscesses, can be readily examined by this means.

The Feces. The number of times that an animal has an evacuation of the bowels depends on two circumstances: the character of the food or the rapidity with which it passes through the bowels. Normally an animal has two or three passages daily, some even less. Diarrhœa is a catarrh of the intestines, and may be due to a variety of causes, such as irregular diet, cold, or to some infectious disease (distemper), some irritant in the food; but it may also be caused by laxative agents independent of catarrh.

Costiveness. Constipation is common in all old dogs and in starved animals; it is also frequently seen in animals that vomit their food and in all peritoneal inflammations.

Complete constipation is seen in all cases of obstruction of the bowels due to twisting of those organs, invagination, hernia, foreign bodies, loss of the vermicular motions, and in all copious exudations from the peritoneum.

Pain during evacuation of the bowels (tenesmus) is seen in inflammation or obstruction of the lower bowels or from the presence of an abscess, from enlargement of the prostate, from splinters of bone or wood in the lower bowel, or from enlargement of the rectal lymphatic glands.

The amount of excrement passed in a given time by an animal depends on the quantity and quality of the food that the animal has taken. In an ordinary sized dog fed on bread the amount of feces passed amounts to 20 per cent. of the amount taken; but if the same animal is put on a flesh-diet the amount of feces is only about 5 per cent. (Ellenberger). In diarrhœa the relative amount is changed; for in this condition the intestinal juices secreted to aid digestion are not reabsorbed, but remain with the feces and are thrown out.

After an obstinate constipation the amount of fluids is also greatly increased, and with it there is also a very offensive smell, due to decomposition of the feces and to the various excrementary matter that has remained in the bowels.

The shape and size of the stools are a rather important matter to consider. In normal health they are cylindrical in form, hard or soft, according to the diet; on meat-diet they are black, on meat and fat mixed they are dark gray-brown, and on bread-and-milk diet they are yellow-brown or almost clay-color. If the animal has eaten much bones, they are whitish. The alimentary matter cannot be distinguished with the naked eye, except bread, which is passed almost as it is taken into the stomach. Of course, there are bodies, such as wood, bony matter, hair, earth, etc., which can also be seen in the feces. Under the microscope

(Fig. 12) we can see numerous particles of food that have passed without digestion in animals that have good health. In impaired digestion we see pieces of muscle, connective tissue, etc., with the naked eye.

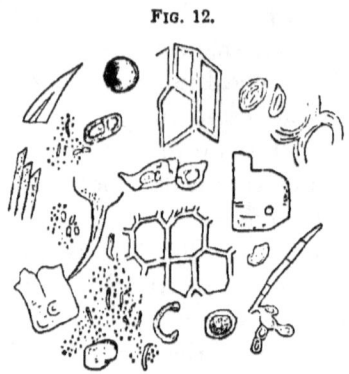

FIG. 12.

Microscopical examination of the feces. Vegetable matter, starch-cells, muscular fibres, epithelial cells, and fungoid growths.

The following deviations in the appearance of the feces may be observed:

1. Pieces of food (muscles and connective tissue) that are easily digested may be seen in the fecal matter. This points to a disordered stomach or may be the entire intestinal canal, as in fevers, catarrh of the lining membrane of the stomach, or from increased peristaltic action due to the effects of purgatives.

2. The feces being thin and light indicate obstinate diarrhœa; they may be yellow, greenish-yellow, or greenish-gray; all point to some disorder of the liver.

3. The presence of mucus, giving the feces a slimy appearance, indicates catarrh of the intestine. If the mucus is mixed with the feces in clot or lumps, it indicates an intense irritation of the intestinal mucous membrane. In this condition the feces are thin; where there are more or less hard fecal lumps mixed with clots of mucus, it is an indication that the large intestine is principally involved.

4. Where the feces are light gray-white or clay-like in color and have a dull gloss (due to the undigested fat they contain) on the outside, it indicates an obstruction of the secretion of bile. When this condition is noticed the mucous membranes, as a rule, are tinged with yellow.

5. Blood mixed in the feces occurs from a number of causes. If the feces are of normal size and firm, the hemorrhage comes from the large intestine; or if coated only on the outside with blood and mucus, it indicates the presence of bleeding hemorrhoids (piles). If the blood is in clots and mixed with the feces, it indicates a hemorrhage of the stomach or small intestines. The blood-clots may vary in color from light red to almost brown-black. As a rule, the further the blood comes the darker it is; if it came from the stomach it would be nearly black, but from the large intestine it is red in color.

6. Pus is sometimes seen in the stools, and indicates the presence of an abscess in the large intestine or perforating into it from some of the adjacent organs.

Physical Examination of the Liver.

It is very hard to make a careful manual examination of the liver, as there is only a small portion of the organ posterior to the ribs that can be reached, and then only in cases where the

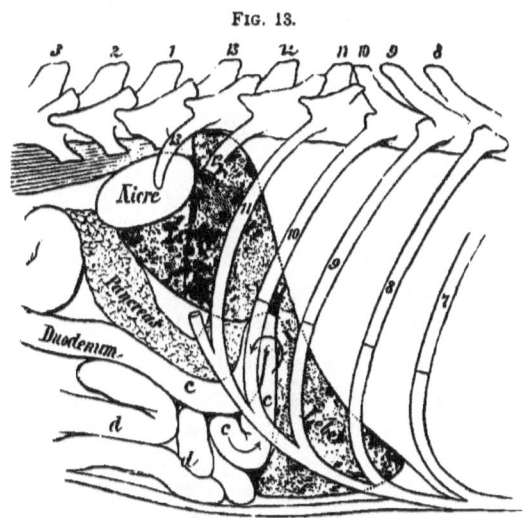

Fig. 13.

Right side of the abdomen, showing the position of the organs.

animal is thin. Fortunately the diseases of the liver in the dog are not numerous and can be detected by other symptoms than that of a direct examination of the gland. Fig. 13 gives a clear illustration of the position of the liver. We may find great tenderness on pressure, which is present in stagnation of bile in carcinoma and in the early stages of cirrhosis or atrophy. Enlargement or displacement of the liver may be seen when cancer, abscesses, or tumors are present; but in making a diagnosis we must take into consideration that the liver varies a great deal in different breeds, and even in individual dogs.

The Spleen.

The spleen of the dog is an organ that is very readily examined by manipulation, as shown in Fig. 8, although in well-fed animals that are fat it is sometimes hard to find. It is frequently enlarged and swollen; this is seen in the majority of infectious diseases, especially distemper. It is seen in leukæmia, or from the presence of tumors or carcinoma.

DISEASES OF THE MOUTH, THE TONGUE, AND SALIVARY GLANDS.

Inflammation of the Mucous Membrane of the Mouth.

(*Stomatitis.*)

ETIOLOGY. The most common cause of inflammation of the mucous membranes of the mouth is by chemical, mechanical, or thermic irritants. The most violent inflammations are caused by poisonous substances of a caustic nature. It may also be seen in all slow fevers and in inflammatory conditions of the surrounding organs, in diseased conditions of the throat, and during "teething" in young animals; mercurial stomatitis is also seen as a result of the absorption from the use of preparations containing the drug.

CLINICAL SYMPTOMS. The first symptom the animal will show will be the slow, careful way it eats; it will leave any large or hard piece of food untouched and swallow small pieces without mastication. The saliva is greatly increased in amount and runs out of the corners of the mouth in thin, glass-like threads or strings. On making an examination of the mouth all the mucous membranes will be found swollen, red, and inflamed; the gums are especially so during dentition; the tongue and soft palate are also inflamed; the tongue is also coated, as a rule. Ulcers sometimes appear in different parts of the mouth.

The duration of the disease depends largely on the causes producing it; as a rule, it is not of much importance and disappears without any medical interference. In some cases where it is caused by bad teeth it is more obstinate, and if it becomes chronic it is apt to become a case of stomacace.

THERAPEUTICS. The animal should be fed lightly, the principal diet being soup or liquid foods, and the mouth should be washed out with permanganate of potassium solution, composed of permanganate of potassium, 1 part; alum, 3 parts; chlorate of potassium, 5 parts, in 100 parts of water; or a solution of boric acid in honey, 1 to 30 parts. Inflamed gums can be rubbed with tincture of myrrh or tincture of catechu, or with a solution of tannin and glycerin, 1 to 20.

Hertwig describes under the name of **aphtha**, or buccal fungi, a diseased condition of the buccal membrane which is seen in young dogs. It commences by the formation of a number of small pustules on the lips, gums, and tongue, about the size and shape of a small pea. They burst in from twenty-four to forty-eight hours and leave a bare, ulcerated surface, which heals up very slowly, often taking from twelve to fourteen days to get well. It is best treated with any of the ordinary mouth-washes. The author has never observed this disease.

Serious parenchymatous inflammation of the tongue is frequently seen. It is generally caused by caustic substances, by wounds on the tongue, splinters of bone, and frequently children put threads, rubber bands, or horse-hair on the tip of the tongue. With the general swelling and inflammation of the part the tip of the tongue is reddish-blue in color, and the color seems to be confined to a certain circumscribed location.

Injuries of the tongue heal very rapidly. If there is much inflammation, it is best to paint the parts with any of the above-named tinctures.

Ulcerous Inflammation of the Mouth.
(*Stomacace.*)

ETIOLOGY. This is a serious inflammation of the mouth, and is generally seen in old, debilitated dogs and associated with the presence of decayed teeth. It is seen, however, in a small proportion of cases where the teeth are perfectly sound and where the animal seems to be in fairly good health.

CLINICAL SYMPTOMS. At first the gums are swollen and red in the neighborhood of certain teeth—generally the incisors and later on the molars. The gums are very red and painful to the touch, and bleed readily. After a few days the inflamed portion becomes green and dark purple on the dividing line with the other tissues. The hemorrhage from the parts is constant and deep abscesses form, involving the alveolar process. This gangrenous inflammation extends, and the teeth become very loose and fall out. In extreme cases the jaw becomes affected, and necrosis sets in and large portions of the jaw exfoliate. This condition may also involve the neighboring tissues; but, as a rule, the tongue is very rarely affected to any great extent. The odor of the mouth is very offensive; there is a bad-smelling, sticky mucus running from the corners of the mouth. Generally the appetite is fairly good, although it is very difficult for the animal to masticate or swallow; and bolting the food whole while affected with this disease has a tendency to upset the stomach.

A favorable termination of this disease is only to be expected in young, strong, healthy dogs, provided it has not become too far advanced. With proper treatment the ulcers clean up gradually, and after two weeks they are all healed up; but sometimes the fever keeps on increasing and the disease becomes septic in character from absorption of dead tissues, causing blood-poisoning and collapse, followed by death. The author has noticed a gangrenous tubular pneumonia from the aspiration of the purulent matter.

THERAPEUTICS. The animal must be fed liberally, but with easily digested food and as soft as possible. Remove all the diseased teeth as soon as you can; wash the mouth frequently with deodorizing mouth-washes, such as permanganate of potassium, 1 to 200. The purulent ulcerations are to be painted with tincture of catechu. Syringe the mouth with a solution of tannin and glycerin, 1 to 20. Chlorate of potassium, 1 to 25, may also be used with safety, as Fröhner has demonstrated that this drug is comparatively harmless in the dog.

Diseases of the Teeth.

Dogs are frequently subject to various dental disorders, such as accumulations of tartar, caries of the teeth, and, rarely, fistulæ of the gums.

We understand by tartar of the teeth a calcareous deposit on the neck of the tooth at the border of the gums. This tartarous substance is deposited chiefly around the canine or molar teeth, and, constantly accumulating, gradually pushes the gums back and often loosens the tooth, which, acting as a foreign body, causes great irritation.

The tartar can be removed by scraping it off with a small cup-shaped instrument or a sound with a leaf-shaped tongue. Some remove it with a hook-shaped pair of pincers. If there is a large amount of tartar, it is best to put the dog under ether, as it can be easier removed and avoid struggling on the part of the animal (see chapter on Removal of Tumors).

Caries of the Teeth. This condition has been observed by a number of authors (Möller, Hoffmann), but is of very rare occurrence.

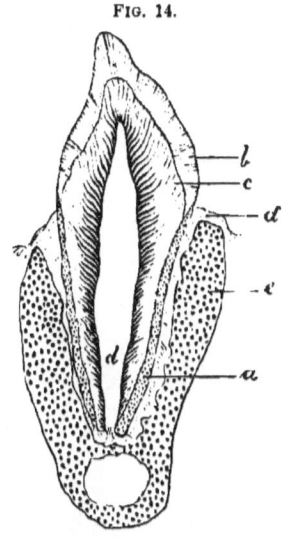

FIG. 14.

Longitudinal section through an incisor tooth: *a*, cement; *b*, enamel; *c*, ivory or dentine; *d*, pulp cavity and alveolar dental membrane; *e*, maxillary bone.

By caries dentum we define an active process of molecular destruction of the enamel and bone of the teeth. This process always begins on the upper surface and mainly in the cavity of the crown of the tooth, forming a grayish or blackish spot. This spot, which is the decaying part of the tooth, advances deeper into the tooth, going on toward the pulp. This penetrates into the tooth until it reaches the nerve, and thus exposing it to the atmosphere, inflames it and makes it very sensitive.

There are certain microbes found in calcareous teeth; but whether they are directly connected with the decay of the teeth is not definitely known. True dental caries is very rare in the dog. Necrosis of the teeth is frequently mistaken for caries. In old dogs we often see an acute inflammation of the periosteum, and the alveolar process becoming inflamed the tooth is lifted out of its socket and finally thrown out. In these cases the alveolar periosteum is destroyed, and the necrotic condition of the tooth causes it to become yellow; this is generally termed false caries of the teeth. Alveolar periostitis commences with the formation of an abscess at the root of the tooth, and the pus formed finds its way to the outside through the alveolar process and the gums. It forms a fluctuating swelling on the gums (abscess of the gums); the opening generally remains so, and if it is in the superior maxillary open fistulous tracts may form under the eye, just below the lower eyelid, and unless carefully examined may be mistaken for a lachrymal fistula. By means of a flexible probe the diagnosis can be made with safety.

In all these cases the animals seem to have a more or less severe toothache; they are irritable, eat very slowly and irregularly, drop more or less saliva, refuse to have the mouth examined, and, if the affected tooth is struck with anything (a key is the best), howl and evince great pain, keeping the mouth open for some time afterward.

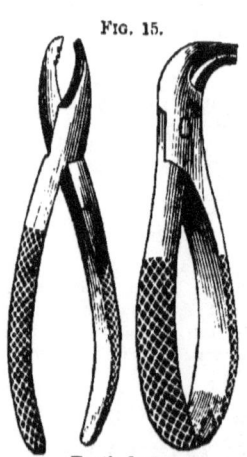

Fig. 15.

Tooth forceps.

When there is more or less pus present the radical treatment is to remove the offending tooth. For this purpose open the mouth by the method described on page 27, or a wedge, and with an ordinary molar-forceps (Fig. 15) extract the tooth, being careful to avoid breaking the crown. The tooth is firmly seized with the forceps as far down on the root as possible; it is first loosened by twisting from side to side several times and then drawn out with a strong pull. The mouth must then be thoroughly cleansed with warm water and the gums pressed firmly together, so as to keep the cavity, if possible, from filling up with a blood-clot. This should be done immediately after extraction.

Dentition.

The first incisors and the eye-teeth (caninea), and the second, third, and fourth molars appear in the dog at the end of five weeks. The permanent teeth begin to come through about the third or fourth month; the canine and middle incisors come through about the fourth month; the remaining incisors about the end of five months, and also the second, third, and fourth molars; the fifth molar about five months, the sixth about six months, and finally the seventh about the end of the seventh month, so that the dog has his full masticatory apparatus at the end of seven months.

During the process of teething the gums become very red and inflamed, with an increased amount of saliva; in some cases the inflammation is intense, with complete loss of appetite. Convulsions may occur from reflex nervous irritation. This nervous irritation may produce a cramp of the lower jaw that is very similar to the paralysis of the jaw in rabies.

These cases are best treated by simple sedatives, and if the gums seem to be tough, they should be lanced with an ordinary gum-lancet, and thus assist the tooth through to the surface.

Malformations of the Cavity of the Mouth.

Malformations or growths on the buccal membrane are frequently seen in the dog, especially located about the edge of the gums and on the inner cheek. They are generally classed as "epulides." They are of various sizes, from the size of a pin-head to a walnut. They are generally pedunculated; very rarely they are seen with an extended base. As a rule, they are hard; they occur in various characters—fibroma, carcinoma, or sarcoma. The author observed a melanotic sarcoma in one case.

The tumors can be removed by the écraseur of wire, as in Fig. 16, or by cutting them with a probe-pointed bistoury. The hemorrhage can be checked by the thermo-cautery or by a solution of chloride of iron; but the hemorrhage is generally so slight as not to require any styptics. It is best to thoroughly cauterize the base, so as to prevent, if possible, the recurrence of the growth; but frequently in spite of it they return.

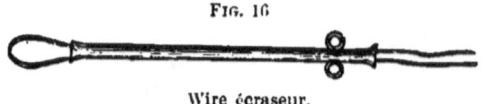

Fig. 16

Wire écraseur.

Besides these tumors of the membranes we have a growth called **ranula**. Often an animal will become very slow in eating, and if the mouth is examined we will find on one side of the tongue and under it a large-sized, fluctuating swelling, reddish-blue in color, and filled with a thick, creamy liquid. Many theories have been advanced as to the cause of this disease; some consider it to be the formation of an ordinary cyst, and others contend that it is due to the plugging up of the ducts of one or more of the salivary glands at the base of the tongue. The author has had five cases under observation which he believes to be ranula. In three of these cases the cause of the trouble was due to the obstruction of the duct of Wharton, which has its entrance into the mouth at the base of the lingual ligament, and in the other two cases it was a cystoid degeneration of a few glands at the base of the tongue, probably due to a plugging of the opening of their ducts and a consequent inflammation of the glands themselves. It therefore seems best to call all the cystoid formations under the tongue, ranula.

It is always advisable to operate on these cysts. Cut down on the cyst with a lancet and make a good-sized opening, and by means of a pair of curved scissors remove a portion of the upper part of the wall, and cauterize the inner walls of the cyst with the thermo-cautery. If Wharton's duct is involved, be guarded in the cauterization, confining it only to the anterior part of the cyst, toward the point of the tongue. The injection of pilocarpine, which has been used in man with success, according to Soffintini's method, has been tried in animals by Hoffmann. It consists in creating a great amount of the salivary secretion, and by force of the collected fluid from the inside break the obstruction of the duct. The author, however, has not tried it.

Inflammation of the Salivary Glands.
(*Parotitis; Mumps.*)

Inflammation of the salivary glands may be caused by the passage of microbes up the duct into the body of the gland through traumatic causes and by direct infection from the blood itself. The author has frequently seen the gland in the region of the ear affected, more rarely the glands of the lower jaw, and least of all the glands of the tongue; he has never seen the glands of the eye affected.

Inflammation of the glands of the ear (parotitis) appears either as a consequence of some mechanical cause, or by infection from the cavity of the mouth from some existing inflammation of that part, or as a disease. The latter requires special mention as a primary idiopathic parotitis (mumps).

ETIOLOGY. This disease is rather rare in the dog, but sometimes it may take the form of an epizootic (Hertwig, Schüssele). In these cases it is probably due to some infecting virus that gets into the gland through Steno's duct. The exact nature and time of incubation of this disease are not known.

SYMPTOMS. The disease begins with a swelling of the glands on one or both sides of the ear. The location of these glands is seen in Fig. 17. They swell rapidly and are very tender to the touch, changing the whole appearance of the head and neck. The animal is very droopy, carries the head stiff, eats with great difficulty, and will swallow only small pieces. The saliva is very thick and forms tenacious bubbles at the corners of the mouth. The fever is seldom high, and in the majority of cases in from five to eight days the swelling decreases and disappears entirely in fourteen days (Hertwig).

In rare cases an abscess is formed in the gland and always in one. The gland swells as in mumps, only the course is much quicker, and the surrounding tissues are much swollen and œdematous. Soon a fluctuating part is felt, which later opens in one or more places, and a thick, creamy pus escapes; the œdema of the surrounding tissues disappears quickly, and the fever, which is rarely of much consequence, goes down entirely and the wound closes in a short time.

The inflammation of the glands of the tongue and lower jaw

generally forms abscesses which open, the pus escapes, and the sore heals up in a short time. The submaxillary generally breaks through the skin and the sublingual into the cavity of the mouth. There is never any serious consequences in any of these cases.

Fig. 17.

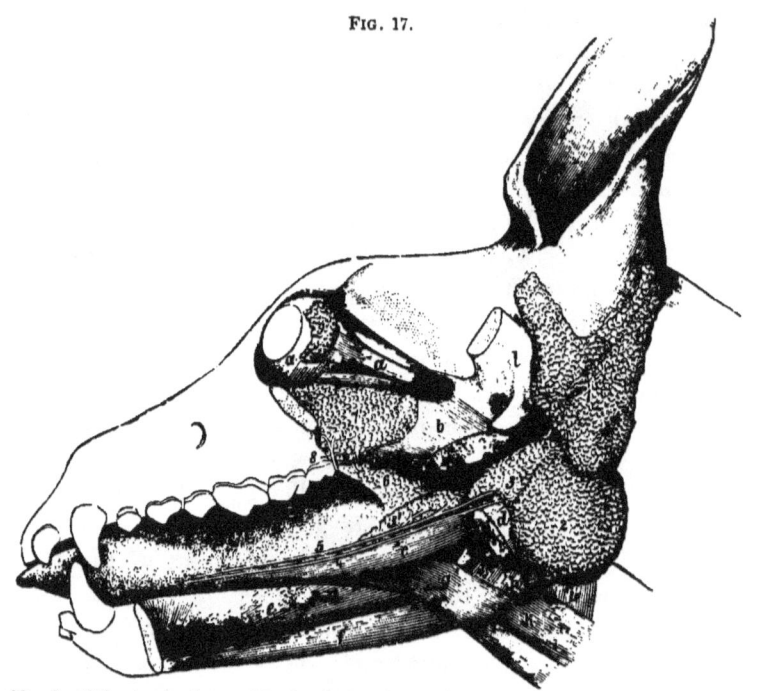

Glands of the head: 1, parotid gland; 2, submaxillary gland; 3, subzygomatic gland; 4, Wharton's duct; 5, Bartholin's duct; 6, palatine gland; 7, orbital gland; 8, Nuckian duct; 9, lachrymal gland.

THERAPEUTICS. In the primary form of parotitis, where we do not have the formation of an abscess, we obtain good results with warm applications. Keep the animals as quiet as possible, and then rub on ointments, such as vaselin and yellow oxide of mercury.

As soon as we see that the swelling is not going down within a certain time, but increasing gradually, we must try and open the abscess as soon as possible and allow the pus to escape. If fluctuation can be felt, cut down on that point; but if not, the skin and fascia have to be carefully cut in the dependent portion, making a good-sized opening. The gland is now exposed, the pus can be detected and opened, a drainage-tube inserted and sewed to the tissues—if not sewed, the animal will shake it out—and cleansed daily with an antiseptic solution. It is better not to bandage the neck, as it interferes with the tube and is a bad place to keep it on. These abscesses heal rapidly if there is exit for the pus.

Inflammations of the other salivary glands should be treated the same way. The abscess of the submaxillary should be opened from the outside through the skin, and the sublingual from the inside of the mouth. In the submaxillary it is not necessary to put in a drainage-tube, but simply to keep the wound clean.

Occasionally we find cysts form in the glands of the tongue. These were first described by Siedamgrotzky as houey-cysts. They are seen on the lower side of the mouth in the region of the larynx, and are covered by the muscles of the neck; or they may be on both sides of the larynx and appear as a conglomeration of small, crowded vesicles with thin, coarse walls filled with a thick, honey-like fluid. In some instances it is very thick, like cheese, and yellow or reddish. They originate in the glands of the tongue, and as their cyst-wall extends into the tissue of that organ they must be classed under the head of ranula.

THERAPEUTICS. In treating these cysts the only practical method to pursue is to remove them entirely, for if they are simply cut into they return in a short time. The method suggested by Siedamgrotzky has been very satisfactory to the author. It consists of making a good, big opening in a dependent part and injecting the parts freely with mild caustic solutions, such as caustic potash or tincture of iodine. If a drainage-tube is inserted into the opening, it is much more satisfactory.

Inflammation of the Mucous Membranes of the Throat.
(*Pharyngitis; Angina Catarrhalis; Sore Throat.*)

This disease is very rare in the dog and not by any means as important as it is in man, and as yet there have not been recognized any cases in the dog that could be compared with diphtheria, angina tonsillaris, and retropharyngeal abscess of man, at least such is the experience of the author. The general affections observed have been common catarrhal inflammations which involved the whole or part of the throat.

ETIOLOGY. The same causes that would produce stomatitis would bring on inflammation of the throat. The most common cause of anginal catarrh is by a continuation of the inflammatory processes from the neighboring organs—for instance, in catarrh of the head, or in laryngitis, and it may appear as a complication of distemper.

PATHOLOGICAL ANATOMY, CLINICAL SYMPTOMS AND COURSE. The changes of the mucous membranes are the same as are recognized in all catarrhal inflammations. The mucous membrane is a diffused red, sometimes spotted, and coated with a dirty yellowish mucus. It is rarely purulent on its surface, except in very grave affections, when especially on its dorsal region there may be seen a number of small, irregular granulations. As a rule, if the inflammation is at all severe, the tonsils are also swollen and protrude out of their membranous pouches in the shape of brownish-red enlargements. We very rarely see any fibrinous (croupal) membranes in any of the severe inflammations of the throat.

The clinical symptoms of catarrh of the throat are similar to acute stomatitis, and it is only by making a careful examination of the throat that we can make a correct diagnosis. The author has found, as a rule, that catarrh of the stomach accompanies all these cases. Catarrh of the nasal passages and pharynx, and slight fever are also seen in these cases. The author has never observed true chronic catarrh of the throat.

THERAPEUTICS. Considering the mild course of the disease little medicinal treatment is desired; a liniment, such as camphorated oil or soap-liniment, should be rubbed on the throat, and sedative mouth-washes, such as boric acid and glycerin. Keep the animal in a dry temperature, not too hot, and give easily digested food.

Sometimes acid or irritating agents may cause acute inflammations of the throat, and if they are so severe as to ulcerate they may be mistaken for diphtheria or croup. In such cases wash the mouth out with a solution of permanganate of potassium, boric or salicycic acid, or paint the throat with nitrate of silver or tannate of glycerin.

DISEASES OF THE ŒSOPHAGUS.

Foreign Bodies in the Œsophagus.

The foreign bodies that become fixed in the œsophagus of the dog are numerous and varied; they consist of portions of food, such as hard, irregular-sized pieces of meat that have been taken in one gulp; long, sharp pieces of bone, such as mutton or fish, pieces of wood, needles, or small stones; sometimes objects are swallowed by accident, such as stones, buttons, glass, or india-rubber balls, corks, etc., and lodged in the pharynx at the entrance of the œsophagus; or if the object is small, it may go to a certain distance into the tube and lodge.

The symptoms vary according to the general character and position of the foreign body. As a rule, the animal is restless and keeps the neck and head extended; it scratches itself with the paws over the spot where the obstruction is located. If it is in the pharnyx, the animal shows signs of choking or may even vomit small quantities of mucus and saliva from time to time. It coughs frequently, and if the obstruction is large it refuses to eat or drink. If water is forced on the animal, it passes down the throat very slowly and evidently with difficulty, or may be vomited immediately after it has been swallowed. If the foreign body is in the pharynx, it can be felt externally with the finger, or opening the mouth and depressing the tongue it can be seen lodged in the pharynx; if it is in the œsophagus, it can be detected by making a careful examination along the course of the tube or by the probang introduced into it, as has been described on page 30. The latter method is the only way to positively determine the presence of a foreign body when it has lodged in the thoracic portion of the œsophagus. In introducing the probang it must be carefully inserted, and if it should come in contact with the foreign body too great pressure must not be made on it, as it is apt to pack the object more firmly or even cause perforation of the tube. When making an examination of the tube externally, should we find a part that is painful we must not consider it the obstruction unless we find a hard swelling with it, as foreign bodies, such as sharp splinters of bone or wood, often go down the tube and lacerate the mucous membrane in its passage and do not become imbedded.

Needles, pins, and small pieces of wood may not be detected even with the probang.

The object, if it goes into the stomach, passes through the intestines and is passed through the rectum, and causes no further trouble. Some authors have observed needles passed per rectum (Friedberger, Kohlhepp). It may, however, lodge in the stomach and cause great irritation and finally convulsions and death. If it is a sharp body, it may perforate the stomach and even find its way out again by perforating the abdominal wall. If it is in the thoracic portion of the tube, it may penetrate the wall and set up septic mediastinitis.

Siedamgrotzky relates a very curious case in a dog in which a piece of bacon-rind, 6 centimetres long and 3 wide, lacerated the œsophagus in the thorax so much as to cause fatal pleuritis. The author has seen the same thing from a splinter of bone. It is also probable that death may occur from the foreign bodies if they are sharp, by penetrating either the heart or one of the large blood-vessels in the vicinity and causing a hemorrhage, or it may also occur from septic inflammation of the œsophagus.

THERAPEUTICS. If the foreign body is in the pharynx or at the entrance of the œsophagus, it must be removed immediately either with the finger or a pair of forceps. If the obstruction is located in the lower portion of the tube, and it cannot be pushed down into the stomach with the probang, it is advisable to attempt to get it up by an emetic—a subcutaneous injection of apomorphia muriate, as per page 34. If that is not successful, then perform œsophagotomy as soon as possible, before the intense swelling interferes with the operation. If this operation cannot be performed on account of the foreign body being located too deeply in the thorax, it is best to give the animal large quantities of lubricating substances, such as olive or any fatty oil. It is better to do this than to use any great force to push the object into the stomach.

ŒSOPHAGOTOMY. This is not very difficult to perform in the dog; the point of operation is directly over the location of the foreign body; the hair is shaved over the part and the first incision is made behind the jugular, making the opening no larger than is necessary to get out the obstruction; the wound in the œsophagus is first sewed up with a continuous suture of catgut ligature, being careful to include the mucous membrane (Hoffmann does not sew the muscular tissue), or the wound can be left open. Our experience has been that we never get union by first intention, even if it is sewn up at once. The external wound is to be left open and filled up with a tampon of oakum and a bandage carried around the neck to keep it in place, and to be changed daily (see treatment of wounds); the bandage must be carefully fixed so that the animal will not injure the wound by scratching it, and must be kept from all food for at least thirty-six hours. These wounds heal up very rapidly, and it is seldom that there is any consequent stricture of the œsophagus or a fistulœ.

We have also in very rare instances an inflammation of the œsophagus (œsophagitis), with or without any ulceration. In the latter case it is due to the irritation of caustic poisons or the laceration of foreign bodies going down the tube. This is best treated with lubricating oils, almond or sweet oil. We may see occasionally a constriction of the œsophagus (stenosis œsophagi) or a dilatation (ektasie and divertikel), but these conditions are impossible to improve by any surgical means that we know of at present.

DISEASES OF THE STOMACH.

Acute Catarrh of the Stomach.
(*Gastritis Catarrhalis Acuta; Gastricismus; Acute Dyspepsia.*)

ETIOLOGY. The following are generally the causes of this disease: hot, fermenting, or decaying alimentary matter; overfeeding; foreign bodies, such as sand, stones, buttons, splinters of wood; and indigestible food, and also parasites. As regards toxic gastritis, that will be taken up later on. We find also that some diseases, such as distemper and some affections of the liver, have acute gastritis accompanying them. It is a question if acute catarrh of the stomach is developed from simple cold.

PATHOLOGICAL ANATOMY. The mucous membranes of the stomach are hyperæmic and swollen; the folds of the membrane are distended and covered with a thick, tenacious mucus. At times there are seen small, hemorrhagic erosions, but often the acute symptoms of intense catarrh are not seen on post-mortem.

CLINICAL SYMPTOMS. The first symptom of acute catarrh is loss of appetite. The animal will be very dainty or pick out certain pieces, generally meat, and eat them very slowly, or, as is generally seen, refuse food altogether. The animal is always very thirsty, drinking large quantities of water. The animal vomits frequently, especially after eating or drinking, but may vomit without anything on the stomach. If after eating, it consists of masses of undigested food mixed with a tenacious mucus; if after drinking, the water is tenacious and forms bubbles of thick mucus—this may be streaked with blood or more or less tinted with bile, according to the condition of the liver. The tongue is coated with a thick, white mucus, and on pressure in the region of the stomach the animal evinces pain. The animal is irritable and wants to keep in the dark and in cool places. The nose is dry, and there may be some rise of the temperature. If the symptoms are of an alarming character, they are generally caused by some toxic condition, due to the formation of poisons generated in the stomach (ptomaïns). With this we have a putrid smell in the mouth, great depression or even complete coma, and evidences of acute narcotic poisoning.

There are always some intestinal complications. There is increased excretion of feces, generally diarrhœa, and occasionally icterus of a catarrhal nature. The animal, as a rule, makes a good recovery. In very rare cases the condition becomes chronic, death never occurring except where some complication other than true catarrh of the stomach is present.

THERAPEUTICS. If the cause has been the eating of some putrid matters, and if you suspect some to be present in the stomach, it is best to give the animal an emetic, such as the hypodermatic injection of apomorphia. Keep the animal on a low diet in the beginning; let the animal do without food for a day, and then give small quantities of milk or finely cut-up meat, soup, or beef-tea; a stomachic, such as tincture of rhubarb or tincture of nux vomica, in small doses; if there is much vomiting, carbonate of sodium or magnesium is to be given in small doses several times daily. We must not administer opium unless the vomiting is persistent. Never give chloral hydrate, as it irritates the mucous membrane of the stomach. Any complication from the intestines will have to be treated according to the directions given later under Diseases of the Intestines. In cases of diarrhœa give tincture of calumbo and subnitrate or subgallate of bismuth. If constipation is present, give small doses of calomel, sulphate of magnesium, and tincture rhei comp.

Chronic Catarrh of the Stomach.
(*Gastritis Catarrhalis Chronica; Chronic Dyspepsia.*)

ETIOLOGY. Chronic dyspepsia is rather common in the dog, especially if the animal has had several attacks of acute dyspepsia. It may also appear as a secondary complication of various diseases, such as cancer of the stomach, gastric tumors, and disorders of the liver.

PATHOLOGICAL ANATOMY. The mucous membrane is covered with a tough, glassy mucus, dirty-white in color. In the early stages the mucous membrane is red, and as the disease continues the membrane becomes blackish-gray in color and more or less swollen, especially if the gastric glands become infected and indurated from the constant irritation.

CLINICAL SYMPTOMS. They are similar to those of acute catarrh of the stomach; but the appetite, while it may be very irregular, is not entirely absent—one day very good and the next absent. Vomiting occurs, but only a short time after eating, and consists of undigested food covered with quantities of tough, glassy mucus, sometimes streaked with blood. Pain on pressure in the region of the stomach, especially after eating, although this is not a constant symptom by any means. The animal becomes thin and shows every symptom of poor nutrition.

We must always take into consideration that mere loss of appetite does not always mean acute or chronic catarrh of the stomach, but is a symptom present in a number of diseases, and every symptom must be carefully examined before coming to a conclusion.

THERAPEUTICS. The washing out of the stomach, so often resorted to in man, is fully explained on page 33. After so doing it is well to irrigate the stomach with fresh water; in anæmic animals with tepid water or with a solution of bicarbonate of sodium, permanganate of potassium (in weak solution), or a weak solution of salicylic acid. As a rule, however, it is not advisable to do this unless you suspect some irritant or poisonous material to be present.

Give the animal a carefully regulated diet, as prescribed on page 56, and internally alkalines, such as bicarbonate of sodium or sulphate or magnesium, a pinch three times daily, and also some anti-fermenting agent, such as dilute nitric acid, creosote, salicylic acid, or a bitter tonic, such as rhubarb combined with bicarbonate of sodium. Calumbo root also gives excellent results. The other bitters are apt to disturb the stomach and digestion, as is also the case with the various agents that are used to counteract catarrh, for instance, zinc oxide, silver nitrate, and bismuth subnitrate.

R.—Rhei rad. pulv. 5.0
　　　Sodium bicarbonas 40.0
M. fiat. pulv. No. x. S.—One three times daily.

R.—Naphthalin 0.3
　　　Saccharum alba 0.6
M. fiat. pulv. No. x. S.—Give one powder three times daily.

Ulceration of the Stomach.
(*Ulcus Ventriculi.*)

When any bleeding occurs from the stomach as the result of some acute inflammatory condition of that organ it always leaves an erosion of the mucous membrane. As a rule, this heals up very rapidly in the dog, rarely leaving any cicatrix on the membrane; abrasions of the mucous membrane from sharp pieces of bone, splinters, or caustic agents also heal up very rapidly.

Occasionally, however, we see the true ulceration of the stomach. The real cause of this condition has not yet been satisfactorily explained, although many investigations have been made on the subject.

The ulcer is generally at the beginning an inflamed circular spot, from which the mucous membrane peels and gradually disappears, extending to the deeper tissues, where it forms a yellowish-red, unhealthy surface, with an irregular, hard, indurated border. Very often they heal up, leaving an irregular cicatrix, generally circular in shape.

In the dog, as in the man, we find that in rare instances the ulceration is so extensive as to perforate the stomach to the serous membrane, and form adhesions to the adjacent organs.

CLINICAL SYMPTOMS. Ulceration of the stomach undoubtedly occurs in the dog, as cicatrixes have been seen on the stomach on making a post-mortem, but during life no symptoms were presented that would enable the observer to make a diagnosis.

The symptoms are irritation of the stomach and occasional vomiting of blood.

THERAPEUTICS. Bicarbonate of sodium, argenti nitras, and bismuth subnitrate. The use of the stomach-pump is contraindicated in this disease, as it tends to increase the hemorrhage.

R.—Bismuthi subnitras	0.3
Saccharum alba	0.5

M. fiat. pulv. No. xii. S.—One powder three times daily.

R.—Argentii nitras	0.6
Argillæ	10.0

F. pilulæ No. xl. S.—One pill three times daily.

DISEASES OF THE INTESTINES.

Intestinal Catarrh.

(Catarrh of the Bowels; Enteritis Catarrhalis.)

Catarrh of the intestines originates frequently from the same causes as catarrh of the stomach, and it frequently happens that the two diseases occur together.

Intestinal catarrh is generally caused by decayed, tainted, fermenting, or indigestible food, and by intestinal parasites or poisons. It also appears in an infectious form, attacking entire kennels and animals of all ages. It is frequently caused by cold or other causes, such as distemper, and from disturbance of the circulation and from disorders of the lungs, liver, or heart.

According to the duration and severity of the disease we determine whether we have acute or chronic catarrh of the intestines. In the acute form the disease lasts from one to two weeks; the chronic often for months.

ETIOLOGY. The causes of acute and chronic catarrh of the intestines are similar; the latter is frequently developed from the acute form, and from a frequent return of the disease the system becomes weakened, and at last, unable to throw off the disease, it remains in a milder but chronic form.

The disease may be located either in the small or large intestine or in both. The small intestine is the most common seat of the disease, but it is frequently found in the large intestine. The various classifications, such as duodenitis, jejunitis, ileitis, typhlitis, colitis, and proctitis, are useful only to the anatomist, but not to the clinical observer. Proctitis is frequently seen in the dog in an isolated form.

PATHOLOGICAL ANATOMY. The effects of catarrh of the intestines is practically the same as in all irritations of the mucous membranes. In the acute form the membranes may be swollen and reddened through the entire intestine, or it may be confined to spots where it is reddened and congested and the membranes raised and covered over its surface with flaky, slimy epithelium. In very bad cases there is a large number of these epithelial masses or spots. These masses of inflamed follicles become grayish-white in color and project from the membrane or finally become ulcerated. In some diseases where there is severe catarrhal inflammation of the mucous membranes we find a sympathetic inflammation of the intestine, in some cases even a necrosis from which ulceration of the bowels follows. The author had one case under his observation where a young dog died from a diphtheritic ulceration of the bowels.

In the chronic form the redness is less intense; the mucous membrane may even be pale or livid gray in color. In rare cases it is slate color. The swelling is more regular and covers over more area, forming a true hyperplasia of the membrane; the inner surface of the bowel becomes irregular and uneven with projections over the entire surface. In some cases the membrane forms true polypus formations, due to circumscribed hyperplasia of the connective tissue. Where there has been cystoid degeneration of the follicles the intestinal secretions are stopped entirely. It is from the chronic form that ulceration of the stomach generally originates.

CLINICAL SYMPTOMS. The most prominent symptom of intestinal catarrh is diarrhœa, especially if it is confined to the large intestine, although there may be no diarrhœa whatever if the inflammation is confined to the small intestine, as it is well known that the absorption of the fluids and the formation of the feces are confined to the large intestine, and we often have intense inflammation of the small intestine, with profuse diarrhœa, without having the large intestine infected whatever. On the other hand, we often have inflammation of the large intestine with no diarrhœa at all.

In making a diagnosis it is well not to identify too closely diarrhœa and catarrh of the intestines—that is, consider each case of diarrhœa as being due to inflammation of the bowels—as there are many causes that increase the peristaltic action and cause diarrhœa that are not due to direct inflammation, such as colds or a sudden chill to an animal that has been kept warm, to poisonous substances, from the administration of laxatives or cathartics, or great exertion in an animal that is not accustomed to it. It is, however, impossible distinctly to draw the line, but a conclusion can be arrived at by the number, amount, and character of the diarrhœic discharges.

In all animals the number of daily stools varies to a certain extent, and their consistency from pulpy to thin, watery evacuations. At first the passages are clearer than natural and yellower, and as the condition goes on they become gray; this color is due to the fact that the passages are so frequent that the liver is not able to furnish sufficient bile to color them, and in a number of cases there is a certain amount of thick, gelatinous mucus mixed in the excremental matter. In some cases the mucus becomes very copious, and that form is passed almost entirely, and in rare cases blood and pus (for further details, see page 40).

In this condition the animal is restless, changing the position frequently, groans or cries, arches the back, or may rest the forepart of the body on the ground and have the hind-quarters elevated. This is an indication of colicky pains. The examination of the abdomen externally does not furnish much information. Sometimes the abdomen is contracted; in other cases it is distended. On applying the ear to the region of the abdomen a great amount of gurgling or rolling is heard in the cavity. This is due to the increased peristaltic action. On pressing the posterior part of the abdomen the animal often evinces pain.

Tenesmus and relaxation of the rectum are generally present in the later stages of this disease. The animal makes prolonged and repeated efforts to pass the excremental matter, and latterly passes only small amounts of mucus after great exertions. In some cases these great exertions cause the lower bowel to be protruded. This, however, is generally seen in young puppies and only in very rare instances in older dogs. If the tenesmus is very great, it indicates that there is great irritation of the lower bowel (as regards the examination of the lower bowel, see page 38).

The other symptoms of catarrh of the intestines are as follows: The color of the urine becomes dark from the tinting of the bile and is lessened in quantity from the drain of fluids from the bowels (Fröhner). Fever is present, but it is generally slight. There is loss of appetite, vomiting, and yellow or icteric coloring of the mucous membranes, great thirst, and the animal becomes weak very quickly and shows great depression. This is specially noticeable when the inflammation is due to eating decayed meat.

Chronic inflammation of the bowels resembles the acute form in many ways, but it is less severe in its symptoms. The feces change from soft to firm, and *vice versa*, the animal becoming weak and thin, showing all the signs of anæmia; but in the chronic cases the appetite is generally very good.

PROGNOSIS. In strong, healthy animals this disease is generally not very serious, but in young dogs or puppies it causes great exhaustion, and they die from collapse before the diarrhœa can be checked. The chronic form in adult animals is generally very hard to control. Often attacks follow one after another, completely prostrating the animal and carrying it off finally.

THERAPEUTICS. In slight cases the only thing to do is to regulate the food, and, as a rule, lessen it in quantity and make it easily digested. Soup or stock mixed with bread or biscuit, rice, etc., friction to the abdomen, and a small quantity of alcohol in the form of whiskey or sherry in weak, delicate dogs. It must be borne in mind that in all cases of this disease the treatment will depend entirely on the causes and symptoms that are observed. If the cause has been due to the ingestion of decayed or putrid substances, internal parasites, the first thing to do is to clean the intestinal canal out by means of a purgative, such as castor oil or syrup of cascara sagrada, or in weak subjects or puppies olive oil. If there is any indication that the liver is disturbed, it is best to first administer a dose of calomel or blue-mass and follow up with an oleaginous purgative. Where there are copious and thin discharges and an indication of excessive peristaltic action it is advisable to use narcotics, and in this instance opium is always indicated. The attempt to substitute extract of belladonna or hyoscyamus and bromide of sodium in this disease has not proved to be very successful. Besides opium we should also use the true astringents, such as tannic acid, calumbo root, and cascarilla bark. If ulceration of the bowels is indicated by the symptoms, acetate of lead or nitrate of silver is to be given, followed up by small doses of naphthalin, salicylic acid, creolin, or creosote. The last drug I have found to be specially useful.

R.—Opii pulv. ⎫
    Acidum tannicum ⎭ . . āā 0.1
    Sacchar. album 0.5
M. fiat pulv. No. xii. S.—One powder every two or three hours.

R.—Acidum tannicum 1.0
    Vini rhei 100.0
S.—One teaspoonful several times daily.

R.—Creosote 0.5
    Aq. destil. 120.0
    Muc. acaciæ 30.0
S.—One tablespoonful every three or four hours.

When the catarrh has affected the lower intestines, it is well to make one or two irrigations of the bowels daily by means of a funnel and a piece of rubber hose with a pipe of hard rubber at the end (Fig. 18), which is inserted into the rectum as far up as possible and the fluid poured into the funnel and allowed to gravitate slowly into the bowel. The best solution to use is a 1 per cent. solution of tannic or salicylic acid in water, the water to be about 30° C. The amount to use is about one or two litres. If this causes much irritation and straining, it must be discontinued; but it is well to give the animal at least one injection by this method, as it helps to clean out the lower bowel and facilitate the action of the medicinal agent.

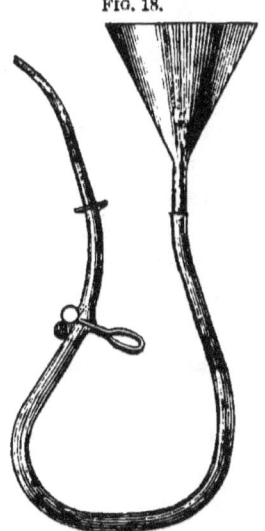

Fig. 18.

Clyster apparatus.

The treatment of chronic catarrh of the bowel is practically the same as the acute. Styptics are generally used, naphthalin, and nitrate of silver, and followed up by subnitrate of bismuth. Tincture of nux vomica is very useful as a tonic in one- or two-drop doses, before meals twice daily. The quality of the food requires special attention. In order to counteract the loss of strength give small quantities of rare or raw meat finely chopped, and also the various peptone preparations. In young puppies the various infant-foods so largely used in children's practice are used as substitutes for milk. Any complication of the stomach will have to be treated by the method advised under Catarrh of the Stomach.

The toxic and mycotic inflammations of the stomach will be described separately.

Toxic Inflammation of the Stomach and Intestines. Gastro-enteritis is caused by the absorption of various acid or irritating substances and also by the excessive use of drastic purgatives, such as aloes, calomel, croton oil.

The intensity of the disease depends on the amount of the drug taken and on the effect it has had on the mucous membranes. The only result may be an attack of acute catarrh, with some loss of the epithelium of the mucous membrane, or there may also be a gangrenous destruction of the walls of the stomach. It is seldom that irritating agents get any further than that organ, wasting their strength there and changing the wall of the stomach into a blackened or tinder-like mass, and all the surrounding tissues are swollen and reddened by hyperæmia or hemorrhages.

We may safely conclude that we have a toxic gastro-enteritis when the symptoms of a serious gastric catarrh appear suddenly, especially after eating, and if the grave symptoms increase rapidly and are accompanied by severe pains taking the nature of colic, and on pressure on the abdomen it is painful, the vomited matter and the passages from the intestines being filled with mucus and blood. (For further details, see chapter on Poisoning.)

The treatment consists, first, in giving an emetic, and after that has had its effect give a laxative—an oleaginous one (olive or linseed oil) is the best; and if the poison can be discovered, use the proper antidotes, which are given in the chapter on Poisoning.

Mycotic Inflammation of the Stomach and Intestines. This is a variety of toxic inflammation of the stomach and intestines. It is due to decayed meat poisoning. This is seen after the animal has eaten decomposed meat, offal, or from drinking brine (Leisering). The active agent in decomposed meat is not definitely known, but it certainly has a toxic agent present in it.

The symptoms of that form of poisoning have been studied very thoroughly by Siedamgrotzky, and are as follows: vomiting of an amount of very offensive, rotten masses of meat and with it quantities of bad-smelling mucus and sometimes bloody passages, intense thirst, and high fever. The author has seen, however, instances where the temperature was subnormal, a small, rapid pulse, great depression, and indifference to the surroundings. Death generally follows with every symptom of collapse. When a case makes a recovery it is very weak a long time, and it is almost impossible to get the animal to eat.

After death the process of decomposition begins almost immediately, and if a post-mortem is to be made it must be made as soon as possible. If this is done, the stomach will present an intense hemorrhagic inflammation of its walls, especially in the dependent portion, as well as severe inflammatory changes in the adjacent organs, liver, spleen, heart, etc.

The treatment has to be symptomatic. In the beginning give an emetic (apomorphia), washing out the stomach, and direct the administration of purgatives, emulsions of castor, olive, or linseed oil. The animal should be fed on light foods easily digested and in small quantities.

Hemorrhoids.

We mean by this name diffuse or knot-shaped (varicose) distentions of the posterior veins of the lower bowel at the anus. According to their location, we call them external or internal hemorrhoids.

The former are located outside the sphincter ani and in the subcutaneous connective tissue. The latter are located inside the sphincter and under the mucous membrane. Sometimes these enlarged veins burst and cause considerable hemorrhage. This, however, rarely amounts to anything, as the mucous membrane is generally more or less inflamed all the time and often the feces are coated with mucus when they are passed. It is a very common affection in the dog.

CLINICAL SYMPTOMS. The act of defecation is painful, the feces covered with mucus and sometimes with blood—either pure blood or blood and mucus mixed. On making a digital examination, which is very painful, the mucous membrane is found to be roughened and uneven, or we may see one knotty lump in the orifice of the anus. In rare instances they appear as bluish-red ulcers which encircle the reddened rectum. The animal is nervous and irritable, sliding the posterior part of the body on the floor, especially on the carpet, so as to rub the rectum, and licking the anus frequently.

The causes can generally be ascribed to a stagnation of the veins from irritation of the membranes from bile or irritants, such as frequent purgation, and in the great majority of instances it will be found that the liver is congested or inactive. In some cases it is due to a disturbance of the circulation from disease of the heart or lungs and from the irritation of habitual constipation.

THERAPEUTICS. The best treatment to pursue is first to use saline laxatives, but not in large enough doses to purge. Sulphate of magnesium or sulphate of sodium and cold enema and the application of an ointment of lead plaster. Any knots may be removed by ligature, scarification, or by the scissors and afterward touched by the thermo-cautery.

Contraction or Stenosis of the Intestines.

ETIOLOGY AND PATHOLOGICAL ANATOMY. Constrictions of the intestinal tract may be formed in any region and may vary in degree. They always produce more or less obstruction to the passage of the alimentary matter, and when the constriction becomes complete the intestinal contents, being unable to pass, usually return toward the stomach again and are expelled by vomiting. In such instances the animals die very quickly. This is noticed in very rare instances where a hernia has strangulated and completely blocked up the canal. (For further details, see chapter on Hernia.)

Constriction may be caused by abnormal conditions of the intestinal contents from alterations of the intestinal walls, by changes in the position of the intestines, and lastly from external pressure.

The bowel is often blocked up by masses of excrement collecting in the lower bowel, gradually blocking up the entire tract from the constant accumulations of excrement coming down from the small intestine. We also see obstructions caused by pieces of wood or splinters of bone that collect masses of feces around them and fill up the bowel—intestinal stones, or calculi (coproliths). These have a nidus consisting of marbles, corks, sponges, or other foreign bodies (Siedamgrotzky). As another cause that frequently causes stenosis of the bowels we must mention ulceration in one case observed by Friedberger. There was an œdema of the mucous membrane of the large intestines, and after extensive ulceration the consequent cicatrix drew the bowel together and caused it to be much less in diameter.

The constriction of the intestine from being inclosed in a hernia and the impaction of the intestinal matters pressing into the part is frequently seen in the dog. The intestine frequently becomes twisted or knotted or even invaginated. This will, however, be taken up under the head of Hernia. These complications, as a rule, occur in the small intestines. External compression of the intestines is frequently caused from enlarged prostate or sarcomas in the pelvic cavity. Sometimes enormous abscesses form in the abdominal cavity, and in very rare instances they are caused by accumulations of fluids in the abdominal cavity, as in the case of ascites. In newly born puppies we see sometimes a congenital obstruction of the rectum (atresia ani). Great masses of fecal matter may accumulate in the anal pouch. This may be due in some cases to a swelling of the anal glands or by the accumulation of masses of the hair gluing around the rectum and preventing defecation. (For further details, see the chapter on Chronic Constipation.)

When a portion of the intestine becomes obstructed the following changes take place: In front of the obstruction an enlargement forms, due to the accumulation of gas and excremental matter, while the portion of the intestine beyond the obstruction is empty and constricted. The accumulation of gas and matter causes an intense inflammation of the mucous membranes, which extends to the muscular coat of the intestines and soon to the serous coat, and quickly the entire intestinal tract is involved in the inflammation, the constricted portion becomes mortified, and perforation follows, allowing the contents of the intestine to escape in the abdominal cavity, causing a purulent peritonitis.

CLINICAL SYMPTOMS. The symptoms of constriction and obstruction of the bowels are so different that they will be described separately.

Symptoms of Constriction of the Bowels. They are not especially characteristic, and resemble chronic catarrh of the stomach. At first the animal is noticed to defecate irregularly; the stools are smaller and passed apparently with more or less difficulty, which is specially noticeable, considering the stools are smaller. The intestine is greatly swollen on account of the accumulation of gas; vomiting is sometimes present. On making an examination of the intestines by the hand we may be able to detect the enlargement.

Symptoms of Obstruction of the Intestines. The animal is irritable and cross, and Trasbot has seen cases where the animal showed symptoms very similar to rabies; or there may be the other extreme, being dull and indifferent to the surroundings, refuse all food, but show great thirst, with no passage of feces whatever. The rectal temperature is slightly increased, the lower portion of the abdomen is inflated with gas and very painful, even on the slightest pressure.

The vomiting is constant and very severe, in the later stages of the disease the animal vomiting whenever it drinks any water. At first the vomited matter is normal, but later on it assumes a greenish color, and finally putrid, containing small pieces of fecal matter.

By examining the abdominal region by the hand we can generally locate the obstruction, which is hard and exceedingly painful on pressure. The swelling can be moved about, showing it to be part of the intestine.

COURSE AND PROGNOSIS. In an ordinary case of constriction of the intestine no definite prognosis can be made with any degree of certainty as to its course and duration. The constriction of the intestine may go on gradually and not cause any serious symptoms for a long time, or it may progress very rapidly and cause a complete constriction in two or three weeks. The prognosis is always serious and generally ends fatally, with the exception of the form of obstruction that will be described below. Foreign bodies, such as pieces of cork, bone, or wood, may be macerated and passed finally without causing any great trouble. It is not difficult, as a rule, to detect the existence of a foreign body in the intestines, but it is very difficult to tell its exact nature.

There is one form of intestinal stenosis that is due to great accumulations of fecal matter in the large intestines. This requires special mention, as it is frequently seen and always in old animals that have little exercise and live on highly spiced food—veal or game—or eat quantities of bones that they are unable to digest. Great accumulation of fecal matter gathers in the colon and rectum. The most marked symptom is the repeated attempts of the animal to defecate without any results or only succeeding in passing a small amount of feces. These are coated with mucus or blood and passed with more or less pain. The stools are small and are generally yellowish-brown in color and in powder-like masses that break up easily, showing no moisture in them. The position of the tail is characteristic. It is carried so as to form a curve at the rectum, the curve being from the base to one-half of the tail. On pressing the fingers into the sides of the abdomen at the entrance of the pelvis up toward the spinal cord we find an elongated, sausage-like body which is extremely sensitive to the touch. This hard mass is found to extend downward and forward toward the umbilicus. When the finger, after being well oiled, is introduced into the anus, there will be found hard fecal masses in front of the sphincter. It is generally impossible to remove them, except to break them up, either with the finger or having first injected a small quantity of oil or glycerin into the rectum, or the handle of a spoon can be used to break up the masses, taking care not to injure the mucous membrane. This is to be followed up by the injection of clysters, or, what is better, glycerin suppositories, and later on administer a sharp purgative, followed by the administration of drop-doses of the tincture of nux vomica.

THERAPEUTICS. As soon as the symptoms of obstruction have been clearly defined, if the stenosis can be removed in a direct way, as would be the case in strangulated hernia, or in the case of accumulations of feces in the rectum due to fecal stagnation, or from ulceration or abscess of the rectum, we will have to treat them as described above; but we might add to that the injection of large quantities of soapy water several times daily, which can be given with the apparatus illustrated in Fig. 18, and a dose of calomel followed by castor or olive oil. The author has not gotten very good results from the use of physostigma or the use of glycerin injections into the rectum. [The translator has either in the form of glycerin suppositories or a solution of glycerin 1, water 10.]

The stenosis of the bowel that is caused by the injection of foreign bodies is best treated with laxatives and not with purgatives; and, if a positive diagnosis has been made, it is best to perform laparotomy with enterotomy as soon as possible, and not to wait until gangrene and peritonitis have set in.

According to Siedamgrotzky, enterotomy is performed in the following manner: Make an incision on the linea alba, and, having located the part of the intestine, pull it through the opening and hold the lips of the wound together. Make the cut longitudinally on the intestinal line, remove the foreign body and prevent at the same time any of the fluids escaping into the abdominal cavity. The operator now takes a fine curved needle and fine catgut and puts in a number of stitches through the muscular and serous tissues, taking care not to go through the mucous membrane, so that when the thread is tightened the two edges of the cut will be brought so as to face into the intestine; these are tied, and another line of stitches is made

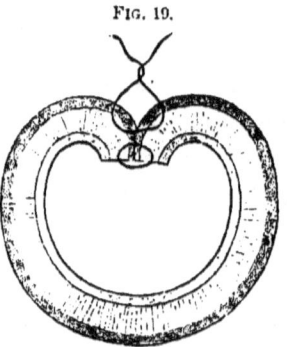

Fig. 19.

Suture of the intestines.

over the first, as is illustrated in the accompanying cut (Fig. 19). The intestine is returned to the cavity, and the wound sewed up with silk and dressed with an antiseptic dressing.

The opening of the abdominal cavity is also to be performed in cases where we can recognize a total constriction of the bowels. In all those cases where the anatomical cause of the disease cannot be clearly established we have no other way to proceed than to treat the symptoms as they present themselves—that is, to give purgatives, or, if there are great irritation and fever, give opium or morphine; but in any case do not neglect to give plenty of watery clysters.

The general treatment must be directed toward keeping up the animal's strength. Subcutaneous injections of tincture of camphor or ether are better than administering them by the mouth, as they are vomited immediately. Do not give the animal any food until the intestinal obstruction has been removed, or at least until there have been free defecation and the passage of the intestinal gas, and the general condition is improved. When the animal does receive food, it must be of the lightest and easily digested, such as soups, milk, finely scraped rare or raw beef, or some of the various foods used as substitutes for milk. Where an animal is subject to fecal obstructions, it is well never to let him have bones if it can possibly be avoided.

Chronic Constipation. This is seen occasionally in the dog. It is due to a lessened or weakened peristaltic action of the bowels. It is seen in all chronic diseases that are accompanied by emaciation and debility, as in chronic catarrh, fevers, icterus, chronic peritonitis, and in many diseases of the nervous system; but it may be observed in many old but healthy dogs, caused by an atrophy of the mucous and muscular membranes of the intestines. This disease is frequently called chronic obstipation, for it causes a form of constipation which would, as can be readily understood, cause just such a train of symptoms as has been described above.

These animals should be fed on non-stimulating, easily digestible food, with or without the admixture of rice-soup, and also plenty of exercise and small doses of tincture of nux vomica. This treatment is far better than the frequent administration of purgatives, especially castor oil, jalap or aloes, and cathartic pills.

Prolapsus of the Rectum.
(*Prolapsus Recti and Ani.*)

PATHOLOGICAL ANATOMY AND ETIOLOGY. The lower bowel is kept in place by the peri-proctal connective tissue, the rectal ring and the coccygeus and obturator internus, and the sphincter ani. By relaxing or distending these supports we have a prolapsus of the mucous membrane, or even the entire rectum may be protruded. If this prolapsus is not relieved soon, it inflames very quickly and becomes torn and ulcerated from great swelling. It may become strangulated and in rare cases gangrenous. It generally results from a relaxed condition of the rectal mucous membrane, or from excessive straining from constipation or diarrhœa, or labor-pains (Hertwig). It is generally seen in young dogs that have catarrh of the lower bowel.

SYMPTOMS. If the mucous membrane is protruded, it is only noticed during defecation or urination. It is seen in the form of dark red wrinkles that protrude from the rectum and return as soon as the abdominal pressure has ceased. If the whole bowel is prolapsed, we find under the tail a cylindrical projection, which protrudes from where the anus was and hangs downward. The mucous membrane that is exposed is wrinkled and congested, and at the centre dependent portion an indentation is seen; this is the opening of the intestines. Through this we can introduce the finger into the intestine. At the anterior end the mucous membrane passes directly into the skin at the anal opening. If there is any invagination, the membrane does not terminate at the anus, but seems to go into the rectum, and the protrusion can be lifted up and passed into the rectum between the swelling and the rectum.

THERAPEUTICS. The first thing to do is to remove the cause, whether it be due to diarrhœa or constipation, and treat it with astringents. The most important thing to do is to reduce the prolapsus as soon as possible: place the dog on his front legs and elevate the hind ones, and having cleaned and oiled the inflamed portion return it to its normal position. If the mucous membrane is very much swollen and inflamed, it is best to scarify it slightly. If the folds of mucous membrane are blackened and decayed from prolonged exposure, they must be trimmed off with the scissors. The author has generally succeeded even in very bad cases in reducing the protrusions by bathing them with cold water or by compressing the protruded intestine by winding on a rubber band, commencing at the external end and winding toward the base of the swelling. It is much more difficult to reduce invaginated intestine, as the more you press on the protruded part it packs into the end of the rectum. A large bougie or candle is inserted in the end of the protruded portion, and it is pressed into its natural position; or, if this does not succeed, perform laparotomy and draw the invaginated intestine back into position from the abdominal cavity. Degive has proven that there is little danger from this operation if it is performed with ordinary caution.

After replacing the intestine it is generally necessary to place a stitch around the perineum, so as to prevent the recurrence of the protrusion. What is called a tobacco-pouch stitch is carried around the anus, and when the strings are drawn it will be seen, as in the cut (Fig. 20), that it prevents the protrusion by drawing the anus together. The sewing of the rectum by this stitch closes up the opening sufficiently to prevent the bowel coming out, but not enough to prevent the escape of liquid fecal matter. It is not advisable to apply cold irrigations or inject astringents, as the dog is very apt to strain more violently after application of either of these remedies. At the same time, if the trouble is caused by diarrhœa, give opium; and if caused by constipation, administer saline purgatives. Stockfleth advises that a series of pins should be placed around the rectum and united with threads,

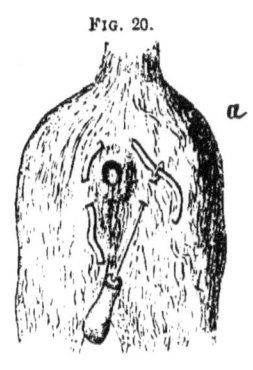

Fig. 20.

Stitching rectum (tobacco-bag stitch): *a*, method of stitching; *b*, stitch tied.

and thus produce a greater constriction from the cicatrix when the irritation heals, so as to hold the parts in position.

Grey made an opening on the median line of the abdomen and drew back the intestine and stitched it to the opening with catgut sutures.

When the prolapsus has been of long duration and reduction seems impossible, it is best to take means to remove the protruded portion of the intestine.

The best method is to place the animal under ether, and having laid it on a table with the posterior extremities elevated, the prolapsed portion is pulled as far as possible out of the rectum. It must then be rubbed in the hands to remove as much blood from it as possible, or a rubber band wound around it from its extremity to its base, and finally ligated at its base, and then by means of a bistoury the protrusion is cut off about one-half of an inch from the ligature.

After the bloodvessels are taken up, by means of a continuous stitch sew up the serous membrane; then afterward sew the muscular and mucous membranes, taking care not to penetrate the mucous membrane entirely through; the continuous stitch is much better, as it makes the union of the lips of the wound much closer; the rubber band is removed, and the stump is pushed back into the opening.

Imperforate Anus.
(Atresia Ani.)

This is a congenital deformity, and consists of a defective formation of the rectum and in some cases of the lower bowel. It is sometimes seen in newly born puppies, and it is usually confined to the cutaneous covering growing over the anus. It can be cut with a small knife and the edge of the wound sewed back so as to prevent it uniting again; but if it is found that the lower bowel is entirely occluded, it is better to destroy the puppy.

INTESTINAL PARASITES.
(HELMINTHIASIS.)

Round Worms. (Ascaris Mystax.)

NATURAL HISTORY. The round worm of the dog is white or yellowish-white in color, and twisted in spirals; there is a difference in the two sexes (see Fig. 21): the males are about 45 to

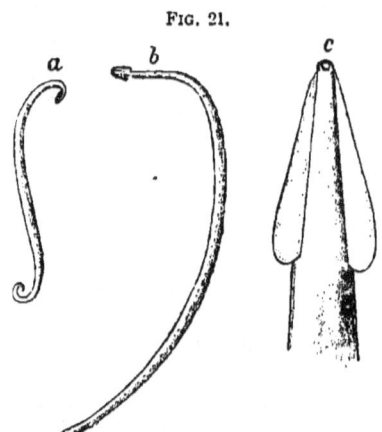

FIG. 21.

Ascaris mystax: *a*, male; *b*, female; *c*, head.

60 mm., and the females from 102 to 130 mm. Their thickness varies from 1 to 1.7 mm. The head is slightly flattened and fitted with two wing-shaped borders, which start from the mouth and enlarge slightly as they pass posteriorly. The mouth is a

small, round opening and fitted with three to six small lips, which cover a number of proportionately large teeth. The caudal end of the parasite is curved and has twenty-six small papillæ on each side. The female is pointed and straight. The sexual organs of the female are peculiar. The vulva is about 36 mm. from the head. In the genital organs there can generally be seen quantities of eggs that on examination are found to have a thick, hard shell, which is marked by numerous small grooves. These eggs are found in enormous quantities in the feces of all dogs affected with the round worm. The development of the embryo is not yet thoroughly understood, but it is generally believed that the embryo passes through several stages before it is ready to enter into the dog's system.

As a rule, the round worm causes little trouble in the dog, but in some instances large masses of these worms collect in a ball and cause considerable catarrhal disturbance of the intestines, or they may even cause symptoms of intestinal stenosis. In rare instances the parasites produce numerous hemorrhagic furrows or indentations in the mucous membrane (Weiskopf). There is no doubt that in some instances round worms cause considerable nervous disturbance, such as cramps or epilepsy. This is generally observed in young animals—puppies under six months old. These nervous symptoms generally disappear with the expulsion of the parasite.

THERAPEUTICS. The principal agent to remove the round worms is santonin, the alkaloid of the plant Artemisia santonica. This is administered and followed up by a dose of castor oil, or the oil may be given with it.

R.—Santonin 0.3
    Ol. ricini 60.0
S.—Divide into three portions and give one every third (3) day.

Tænia.

NATURAL HISTORY. The cestodes are flat, tape-like worms, with or without intestines. They grow from one parent or head and adhere together in a long, ribbon-like colony. The head is furnished with sucking cups and hooks, by which means it adheres to the mucous membrane of the intestine. The parasite is thin at the neck, and at its termination it consists of a number of matured segments that separate from the parent parasite when they are fully developed and are carried out among the feces. Each segment is complete in itself, having both male and female genital organs. This order are hermaphrodites, and are peculiar from the fact that they produce the germs of new nursing mothers in the shape of eggs, while the nurse remains sexless. The ripe segments (proglottides) are soon detached and passed either into manure or in water where there are aquatic plants. They then go through several forms and are taken up by a new host. The eggs are covered with a hard, tough shell, inside of which is a six-hooked embryo. If this egg is taken into the stomach, the acid gastric juice dissolves the shell, the embryo is liberated, and immediately fastens the hooks into the mucous membrane, and from there perforate into the connective tissue of some of the adjacent organs, where they lose their hooks and form a sac-like cyst. These contain fluid, and are termed bladder-worms. These cysts form bladder-like excrescences on their sides, which develop and increase in size, and are named, from their shape and size, cœnurus when empty, and cysticercus or cysticercoid when they contain fluid. In each of these bladders we find the individual tænia head, furnished with the ring of hooks and the sucking cups. These bladders divide and subdivide into numerous daughter-cysts or breeding buds, all of which produce the little heads of the tænia. This is frequently seen in the echinococcus, where enormous masses are formed. If any domestic animal gets one of these ripe bladder-worms into the stomach, the gastric juice dissolves its covering and it finds its way to the duodenum, when it fastens itself by means of its hooks and sucking apparatus and instantly becomes a breeding parasite.

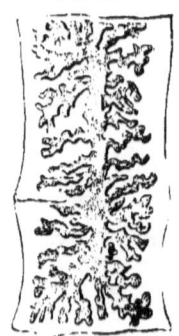

Fig. 22.

Uterus of the tænia cœnurus (enlarged).

The anatomical structure of the cestodes (Figs. 22, 23, and 24) is very simple. The body is divided into two layers, an external and an inner covering. In the latter we find the sexual organs.

The external layer is chiefly muscular, and contain also a mass of calcareous nodules that replace the defective bony structure of the cestodes. The surface of the head is covered with a skin or cuticle from which the hooks originate. The digestive system and bloodvessels are absent, but in the inner layer we find a system of very much branched vessels which connect with two elongated canals united at each joint by a cross system of similar canals, which is said to serve as an excretory apparatus. The branches running into these canals end in a common orifice. Each link or segment has an independent male and female sexual apparatus. The male apparatus consists of numerous pear-shaped testicular bladders with a canal of exit. The end can be turned up into the female opening. In the female portion we can distinguish ovaries, uterus, and vagina. The uterus is remarkably well defined in each segment.

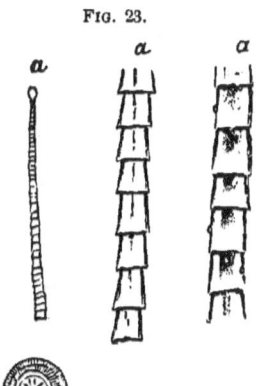

Fig. 23.

Tænia serrata: *a a a*, natural size; *b*, egg, greatly magnified.

The following varieties are seen in the dog:

Tænia Serrata. This variety is from 0.5 to 1 m. in length and about 0.5 cm. in width when fully developed. The head is large proportionately, often four-sided, and is fitted with two rows of hooks and also sucking disks, which are oval in shape. The anterior border of the segments is much narrower than the posterior. The edges are serrated or saw-like, hence the name. The genital orifice is situated on the border, sometimes on the right and sometimes on the left. The full-grown segments are nearly square, or may be broader than long. The uterus has a large central body, with eight branches on each side. The eggs are indented on the sides and have a hard, tough shell. The bladder-worm is found in the liver of the hare, called cysticercus pisiformis. This club-shaped cyst, which is from 8 to 13 mm. in length and 4 to 6 mm. in width, has been found by Lesbre in the brain of a dog affected by tænia serrata. This was probably caused by self-infection.

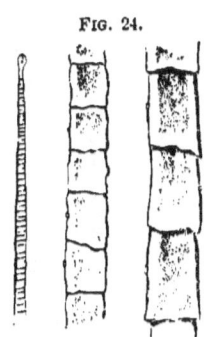

Fig. 24.

Tænia marginata (natural size).

Tænia Marginata. This is the largest tænia of the dog, being from 1.5 to 3 m. in length. In rare instances it has been found to be 5 m., and the width of the developed segments is about 0.5 cm. Its head is nearly square, with four small, sucking disks and a double crown of thirty-six hooks. The segments are nearly square. In the middle of the colony they may even be broader than long, with irregular edges. The sexual orifice, which is mobile, may be alternately on the right or left side. The uterus has a broad central body and has five branches on either side, which are intertwined. The eggs are oval and enveloped in a tube-cast. The bladder-worm of the tænia marginata is the cysticercus tenuicollis, and is found in the serous tissues of the sheep, cattle, goat, and pig.

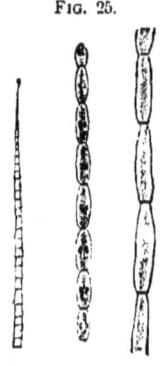

Fig. 25.

Tænia cucumerina (natural size).

Tænia Cucumerina. (Fig. 25.) This is a small tænia from 5 to 30 cm. long and 2 mm. wide. It has a small, elongated head, with sixty hooks; the segments are rounded at the corners and are the shape of a cucumber, hence the name, and have a small sexual orifice at each corner. The uterus is irregular, with double-shelled, rounded eggs, six to fifteen massed together in elongated cocoons. The primitive stage of this tænia, which is very common in the dog, is in the abdominal cavity of the dog-louse (trichodectes canis) (Melnikoff) and also in the common dog-flea (ceratopsyllus canis).

Tænia Cœnurus. (Fig. 26.) This tænia is generally about 40 cm. long, although in rare instances it may reach 1 m. It has a small, pear-shaped head, with twenty-eight to thirty-six hooks and four sucking disks. The anterior links of the colony are always very short, and those at the extreme end are elongated and narrow. The uterus has a long central body, with eighteen to twenty-six side branches. The eggs have a hard shell, with an indurated border. The larval state of this tænia, which is the cœnurus

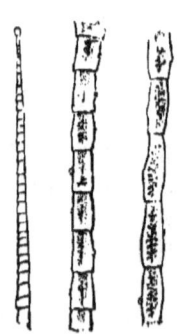

Fig. 26.

Tænia cœnurus (natural size).

cerebralis, varies in size from a small seed to a large egg, and has a number of nursing or daughter-cysts or bladders on its inner wall. It is generally located in the brain, and in rare instances the spinal cord. It is seen in all ruminants, especially sheep.

Tænia Echinococcus. (Fig. 27.) This is the smallest tænia of the dog. Its greatest length is 4.4 mm., and it has three and in rare instances four segments. The last segment is the largest and the only one to possess sexual organs. The uterus is large and irregular, without any central body, and a sexual orifice which is located at the border. The head is round and has four sucking disks and twenty-eight to forty-six small, imperfectly developed hooks, arranged in two rows. The eggs are round and slightly elongated, the shell being formed in several layers. The bladder-worm is the echinococcus polymorphus; the bladder is filled with a non-albuminous fluid, and generally has daughter-cysts on the sides. These cysts may assume enormous proportions, ranging in size from a pea to a man's head or even larger. It is found in the pig, cattle, and sheep, and very rarely in the horse, but quite frequently in man, especially in Iceland and Australia. It is generally found in or attached to the liver or peritoneum, but it has also been found in the lungs, kidneys, spleen, muscular system, pleura, bones, and the brain.

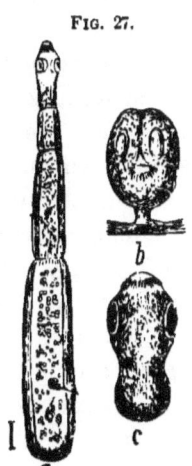

FIG. 27.

Tænia echinococcus: *a*, tapeworm, enlarged twelve times; *b*, cyst containing head; *c*, immature head.

CLINICAL SYMPTOMS. When tapeworms are present they generally cause more or less disturbance in the host. Often they produce the same symptoms as ascarides, but, as a rule, they cause much more trouble than the round worms. Schieferdecker found that in the duodenum, where the tæniæ cucumerina are generally found, the mucous membrane had numerous small tunnels, through which the tæniæ passed in and out, and a peculiar hypertrophy of the papilla. In some cases they were four or five times their own length. In other cases Lieberkühn's glands were sunken and collapsed and in several cases had completely disappeared. The tæniæ echinococcus, when they are present in large numbers, cause great irritation of the intestines, with hemorrhagic infarction of the tissues. In irritable animals they cause epileptic spasms or even symptoms of rabies, such as change of voice, paralysis of the lower jaw, dulness, and indifference to surrounding objects. Friedberger and Fröhner have also observed similar symptoms in dogs that have been infected with tænia cucumerina. In rare instances the tæniæ have been known to penetrate the intestine. According to the observations of Cadéac, the perforation was made by two of the tæniæ serrata. In a great number of instances it is impossible to say positively that the animal has tapeworm unless the segments are observed in the feces, and the most dangerous to man (the tænia echinococcus) is extremely hard to find on account of the small size of the segments. The other tapeworms are comparatively easy to find, as the segments are readily seen on the outside of the stools or catch in the anus and hang out, the dog frequently drawing attention to them by licking the anus or drawing the hind extremities along the floor by means of the front legs. In doubtful cases it is well to give a small dose of some tæniafuge, and the animal will generally pass a few segments.

THERAPEUTICS. The most important of the numerous tæniafuges recommended are as follows:

1. *Extract of Male Fern* (*extractum filix mas*), according to the experience of the author, is the best agent to use. It is to be given on an empty stomach (in the morning being the best time), in doses of from 1 to 4 grammes in pill-form or in capsules. As this drug has no purgative properties it must be followed up three hours afterward by a dose of castor oil (30 to 50 grammes). It must be borne in mind that male fern in large dose is a poison, and the maximum (4 gms.) must not be exceeded in the largest dog.

2. *Kamala.* This is to be given in doses of 2 to 8 gms., mixed with honey or syrup. It must be repeated in one hour after the first dose, as it has purgative properties, and it is not necessary to follow it up with any other drug, which is an advantage.

3. *Kusso* (*flores koso*). This is to be given in doses of from 3 to 5 gms., diluted with milk, repeated three or four times at intervals of three-quarters to one hour. This should be mixed or followed with a small dose of castor oil.

Pomegranate (*cortex granati*), in the shape of the macerated decoctions of 30 to 100 gms.; pumpkin-seeds crushed and macerated in hot water; areca-nut grated up fine, in from 20 to 30 gms.; oxide of copper, picronitrate of potassium, turpentine, chloroform, are all tæniafuges. These agents are only used to a slight extent, as they are much less efficient than the first three preparations mentioned.

The preparation of the animal for the tæniafuge is always an important proceeding, and must always be followed. It consists in letting the animal go hungry for at least one day and giving him also a mild purgative to cleanse the intestines, making a clear way for the expulsion of the parasite. After the animal has passed the parasites they ought to be picked up on a shovel or other object and the passage put in the fire to destroy the segments, especially if you have reason to suspect that the tænia echinococcus is present, on account of its danger to man.

 R.—Kamala 8.0
  Mel. . . . . . q. s.
 Fiat elec. S.—To be given in two doses.
 R.—Ext. filix mas. . . . 2.0
 Capsule gelatine No. 1. S.—To be given in one dose.

Oxyuris Vermicularis.

By this name (Fig. 28) we mean a small, white, thread-like, round worm. The female is from 9 to 13 mm. in length and the male from 3 to 4 mm. in length. They are generally located in the rectum and lower large intestines. They cause great itching of the anus, and the animal is observed to lick that part constantly and also to frequently pull the hind-quarters over the floor.

FIG. 28.

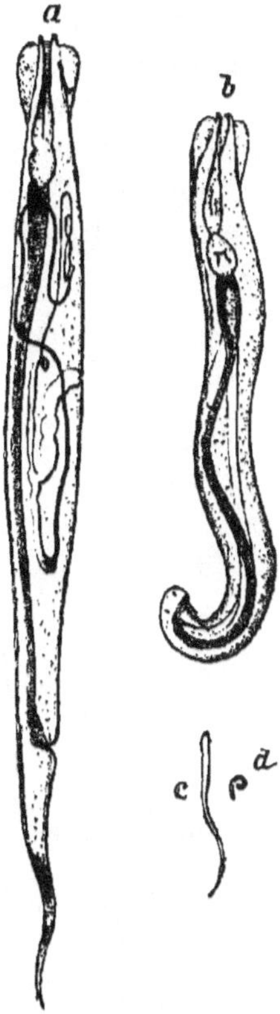

Oxyuris vermicularis: a, magnified diagram of the female; b, the male, magnified; c, natural size of the female; d, natural size of the male. (VIERORDT.)

These harmless parasites are removed by clysters composed of solutions of salt-water, quassia bark, vinegar, or a weak solution (1 : 1000) of corrosive sublimate.

Dochmius.

Dochmius (anchylostomum) (Fig. 29) is a small, thread-like parasite which belongs to the family of strongylides. The end of its head is like a bell-shaped capsule having two small, curved teeth on its dorsal border and four teeth on its ventral border. By means of the bell-shaped disk and the teeth on the inner part of its mouth it sucks and buries into the mucous membrane of the intestine and sucks blood. The three forms of this parasite found in the small intestine of the dog and described are as follows: the dochmius duodenalis; the male is 10 mm. long and 1 mm. thick; the female is 12 to 18 mm. long; the dochmius trigonocephalus; the male is 8 mm. long and 0.3 mm. thick; the female is 12 mm. long and 0.5 mm. thick; and the dochmius stenocephalus; the male is 6 to 8 mm. long and 0.24 mm. thick; the female is 8 to 10 mm. long and 0.38 mm. thick.

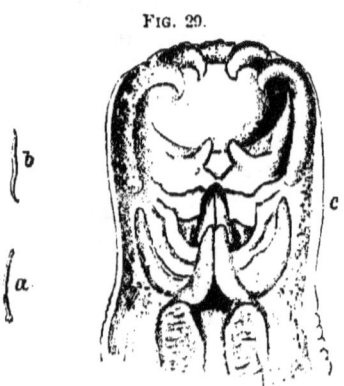

FIG. 29.

Dochmius duodenalis: a, male; b, female (natural size); c, magnified head. (JAKSCH.)

Animals affected with this parasite become anæmic, weak, and thin, and have a peculiar discharge of a thin, bloody mucus from the nose (Mégnien, Raillet).

The presence of this parasite is recognized in the same way as one would locate the tænia—by the presence of the eggs in the feces. They are easily recognized, the eggs being similar to the ascarides.

Besides the already mentioned parasites we also find in the intestines the trichocephalus depressiusculus in the cæcum and the bothriocephalus latus, cordatus, fuscus, reticulatus, and bubius in the small intestines; and we also find a coccidium (the coccidium perforans), which may produce a diphtheritic inflammation of the intestines (Rivolta and the author). They have been known in rare instances to produce rabiform symptoms.

DISEASES OF THE PERITONEUM.

Inflammation of the Peritoneum—Peritonitis.

ETIOLOGY. Peritonitis is generally seen as a secondary disease due originally to some irritation or injury of some of the other organs of the abdomen: From toxic gastro-enteritis, ulceration of the stomach or intestines, accumulations of fecal matter in the intestines; from metritis or parametritis after labor; from inflammation or abscess of the liver; from purulent inflammation of the kidneys or from purulent pleuritis; from rupture of the intestines and the escape of food or feces into the abdominal cavity. It may also occur from a general inflammation of all the serous membranes of the body, as is sometimes observed in infectious diseases; to pyæmia or metastatic peritonitis; from the breaking down of tubercular masses that have collected on the peritoneum, or from cancer. Primary peritonitis is always caused by some injury to the abdominal wall—shocks, blows, or by penetration of the abdominal walls, or after some operations. It is a question whether cold will cause the disease; the author doubts it very much.

PATHOLOGICAL ANATOMY. According to the extent of the disease we call it either partial (circumscribed) or general peritonitis (diffused); according to its course acute or chronic; and according to its character we call the exudate serous, fibrinous, purulent, putrid, or hemorrhagic. The purulent form of the disease is the most common, and on account of the extensive irritation that any inflammation causes in the peritoneum it is apt to take the diffuse form of the disease; and when it starts originally as circumscribed the disease generally becomes diffused in a short time. The peritoneum is first injected and ecchymosed, becoming dull-red and velvety, due to the removal of the endothelium and partially to the exudate, which contains more or less fibrinous substances. This collects as a thick layer over the peritoneum; the exudate unites the intestines to each other, to the different organs in the abdominal cavity, or to the sides of the abdominal walls. In recent cases these adhesions are easily pulled apart, but later on they become firmly united and very hard to separate (adhesive peritonitis). There is also a quantity of a fibrous exudate thrown out, accompanied by more or less liquid. This varies from a small quantity to several litres. There is always some œdema of the serous wall of the intestine, which becomes soft and friable.

The chronic form may start out at the onset, but generally it follows an acute attack; the peritoneum becomes very much thickened and adhesions form with the intestines and the adjacent organs, at times contracting the intestinal walls and lessening the diameter of the intestinal canal. In the chronic form the exudate is not purulent, as a rule, but is composed of thick, hemorrhagic serum. In the dog we sometimes observe a form of ascites (see page 86) in which we have a chronic thickening of the peritoneum and a collection of a turbid, fibrinous exudate (inflammatory ascites).

A circumscribed peritonitis may be caused by a local ulceration of the intestine or stomach and the irritation extend to the serous coat. We often find small circumscribed deposits on the spleen and liver that have originated from slight peritonitis. In cases where there is a small amount of purulent peritonitis the inflammation remains in one locality and becomes encysted. As a rule, with the exception of circumscribed peritonitis, death generally occurs in the first stages of the disease; and it is only in mild cases, where the exudation is very slight, that there is any chance of recovery. The exudate breaks down and is reabsorbed, but, as a rule, there is such an extensive thickening and adhesions formed that it is only in rare cases that the animal ever is restored to perfect health.

CLINICAL SYMPTOMS AND COURSE OF THE DISEASE. When the disease is caused by some traumatism, by perforation either from the intestines or externally, the symptoms appear very rapidly. At first there are colic, great restlessness, and a stiff, unnatural gait. The posterior extremities are carried out from the body and not flexed. The animal groans and cries. The pain is continual; the abdomen is very sensitive on manipulation, the slightest touch producing great pain. The author has seen several cases, however, where the animal showed very little pain in this disease, but it has been in cases where there was great debility. The abdomen becomes distended in the first stages of the disease, due to inflation of the intestinal tract from gas and later on by the collection of the exudate. When the abdomen is distended, on percussion, if gas is present, the sound is hollow, and when the exudate is present the sound is dull. The exudate, of course, lies on the floor of the abdominal cavity; but where the exudate forms very rapidly the whole abdomen is filled up, causing great dyspnœa.

In the early stages of some cases the abdomen is tucked up, the walls are tense, firm, and painful to the touch, and it is some time before the abdomen begins to enlarge from the collection of the exudate. As a rule, the bowels are constipated, except where there has been some diarrhœa present before the disease started, which is seen in those cases where there is ulceration of the mucous membranes. Vomiting is always present, the vomited matter being greenish-yellow mucus. There is total loss of appetite. The temperature rises to 40° C. or above. If the disease is not so severe as to cause death in a day or two, the temperature fluctuates, being high at one part of the day, and then it becomes subnormal, its character being remittent. The pulse is fast, thin, or wiry, and finally imperceptible.

The great majority of cases are fatal, the animals dying in from one day to a week, according to the intensity of the disease. They usually die in a condition of collapse; in rare cases from heart-failure or suffocation from the collection of the exudate.

Circumscribed or chronic peritonitis produces less marked symptoms and is harder to recognize, the symptoms of diffuse chronic peritonitis being those of ascites. The best way to confirm a diagnosis is to puncture the abdomen with a small trocar and see the character of the fluid.

THERAPEUTICS. Acute diffuse peritonitis should be treated with constant applications of cold-water compresses to the abdomen, and, if the irritation is very intense, the application of a counter-irritant, such as mustard poultices or mustard oil; the latter is the best. Take 30 to 50 grammes of a mixture composed of mustard oil, 10 parts, and olive oil, 100, rubbing it well into the abdomen. Opium is to be given internally in doses of 0.1 to 0.5 gramme, and when there is collapse give whiskey and spirits of camphor. If there is any obstruction of the bowels, give injections of warm water. The exudate can only be removed by puncture of the abdomen, when the acute symptoms have subsided. It must be always borne in mind (and this holds good in inflammation of other serous membranes) that the production of a serous exudate is a process that assists the existing conditions because the liquid helps to keep the intensely inflamed parts separated and prevents friction and its complicating inflammation.

Abdominal Dropsy.
(*Hydrops Ascites; Ascites; Hydrops Abdominis; Hydrops Peritonii.*)

By this is meant a collection of a serous liquid in the abdominal cavity that originates without inflammatory symptoms, being solely due to transudation. The amount of liquid collected varies very much. In some cases there are only a few spoonfuls collected, while in a very large dog the author found 21 litres of fluid.

The color of the fluid is sometimes as clear as water, but it is generally reddish-yellow. It may also be filled with fibrinous flakes, which indicate chronic peritonitis. When exposed to the atmosphere it becomes firm and jelly-like. It is thin and watery and slightly sticky when pressed between the fingers, and about the specific gravity of blood-serum. At first the peritoneum is normal, but, if this condition lasts some time, the peritoneum becomes pale or dull white, and finally a fatty degeneration sets in; when the animal has been repeatedly punctured inflammatory processes take place, and are followed by adhesions.

ETIOLOGY. Ascites never appears as an independent disease, and can only be regarded as the symptom of another disease. As the peritoneal veins belong to the mesenteric system, any obstruction of the portal veins causes these serous collections, as in cirrhosis of the liver or tumors of that organ, or from compression of the mesenteric veins by tumors, abscesses, etc. Ascites is also seen as a symptom of general dropsy from disease of the kidneys or lungs, and from defective action of the heart. It may also be caused by local diseases of the peritoneum, from tuberculosis, carcinoma, or from chronic inflammatory conditions. It is, therefore, best to draw a direct line between transudate and inflammatory exudates.

Friedberger and Fröhner could not find a trace of ascites in a dog ten years old that had carcinomas in nearly all the abdominal organs and peritoneum.

CLINICAL SYMPTOMS. The chief clinical symptom of this disease is the presence of fluid in the abdominal cavity. Small amounts very frequently are not noticed, and in fact cannot be determined by any means except by tapping When there is a considerable collection of serous fluid the abdominal wall is distended, and, from the fluid being in the lower portion of the abdomen, the outlines of the trunk resemble those of a pear; there is a peculiar sunken appearance of the flanks. When the tips of the fingers are struck against the distended abdomen there is a fluctuating movement, and when there is a large quantity of fluid present the sound of the fluid can be heard when the side of the abdomen is struck sharply with the flat of the hand. With percussion we can tell to a certain extent the amount of fluid present. The animal should be made to stand, thus having the fluid lying in

FIG. 30.

Section through the abdomen of the dog showing the distribution of the peritoneum: *a*, kidney; *b*, aorta; *c*, vena cava; *d*, intestine; *d'*, duodenum; *e*, pancreatic gland; *f*, spleen; *g*, liver; *h*, subperitoneal fat.

the base of the abdomen. By percussing, beginning at the lowest part of the abdomen and moving upward on the wall, where there is fluid, we will get a dull sound, and when the line of fluid is passed we get the intestinal or tympanitic sound. It is very important that the animal should be in a standing position, as it can be readily understood when the animal is lying on its side, the fluid being beneath, we would get a clear tympanitic sound all over the wall on the upper side and still have a large quantity of fluid in the cavity.

The higher the fluid collects the greater is the pressure on the abdominal organs and the diaphragm, interfering with regular respiration. The urine is generally normal but reduced in quantity, the digestion impaired, and the bowels disturbed. In the majority of cases diarrhœa is present, and occasional vomiting.

While it seems very easy to make a diagnosis when the above symptoms are present, still the following diseases may present several or all of the symptoms above described.

1. *Acute or Chronic Peritonitis.* When one reads the symptoms of acute peritonitis the diseases can be readily separated, but in the latter part of the disease, when the effusion has collected, or where the chronic stage of peritonitis is present, it is a little difficult to separate them, the only positive means being to puncture the walls with a small trocar (hypodermatic) and obtain a small portion of the fluid; and it is rather common to see ascites associated with chronic peritonitis.

2. *Fatty Deposits in the Abdomen.* This disease is present quite frequently in old dogs; but a differential diagnosis can be made from the fact that where there are enormous collections of fat present the abdomen is round in appearance, and does not become pendulous whether the dog is standing or recumbent. It is well not to puncture in these cases, as it gives no information.

3. *Abnormal Collection of Urine in the Bladder.* In these cases we feel a ball-shaped body in the posterior portion of the abdomen; this swelling does not follow the changes in the position of the body, and is not indicated by percussion. A good way to make a differential diagnosis is to lift up the animal by the posterior extremities, and if it is ascites the liquid will settle on the diaphragm and interfere with the respirations; if the bladder is filled we do not have the dull percussion-sound. To further confirm the diagnosis pass the catheter.

4. *Distention of the Bowels with Gas.* In this instance there is an absence of the fluctuation and the clear tympanitic sound all over the abdomen.

5. *With Collections of Urine in the Abdomen after Rupture of the Bladder.* On the passage of the trocar the clear urine is passed, which can easily be recognized by the color and odor.

6. *In Advanced Gestation.* By careful manipulation the fœtuses can be easily distinguished in the abdomen.

Besides the above conditions, we may also have to distinguish between ascites and tumors of the abdominal cavity (hydrometra, pyometra). All these affections can be recognized by carefully considering the history of the case and the accompanying symptoms.

It is always well to carefully study the exciting cause of the disease, as the course-treatment depends on it. This, however, is rather hard to do. If it is the heart or lungs, it can be recognized; but often we have affections of the liver and spleen that are never recognized during life. To make an examination of these organs it is well to do it just after the animal has been tapped and the fluid has been removed; the walls are then collapsed, and the organs can be manipulated at the same time. If tumors are present, they can be recognized.

Notwithstanding all the etiological conditions described, there are often cases where the cause can only be guessed at.

PROGNOSIS AND THERAPEUTICS. As a rule, the prognosis is unfavorable, as we are unable to remove the exciting cause. The cases that recover are generally in young dogs (Friedberger and Fröhner, and author). Our first effort is to remove the exciting cause, if it is recognized, and then remove the dropsical effusion. This can be done in the following ways :

1. *By Purgatives.* This method is to be followed where there is constipation associated with the disease. Saline purgatives are the best, and those only in sufficient doses to cause a laxative action, so as not to interfere with the appetite.

2. *By Means of Diuretics.* These must only be used where there is positive evidence that there is no previous irritation of the kidneys. The best diuretics are the vegetable, such as digitalis, juniper berries; the only saline drugs are acetate of potassium and sodium.

℞.—Tinc. digitalis fol.	1.0
Sodium acetate	2.0
Oxymel scillæ	20.0
S.—One teaspoonful three times daily.	
℞.—Potassium acetate .	1.0
Spiritus juniperi .	20.0
S.—One teaspoonful three times daily.	

3. *Hydrochlorate of Pilocarpine.* We sometimes obtain very good results with this drug. The injection of the solution subcutaneously is made once daily (0.005 to 0.01 of water). Zahn gave

three drops of the 1 per cent. solution on the tongue three times daily. With this drug the amount of saliva is greatly increased, and the amount of fluid exudated greatly decreased. This must never be administered where there is any disease of the lungs or air-passages.

4. *Tapping or Puncturing the Abdomen.* This is indicated where there is a large collection of fluid that is pressing on the diaphragm, and also as a diagnostic procedure. Whether it is best to remove the fluid in all cases is a question that has not been decided; yet the author is of the opinion that the fluid should be removed, provided the animal is robust and not too old, especially as the operation is comparatively harmless, and has the advantage over purgatives and diuretics in that the accumulation is removed quickly. In a number of cases the fluid has not accumulated after one or more punctures. Friedberger and Fröhner have seen old dogs that have died during or shortly after the operation. The method of puncturing is to take the ordinary trocar (Fig. 31); a narrow calibre one is the best, even if it takes a long time to drain out. We also avoid unconsciousness, which sometimes occurs where a large quantity is drained out suddenly.

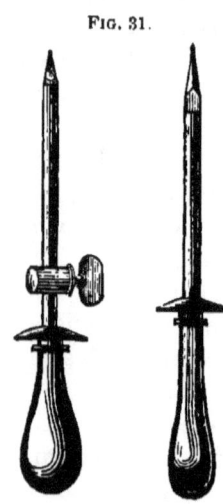

Fig. 31.

Trocars for ascites.

The method of operating is very simple. The place to insert the catheter is generally about the umbilical region, on or to one side of the linea alba. The animal should be placed in a standing position. Should the canula become plugged either by the omentum or intestines coming against the opening of the canula, it is best to introduce an elastic catheter and push them to one side.

DISEASES OF THE LIVER.

Catarrhal Jaundice.
(*Icterus Catarrhalis; Icterus Gastro-duodenalis.*)

ETIOLOGY. In catarrh of the stomach we often have symptoms of jaundice with that disease, especially where the inflammation of the mucous membranes extends to the duodenum, and the ductus choledochus becomes closed by the swelling of its mucous membranes and prevents the exit of bile. As soon as such an obstruction occurs the bile can no longer flow into the intestines; it becomes stagnant and dams back, causing a pressure in the bile-ducts, and being unable to escape it finally enters the lymphatic vessels of the liver, from them into the blood through the thoracic duct. After this there follows a series of symptoms that have been named jaundice (icterus). In the earlier stages of the disease we have to deal with an icterus that is produced by stagnation of the bile. This has a number of names—stagnating icterus, icterus of reabsorption, or hepatogenous icterus. While the swelling of the mucous membranes is generally the cause of this disease, still there are a number of other causes that may also produce it, such as foreign bodies in the ducts (parasites, gallstones), and also from ulceration of the mucous membrane, by the cicatrix of tumors, abscess in or near the liver. The stoppage of the flow of bile sets up an inflammation of the tissues and sometimes forms abscess of the liver; but as the great majority of cases are caused by the catarrhal form, we will describe that. Any cause that will produce catarrh of the stomach will finally produce icterus—improper food, especially when it is frozen; cold drinks after over-heating, decayed meat, salt fish. That form of icterus that is often seen during distemper is very likely to be catarrhal.

PATHOLOGICAL ANATOMY. The symptoms of catarrh of the duodenum are always present; the vessels are more or less injected, and the mucous membrane swollen. As a rule, the mouth of the duct is closed, and it is only by very strong pressure on the gall-bladder that we are able to open it and force out the bile in the duct. In some cases a white clot of mucus is forced out, but Siedamgrotzky has found that in the great majority of cases it is due to swelling of the intestines and not to catarrh of the mucous membrane of the duct.

In some post-mortems we may not find any swelling in the region of the duct, but very frequently the post-mortem changes are so quick as to be hardly recognizable at the autopsy. Another fact to be taken into consideration is that the canal is so very narrow in the dog that it takes a very small amount of swelling to obstruct it.

The body of the liver may be changed; it is generally enlarged and anæmic, and varies in color from a yellow to a yellowish-brown. The color is not regular, but spotted like a nutmeg. The cells of the liver are infiltrated and filled with drops of fat, colored with brownish pigment in the shape of granulated clots. The cadaver is generally anæmic; the blood is either clotted, and in the heart and large bloodvessels we find large lumps of hard reddish-yellow coagula, or the blood may be stained yellow and contain white blood-corpuscles in increased quantities. The red blood-corpuscles are not much changed, but vary in size. All the tissues of the body, except the white substance of the brain, the spinal cord, and the corneal tissue, are stained more or less by the bile-pigment. The muscles of the heart undergo a certain amount of fatty degeneration. The kidneys are anæmic; in the pale portion of the kidney we see extensive whitish stripes running in the direction of the urinary canals; this is caused by an irregular fatty degeneration and pigmentary infiltration of the canals (Siedamgrotzky).

CLINICAL SYMPTOMS AND COURSE OF THE DISEASE. As this disease is generally associated with catarrh of the stomach, the first symptoms in jaundice will be of that disease—loss of appetite, vomiting, coated tongue; in some rare instances, however, these may be absent. The first symptom being that of jaundice (yellowness of the mucous membranes), when the bile and bile acids enter the blood the following symptoms are observed:

1. By the entrance of the coloring-matter of the bile into the tissues these become more or less yellow, the first being the yellowness of the conjunctiva and the sclerotic coat; later the whole cutaneous covering becomes tinted. The yellowness may be very plainly seen on the abdomen, on the inner fascia of the thighs, and the mucous membranes of the mouth and throat; the color may range from a light yellow to a dirty orange-yellow; the latter color generally spreads over the entire body in the later stages of the disease.

2. On account of the coloring-matter being present in the urine it is changed from the normal to a yellowish-green or to a dark greenish-brown color; when put in a vessel and agitated it foams very easily; and if a piece of paper or linen is placed in it, it becomes tinted the color of bile. It is also easy to detect the

presence of bile color of urine by chemical examination. (For further details, see the chapter on the Examination of the Urinary Apparatus.) Besides the bile acids the urine almost always contains albumin, short hyaline casts, pigment granulations, and epithelium of the kidneys.

3. On account of the stoppage of the flow of bile into the intestines the feces become gray or clay colored and contain much undigested fat, and hydrobilirubin is present. The fat substance not being digested, the feces become very fetid; this change is also due to a certain extent to the antiseptic effect of the bile, and as the food is passed along the intestine the tonic effect of the bile is wanting.

4. The bile acids present in the blood produce a certain amount of depression on the nerve-centres, and for this reason we find that the pulse and respirations are subnormal in action, and the temperature is reduced. Other symptoms of the narcotic effect of the bile are seen in some cases where there are depression, great muscular debility, indifference to surroundings, somnolence, and finally deep coma.

The local examination of the liver gives little satisfaction. The author has never been able, except in one case, to find any perceptible enlargement of the liver. Any manipulation of the liver does not seem to give the animals pain even in the later stages of the disease. The prognosis in the dog is generally unfavorable. The yellow coloration gradually becomes deeper, the temperature falls in the majority of cases, the pulse becomes weak and irregular, and finally death occurs with general paralysis. If the case progresses favorably, the first sign is a lessening in the coloration of the urine and a darker hue to the feces, the pulse becomes fuller and more regular, the temperature increases, the animal shows more animation, and the color in the mucous membranes and skin becomes lighter until it finally disappears. If there is a relapse, it is generally caused by improper feeding.

THERAPEUTICS. We must first aim to reduce the irritation of the duodenum, also the bile-ducts. This is first gotten at by regulating the diet: Small quantities of lean meat and alkalies in the form of carbonates and carbonic acid. Strong purgatives have been recommended, such as calomel, castor oil, and infusions of rhubarb; but they are of no particular value—in fact, in the majority of cases, they do more harm than good; but enemas of warm water two or three times daily are very useful. We can also try to empty the gall-bladder mechanically by pressing the abdomen between the fingers in the region of the kidneys; also by faradization—a strong current is to be applied in the region of the liver on both sides of the abdomen; this is to be kept up for ten minutes at a time twice daily. Or by emetics, it being claimed that the compression of the liver during emesis by the abdomen will often empty the gall-bladder. We can also try to carry the bile out of the system by the kidneys. The best drugs to use are mild diuretics, such as acetate of sodium or potassium. Where there is great debility or depression we can use spirits of camphor or ether. [Boldine, the alkaloid of the *Penmus boldus*, has recently been spoken of as producing good results in jaundice; it is given in dose of 0.08 gm. daily.]

The other affections of the liver are of slight importance and are rarely met with during life, consequently they will be only mentioned briefly.

Hyperæmia of the Liver.

This may be caused by either an increased or obstructed flow of the bile, and, therefore, it is important to be able to distinguish between the two.

Congestive hyperæmia of the liver is a normal condition during digestion, but it may be abnormally increased by eating large quantities of food, especially if it is rich and irritating, and from want of exercise; decayed or tainted food may also cause this condition.

Stagnating hyperæmia of the liver may be caused by defective valvular action of the heart or a weakened condition of that organ; in the later stages of acute diseases, such as the lungs; in cases where large numbers of the lung capillaries become atrophied and useless; in great pleuritic exudations; in extensive induration of the lungs, with emphysema; and also in dropsy of the pericardium.

PATHOLOGICAL ANATOMY. The liver is greatly enlarged and very hard; when a section is cut in it the blood seems to run out of it in large quantities. This blood is generally dark colored, especially if the stagnation has been prolonged. The liver tissue may be spotted, the surfaces corresponding with the central veins, which are located in the centre of the acini; or we may notice peripheric zones (nutmeg liver) alternating with lighter colored spaces. The liver gradually becomes smaller and its surface dull, and later on the parenchyma becomes finely granular.

CLINICAL SYMPTOMS. It is not possible to make a positive diagnosis of this disease, we can only suspect it by great tenderness on pressure in the region of the liver, and perhaps slight icterus; but as these symptoms may all be caused by catarrh of the bowels, it is well to be very cautious before making a positive diagnosis.

THERAPEUTICS. This consists in mild purgatives followed by saline laxatives.

Inflammation of the Liver.
(*Hepatitis.*)

This disease appears in two forms—acute parenchymatous and chronic interstitial.

1. **Acute parenchymatous hepatitis** accompanies various infectious diseases, probably in the same way that we see congestive hyperæmia of the lungs; it is also seen as a symptom of acute phosphorus-poisoning.

The pathological-anatomical alterations are as follows: Enlargement, softening, and a friable condition of the tissue, which breaks easily to the touch. At first it is dark red, but later on it becomes a yellowish clay color, with a roughened appearance of the external surface, due to the enlarged acini; the capsule (Glisson's) is dull and thickened, due to a certain amount of peri-hepatitis. If the disease lasts any time, the volume of the liver is greatly lessened.

The clinical symptoms are: Evidences of catarrh of the stomach, pain on pressure in the region of the liver, icterus.

The therapeutic treatment consists of light, easily digested food, with little fat, and saline laxatives.

2. **Chronic Interstitial Hepatitis (Cirrhosis of the Liver).** This disease originates from causes that are at present unknown. Friedberger and Fröhner surmise that it is caused by valvular disease of the heart.

PATHOLOGICAL ANATOMY. There are two stages of change in this disease. In the first stage the liver is very much enlarged and hard, the edges of the lobes are blunt, on the surface there are a number of uneven depressions. On making a transverse section we find a network of reddish-gray tissue that surrounds the acini; later on this involves the acini. In the second stage we find a cicatricial retraction of the newly formed tissue, and at the same time a disappearance of true tissue of the liver. The liver then becomes gradually smaller and has a very irregular surface; the capsule is thickened and in some places depressed; the tissue is hard and tough when cut with a knife.

CLINICAL SYMPTOMS. The disease generally starts without any visible symptoms, although it is a common disease in old dogs that have lived well. When the disease becomes pretty well advanced we find evidences of an interference in the portal circulation by the appearance of ascites and chronic catarrh of the stomach. With these symptoms we also find a tendency to constipation with occasional changes to diarrhœa. In rare cases a certain amount of icterus is present. This is due either to interference with the passage of bile from the gall-bladder by catarrh of the duodenum, or to a contracted condition of the small bile-ducts. There is no pain on pressure in the region of the liver, even in the advanced stages of the disease.

The disease is generally very slow, but ends fatally, and when there are ascites and some œdema of the extremities present the end is not far off.

THERAPEUTICS. This consists in treating the case as if it were one of catarrh of the stomach, by means of saline purgatives, and the ascites by puncture.

3. **Purulent Inflammation of the Liver (Abscess of the Liver).** This may be caused by injuries, such as blows or kicks externally, or from foreign bodies or perforating abscesses coming from the stomach, from metastasis, from phlebitis and the thrombus undergoing purulent destruction, and from pyæmia in abscess of the stomach.

PATHOLOGICAL ANATOMY. Abscesses of the liver appear singly or in large numbers; the traumatic abscess is generally solitary and the metastatic multiple. The pus is cream-like, and in some instances fetid and reddish-green in color. Small abscesses may heal by reabsorption, but the large ones open into the abdominal cavity and cause a fatal peritonitis.

CLINICAL SYMPTOMS. Icteric symptoms, with frequent chills, point to abscess of the liver. Treatment is useless.

Fatty Liver.
(*Hepar Adiposum.*)

This is an abnormal diffuse fatty infiltration of the cells of the liver. It is hard and seems anæmic when a section is made through the organ. The cells are found to be filled with numerous fatty drops.

This condition is seen in old animals that have been fed well and had little exercise, and is a natural fatty infiltration. It must, however, be distinguished from the fatty degeneration that is found to follow several poisons, and in the later stages of consumption. In fatty infiltration the blood of the portal vein carries abnormal quantities of fat into the liver which is deposited in the cells. In fatty degeneration the fat originates in the cells themselves; this is due to the albumin separating into two atoms. One contains nitrogen, while in the other nitrogen is absent. This latter part undergoes fatty degeneration.

The treatment of fatty liver is the same as any adipose condition.

Neoformations of the Liver and Gallstones.

The neoformations found in the liver of the dog are sarcomas, carcinoma, and adenoma. These cause irregular enlargements on the body of the liver, and produce symptoms similar to those of cirrhosis of the liver.

All treatment is useless.

Gallstones are very rare in the dog; the only way that they might be recognized would be the appearance of icterus, produced by retention, with intense colic, which disappears in a short time.

The following parasites have been found in the liver: Distoma lanceolatum and distoma campanulatum. In the bile-ducts Ercolani and Lissizin found a fully developed male strongylus gigas in the liver of a young dog which had died of severe convulsions.

Amyloid and Lardaceous Liver.

Amyloid liver, as a rule, is a symptom of a general amyloid condition developed from a cachectic state from prolonged suppurating wounds or from chronic inflammation of the pectoral membranes.

The liver is very much enlarged and blunt on the edges of the lobes. It is tough and firm on section, the cut surface speckled and grayish-brown in color. On microscopical examination the walls of the capillaries will be found to have undergone amyloid degeneration; the cells are atrophic and show partial fatty degeneration. These parts become blue when brought in contact with iodine or sulphuric acid, reddish-brown with tincture of iodine, and methyl-violet turns them intensely red.

Lardaceous liver is developed when we have a disease that has a tendency to produce amyloid degeneration. The liver becomes very large. With it we generally have amyloid kidney with albumin in the urine, and we also may have amyloid spleen.

This disease is generally impossible to diagnosticate and useless to treat.

POISONS.

A short abstract on poisons, together with their symptoms and treatment, is here given:

Poisoning by Arsenic. The poison may be given intentionally or by eating some of the various rat poisons. There is a violent inflammation of the stomach and intestines, with great restlessness, bloody diarrhœa, vomiting, and dyspnœa, great weakness, and finally collapse, death occurring in a few hours.

THERAPEUTICS. Emetics and ferruginous agents, the hydrated peroxide of iron in water every quarter of an hour; carbonate of magnesium, a teaspoonful every fifteen minutes, followed by alcoholic stimulants. The stomach-pump can also be used if there is not prompt emesis.

Poisoning by Hydrocyanic Acid (Prussic Acid). This is generally given intentionally in the form of cyanide of potassium or the pure acid. There is an odor of bitter almonds on the breath. The symptoms are vomiting, yelping cries, dyspnœa, convulsions of the legs, and death in a short time. If the dose should be small there are great restlessness, fear, vomiting, dyspnœa, dilated pupils, convulsions, especially of the extremities, fall in the temperature, marked depression of the pulse and respirations, cyanosis, and unconsciousness.

THERAPEUTICS. Emetics, artificial respiration (rhythmic pressure of the lower abdominal walls), bathing in cold water, stimulants, chlorine water, and atropia.

Poisoning by Carbolic Acid. This is generally produced by licking applications containing carbolic acid, tar, or creosote that have been applied to the skin, or through absorption through the skin from a wound, or through some mucous membrane (uterus), and by mistakes in giving it internally. The urine is a dark olive-green; there are light colic, pain on pressure of the abdomen, vomiting, diarrhœa, great inflammation and redness of the mouth, weakness, slight decrease in temperature, twitching of the muscles, total paralysis, convulsions, and collapse.

THERAPEUTICS. Glauber's salt, white of eggs, stimulants.

Poisoning by Iodoform. This may be caused by licking wounds dressed by the drug (Albrecht, Fröhner, and author), and injections of iodoform solutions into cysts. In the acute form we have great gastric disturbances, small and frequent pulse, decrease of the internal temperature, suppression of urine, albuminuria, dulness, and convulsions, alternated with great excitement, collapse. In the slow form we have catarrh of the mucous membranes, emaciation, and skin eruptions.

THERAPEUTICS. In the acute form, first give emetics, followed by carbonate of potash, large quantities of starch, atropia; in the slow form, saline laxatives and tonics, and remove the cause.

Poisoning by Phosphorus. This may be caused by eating some of the various roach or bug poisons that have been spread on bread and eaten by the animal. There is constant vomiting; the vomited matter has an odor of phosphorus; if taken into a dark place it is luminous. There are great restlessness, howling, whining, great heat, and indications of intense irritation of the mouth and throat; the saliva is thick and copious. After these symptoms have been present for some time the animal becomes quiet, the mucous membranes become dirty yellow, great pain on pressure of the liver, stomach, and intestines. The feces are tinged with blood and albuminuria, and, according to some authors, if there is any icteric coloration, it is a positive symptom; finally paralysis and collapse.

THERAPEUTICS. Use sulphate of copper as an emetic, turpentine in emulsion, and treat any other symptoms as they appear.

  R.—Cupri sulph. 1.0
   Aqua destil. 50.0
  Sig.—A tablespoonful every ten minutes until you get emesis.

Poisoning by Mercury. 1. Acute poisoning by corrosive sublimate is very rare; the symptoms are intense inflammation of the entire intestinal tract, vomiting of blood, and bloody diarrhœa, with intense local irritation, symptoms of paralysis, and death.

THERAPEUTICS. Albumin and iron preparations, followed by stimulants.

2. Mercurial poisoning taking a slower course may be caused by calomel or mercurial dressings, especially from mercurial ointment when it is applied externally. We have salivation, catarrh of the stomach, profuse diarrhœa, emaciation, with marked muscular debility.

THERAPEUTICS. Sulphur, iodide of potassium, stimulants, and nutritious food, and clean the mouth with a wash containing chlorate of potassium.

Poisoning by Strychnine. This is generally administered intentionally, although it may be caused by giving repeated small doses of nux vomica, the dog being particularly susceptible to this poison. There are violent tetanic spasms, trismus, and opisthotonus. The convulsions are clonic, having intermissions between them.

THERAPEUTICS. Give narcotics, chloral hydrate in clysters, 2.5 grammes to 50 of water; morphia, also tannin and tincture of iodine. Never administer chloroform or ether.

Meat- and chloroform-poisoning will be mentioned later on.

DISEASES OF THE RESPIRATORY ORGANS.

PHYSICAL EXAMINATION OF THE RESPIRATORY APPARATUS.

In making an examination of the respiratory apparatus the following points are to be considered:

Examination of the Nose.

It is a rather hard thing to make an examination of the nose on account of the anatomical conformation of that part, and we are practically restricted to the aid a nasal mirror can give us and the character of the nasal secretions. The external portion of the nose is damp and cold in health, and dry and warm when a dog has any fever or elevation of temperature, in the first stages of nasal catarrh, and any inflammatory condition of the eyes. This should not be taken as a positive evidence, as frequently cases are seen where this is no guide, the nose being cold when there is great fever.

Swelling, redness, and excoriation at the entrance of the nasal chambers indicate an inflammatory and purulent condition of the nasal mucous membrane.

Any discharge from the nose, beyond a natural moistness, indicates some diseased condition. In cases of acute nasal catarrh it is clear and thin, nearly pure serum in the beginning, but later on it becomes mucous, and finally muco-purulent. In chronic catarrh it is compact, sticky, and finally very tenacious, and sticks to the external opening of the nose, often entirely closing it up and eroding the skin where it comes in contact with it. In distemper it is yellowish to yellowish-green in color; sometimes it is streaked with blood or pus, and in rare cases it has a fetid odor. (For further particulars, see chapter on Distemper.)

When the discharge is copious, especially when the head is jerked downward with a sneezing cough, it is generally a sign of some irritation of the frontal sinuses. A nasal discharge following coughing generally comes from some trouble in the deep sections of the air-passages, larynx, windpipe, bronchia, or the lungs; a rusty yellow discharge indicates croupous pneumonia; this is, however, very rare. Frequent sneezing, with a copious purulent, bad-smelling discharge mixed with blood, points to the presence of pentastoma tænioides in the frontal or nasal cavities. In cases of acute catarrh of the throat, foreign bodies, paralysis of the larynx, or large tumors in the throat, the discharge may be mixed with some of the contents of the stomach. These affections are extremely rare in the dog compared with other animals. True cases of bleeding of the nose are seen in hemorrhagic catarrh of that organ, in suppurating conditions of the nasal cavities from the pentastome, and also in distemper. Hemorrhage of the lungs is indicated when there are large masses of frothy blood discharged from the nose and mouth. Wheezy respiration is generally due to some contraction of the nasal cavities. For instance, as a consequence of violent nasal catarrh, tumors, fractures of the nasal bones, narrowing of the nasal passages, pressure from some of the neighboring organs, solid collections of matter. In some breeds of dogs, such as pugs and bulldogs, the passage is so narrow that a slight contraction may cause them to breathe through the mouth. The nasal sound is like a snore when copious accumulations of mucus have collected on the mucous membranes, as in distemper, or the later stages of simple catarrh of the nose. In all the affections named many animals seem to have intense itching, which they indicate by rubbing the nose against solid objects or wiping it with the paws.

Physical Diagnosis of the Larynx and Windpipe.

The symptoms include the bark, cough, and respiration, as well as the local symptoms. The bark is always rough, hoarse, or shrill in all affections of the internal larynx, and is always of great importance in rabies (barking howl). The cough is an accompaniment of all affections of the larynx; it is generally loud and either short, raw, hoarse, bark-like; and in the later stages of catarrh, where there is much mucus, it is loose, moist, and rattling, and may be produced by slight pressure on either side of the larynx, by cold, pressure, or after drinking; in any chronic irritation of the larynx, any excitement, such as the pleasure of meeting a person they know, will start a severe coughing spell. The respiration is always dyspnœic and accompanied by a stenotic bruit when from the results of some diseased condition there is a contraction of the larynx. Auscultation of the larynx is performed by placing the ear directly on the larynx. Normally the sound is a slightly wheezy respiration. Rubbing, creaking, or rattling sounds indicate more or less liquid accumulations (mucus, pus, or blood); wheezy, gasping, snoring sounds indicate severe swelling of the mucous membrane or tough mucus (chronic catarrh); it may also indicate the presence of tumors, membranous accumulations, and paralysis of the muscles of the larynx.

A local examination of the larynx can be made both externally and internally. Externally the larynx can be examined for fractures or dislocation of the cartilages, for œdematous, phlegmonous, or emphysematic swellings of the part or its surroundings, and sensitiveness to pressure always indicates some irritation of the larynx.

The internal examination of the larynx is very easy and simple, except in cases where the animal is very vicious; the method of keeping the mouth open is fully described on page 27, and then by means of a spatula or the handle of a spoon the tongue can be depressed or pulled out of the mouth with a pair of blunt forceps; the examination should be made near a window or by means of a lamp; the light can then be thrown into the posterior portion of the throat. In vicious animals, they can be put under ether or stupefied by morphine. When the mouth is opened and the tongue depressed we can easily see the entire pharynx and the upper wall of the larynx, and in some cases a part of the windpipe. In acute catarrh the mucous membrane of the larynx is injected and red, and covered with slimy white or yellowish mucus. In chronic catarrh it is not so red, but the mucous membrane has a number of bluish-red vessels running through it, and covered with tough, glassy, or purulent mucus; the membranes are sometimes granular; we may also find at the entrance of the œsophagus foreign bodies, tumors, or abscesses.

Physical Diagnosis of the Lungs.

The lungs of the dog consist of a number of layer-like portions which are united by the bronchia and connective tissue; the ana-

104 DISEASES OF THE RESPIRATORY ORGANS.

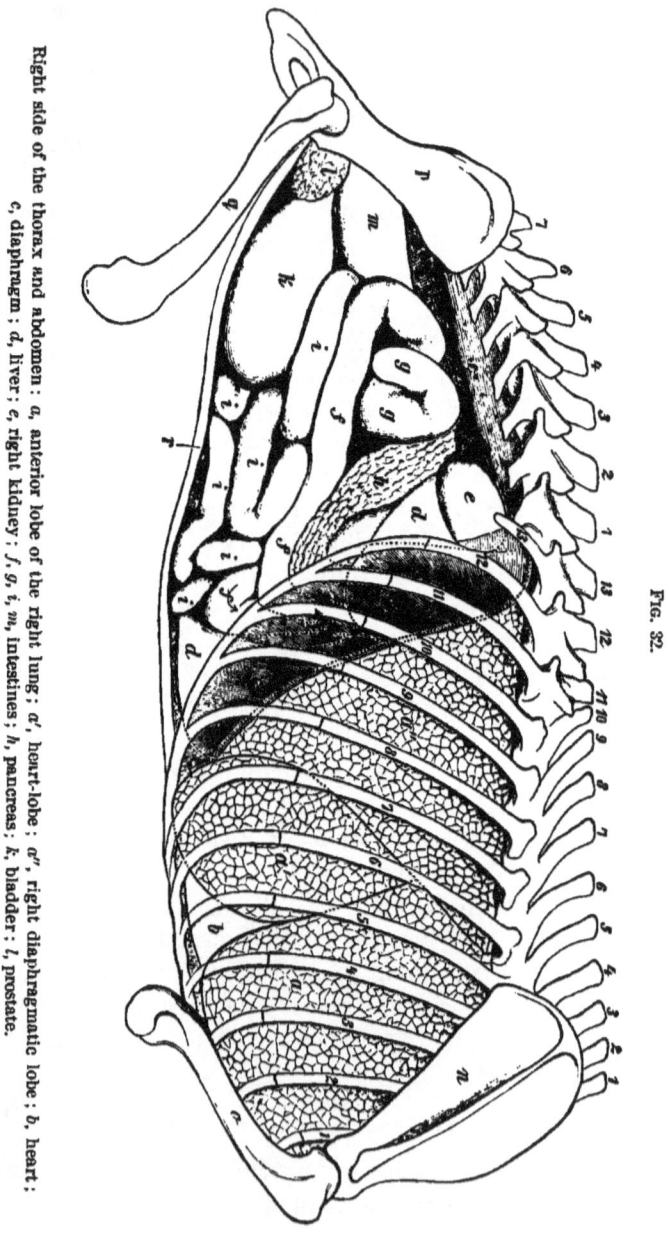

FIG. 32.

Right side of the thorax and abdomen: *a*, anterior lobe of the right lung; *a'*, heart-lobe; *a''*, right diaphragmatic lobe; *b*, heart; *c*, diaphragm; *d*, liver; *e*, right kidney; *f, g, i, m*, intestines; *h*, pancreas; *k*, bladder; *l*, prostate.

tomical positions of the lungs are shown in Figs. 32 and 33. The left lung is divided into two portions or lobes, an anterior and a

PHYSICAL DIAGNOSIS OF THE LUNGS.   105

posterior; the former is again subdivided in two; this division is not very distinct in some cases. The section that divides the large

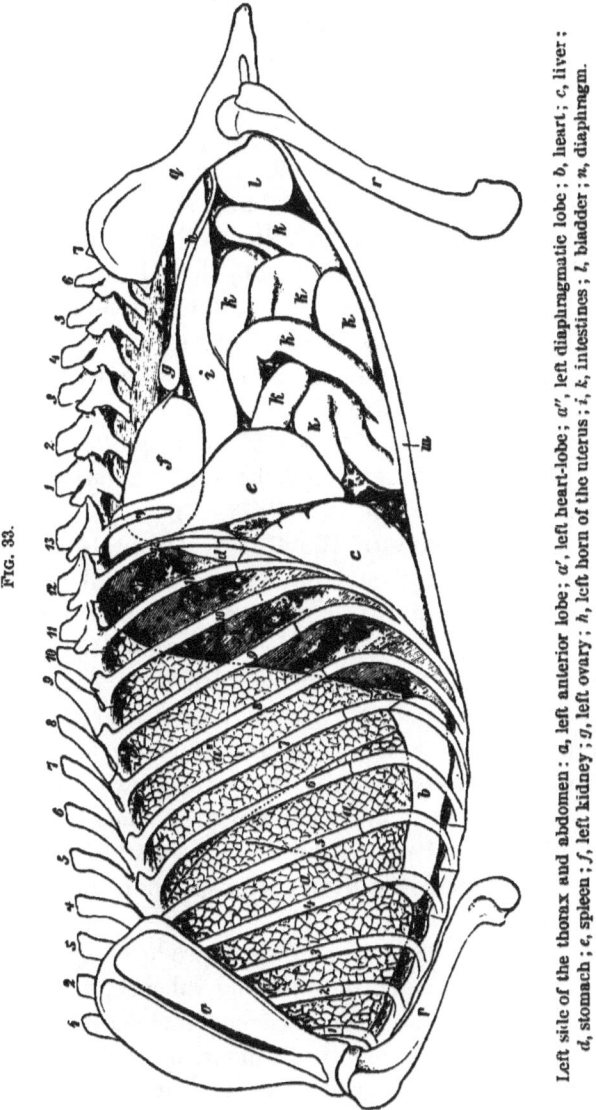

Fig. 33. Left side of the thorax and abdomen: a, left anterior lobe; a', left heart-lobe; a'', left diaphragmatic lobe; b, heart; c, liver; d, stomach; e, spleen; f, left kidney; g, left ovary; h, left horn of the uterus; i, k, intestines; l, bladder; m, diaphragm.

lobes begins opposite the fourth or fifth vertebra and runs downward and backward as far as the sixth rib; the anterior lobe extends as far as the first rib, and anteriorly and posteriorly to the sixth rib; the large posterior lobe extends back as far as the eleventh or twelfth vertebra, where it extends upward and lies between the vertebra and the diaphragm. The left lung has a small incision near the heart called the heart incision. The right lung is somewhat larger than the left, and extends as far back as the twelfth or thirteenth vertebra; it is divided into four lobes; the posterior lobe is considerably larger than the corresponding lobe of the left lung. The cardial lobe lies upon the heart, almost surrounding that organ; the other lobes hold the same relation as they do in the left lung. The middle lobe of the lungs is a club-shaped portion that lies in a special groove in the mediastinum, extending anteriorly as far as the heart and posteriorly to the diaphragm.

In making an examination of the lungs we must take into consideration the shape of the cavity of the chest, sensitiveness to pressure, the number and character of the respiratory movements, the character of the cough, and the information derived from auscultation and percussion.

Shape of the Cavity of the Chest. In healthy animals the two sides of the chest should be symmetrical. A depression on one side means pain in that portion of the chest, dry pleuritis, recent fractures of the ribs, one-sided contraction of the lung after a rapid absorption of the exudate of pleurisy. In a case where there is a fractured rib there may be a protrusion in one place, an inflammatory condition of the ribs, and tumors of the wall of the chest; when the whole chest seems swollen it indicates double pleuritis, with a great amount of exudate present; when only the posterior half of the thorax seems distended and we find the abdomen enlarged, it indicates ascites, tumors, or collections in the abdominal cavity.

Sensitiveness to Pressure. This is produced by a number of inflammatory conditions of the skin and subcutis, the ribs, or the intercostal muscles in cases of muscular rheumatism, in fracture of the ribs, and quite frequently in pleuritis.

Number and Character of the Respiratory Movements. Normal breathing is performed in the dog, as in other animals, through muscular action in inspiring, and the elasticity of the tissue of the lungs and the walls of the chest in expiration; this is also aided by the pressure of the intestines on the diaphragm. It is only when the respiration is obstructed that the assistance of the muscles of respiration is required in expiration. The works on physiology give more minute details on this subject. The normal respirations are from twelve to eighteen per minute, the size of the animal making a slight difference, in the smaller dog of course being more. Various conditions tend to alter the above number, such as running, physical excitement, overloading of the stomach, and advanced pregnancy. While the respirations in the dog are regular, yet they are disturbed more quickly by physical excitement than in any other animal.

A pathological lessening of the number of the respirations may be seen in all serious affections of the brain and its membranes; in acute infectious diseases, such as septicæmia and distemper; and in cases of contraction of the air-passages.

A slight increase in the respirations may follow any increase of temperature; they are also increased when any pain is present, in circumscribed pleuritis, in the commencement of peritonitis, in fractures of the ribs, and in rheumatism of the intercostals. Laborious respiration (difficulty in breathing, dyspnœa) is seen where there is any contraction of the pharynx, larynx, or windpipe; for instance, from the swelling and inflammation of the mucous membrane in those organs, foreign bodies, tumors, etc. We see laborious breathing, with great increase of the number of respirations, in any irritation of the bronchial tubes where they become contracted or filled with mucus, and in all diseases of the true lung-tissue; in all exudates into the pleuritic cavity, or in diseases of the abdomen where there are collections of solids or fluids in the abdominal cavity that press on the diaphragm; in cramp, or spasm of the muscles of respiration, as in strychnine-poisoning, tetanus, or eclampsia in nursing bitches; in diseases of the heart where there is stagnation of the thoracic circulation. In all cases of dyspnœa in the dog the animal rarely lies down, but prefers to assume the sitting position with the front legs spread wide apart.

Cough. The nature and form of cough are very important symptoms in all diseases of the respiratory organs. Cough is produced by reflex action from all parts of the mucous membranes of the pharynx, windpipe, bronchia, and also by an inflamed pleura. The pulmonary tissue never produces cough by reflex irritation. The so-called "stomach cough" is only imaginary, no such thing can truly be said to exist. Cough is generally absent in diseases of the brain or in cases of carbonic-acid poisoning, as well as in cases where the glottis and the muscles of respiration are paralyzed; in such cases it is impossible to produce coughing by manipulation of the throat. Dogs do not cough intentionally, but if it is very painful they can suppress it.

An animal can be made to cough by pressing the sides of the pharynx between the fingers; if the throat is pressed hard, an animal will cough and make motions of the throat very similar to those of vomiting.

Occasionally an animal is found in whom the most severe pressure will not produce any signs of coughing, although it may make a swallowing movement.

Several spells of coughing after a slight pressure on the pharynx point to a diseased condition of that organ; if the same pressure is made on the windpipe, and the animal coughs violently, it also indicates a diseased condition of those parts. In bronchitis and catarrhal pneumonia coughing can be produced by tapping on the wall of the chest.

In the beginning of acute bronchitis and in pleurisy the cough is dull, weak, usually frequent, dry, and husky. In chronic bronchitis, catarrhal or croupal pneumonia, emphysema and œdema it is very much the same, but not so frequent, and in tuberculosis it is hollow and dull. There are many exceptions to this rule; for instance, in cases where foreign bodies enter the lung through the mouth or by vomiting, the cough is convulsive and violent, resembling whooping-cough (chronic pharyngeal catarrh) in its intensity. As a rule, dogs cough more frequently at night than during the day.

The expectorations cannot be examined in the dog as they are in man, as the animal generally swallows all the secretions; in rare instances there may be a small portion of the mucus thrown out of the mouth in coughing. We can often see the animal chewing or swallowing after a fit of coughing, which indicates that the animal has brought up a piece of mucus into the mouth or pharynx; this is seen when the cough becomes loose, moist, or rattling, and is what is termed "looseness" of the cough, being seen generally in pharyngeal, tracheal, and bronchial catarrh. The largest amount of excretion is seen in bronchial and tubercular diseases; while in catarrhal and croupous pneumonia, and also in certain forms of bronchitis, we find the excretion is thick and firm, and accompanied by dry, laborious coughing-spells, and at the end of the cough there is a swallowing movement. In hemorrhage of the lungs the cough is accompanied with more or less foamy blood from the nostrils and mouth, and in some cases symptoms of choking; a slight hemorrhage may escape our observation, as the blood is generally all swallowed.

Percussion of the Thorax. Percussion (tapping) is performed by means of a percussion-hammer and an ivory or metal plate (pleximeter) (Fig. 34). Lay the plate close to the wall of the chest, and, with the hammer in the other hand, strike the plate a number of light, quick taps; the fingers can also be used, and are preferred by some. Place the index or middle finger of the left hand firmly on the chest-wall, and with the index-finger of the right hand tap on the finger of the left hand.

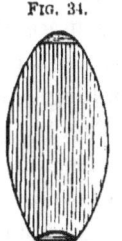

Fig. 34.

The limits of percussion are given in Figs. 32 and 33; but it must be taken into consideration that on expiration the posterior limit of the lungs is carried forward of the dotted line and not extending to the last rib; and, also, when the stomach or intestines are very much filled with gas, crowding the diaphragm forward, lessens the extent of the lungs. In percussion we make the distinction between a clear, loud, normal lung sound and a tympanitic, dull, or solid sound of disease. The clear normal sound of the healthy lung is heard all over the thorax, the volume of sound depending on the thickness of the lung at the particular part being examined. The muscular layers of the

Pleximeter.

chest have a certain effect on the sound, very thick walls lessening the sound to a certain extent; the sound is more or less dull over the shoulder-blade, sternum, and back; the posterior borders of the lungs often have no perceptible sound, as they are so thin.

A dull, muffled sound, which has been mentioned in the above classification, is heard in the following conditions: In the tissues of the lung where the air cannot reach, as in hepatization; in croupal pneumonia; in tuberculosis, provided that the diseased centre is not entirely surrounded with tissue containing air; in tumors of the lungs; in hemorrhagic infarction; in sections of the lungs that are compressed by pleuritic or pericardial effusions. Œdema of the lung is only accompanied with dulness when it is well advanced.

The dull sound is present when an abnormal medium is between the lungs and the pleximeter, as in the various pleural diseases; tumors of the pleura; pleuritic or dropsical effusions; and also in certain pathological alterations of the chest, as in œdema, tumors. The more the tissues fill up near the walls of the chest and the greater the density of the medium between the pleximeter and the lungs, the more indistinct and muffled the sound becomes.

The tympanitic sound is heard where there is any cavity or hollow in the lungs, as in pneumothorax. In the alteration of the tension of the parenchyma of the lungs we find it above pleuritic exudates and in the neighborhood of large tumors of the lungs, or in compression of the lungs from the pushing forward of the diaphragm due to tumors, ascites; also moistening of the alveola by fluids and reduction in the contained air, as in the loose moist stage of croupal pneumonia; also where there are many small tubercular centres in the tissue of the lungs, which are hollow in the centre and contain air, and sometimes in œdema of the lungs. Cutaneous emphysema of the walls of the chest gives a clear tympanitic sound. There are several modifications of this sound, as the cracked-pot or metallic tinkling percussion-sound; but these are not of much diagnostic value, as they appear only when there may be large cavernous spaces in the walls of the chest.

Fig. 35.

Stethoscope.

Auscultation of the Thorax. This is performed either by putting the ear directly against the walls of the chest over the affected region (direct auscultation), or by using a stethoscope (Fig. 35) (indirect auscultation). [A form of stethoscope called the "Phonendoscope," a modification of the phonograph, has lately been introduced and used in the larger animals with considerable success, but the translator finds that on account of its size it is not of much practical use in the dog.] The first method is the best, especially with restless animals.

The ear distinguishes the true respiratory and accessory sounds. In the former we hear a vesicular respiratory bruit, which has a lapping character; and the bronchial respiratory bruit, which is a blowing murmur; and, lastly, an indistinct respiratory bruit, which is a slight soft murmur.

The vesicular respiratory bruit is heard when any portion of the lung that is filled with air lies against the wall of the chest. In normal inspiration the sound is a smooth, regular murmur, the air going directly into the alveola without any resistance. This sound can be increased very much even during health by active movements or during excitement; it is also much clearer and louder in emaciated animals where the walls of the chest are thin. The vesicular murmur is always much louder in young animals, and especially in puppies; the murmur is also noted in expiration in animals under nine months. According to the amount of irritation, the vesicular murmur is lessened in bronchial catarrh where there is much swelling of the mucous membrane and secretions collected; in stenosis of the upper air-passages; in emphysema of the lungs; in certain stages of catarrhal pneumonia; in pleuritic or dropsical exudations; in thickening of the pleura from the deposit of lymph-masses, tumors, or œdema.

It disappears entirely in croupous pleuritic effusions, in pneumothorax, and in closure of one of the large bronchial tubes.

The vesicular murmur is increased in dyspnœa in portions of the lungs that are healthy when other parts are diseased, the healthy portions doing all of the work; this is especially seen in bronchitis, where the smaller bronchia are plugged up with secretions. We occasionally find an irregular vesicular murmur in healthy dogs, but it is also heard in cases of bronchitis; this murmur is only heard on inspiration.

The murmur of expiration is very slight; in normal cases it can hardly be heard; it is quite plain when the breathing is strong after excitement, action, etc., especially in young dogs and those animals that have a thin chest-wall. According to the diseased condition, the sound is strengthened, varied in tone, and prolonged.

The bronchial respiratory bruit (bronchial breathing, wheezing sound) may be heard in the normal respiration of the pharynx, windpipe, and the anterior part of the chest in diseased conditions; it appears where any part of the lung is deprived of air, and the disease has plugged up the smaller bronchia and extended to the larger-sized bronchia. This is the case in the various pulmonic affections, where we find large sections of the lungs are obstructed, or in compression of the lung by a pleuritic exudate or by tumors, and in rare cases by the pressure of the diaphragm where it is pushed forward from the collections of fluids in the abdomen. It is also heard when a quantity of mucus is coming up the bronchial tubes; this sound disappears when the mucus is coughed up. Lastly, we find it in cases where the lung has large cavernous spaces in it.

Indistinct respiratory bruits are heard in lobular pneumonia, where the diseased lobules are located among clear tissue that the air is passing into, and where the true character of the respiratory bruit is not heard on account of the loud rattling of the air going through the contracted bronchial tubes. Indistinct respiratory sounds are also heard where there is more or less mucus in the bronchial tubes and after the animal has had a coughing spell the true bronchial sound is heard.

Irregular bronchial sounds (rattling bruits) are caused by the movement of the mucus or fluids that are in the air-passages, being carried to and fro by the passage of air. They are dry (snoring, wheezing) where a small quantity of sticky mucus collects in the bronchial tubes, as is seen in some catarrhal affections, and in cases where the mucous membrane is considerably swollen. The snoring sound is generally heard in the large bronchial tubes. The wheezing sounds occur in the smaller bronchial tubes. A spell of coughing produces considerable change in the character of the slight, rattling sounds of the chest. The rattling sounds are moist when the secretions are liquid; the thicker they are the duller the bruits become. We hear moist, rattling sounds when the secretions are collected in the large bronchia; this sound is also heard when there are cavernous portions in the lungs. We find much less when this is the case in the middle bronchia, and a very low bronchial bruit when the small bronchia are involved. By this means we can distinguish in what position the irritation lies in the bronchia; this is rather important in diagnosing a case of bronchitis. When the fine bronchioles are involved it has a cracking or crepitant sound and sibilant bruits; this is only heard during inspiration. This sound may sometimes be heard in the alveolar passage and in the alveoli themselves when they are filled with mucus or closed up, and where the air can only reach them by strong inspiration. This is seen in the first and third stages of croupal and catarrhal pneumonia, in œdema of the lungs, and in capillary bronchitis; in the last the crepitation is mixed with an irregular rattling sound. We have also the friction-sound of the pleura; this is not heard in the normal condition, but in disease; it is either crepitating, scraping, or scratching. It is heard in pleurisy; as a rule, it is louder on inspiration than expiration; it is produced by collections of fibrinous accumulations on the pleura. These sounds are not heard when the pleura is separated by the presence of an exudate; the sound is plainest at the commencement of the disease and when the exudate is being absorbed. This sound is not altered by coughing, and in this way can be distinguished from rattling sounds, which are heard when it is a case of pleuro-pneumonia. The rubbing sound caused by the broken ends of a fractured rib is indicated by the crepitation on movement of the ends of the rib.

DISEASES OF THE NASAL CAVITIES.

Catarrh of the Nose.

(*Cold in the Head; Coryza; Rhinitis; Nasal Catarrh.*)

ETIOLOGY. Catarrh of the nose (catarrhal inflammation of the nasal mucous membranes) occurs very frequently and originates from local causes (dust, smoke, pentastomum tænioides) or by cold. Cold in the head is also a symptom of distemper, and may appear secondarily in any inflammation of the other mucous membranes of the head.

CLINICAL SYMPTOMS AND COURSE. These are sneezing, wiping the nose with the paws, or rubbing it against some object. Later, a nasal discharge, which is watery and liquid at first, and later becomes turbid, thicker and more tenacious; and it may become purulent, according to the complications that may appear later on. If the cavities in the upper chamber of the nose are affected, the discharge is very profuse and there is more or less disturbance of the general system. When the catarrh is confined to the anterior chambers the nasal cavities are often very much contracted and we hear a snuffling nasal bruit; and if the chamber is very much contracted we may see dyspnœa, and the animal is compelled to breathe through the mouth. This is apt to occur more in those dogs that have narrow, twisted, or curved nasal chambers, as in the case of the pug and bulldog. True bleeding of the nose (epistaxis), or mucus streaked with blood, is very seldom seen. The duration of a case of nasal catarrh is about a week; we may, however, occasionally see a case where there is a tendency to a chronic condition; in such a case the secretion becomes purulent and has a tendency to dry around the nose, forming dirty crusts around the nostrils and the upper lip. In very bad cases the secretion is purulent, with a very bad odor, and in rare instances streaked with blood. This is specially the case where the pentastomum tænioides (*Linguatula tænoïdes*) is the cause of the diseased condi-

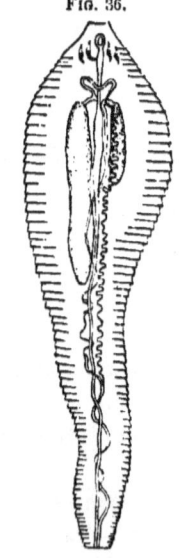

Fig. 36.

Pentastoma tænioides.

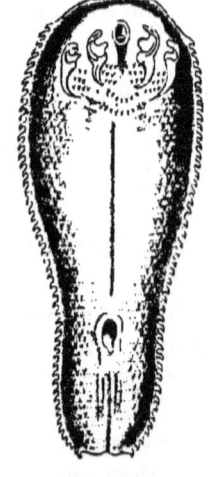

Fig. 37.

Pentastoma denticulum.

tion of the mucous membrane. This tænia-like parasite, which belongs to the class of arachnides, has a flat, curved body which is indented at its borders, and fitted with hook-shaped claws, which can be extended forward, and between them it has a buccal orifice, which is surrounded by a horny ring; there are no organs of sight, respiration, or circulation; the female is 26 to 130 mm. long and 3 to 4 mm. wide; the male is about 20 mm. long and the same width as the female; toward the posterior part of the body both sexes are about 1 to 2 mm. wide. (See Fig. 36.)

These parasites are found in the sinuses of the forehead and the upper nasal chambers; they may also find their way into the pharynx, and are developed sexually. The eggs are yellowish-brown, as many as 500,000 being found in one female; these eggs are mixed with the nasal mucus and passed out where they become attached to some vegetable substance eaten with the vegetable food by a herbivorous animal or man. In the stomach it becomes free when the shell is dissolved off and reaches the liver in various ways. It may be found in the spleen, kidneys, peritoneum, where it becomes encysted; this is the sexless larva-form, pentastomum denticulatum (*Lunguatula denticulata*) (Fig. 37). It resembles the sexed parasite in general shape, except that it is much smaller, from 4 to 5 mm. long, and in its anterior part about 1.5 mm. wide. It lies in a detached cyst, which is about 5 mm. long. In six months it becomes sufficiently developed to break through the cyst-wall and by direct migration finds its way to the bronchial tubes; it is coughed up from the lungs by the host, and finds its way into the nasal cavities of the dog through the food or is carried into the nose in respiration and crawls up into the nasal cavities. Hering has seen the disease but once; Friedberger and Fröhner have seen it in a few cases; but Colan has seen sixty-four cases, and found from one to eleven parasites in the nasal chambers of each case.

Pentastomum catarrh is different from ordinary nasal catarrh from the fact that there is a more or less bloody nasal discharge which is very purulent and putrid, and that there is a great depression noticed in the animal; it becomes emaciated and sneezes a great deal oftener than in ordinary catarrh. An instance is recorded where the parasite penetrated the hard palate, causing a great flow of saliva. In some cases the inflammation has extended from the nasal cavities to the cranial cavity and produced meningitis, with severe cerebral symptoms, great excitement, restlessness, and a tendency to biting or snapping, and also paralysis of the lower jaw and several symptoms very similar to rabies.

Friedberger and Fröhner advise that in all cases where there are symptoms of rabies that the frontal sinuses be examined, as there is often a case where the pentastomum is present and it may produce cerebral symptoms and even death without any marked alteration in the mucous membranes of the nasal passages. At the same time, it is possible to accidentally find a pentastomum in a dog that has died from true rabies. The author may also mention that he has found cerebral symptoms in an animal that has been suffering from purulent (non-parasitic) nasal catarrh.

THERAPEUTICS. Nasal catarrh will generally disappear without any special treatment. To protect the neighboring tissue from the excoriation of the tissues caused by the discharge, it is well to keep it clean with tepid water and a little borax, or to coat the part with vaseline or oxide of zinc ointment. In all mucous, purulent, or chronic catarrhs spray the nose with a 2 per cent. solution of creolin, or coat around the nostril with vaseline or oil. In acute catarrh it is best to spray the nostril with an atomizer, using either of the following solutions: creolin, 2 per cent.; carbolic acid, 2 per cent.; boric acid, 3 per cent.; the inhalation can be given in the form of warm solutions, allowing the animal to inhale the steam from them by the method described in the treatment of Chronic Catarrh of the Larynx, on page 119, or with an atomizer; infusions of chamomile, carbolated water, tar water, and oil of turpentine have been used with good results.

Violent bleeding at the nose can be controlled by injections of cold water or a 3 per cent. solution of chloride of iron into the nostril. It is impossible to place a tampon in the dog's nose that will be efficient on account of the anatomical peculiarities.

When the pentastomum is present the only efficient way to get at it is to trephine the frontal bones so that agents can be injected directly into the location of the parasite. For this operation we would refer you to the text-books on surgery.

DISEASES OF THE LARYNX.

Acute Laryngeal Catarrh.

(Acute Laryngitis.)

ETIOLOGY. The most common cause of catarrh of the larynx is cold; laryngitis rarely originates from direct irritation of agents that affect the mucous membrane of the larynx, such as smoke, dust, etc. It may result from constant barking, as when an animal is taken to a show and barks constantly, or lying near a fire and getting very warm, and then going and lying at the door, when the draft will come on the head and throat. Laryngitis appears as a secondary symptom of acute inflammation of the nose, throat, and large bronchials, and it is generally present in distemper.

PATHOLOGICAL ANATOMY. The mucous membrane of the larynx is reddened and inflamed, swollen, and covered with mucus over its entire surface; in some cases the membrane is eroded or ecchymosed.

CLINICAL SYMPTOMS. The first symptom is a cough; this may be very violent, according to the condition; it is always coarse, hard, and dry in the beginning; later it becomes softer and more moist as it is accompanied with the secretions of mucus.

By a slight pressure on the larynx we can make the animal cough, and it seems to be painful to manipulation; running, excitement, drinking cold water, or the administration of medicines all produce coughing. Difficulty in respiration is seen in certain forms of laryngitis where there are intense inflammation and great swelling of the mucous membrane; it is also accompanied by more or less wheezy or rattling sounds, which can be heard by placing the ear on the larynx. There is not much constitutional disturbance in this disease; the animal is depressed and eats slowly; this is probably caused by a certain amount of the irritation extending to the muscles of deglutition and swelling of the mucous membrane, or from some form of pharyngitis which may be present at the same time; if so, it is generally accompanied by a slight rise of temperature.

The disease generally lasts only a few days, although we find some cases that do not respond to treatment, and they are apt to remain irritable and become chronic.

THERAPEUTICS. The first thing to do is to remove the animal from cold or draughts and friction with some mild liniment over the larynx; also the application of a moist warm compress over the larynx and the inhalation of medicated warm water, such as chlorate of potassium, 0.50; water, 20.0; or Listerine diluted one-half with water, from an atomizer, and internally the administration of some calmative or narcotic; of the latter, morphine is the best, as it lessens the cough and irritation. The following prescription is very useful where the animal is a small pet dog—that is, kept in the room; it is very useful to prevent the cough, as it is always worse at night:

 R.—Morphiæ sulph. 0.1
   Aq. amygdalæ amaræ 24.0
 S.—Half a teaspoonful three times daily.

 R.—Morphiæ sulph. 0.12
   Potassii cyanid. 0.15
   Syr. pruni Virgin. 96.00
 S.—One teaspoonful four times daily.

 R.—Ext. hyoscyamus 1.0
   Liq. ammon. acetatis 20.0
 S.—Twenty drops every half hour.

Chronic Catarrh of the Larynx.

(*Chronic Laryngitis; Convulsive Cough; Chronic Irritable Cough.*)

ETIOLOGY. Chronic laryngitis generally results from an acute attack of laryngitis or from some severe irritation of some of the other organs of the air-passages; it generally comes on gradually, the cough getting more frequent; it may also follow ulceration of the larynx or the formation of a tumor in that part.

PATHOLOGICAL ANATOMY. The mucous membrane is thickened, but not so red as in acute laryngitis; it is marked with fissures and elevations from enlarged tissue; and here and there may be noticed a dirty bluish-red coloration. The surface is granular on account of the swelling of the inflamed mucous glands; in rare cases we may see small papilliform elevations or small eroded ulcerative places which mark a breaking down of some of the mucous glands; the secretion which covers the parts is thick, slimy, and tenacious; in some cases it is yellow, like pus.

CLINICAL SYMPTOMS. The symptoms are similar to acute laryngitis, except that they are not so severe; the larynx is slightly sensitive to pressure; still the irritation is there; the animals will cough after manipulation, but not to such a marked degree; they do not try to get away from the pressure as they do in the acute form; there is no disturbance of the general system. The cough sounds dry, hoarse, and rough, seldom moist; the cough, which is frequent, is quite loud, and accompanied by a wheezy inspiratory sound, the night being the time it is mostly heard, or when the animal runs about and plays, and his master is going to take him out for a run; in some cases the cough resembles the whooping-cough of children (tussic convulsiva).

THERAPEUTICS. As a rule, the treatment of this disease is unsatisfactory; of course, this depends to a large extent on the animal. Being removed from the conditions that have originally caused the disease, the first thing to do is to keep the animal perfectly quiet and protect it from cold. Among the agents used in general treatment the following are best: Inhalations of hot medicated solutions, carbolic acid, tar, oil of turpentine or powdered salt, chlorate of potassium, alum, and tannic acid. Inhalations with these agents by means of an atomizer should be made twice daily for ten or fifteen minutes. When the larynx is very sensitive powdered bromide of potassium should be blown up the nose.

It is readily understood that inhalations are rather hard to administer in the dog, as the animal cannot be kept still while the medication is being made, and also because the dog breathes through the nose, and if prevented from doing so the vapor is carried into the throat and again into the mouth. The only practical way to get an animal to inhale a vapor is to put him in a close box and through an opening introduce steam that fills up the apartment, and the animal has to inhale it. This, however, can only be practised in a hospital. But where the animal is at home the best method of procedure is to place the animal on a cane-seated chair, and having placed the medicated agent, steaming hot, under the chair, cover the animal with a sheet and hold him for ten or fifteen minutes; or we may also hold the steaming vessel under his nose and cover the head. It is only with the greatest difficulty that the laryngeal mucous membranes can be painted with any medicinal agent. This is to be regretted, as it is the only direct way that that membrane can be treated with any certainty. The intratracheal method of administration of medicinal agents which has so largely been used by Dieckerhoff in the horse has been tried by the author, but has not been of much value, and especially in animals that are fat or have short necks.

Frequently in chronic catarrh we use narcotics to stop the severe cough produced by irritation of the membrane—morphine and extract of hyoscyamus, and in rare cases bromide of sodium or chloral hydrate. Expectorants are not of much use in the dog. The laryngeal inflammation so frequently observed in man, namely, **Croupal and Diphtheritic Laryngitis,** has not been observed in the dog. Esser and Friedberger have each seen a case of partial paralysis of the laryngeal muscles which was accompanied with great difficulty in breathing and roaring sounds during inspiration. On post-mortem there was great hypertrophy of the muscles on the posterior side of the larynx, and the atrophied muscle was produced by pressure on the left recurrent nerve. The author has also seen such a case of laborious respiration in a large-sized German bulldog.

DISEASES OF THE AIR-PASSAGES AND BRONCHIAL TUBES.

Catarrh of the Windpipe and Bronchia; Bronchitis.
(*Trachealis and Bronchial Catarrhalis.*)

ETIOLOGY. Catarrh of the air-passages and of the bronchia occurs very frequently in young, weakly, debilitated dogs. It sometimes originates primarily, but, as a rule, it occurs as a secondary disease. It is caused by cold, especially by breathing cold air when warm; and in pet dogs we see it quite often where the animals will lie near the register or an open fire until they are very warm, and then go to the outside door and lie on the floor where the draught can strike on them and get cool very rapidly, and repeat this a number of times. It is also caused by mechanical or chemical irritations, such as smoke, dust, parasites, strong gases, or, secondarily, from the extension of inflammations from neighboring organs, as the larynx or lungs, or from defective blood-circulation of the lungs produced by weakened heart-action. Catarrh of the trachea and bronchia is very often seen as a complication of distemper, as well as many serious internal diseases, especially in affections of the brain. The latter cause is generally traced to the fact that there is an accumulation of particles of food and secretions which collect in the mouth and throat, decompose, and are respired into the trachea and produce an irritation.

There is no doubt that infectious influences play a certain *rôle* in the cause of this disease, for there are often cases occur where it cannot be due to cold or exposure, especially in the spring and fall months, and it is sometimes seen where a number of puppies are housed together, or in some cases attacking older dogs. In some of these outbreaks it is quite difficult to distinguish it from distemper. (See Infectious Bronchial Catarrh.)

PATHOLOGICAL ANATOMY. In describing any catarrh of the trachea it should be classed under the head of bronchitis, as it is impossible to draw the line of distinction between the two. In bronchitis the mucous membrane is diffused, red, swollen, and tears easily to the touch. In the earlier stages of the disease there is little mucus found on it, but as the disease goes on to the later stages the secretion becomes more copious and turbid or yellow with pus-corpuscles; later on it becomes more or less colored with blood-corpuscles.

Chronic Catarrh. In this condition the color of the mucous membrane is brownish-red or violet and the membrane is frequently uneven and thickened; the secretion is clammy, slimy, or shining, in some cases bad-smelling or even putrid.

In old chronic cases of bronchitis there may be some stenosis of the tubes, and also, from the constant irritation of the bronchia, emphysema of the lungs.

Stenosis (contraction) of the bronchia may be caused either by swelling of the bronchial mucous membrane or by the collection of masses of thickened secretion in the tube. In some cases the two causes acting together exclude the air from the alveoli of that part of the lungs to which the affected bronchia carry the air, causing the lung-tissue to collapse. This condition, which originates in the manner described, does not change in its structure, but soon becomes solidly filled with blood.

In all chronic conditions we also find the opposite of stenosis— that is, Bronchiectasis (widening of the bronchial tubes); this is caused by a relaxed condition of the bronchial walls, due to the chronic irritation and also to the pressure of collections of the secretions. This dilatation of the tubes may be either cylindrical or spindle-shaped.

Emphysema of the Lungs. This is found near the atelectasic centres and on the borders of the lungs; this condition is supposed to be caused by violent coughing spells and also by bronchitis.

The affected parts do not collapse, but appear clear and bloodless, soft, and collapse quickly on incision.

CLINICAL SYMPTOMS AND COURSE. These vary according to the amount and location of the irritation, whether it is in the trachea, large, medium, or small bronchia, and whether it is acute or chronic.

Acute Catarrh of the Large Bronchia. This commences with slight and frequent chilly spells, accompanied by fatigue, indifference, depression, and sometimes with a stiff and strained gait and slight rise of temperature. Soon afterward the animal commences to cough; this is one of the principal symptoms of the disease. In the beginning it is dry and dull; later it becomes moist and more frequent. It can easily be started by slight pressure on the trachea, and also by tapping on the chest close behind the shoulder.

Percussion gives negative results. On auscultation in mild cases we hear an increased vesicular respiration in the trachea and large bronchia, and when the medium-sized bronchia are affected and there are large accumulations of mucus in the tubes the vesicular murmur is increased. This is due to the fact that while the bronchitis is in the dry stage the sounds are roaring or snorting in character, and when the fluid mucus has accumulated the sounds become rattling, as if the air was passing through a thick mucus. When the small bronchia are affected these sounds are much more decided, and in this condition there are high fever and general disturbance of all the functions, and also a marked difficulty in respiration. One prominent symptom in the dog is the inflation of the cheeks with each expiration. Any pressure on the walls of the chest will immediately produce a fit of coughing. The cough is first dull and weak, and as the disease increases it becomes looser and easier, the vesicular sounds being very wheezy. Capillary bronchitis in young animals is very apt to terminate in catarrhal pneumonia; but even if this grave complication does not occur, it is still a very dangerous disease and is apt to prove fatal. The course of the disease is never less than two weeks, and may often last several weeks before a favorable termination is reached.

Chronic Bronchial Catarrh; Asthma. This disease is common at two periods of an animal's life—when it is very young and after it becomes old—and is a consequence of acute bronchial catarrh. In old animals it very often takes the chronic form at the onset.

This disease, or the results of it, is what is generally termed asthma, so often seen in old well-cared-for dogs. The disease is characterized by a certain amount of difficulty in respiration, which is increased by running or any excitement, and is generally accompanied by a severe attack of coughing, which in severe cases ends with every evidence of choking or even vomiting. The cough is generally moist, and may be accompanied with a certain amount of rattling. In the majority of cases, where the disease is not far advanced, the animals enjoy good health and rarely exhibit any fever. In old cases the expired air may be bad-smelling or fetid.

Percussion gives no definite results. Auscultation gives sounds that depend on the number and size of the diseased bronchia and the character of the mucus accumulated in them. We may find either moist or rattling sounds which vary in character; and a heightened vesicular respiration or else an indistinct mucous sound.

THERAPEUTICS OF TRACHEAL AND BRONCHIAL CATARRH. Keep the animal in a moderately warm place where it is dry and free from draughts, but well ventilated. In the early stages of the disease give a mild expectorant, such as syrup of tolu or wild cherry. Local inhalation of vaporized drugs is not of much use, as very little of the drug is carried into the bronchial tubes, especially the small ones. We may administer medicinal vapors by putting a teaspoonful of turpentine in a quart of boiling water and hold it so that the animal will inhale the steam.

In the chronic cases we generally get good results from the administration of expectorants, such as apomorphia, ipecacuanha, and spiritus ammonia mindererus; and where there is a violent cough add narcotics, such as morphia, extract of hyoscyamus, or dilute hydrocyanic acid and cyanide of potassium. When there is fever present a few doses of antipyrine (0.5 to 1.0 gramme, twice daily) will generally suffice.

Tartar emetic, chloride of ammonium, and sulphuretted antimony are of little use; in fact, do more harm than good, as they often destroy the appetite. In the early stages of the disease the cough does not amount to much, but in the later stages it is constant and very disagreeable, especially at night, and it is in such cases that expectorants are useful to remove the accumulations of mucus. The addition of morphia to the apomorphia solution has the tendency to counteract the emetic effects of the latter drug.

    R.—Apomorphia 0.01
        Morphiæ hydrochlor. 0.06
        Ac. hydrochlor. dil. 0.3
        Aqua destil. 100.0
    S.—One-half to one tablespoonful every three hours.

    R.—Inf. senegæ rad. 10.0
        Liq. ammon. acetas . . . 4.00
        Syr. simplex 15.0
    S.—One tablespoonful every four hours.

    R.—Syr. ipecacuanhæ ⎱
        Syr. althææ   ⎰   āā 20.0
    S.—One small teaspoonful every three hours.

In chronic bronchial catarrh inhalations of medicated vapors are very useful, and especially the vapors of turpentine, where there are great accumulations of mucus and a fetid breath. Inhalations of the vapors of tar and carbolic acid are also useful. Internally the author has found that a small pinch of bicarbonate of sodium or Rochelle salt given daily in a teaspoonful of warm water is very useful. In broncho-blennorrhœa the oil of turpentine has given very good results. The action of tar is a little irregular and destroys the appetite. Ichthyol and thiol are given in doses of 0.2 to 0.5 gramme several times daily. Narcotics should be administered only when the cough is very severe. Intratracheal injections, which are used by Dieckerhoff in the horse, after Levi's method, may be used in the dog (solutions of iodide of potassium or nitrate of silver); but the author has found that form of medication very difficult.

    R.—Terebene . . . 2.0
        Spts. vini rect. ⎫
        Aqua destil.   ⎬   . āā 500.0
        Spts. menth. ⎭
    S.—Several dessertspoonfuls daily.

DISEASES OF THE LUNGS.

Catarrhal Inflammation of the Lungs; Pneumonia.
(*Catarrhal Pneumonia; Lobular Pneumonia; Broncho-pneumonia.*)

ETIOLOGY. Catarrhal inflammation of the lungs generally originates as a secondary disease following bronchitis, by an extension of the inflammation of the small bronchia into the alveola, or from the obstruction of the bronchial tubes. The causes of lobular pneumonia are from accumulations of mucus in the trachea, which may be only imperfectly coughed up, or in very weak cases, lying in the tubes, become decomposed and putrid, and act as an irritant. These, on inspiration, are carried into the deep portions of the lungs directly on the alveoli, and from a capillary bronchitis it may become converted into a catarrhal pneumonia. In some cases particles of food, medicines, especially thick mixtures, get into the larynx, when the animal is unconscious or where there is partial paralysis of the throat. These substances penetrate into the lungs, and are very difficult to dislodge from the bronchia. This form of the disease is generally termed traumatic or aspiring pneumonia.

PATHOLOGICAL ANATOMY. In a lung affected with catarrhal pneumonia we always find all the characters of bronchitis, and as the disease advances the groups of alveoli that belong to the affected bronchia are rapidly filled with the catarrhal deposit, preventing the air from penetrating into them. Soon we see an intense hyperæmia of the walls of the alveoli and the exudation of a thin, non-curdling fluid and numerous white blood-corpuscles which soon become pus-corpuscles, and the commencement of a fatty degeneration and detachment of the alveolar cells. The alveoli and the small bronchia become entirely filled with pus-corpuscles and a certain number of blood-corpuscles and broken-down epithelial cells, and the inflamed portion of the lung can easily be distinguished from its healthy surroundings. They form hard, tough, roundish or lobulated lumps which vary in size and number, projecting slightly above the surface of the lung, and on making a cross-section of the diseased portions in the earlier stages of the disease they are seen to be dark bluish-red and later on become gray, while the surrounding tissue that is not diseased is normal, or, what is more frequent, is slightly congested with blood. The detached centres which show plainly in the early part of the disease soon become confluent, so that finally we have large sections of the lung involved. In rare cases we find fibrinous (croupal) centres in connection with the catarrhal pneumonic centres, and extended vesicular emphysema in the neighborhood of the affected centres, and at the borders of the lungs, is often seen. We may also have subpleural and interstitial emphysema and sero-fibrinous or pussy pleuritis about the broncho-pneumonic centres.

CLINICAL SYMPTOMS. It is very difficult to make a sharp distinction between capillary bronchitis and lobular pneumonia on account of the close relation between these two diseases. If the disease has affected the alveoli, there is a marked acceleration of the respirations, in some cases as high as 60 per minute, and also inflation of the cheeks with each expiration; the cough is short, frequent, and apparently very painful; the pulse running from 150 to 170. On making a physical examination by percussion there are a number of dull centres through the lungs; in some instances the whole of the lung gives dull sounds. According to the stage of the disease, strong vesicular breathing, snoring, fine or loud bruit, and where there is extended infiltration we hear bronchial respiration.

The temperature often goes up to 40° or 41°; this high temperature usually commences early in the disease, or it often makes a rise when the disease has become converted into catarrhal pneumonia. If this complication does not occur, the temperature will not make any marked change, but follow a regular course, which is to rise quickly at the onset, and gradually fall as the disease decreases and the animal goes on to convalescence.

COURSE AND PROGNOSIS. The course of catarrhal inflammation of the lungs is rarely less than three weeks, and often prolonged over several months, with varying degrees of intensity. Traumatic pneumonia is the only form of the disease that runs its course quickly.

The terminations of the disease are : Recovery by resolution, in which the inflammatory products which fill the smallest bronchia and the alveoli are changed into a kind of emulsion and are either reabsorbed or coughed up. Or in the secondary disease, for instance; chronic interstitial inflammation of the lung, or in rare cases the formation of purulent gangrenous centres. Third, death, which may occur at any stage of the disease, in the early stages as a consequence of great extension of lobular pneumonia, or at any time as a result of œdema of the lungs.

Chronic Interstitial Pneumonia.

(*Chronic Induration of the Lungs; Cirrhosis of the Lungs; Phthisis.*)

When the disease terminates in this pathological condition we find an inflammatory deposit in the interlobular and interstitial connective tissue; this deposit compresses the alveoli and small bronchia, and they lose their functions and are finally absorbed, and on section of the affected portion of the lung it is found to be coarse, rough, and irregular on its surface, the tissue varying from yellow to yellowish-red in color. The bronchia surrounding the affected portion are distended and pocket-shaped, and there are also a certain number of spots of localized emphysema.

The clinical course of the disease shows very little fever, but the animal is never entirely restored to health; the respirations are short, labored, and with a quick, weak cough. They finally become emaciated, complicated with dropsical effusions, and finally die from exhaustion.

In some cases of lobular inflammation of the lungs the inflamed portions form abscesses, or we may find gangrenous portions. These terminations depend on the nature of the irritant, and generally occur after traumatic pneumonia (foreign bodies). When an abscess is formed a pear-shaped body is found in the centre of the infiltrated lobule, and surrounding it is a thin, delicate layer of yellowish tissue, and over that a tough red layer of inflamed pulmonary material; large abscesses may be formed by the fusion of all the infiltrated pulmonary tissue.

When gangrene is formed the inflamed catarrhal centre becomes dirty greenish-brown in color, or in severe cases almost black. In the early stages the diseased portion is hard and fibrous, but it soon becomes soft and pulpy and filled with a turbid, fetid, greenish serum. When the disease is slow and chronic the gangrenous spots are limited in size, but generally when the disease assumes the gangrenous form it becomes diffuse, and the animals die rapidly from exhaustion.

We recognize the gangrenous form when the breath becomes

putrid, for in the dog it is almost impossible to get any of the discharge that is coughed up, the animal generally swallowing the mucus. When the animal has a putrid breath we always find a course of alarming symptoms accompanying it—septic fever, chills, and a high temperature. If the sputa were examined, we would probably find numerous micrococci, bacteria, and portions of broken-down lung and elastic tissue.

Œdema of the Lungs. This is apt to follow all debilitating diseases that weaken the left side of the heart, and that organ is unable to force the venous blood through the lungs. There is a regurgitation of the blood, and the alveoli and bronchia become filled by a serous fluid which exudes from the bloodvessels.

The œdematous lung is distended and much larger than normal; on pressure with the finger the indentation remains some time. On section of the lung a large quantity of reddish foamy fluid exudes from the tissues and the bronchial tubes.

When œdema of the lungs follows catarrhal pneumonia it generally begins with great difficulty in respiration, labored or stertorous in character, a short, faint cough, and in rare instances a quantity of thin reddish fluid comes from the nose or mouth. On making a physical examination, percussion gives no results but those found in catarrhal pneumonia. On auscultation we hear rattling bruits all over the chest, especially in the anterior part, and also in the trachea; the blowing sounds may be very loud in some cases and can be heard some distance from the animal. Death occurs in a short time. Some time before the actual symptoms of œdema appear the exhausted condition of the heart is indicated by the pulse being irregular—that is, weaker at inspiration than at expiration.

THERAPEUTICS. In treating lobular pneumonia we use the same general course as we do in bronchitis. The author obtained the best results with Priessnitz's compress, and by the remedies recommended under the treatment for bronchitis. The good effects of moist, warm compresses can be much increased by sharp friction with a small quantity of mustard-oil to the sides; but it must only be applied in young, strong, healthy animals. The best method of application is to make a liniment of 3 parts of oleum sinapis æthereum in 45 parts of olive oil, and divide it into two parts, and apply one-half to each side of the chest, then wind a dry bandage around the chest-walls, and ten to twelve hours later apply Priessnitz's compress.

In cases where there is great accumulations of mucus it is advisable to give the animal an emetic (apomorphia is the best). Narcotics are to be given when the cough is constant and distressing. Where there is much debility stimulants are indicated, such as wine, ether, and give the animal small, often-repeated quantities of chopped meat, broth, milk, and the peptone preparations.

Very little good is to be derived from inhalations in this disease. When the breath is offensive we advise inhalations of turpentine or a 1 to 50 solution of creolin. Inhalations of carbolic acid are recommended, but on account of the danger of poisoning by that drug they are to be used with extreme caution. In septic fever, after the appearance of gangrene of the lungs, give subcutaneous injections of ether or camphor.

When œdema of the lung is recognized, it must be regarded as a grave symptom and generally fatal. We must, therefore, take very energetic measures—active stimulants, such as mustard oil, to the sides, and also injections of ether or camphor subcutaneously. Bleeding and the use of cardiac stimulants, such as digitalis or caffeine, are useless.

Catarrhal pneumonia is the only grave important disease of the lungs in the dog; the others are of small importance.

Croupal inflammation of the lungs, as we understand it, is a firm, hemorrhagic exudation in the alveoli of the lungs and small bronchia. This is very rare in the dog. The author has never seen a case of true lobar pneumonia, but has seen a few cases of croupal lobular pneumonia, the course of which is very similar to catarrhal pneumonia in all its symptoms, the difference only being detected on post-mortem. Roll makes the statement that croupous inflammation of the lungs is common in the dog, but he probably meant croupal lobular pneumonia.

Anthrakosis pulmonum (blackening of the lungs) is quite common in the dog, but it has no pathological significance.

Emphysema of the lungs is not such an important disease in the dog as it is in man and the horse. That form of emphysema which appears in bronchitis and pneumonia, characterized by an extreme distention of the alveoli, has been mentioned under these diseases. If the irritation is constant, the disease becomes chronic, and a progressive atrophy of the alveolar walls takes place until they are entirely closed up, the neighboring alveoli become absorbed or altered, and finally cavities are formed, and the bloodvessels become atrophied. On section of the lung the edges of the cavities are pale, soft, and the bloodvessels are stained with pigment. Sometimes laceration of the alveolar walls allows air to penetrate into the interlobular, interstitial, or subpleural connective tissue; this is generally caused as a result of severe and continual coughing spells, and where animals have died from some form of suffocation. Siedamgrotzky describes a case where an old emphysematous dog had a severe fit of coughing and the lung was lacerated, causing pneumothorax.

DISEASES OF THE PLEURA.

Inflammation of the Pleura; Pleurisy.
(*Pleuritis.*)

ETIOLOGY. The disease is divided into two forms—primary and secondary pleuritis. The primary form may be caused by cold, from traumatism, etc.; the secondary from the extension of inflammations from the surrounding organs, as in pneumonia, gangrenous pericarditis, peritonitis extending through the diaphragm, fractured ribs, injuries to the walls of the thorax, or perforation of the throat by foreign bodies. We also see it in all forms of pyæmia and tuberculosis.

PATHOLOGICAL ANATOMY. The pleura is dull and swollen and very much injected, rough on the surface, due to it being covered with fibrinous accumulations (small button-like elevations), and in the advanced stages large masses of fibrinous substances. When there is no accumulation of fluids it is called pleuritis fibrinosa. But generally we find a more or less copious secretion of fluid from the capillaries. This fluid (pleuritic exudation) accumulates between the pleural folds in copious fibrinous masses; it is usually serous or sero-fibrinous, appearing as a slightly yellowish turbid fluid, with more or less fibrinous coagula swimming in it. Chemically it is almost like blood-serum. This liquid contains red blood-corpuscles and round cells; if the former is in large numbers, the hemorrhagic exudation is found; but if the cells are present in quantities, the purulent or suppurating form is seen. True purulent exudation is always caused by the presence of a specific purulent poison, and becomes fetid as soon as decayed or gangrenous agents find their way into the pleural cavity, as in gangrene of the lungs, perforation of the throat by foreign bodies, in deep wounds of the chest, and in perforation of the œsophagus in the thoracic cavity.

The excretion which collects rapidly crowds the lung of the affected side and finally presses it against the spinal column and mediastinum, pressing the lung into an inert mass. The opposite lung is the seat of considerable collateral hyperæmia, which may lead to œdema, according to the severity of the condition. When compression of a lung is continued for any length of time the alveoli lose entirely their functional activity, their walls collapse and become adherent if the fluid exudated finally becomes absorbed. After this has occurred it can readily be recognized by the depressed appearance of the ribs. In cases of primary pleuritis which were seen by the author the inflammatory process was always restricted to one side, and that, as a rule, was the left side. The cases of secondary pleuritis were generally double-sided, but the inflammatory conditions are never of equal intensity on both sides, one side being always a little worse than the other. Besides having the results of pressure shown on the lungs, we also have the heart pushed toward the healthy side of the mediastinum or the diaphragm.

The conclusion of pleuritic inflammation depends on the intensity and duration of the disease and the character of the exudate. In favorable cases the latter is reabsorbed and good results follow. In serious cases only part of the liquid portion of the exudate is absorbed, while a fibrinous exudate covers the pleura; this becomes converted into a granular tissue, containing numerous vessels, and later into a stringy cicatricial tissue, called a pleuritic sward, and more or less adhesions of the pleura between the lungs and inner wall of the thorax and between the lungs and diaphragm. Although the sward formations may be very extensive, it is possible for the lung to regain its normal extension, but it takes a long time. Thin adhesions sometimes tear; extended adhesions offer a constant hindrance to the unrestricted use of the affected part of the lung. Purulent exudates are sometimes reabsorbed; but, as a rule, if the pus is not removed at the proper time by surgical interference, it breaks out, either through the pleura into the lungs and then through the bronchia, or it forms abscess somewhere in the cavity of the chest, generally in the region of the sternum, by undermining the pleura and muscles of the walls of the chest.

CLINICAL SYMPTOMS. In the primary form of pleuritis, when its origin is from cold, etc., it is ushered in with more or less fever and increase of temperature, the pulse increases in frequency, and at the onset the animal generally has a chill; the temperature remains high, and the pulse small, weak, and thready. Primary pleuritis with purulent or putrid effusions is rare, and when it does occur it is always accompanied with a high intermittent fever.

The general health is very much disturbed. They are stiff and sore in moving about; little or no appetite, but intense thirst. The visible mucous membranes are reddened and congested, and in cases where there is much exudation the membranes are dark bluish-red. The feces are dry and hard. The urine presents some symptoms that are diagnostic: While the exudate is forming and collecting the urine is scanty and thick, and albuminous in reaction. When the exudate is commencing to be reabsorbed the urine increases very much in quantity, and is very clear and white (see chapter on Examination of the Urine).

There is also a marked dyspnœa. In dry pleuritis the respiration is superficial and rapid, and where there is great exudation the respirations are short and painful and the animal has all the symptoms of smothering. A characteristic symptom is the way the animal endeavors to assist respiration by assuming a sitting position, with the front legs spread out as far apart as possible, and using the abdominal muscles, and shows pain on pressure of the abdominal muscles of the affected side. The animal has a dull, dry, weak cough; this may, however, be absent.

The physical symptoms are characteristic. On percussion at the onset of the disease there is little change of sound, but when the exudate has reached a certain height the lower parts of the chest give a dull sound which seems to be limited in a straight line, according to the position of the animal. Above the excretion the sound is tympanitic on account of the retraction of the lung. Auscultation gives a friction bruit in the onset, and when the fluid begins to be reabsorbed and the pressure of the exudate against the lungs is lessened the respiratory bruit is altered. In the earliest stages of the disease the sounds are vesicular, but as the exudate collects the sounds become indistinct or blowing and finally only bronchial, and when the bronchial tubes are affected sound is lost entirely. In the healthier parts of the lungs we have increased vesicular breathing.

COURSE AND PROGNOSIS. Primary pleuritis is generally slow in its course; the time taken by the exudate to become reabsorbed is very long, unless it is removed in an operative way. When the exudate commences to be reabsorbed the percussion-sound becomes less dull and the respiration bruit more distinct, and if the exudate becomes quickly reabsorbed the diseased side is less in circumference, or it can be better described as being flatter.

Death may occur during the critical period of the disease by collateral hyperæmia and œdema of the non-affected sections of the lungs, by carbon-dioxide-poisoning from defective function of the lungs, by total stagnation of the circulation of the blood from pressure of the exudate on the large bloodvessels and the heart; later on by exhaustion and by secondary diseases. To this class belong dropsy caused by stagnation of the blood circulation from weakness of the heart, and amyloid degeneration of the kidneys, liver, and spleen. Death may also occur from complicating diseases, such as bronchitis and lobular pneumonia.

The prognosis is generally favorable; as a rule, very severe cases of primary pleuritis make good recoveries. In secondary pleuritis the prognosis depends on the original disease.

THERAPEUTICS. The treatment of secondary pleuritis is the same as the primary; but in the former we must take into consideration the treatment of the original disease. In the early stages of the disease, when the exudate is collecting, we must apply counter-irritants, such as liniments or plasters of mustard. When a copious exudate has been formed we try to get its reabsorption by stimulating the kidneys by means of acetate of potassium, acetate of sodium, and juniper berries. When the heart is weak we use digitalis and squills. Small doses of calomel are also useful.

R.—Hydrarg. chlor. mite 0.03
Digitalis pulv. 0.05
Saccharum lactis 0.5

Fiat pulv. No. vi. S.—One powder three times daily.

Diuretics and cardiac stimulants have only an indirect influence on the accumulations, and when the exudate is gradually absorbed we can hardly credit these drugs with accomplishing the results, as the exudate is usually re-absorbed when the acute inflammatory stage of the diseases has passed. The best method of treatment is the removal of the secretion by surgical means—that is, to puncture the chest-wall. This operation is not at all dangerous in the dog, and is generally successful unless the adhesions are too thick.

The operation must be performed where there is a very large exudate and the dull sound can be heard over the entire lung; where there is œdema of the lung; in intense dyspnœa caused by the pressure of the exudate; and where there is deficient reabsorption, as is seen when the fever has entirely disappeared and the fluid does not show any signs of becoming reabsorbed.

Puncture of the cavity of the chest: The trocar used in this operation is an ordinary sized trocar, seen in Fig. 38, or, if we wish to make first an exploring puncture, we use the needle of the ordinary hypodermatic syringe. The needle, after having been disinfected, is introduced into the lower third of the wall of the chest, between the fifth and ninth rib, the patient being in a standing position. The entrance of air into the thoracic cavity must be avoided, and to prevent this we must use a trocar that has a faucet, or else when the flow of fluid becomes stopped at any time from some obstruction at the end of the trocar it is well to put the finger over the end of the opening to prevent the air from being sucked into the cavity. It is well to empty the cavity slowly and never entirely, as the affected pleuræ come in contact with each other and rub, often causing acute hemorrhage. After withdrawing the trocar it is well to paint the opening with some iodoform collodion.

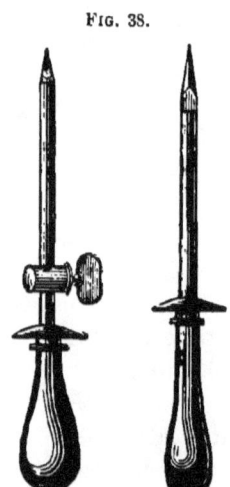

FIG. 38.

Trocars for puncture of the thorax.

When the fluid obtained is purulent, it generally requires several punctures to empty the cavity. The animal should have a nutritive but easily digested diet—soup, beef-tea, lean meat; and when the fever is high, antipyrine in doses of 0.5 to 2.0, according to the size of the dog.

Dropsy of the Chest.
(*Hydrothorax*.)

Any accumulation of serous fluid that is not dependent on an inflammation of the pleura (that is, of a transudate) in the cavity of the thorax is called hydrothorax. This is often a symptom of general dropsy, or it may arise from chronic disease of any of the organs (see ascites). In such cases the effusion first shows itself in the chest when dropsy of the skin (anasarca) exists.

PATHOLOGICAL ANATOMY. Hydrothorax, as a rule, affects both sides of the chest. Fröhner records a case where one side only was affected. We find in the cavity of the chest a clear yellow fluid, sometimes mixed with blood; the pleura is œdematous, swollen, and in long-continued cases it has a flaccid or macerated look. The lungs do not present any change, except the signs of partial compression. The other organs of the body are anæmic.

CLINICAL SYMPTOMS. The physical examination of this disease presents symptoms very similar to pleuritic exudates, but in dropsical transudates both sides of the thoracic cavity are filled, and on changing the position of the animal the fluid moves about much more quickly than a pleuritic exudate would, and the sensitiveness of the animal to pressure on the walls of the chest and the rubbing or crepitating bruit of pleuritis are absent.

THERAPEUTICS. The treatment, as a rule, is of a palliative character, as it is only in very rare instances we succeed in removing the original disease; we use the same agents as in ascites. The operation of tapping the chest-wall (see Puncture of the Cavity of the Chest, page 134) is only to be resorted to when the fluid has collected in large quantities and the animal is threatened with suffocation; but this only affords temporary relief.

Pneumothorax.

ETIOLOGY. The cause of pneumothorax—that is to say, the accumulation of air in the thorax—is produced in several ways. By perforating wounds of the chest, by the breaking into the pleural cavity of a collection of pus from the lung, tearing of the lung-tissue from great exertion, and from perforation of the œsophagus.

PATHOLOGICAL ANATOMY. On making an opening into the chest with trocar and canula the air escapes with a hissing sound; if the collection of air is great, the lungs are pushed out of position, interfering greatly with respiration. If this condition exists for any length of time, a purulent, and, in rare cases, a sero-purulent, pleuritis is developed, caused by the presence of some irritant agents that have gained admittance into the cavity with the air.

CLINICAL SYMPTOMS AND COURSE. There is great difficulty in respiration, and the affected side of the chest-wall is visibly distended, and during respiration it remains almost stationary. When the heart is pushed out of position there is a peculiar tympanitic sound, the pulsations have a metallic echo, and the respiratory bruit is absent. In some rare cases we hear a metallic bruit, which is caused by the entrance of air directly into the pleural cavity with each inspiration.

Animals in this condition generally die rapidly, although we may find rare cases where recovery takes place by an absorption of the air or by the accumulation of a fluid, which in turn becomes rapidly absorbed itself. The treatment consists in tapping the chest-wall.

Hæmatothorax.

In consequence of the destruction of some large vessel or vessels in the lungs or the pleural cavity, from the presence of growths, we have extensive hemorrhage into the thoracic cavity. The physical symptoms are similar to those of other pleural exudates; but this condition comes on very rapidly, and also in this condition the mucous membranes become very pale. When the symptoms are not pronounced the operation of puncture will determine the condition positively. Normal hemorrhages are easily and quickly absorbed, but often there is more or less pleuritis connected with them. Where there is great dyspnœa puncture is always advisable.

DISEASES OF THE CIRCULATORY APPARATUS.

EXAMINATION OF THE CIRCULATORY APPARATUS.

Examination of the Heart.

ANATOMY OF THE HEART. The normal position of the heart may be seen in Fig. 39. It lies on the left side, but not so far as is seen in other domestic animals. The direction of its axis is not vertical, but extends slightly in a posterior direction, with a slight curve toward the left side. The base of the heart extends from the third to the seventh rib; the apex extends backward toward the diaphragm. Superiorly the heart lies close to the large

FIG. 39.

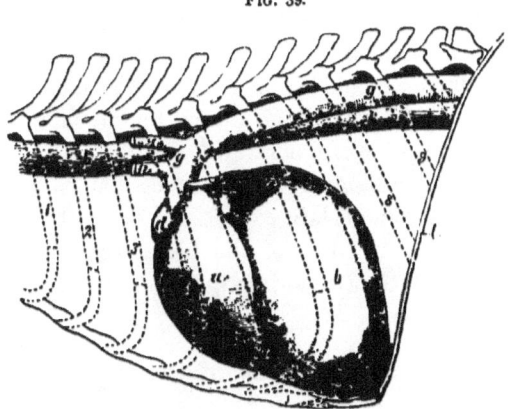

The heart in position: *a*, right ventricle; *b*, left ventricle; *c*, left auricle; *d*, right auricle *f*, pulmonary artery; *g*, aorta; *k*, œsophagus; *l*, diaphragm.

vessels—the trachea and the œsophagus—and lies close on all sides to the lobes of the lungs. In its inferior portion it lies close to the chest-wall, extending from the third to the seventh rib. In the heart-sections we find the following arrangement: the right section lies in a right anterior direction from its axis and the left lies in a left posterior direction.

The size of the heart varies greatly in different animals, even when in a normal condition, and it is, therefore, impossible to lay down any relative rule as to its size or dimensions. According to Colan, the weight of the heart compared with that of the body is 1 to 90; and according to Rabe, it varies from 1 to 4 to 100, and taking relatively all the breeds of dogs, and also sex and age, the relative size is 0.6 and 2.2 to 100.

It is difficult to make an examination of the heart on account of its position, lying as it does hidden between the lobes of the lungs, and only a small portion of its surface exposed where it can be heard, and from the fact that it varies in size not only in the various breeds, but also in individuals. We find that in animals affected with the various heart-affections and also in perfect health the pulmonary bruit may be so increased that it is impossible to detect when there are weak heart-sounds, as the largest portion of the heart is covered by portions of the lungs, and these parts making sounds the ears cannot detect the sound, as the restlessness of the animal during examination and the movements of the cutaneous muscles and the coat of the animal are all factors that assist in preventing a proper examination of the heart.

The following details must, therefore, be looked upon as theoretical in character to a certain extent.

In making an examination of the heart we must consider the position and size of that organ, its palpitation sounds, and character of the pulsations.

Position and Size of the Heart.

Both are to be detected by percussion, but for the reasons above explained it rarely answers our expectations. In percussion over where the heart lies we find in normal conditions a dull sound, which lessens in deep respiration, and also the position, either standing or recumbent, may make a decided difference.

Animals having a small heart the sound is often entirely absent. The sound of that section of the lung that lies between the heart and the chest-wall is also a factor that makes the dull sound, and it is only by strong percussion that any sound can be detected at all, so that it may hardly be said to be of much diagnostic value.

There may be an abnormal dulness in the heart's action in hypertrophy, in dilatation, in exudates and transudates around the heart, in retraction or contraction of the lobules of the lung surrounding the heart; but we may often be deceived by abnormal processes that surround that organ, such as thickening of the lung-sections or swards on the pleura.

The dull sound is absent in enlargement of the lungs by emphysema, when air has entered the pericardium, after injuries, in one-sided pleuritis, in pneumothorax, and the sound is anteriorly situated in the chest when there is intense meteorization of the stomach or intestines, and in ascites.

Character of the Heart-pulsations.

The pulsations of the heart can be distinguished by putting the hand on the inferior portion of the chest near the sternum, about the fifth rib (on the right side the pulsation is a little more anteriorly situated). The pulsation makes a distinct vibration of all the adjacent parts, and in emaciated animals there can be noticed with each pulsation a distinct swelling or motion of the lower portions of the ribs; this vibration may be greatly lessened by the presence of layers of fat on the sides of the chest. After great exertion or excitement the strength of the pulsation against the chest-wall is greatly increased.

The pulsations of the heart are increased by disease in the following manner: After considerable loss of blood, in any case of fever, in palpitation of the heart, in some forms of heart-disease, in hypertrophy of the heart, by the influence of some poisons, like digitalis or aconite. It is almost imperceptible in degeneration of the muscle of the heart, in the later stages of acute diseases, in cases of poisoning, in fatty degeneration of the heart and when the heart has become compressed by the effects of hydrothorax, pneumo-pericarditis, or emphysema of the lungs. It is distinguished only on the healthy side in lateral pleuritis.

Character of the Heart-sounds and Bruits.

In order to distinguish the heart-sounds we must put the ear close to the side directly over the heart where the beats are loudest; it is better to cover the place with a handkerchief or cloth, or we may use a stethoscope. We should hear two sounds in each heart-beat—a systolic, which corresponds to the ventricular contraction, and a diastolic, which corresponds with the beginning of the diastole. Both these sounds follow each other with short intervals between. The pause between the first and second sound is short, but between the second and the next first the sound is much greater. The first sound is a mixed muscular and valvular sound of the mitrals and tricuspids, and the second is a semilunar valvular sound.

Unfortunately these sounds are indistinct and incomplete in the dog, even in perfect health. In very fat dogs we may not hear any heart-sound, or we may only hear the first one. In well-fed dogs it is not rare to hear the first sound, which is a great deal louder than the second, only on the left side. In thin animals we can hear the sound distinctly on both sides. With the respiratory bruit we lose to a certain extent the full strength of the sounds, and often only the first sound is heard. After great activity the heart's action is increased so much that the sounds follow each other so rapidly that it is impossible to distinguish one from another.

In pathological conditions the heart-sounds may be increased by a number of causes, as in the beginning of certain fevers; but generally it is an indication of hypertrophy. A lessened heart-sound is found in any heart-weakness, as in degeneration of the heart-muscle, in accumulations of exudates around the heart in the pericardium, or in emphysema of the lung-sections, etc. In such cases, as a rule, the heart-sound is imperceptible.

As can be readily seen, it is by no means easy to hear the heart beat in its normal condition, and the condition becomes more complicated when we have to distinguish pathological sounds—"heart-bruits." We distinguish between endocardial heart-bruits, which originate in the heart direct, and pericardial heart-bruits, which come from the arterial part of the heart and its envelope. The former are divided into organic and inorganic bruits. The organic heart-bruits are produced by stenosis (contraction) of the ring and by insufficient or imperfect closing of the valves, which may occur either in systole or diastole, making the heart-sound indistinct, or it may be entirely absent, and the bruit takes the place of the heart-sound. The systolic bruit is buzzing or blowing in character, and indicates an imperfect closing of an arterio-ventricular valve (in most cases of disease of the mitrals). The diastolic bruit is rushing or wheezing in character, and indicates a stenosis of the arterio-ventricular ostia, or the imperfect closure of an arterial valve. The inorganic heart-bruit is seen in man in all forms of anæmia, and occasionally in fevers. The pericardial bruits are very similar to pleuritic friction-sounds—that is, a scratching or scraping sound.

They are located in a sharply defined locality and do not occur in direct rhythm with the heart-sounds, but seem to occur between them. They are noticed in pericarditis as soon as there is any fibrinous deposits present and there is not sufficient pericardial fluid present to keep the folds free from contact with the heart. A change in the position of the animal makes quite a difference in the character of the bruit, and they may easily be distinguished from endocardial sounds. The pericardial friction-sound is distinguished from the pleural friction-sounds from the fact that it is entirely independent of the movements of respiration.

Character of the Pulse.

The pulse is best examined in the femoral artery inside of the thigh, and it may also be felt inside of the forearm. In the examination of the pulse we must take into consideration its frequency, its cadence, and its quality.

The normal pulse varies greatly, according to the breed, age, and size of the animal, and is rapidly increased from such causes as physical efforts, fear, fright, pleasure, etc. The general pulse is from 70 to 120—large animals being less, and very small animals having a correspondingly frequent pulse-rate. The rhythm (cadence) should be regular in a healthy animal, and physical causes make it irregular; but an irregular pulse in perfect health is very common in the dog; in fact, perfect rhythm is rare, as can be easily demonstrated by taking the pulsations frequently, the irregularity being well marked in very young or old animals. In normal conditions the pulse must be similar in both thighs.

We find a lessening in the pulse in some forms of poisoning, following hemorrhages, in affections of the muscle of the heart, in starvation, diseases of the brain, meningitis and hydrocephalus, in hepatogenous icterus, also in collapse and in diseases characterized by a continued high temperature.

An increase of the pulse is found in all fevers, in cases of valvular defects, in heart-weakness and paralysis or collapse of that organ from continued high fever. When the temperature increases the pulse rises. The pulse is irregular (arhythmic) in some diseases of the heart (incompensated valvular defects, myocarditis), after large doses of digitalis, and in heart-weakness. It is only intermittent (as a forerunner of entire irregularity) in slight cases of valvular defects, in some diseases of the brain, and in gastrocism. The pulse is full and distended where great physical exertion is used; small and collapsed after severe hemorrhage and in enteritis. In intense heart-weakness and collapse it becomes thread-like and imperceptible.

The venous pulse—that is, the apparent increase in the amount of blood in the jugular at its entrance into the chest—is often seen in the dog. It is generally a symptom of some chronic heart-affection, such as imperfect closing of the tricuspid valves, and of heart-weakness.

DISEASES OF THE HEART.

Valvular Defects.

GENERAL NOTES ON VALVULAR DEFECTS. By valvular defects we understand such anatomical alterations in the valves and openings as lead to an irregularity in the circulation of the blood, becoming apparent by visible symptoms in the pulse or general condition; but those slight valvular defects so often seen in postmortems and never noticed during life, are not to be considered.

Valvular defects appear in two forms: first, when the valves close imperfectly; or, secondly, when the openings become contracted, causing stenosis. Imperfect closure of one valve causes a certain amount of blood to flow back into the portion of the heart from which it has just come; for instance, when we have imperfect action of the mitrals or of the tricuspids in systole, part of the contents of the ventricles run back into the auricle, and when there is insufficient action of the semilunar valve in the diastole a part of the blood that has been thrown into the artery returns into the chamber again.

Stenosis of one opening retards the passage of blood, when we have a contraction of an arterio-ventricular opening. At the time of diastole the blood is kept back at the entrance of the affected ventricle, and it is imperfectly filled; while in the aortic opening in pulmonic stenosis the exit of the blood out of the ventricles (Fig. 40) in systole is retarded. In any of these conditions there is imperfect heart-action; every defect of an arterial opening interferes with perfect ventricular action and every defect in a venous opening causes a corresponding lessening of power in the auricle.

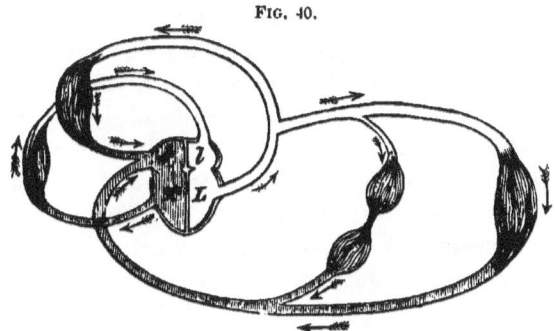

Fig. 40.

Diagram of the blood-circulation.

An abnormal pumping of the blood in this manner is sure to cause more or less disturbance of the entire organism, but there are certain compensatory processes in the heart itself that tend to overcome this. As a consequence of the impaired flow the heart-muscle is worked much harder and becomes hypertrophied (compensating heart hypertrophy). We often see cases where defects of the aorta become equalized by a hypertrophy of the left ventricle. In valvular defects of the mitrals the stagnation of the blood occurs in the veins, capillaries, and arteries of the lungs, and as far back as the right ventricle, which becomes dilated and hypertrophied while trying to take up the extra work thrown on it. In course of time we also see hypertrophy and dilatation of the left ventricle, and during diastole the stagnated blood runs in great quantities into it out of the dilated auricle.

These compensating processes of the heart are apt to prevent for a long time any great functional disturbance, provided the heart receives its proportional nutrition. If this is not the case, for instance, in anæmic and cachectic, feverish animals, the compensating heart hypertrophy is not present or is only developed to a slight degree, and also in cases of insufficient nutrition, due to some alteration in the coronary artery, the heart is no longer able to satisfy the demands claimed from it and tires out, and all the effects of blood-stagnation rapidly show themselves.

Etiology of Deficient Valvular Action of the Heart. The most common causes of valvular defects are endocarditic processes, which are developed on the valves and take an acute course, according to the amount of the irritation, and cause a fibrinous, rigid thickening of the valves. Sooner or later we have an imperfect closing of the valvular opening through cicatricial retractions; also adherences to the lobula of the valves or in their neighborhood. We may also see deposits of lime salts, and a contraction of the opening belonging to the affected valve. In rare cases there are heart-weakness and imperfect valvular action; it may be caused by a dilatation of the opening, and, becoming abnormally distended, the valves cannot meet and make a complete closure. Atheromatous processes may also produce this condition.

General Symptoms of Deficient Valvular Action of the Heart. The symptoms which appear at a certain time in all valvular troubles are: Increase of heart- and pulse-action (after slight exertion it is abnormally increased); palpitation of the heart; difficulty in respiration; cyanosis of the visible mucous membranes, especially of the head; venous pulse; dropsical effusions, such as œdema of the legs, abdomen, or testicles; hydrothorax; ascites; albuminuria, with lessening of the amount of urine; complications of the digestive organs of various kinds; and, finally, general nutritive disturbances, anæmia, emaciation, etc.

Symptoms of Valvular Deficiency in One Opening. *Deficiency of the Mitrals.* The imperfect closing of two of the valves occurs very frequently in the dog. Besides the alterations of the valves we find hypertrophy and dilatation of the left auricle of the right heart, and in the later stages the right ventricle also.

The clinical symptoms are: Increase of the pulse and distention of the artery, systolic bruit of the left wall of the chest, increase of the second (pulmonic) sound, weak, frequent pulse, shortness of breath, and later dropsy, etc.

Stenosis of the Left Venous Opening. This is generally accompanied by mitral insufficiency. It leads also to dilatation and hypertrophy of the left auricle and the right ventricle, and the left ventricle is generally small, narrow, and contains little blood.

The clinical symptoms are: Slight increase in the pulse, diastolic bruit (this is absent in some cases); considerable increase of the second (pulmonic) bruit; very small, irregular pulse; great difficulty in respiration; and dropsy makes its appearance early in the disease.

Disease of the Aortic Valves. This condition of the semilunar valves causes a dilatation and hypertrophy of the left ventricle and flattening of the papillary muscles.

The clinical symptoms are as follows : A very strong heart-beat; increase of the heart-dulness on the left side; a full, bounding pulse is very frequently noticed. This character of the pulse is also noticed in small arteries that in normal conditions have no distinct pulse. Shortness of breath, œdema, and dropsy of the dependent parts.

Stenosis of the Aortic Opening. Rare in the dog.

The clinical symptoms are a systolic bruit, a very slight sound of the aorta, small, weak pulse, general anæmia, etc.

Imperfect action and disease of the tricuspid valves cause distention of the right auricle, and it also has a systolic murmur on the right side and a strong, venous pulse. Stenosis of the right venous opening and defects of the pulmonary valves are extremely rare.

We very frequently have a combination of a contraction of an opening and also a deposit on or retraction of the valve at that opening and also a single valvular defect, and the two make a combination of symptoms that are rather hard to separate.

PROGNOSIS AND THERAPEUTICS OF VALVULAR DEFECTS OF THE HEART. A diseased valve must be considered incurable, but it may exist for a long time without causing any decided disturbance of the general circulation. It is impossible to predict how long a "compensating" state will continue. Mitral defects seem to last the longest. This conclusion is arrived at from the fact that it is quite common to hold post-mortems on dogs that have been apparently healthy during life and find serious heart-defects.

Compensating heart-defects do not require any treatment. We try to aid the heart in its efforts by giving nutritive diet and removing all exciting causes, such as great or prolonged exertion.

As soon as the heart begins to weaken and the difficulty in respiration increases, accompanied by œdema, palpitation, etc., we must use heart-tonics—digitalis, strophanthus, caffeine, etc.

℞.—Tinct. strophanthus sem. 15.0
S.—Ten to twenty drops morning and evening.

℞.—Caffeine citrate 0.05
Fiat M. No. x. S.—One powder morning and evening.

℞.—Tinct. digitalis 4.0
Aquæ 64.0
S.—One teaspoonful twice daily.

If we succeed in re-establishing a compensating action, the symptoms gradually disappear, and we need not use diuretics; if, however, we do not get the desired result and there should be any œdema, we must treat it symptomatically. (See Dropsy of the Abdomen.)

The symptoms above described are sometimes found in dogs that do not present any marked alterations in the valves or openings either during life or on post-mortem. These are due either to simple idiopathic hypertrophy and dilatation or to alteration of the heart-muscle.

Idiopathic Hypertrophy and Dilatation of the Heart: On post-mortem we find, as a rule, a hypertrophy of the left ventricle; but occasionally it is in both ventricles. At the same time we do not find any alteration of the lungs or kidneys which might produce secondary hypertrophy of the heart-muscle. The causes are extreme and constant exertion, cold, abnormal excitability of the heart (in closely bred animals), overfeeding, and too much rich blood (as in pet animals).

A condition called Callous Indurative Degeneration of the Heart is often mistaken for valvular defects. In this condition the heart is greatly enlarged and dilated and the walls are hypertrophied. The body of the heart-muscle is filled with a number of whitish, hard bodies, which on examination are found to be cicatricial connective tissue. The left ventricle is the favorite seat of these bodies.

The cause of these bodies has not been fully determined, but they are due either to Myocarditis or to defective nutrition of the heart-muscle as a consequence of contraction or closing of the coronary artery.

The clinical symptoms presented are as follows: The heart becomes weak, palpitation, increase in the number of pulse, dropsical effusions.

Auscultation gives nothing but pure heart-sounds, and with the above symptoms you may have a callous degeneration of heart or a pure idiopathic hypertrophy; during life it is impossible to determine which; as the treatment in both cases is the same, it is of no practical value. This consists of protection against excitement or great bodily exertion; give nutritive, easily digested food; and, if the heart is irregular, heart-tonics.

DISEASES OF THE PERICARDIUM.

Pericarditis.
(Inflammation of the Heart-envelope.)

ETIOLOGY. Inflammation of the pericardium may originate in a primary way by traumatisms or cold, or, secondarily, in connection with infectious or inflammatory diseases of the neighboring organs, especially pleuritis or pleuro-pneumonia.

PATHOLOGICAL ANATOMY. It either occurs in the acute or chronic form. The anatomical alterations that it produces on both surfaces of the pericardium correspond to those on the pleura caused by pleuritis. The most common form is sero-fibrinous pericarditis, with copious liquid exudates in the pericardium and masses of fibrinous lymph attached to the surface of the pericardium; in very rare instances the folds are attached to each other. When this condition has been present some time the pouch becomes dilated and relaxed and the heart-muscle shows more or less atrophy.

CLINICAL SYMPTOMS. Slight pericarditis rarely shows itself to any marked degree; but in severe cases there is decided palpitation, the pulse becoming weak and indistinct, with marked irregularity in the rhythm. On auscultation there is great dulness all over the region of the heart; finally, the heart-sound is entirely lost or simply a pericardial rubbing bruit is heard. When the pericardial folds are attacked or when they are separated this sound disappears.

There may be an increase of temperature, caused by the compression of the lungs, and the slightest exertions cause marked increase in the respiration (Siedamgrotzky and others). As soon as the disease becomes advanced the same symptoms that are seen in any case of defective heart-action are noticed; the lessened arterial pressure causes irregularity in the action of the urinary apparatus, and from venous stagnation dropsy shows itself in different parts of the body, especially in the extremities.

THERAPEUTICS. Keep the animal as quiet as possible; give nutritive, easily digested food (meat-diet), and such agents that will lessen the fever and tone up the heart. The Priessnitz compress and cold-water compresses might produce better effects, but they excite the animal and produce more harm than the good they do. Laxatives (sulphate of magnesium or sodium, calomel). As heart-tonics give strophanthus, digitalis, etc. When the exudate accumulates to an alarming extent we must resort to surgical means and empty the pericardium by means of the trocar, as in pleuritic effusions (see Fig. 38), using as long and as thin a trocar as possible; an aspirating syringe-needle is the best. Select a space over the dullest part of the heart and insert the trocar low down in the left chest wall, taking care not to put the point in too deep and injure the heart itself.

The treatment of pericarditis is generally symptomatic.

Dropsy of the pericardium (hydro-pericardium) is a collection of serous fluid in the pericardium without any direct inflammation of the pericardium.

In health the pericardium always contains a small amount of fluid, and it is only when we recognize by physical means a very much increased amount of fluid in the sac that it can be called Hydro-pericarditis. Dropsy of the pericardium may appear as a symptom of various diseases (defects of the valves, inflammation of the heart-muscle, diseased conditions of the coronary arteries, disease of the kidneys, and acute anæmia) as well as in connection with inflammation of the pericardium, and is generally accompanied with all the symptoms of general dropsy.

The clinical symptoms are those of pericarditis; the friction-bruit and the increase of temperature are absent, however. The treatment consists in removing the original causes, and, if this cannot be cured, to puncture; diuretics (digitalis) are to be administered; but these, as a rule, produce only a temporary effect.

Hemorrhage into the pericardium (hæmopericardium) is rarely seen. It may be caused by gunshot-wounds, by a bursting aneurism, or by laceration of one of the coronary arteries. Death generally occurs in a short time by compression of the heart. Where fatal results do not occur for a short time—that is, where the blood oozes out slowly and fills the sac gradually—it is impossible to make a certain diagnosis. This is also the case when air or blood (pneumocarditis) penetrates into the cavity from the lungs in cases of some traumatism of those organs.

Filaria in the Blood.

Three kinds of parasites have been found in the blood, namely, filaria immitis, spiroptera sanguinolenta, and strongylus vasorum.

Filariæ Immitis (males 130 mm. and females 250 mm. long; both 1.5 mm. thick). They generally lie in the right side of the heart; very rarely in the left. Its embryos, which are 0.25 mm. long and 0.05 thick, inhabit the blood directly in the circulation (Delafond, Nocard, Gruby, Ruether, Johne, Rieck, Deffe, and others). This parasite is generally found in Indian, Chinese, and American dogs, especially in the Southern States. Wheeler rarely made a post-mortem that he did not find it, often without presenting any observable symptoms during life. It is rarely found in Europe. The characteristic symptoms are emaciation, epileptiform convulsions, unconsciousness, dyspnœa, and rabiform symptoms. How the parasites find their way into the blood is rather interesting. The embryo is passed in the urine and carried by air or water into rice-fields or swampy places, and the parasite finds its way into the system by the dog drinking the water. Some authors contend that the larvæ get into the blood like the larvæ of the filaria sanguinis, by being first absorbed by the mosquito and then developed and passed again to the dog. The only case observed by the author was a dog which had been imported from India and brought to the hospital to be treated for a large wound. The subject was emaciated and anæmic, but seemed to be very healthy otherwise; he had a good appetite, so that we did not consider it necessary to make an examination of the circulatory apparatus. One morning the patient died in his box. On post-mortem there were all the symptoms of imperfect circulation of all the veins of the posterior extremities, distention of the base of the heart, and distention of the right ventricle, the wall being thickened about 1 or 2 cm.; the chamber was filled with dark red blood-clots, and in

150 DISEASES OF THE CIRCULATORY APPARATUS.

this clot was found five fully developed filariæ—three females and two males. The number of embryo filariæ found in the blood was enormous; Reicke estimated them to be about one million. The affected heart is shown in Fig. 41.

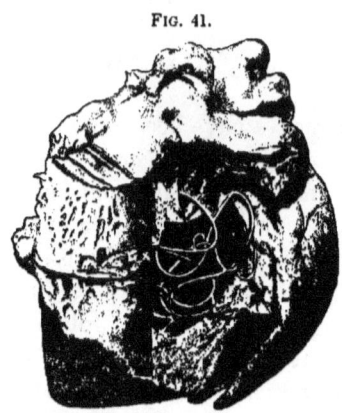

FIG. 41.

Heart, with filaria immitis in the ventricle (photograph).

The clinical symptoms of this disease were very plainly seen in a case described by Deffe. This was a five-year-old Japanese dog. On post-mortem the right heart showed several dark red blood-clots and thrombus and nearly fifty examples of the filaria immitis, ranging from 12 to 30 cm. in length and gathered in balls. He found also enormous quantities of the embryos in the blood; as many as fifty could be counted under one microscopic glass-slide. The following changes were found in the right heart: Hypertrophy, thrombus, endocarditis, and thrombus in the arteries of the lungs; chronic interstitial nephritis in the kidneys, and a number of embryos in Bowman's capsule and the canals hollowed and distended in different portions.

The most important clinical symptoms were great emaciation, notwithstanding plenty of good food and a good appetite (the appetite afterward disappeared); cough, weakness of the heart's action (small, irregular pulse, varying in force); polyuria (the urine was light and contained epithelium of the kidneys and bladder); hyaline and granular cylinders; albumin; triple phosphate crystals; pain in the posterior portion of the body, especially in the region of the kidneys, and slight paralysis.

Spiroptera Sanguinolenta (*Filaria Sanguinolenta*) (male 30 to 40 mm., female 60 to 70 mm., and about 0.5 mm. in width). These have been found by Megnin, Raillet, and others in aneurism of the aorta and (very rarely) in the blood. This parasite is occasionally found in the walls of the stomach and the mucous membrane of the œsophagus, and in the bronchial lymphatic glands. Eggs and embryo are found in great numbers in the blood. The intermediate host of the spiroptera, according to Grassi, is the kitchen moth (blatta orientialis). When the spiroptera locates itself in the walls of the œsophagus it causes more or less disturbance of the system and rapid emaciation (Driessen, Littlewood, and others).

Strongylus Vasorum (*Hæmatozoon Subulatum*) (male about 1.5 mm., female 1.5 to 2 mm., and 0.080 thick). According to Laulanić, they are located in the right ventricle and the pulmonary artery. The eggs reach the capillaries of the lungs through the circulation, and from these the liberated embryos enter the alveoli and bronchioles and form transparent nodules which look like tuberculous masses. Leisering found sexually ripe parasites in these nodules in the alveoli and also in the prostate and spongy portion of the penis. Both observers found numerous embryos in the blood.

DISEASES OF THE URINARY AND SEXUAL APPARATUS.

EXAMINATION OF THE URINARY APPARATUS.

This comprises the examination of the prepuce, urethra, prostate, bladder, and especially the urine.

Examination of the Prepuce and Urethra.

If a glossy or purulent discharge comes from the prepuce, it indicates a catarrhal condition of the part (catarrh of the foreskin or gonorrhœa of the prepuce). If the discharge is purulent, bloody, and has a fetid odor, we will find wounds or ulceration on the prepuce or the glans. Catarrhal affections (urethral, gonorrhœal) of the urethra are very rare in the dog. They are recognized by a discharge of purulent mucus from the urethra, by difficulty in urination, and the animal shows great pain on catheterization. In cases where there is great difficulty in passing urine, or where it is retained entirely, it becomes necessary to pass the catheter or sound. When this retention of urine occurs it is generally due to the presence of a stone in the bladder, a collection of stones in the urethra, or swelling of the prostate.

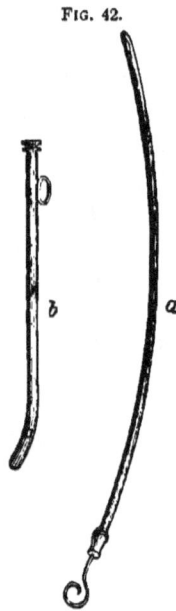

FIG. 42.

Catheters: *a*, male catheter; *b*, female catheter.

Passing the catheter in the dog: It is best to use an ordinary rubber catheter in the male dog (about 2 to 5 mm. in diameter and the ordinary length). The subject is laid on the left side or back and held in that position by an assistant. The prepuce is shoved back behind the swelling of the glans and held firmly with the left hand (see Fig. 43). Now grasp the catheter with the right, and, of course, first see that it has been well lubricated with some oil or cosmoline and that it contains the wire-stylet, and introduce it into the urethra; if it is pushed forward up the canal and meets with an obstruction at the posterior end of the bone of the penis, it is due to a flexure of the canal and also to the fact that

EXAMINATION OF THE PREPUCE AND URETHRA. 153

the diameter of the urethra is less and the part at that portion has slight contractile properties. By a gradual pressure the stricture is overcome and the catheter passes upward to the arch of the perineum; here the

FIG. 43.

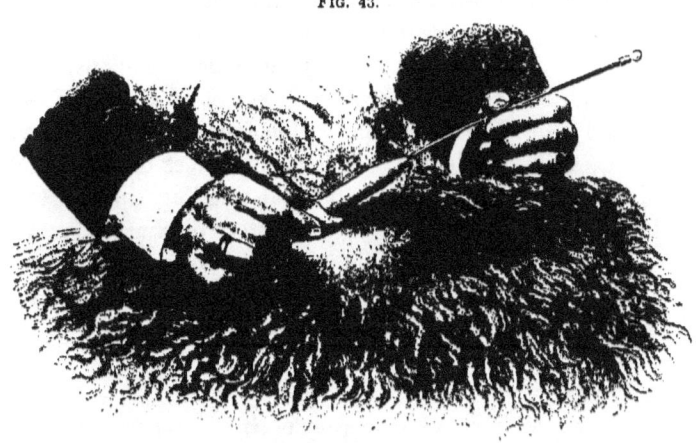

Passing the catheter.

wire-stylet must be withdrawn from the catheter at least one-third, so as to allow the catheter to make the curve; a gradual pressure soon brings it into the bladder, when the wire can be removed entirely.

FIG. 44.

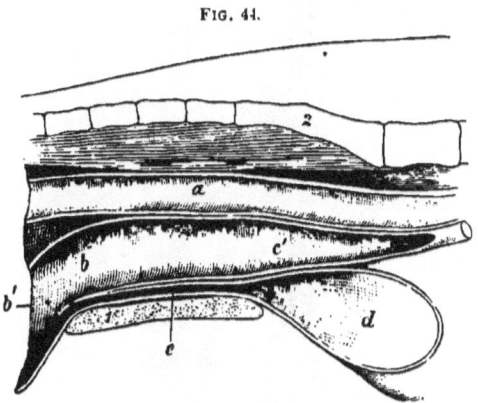

Median section through the pelvic cavity; *a*, rectum; *b*, vagina; *b'*, vulva; *d*, bladder; *e*, urethra; *l*, pubic symphysis.

In the bitch we generally use a metallic catheter, either silver or German silver (Fig. 42, B). The instrument is passed up on the floor of the vagina until it comes in contact with the urethral opening (see Fig. 44); this is closed with a slight sphincter (the so-called urethral valve); this is soon overcome and the catheter passes into the bladder without difficulty, except in cases where the urethral opening is extremely small.

It is only in exceptionally large animals that we have an opportunity to make an examination of the urethra. In the bitch certain discharges from the vagina are of diagnostic value. During the period of "heat" (menstruation) we have a copious, bloody discharge, and during the preparatory stages of labor we see a thick, clammy discharge, and the lochia commences with a nonfetid, serous, slimy discharge, which soon changes to a thick, yellowish fluid. Purulent, putrid, and bad-smelling discharges are generally found in inflammatory or ulcerative discharges from the vagina or uterus. It may also be observed when a carcinoma is present. In such cases it is best to introduce a mirror-speculum into the vagina and make a specular examination.

Examination of the Prostate.

This body varies in size, but in the dog it is large in comparison to the relative size in other animals. It is a round, ball-like body

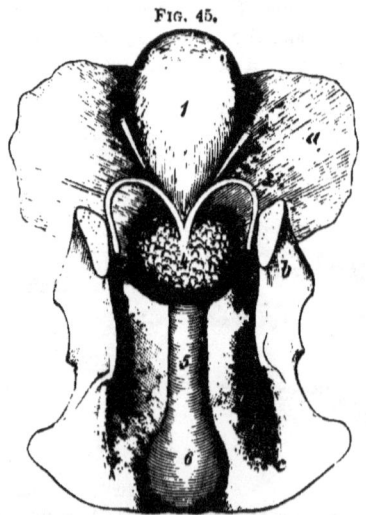

FIG. 45.

Section through the pelvis of the male: 1, bladder; 2, opening of the ureters into the bladder; 3, spermatic ducts; 4, prostate gland; 5, urethra, showing Wilson's muscle; 6, arch of the urethra; c, pelvis.

cut into two portions, lying on the neck of the bladder where the urethra commences. It lies about the anterior portion of the pubic bone, and being free to a certain extent it can be pushed into the abdominal cavity by the finger. When we have hypertrophy of that organ we distinguish it by a hard enlargement extending in all directions in the pelvic cavity.

Examination of the Bladder.

The bladder is almost entirely covered by peritoneum and lies just anterior to the brim of the pelvis, or in some cases it lies entirely in the abdominal cavity. When the bladder is very much distended it extends as far as the umbilicus and fills up the lower portion of the abdomen; it can be distinguished by manipulation. It is a round, distended, tumor-like body, with a dull sound on percussion. On examination per rectum we not only feel the neck of the bladder and the prostate, but the bladder itself can be easily distinguished. Tumor or stones in the bladder can be felt by pressing down toward the wall of the abdomen, and the animal evinces more or less pain when the bladder is distended and any pressure put on it.

It is very hard to make any examination of the kidneys that is of any practical value, as will be seen from the plates on Figs. 32 and 33, as they lie high up toward the spine and are well protected and covered by the intestines and also by large collections of fat. In some animals with loose, flabby abdominal walls, or when a large collection of fluid has been removed from the abdominal cavity, we can examine the kidneys. We can, however, distinguish any specially large body, such as tumors of the kidneys or perinephritic abscesses, by manipulation.

Examination of the Urine.

The urine has to be examined as to its amount, color, transparency, reaction, weight, odor, and the presence of certain foreign or chemical substances.

The properties of normal urine are described in all works on physiology, and concerning pathological urine the author would refer you to such works as the *Treatise on Microscopy and Chemical Diagnosis of Diseases of Domestic Animals*, by Siedamgrotzky and Hofmeister; the *Comparative Physiology of Domestic Animals*, by Ellenberger; and also a *Text-book of Clinical Methods of Examination*, by Friedberger and Fröhner. The author will confine himself to a slight summary of the distinguishing characters of urine, both normal and pathological.

Amount of Urine. The amount of urine passed in one day depends largely, of course, on the size of the animal, the quantity of fluids it drinks, and the temperature of the atmosphere. The average amount of urine passed by a dog is from 0.5 to 1.5 kilogrammes daily. A decrease in the amount of urine passed indicates that the water of the body is being taken up through some other channel, as in violent diarrhœa, great salivation, during the formation of pleuritic or peritoneal exudates, or in dropsy, in fevers, in decrease of the pressure of the heart, as in valvular defects, myocarditis, etc. An entire stoppage of the urine may occur in inflammation of the kidneys, in obstruction of the urethra, paralysis or rupture of the bladder, from calculi in the bladder or urethra, from stricture of the urethra, or from swelling and pressure of the prostate.

An increase of the amount of urine (polyuria) may be due to the presence of a large amount of water in the blood (anæmia, hydræmia), in atrophy of the kidney, where there is great reabsorption of exudates; in diabetes mellitus (a condition that corresponds to diabetes insipidus in man). This, however is extremely rare in dogs. We may see it after the administration of the different diuretics. It is frequently seen in convalescence from acute diseases.

Constant dribbling of urine indicates paralysis or weakness of the bladder.

The Color of the Urine. This varies in the healthy dog from pale yellow when it is thin, to dark yellow when it is concentrated. Food also has a certain influence on the color. After eating fat it is reddish-yellow, and after meat it is light yellow; after eating sugar and bread it is dark yellow, and when the animal is starved it is deep yellow. Disease has also a great effect on the color. It is a deep yellow color in fevers, and pale or colorless in diabetes, general anæmia, and atrophy of the kidneys; a green or light brown in diseases of the liver and catarrh of the duodenum; a greenish-black color after the absorption of tar preparations or carbolic acid ; a red color from santonin, rhubarb, and senna (in these cases there is always an alkaline reaction). The appearance of blood in the urine indicates grave conditions. In hæmaturia we may see the color vary from bluish-red to almost black, the color corresponding to the number of blood-corpuscles present, and in hæmoglobinuria the coloring-matter is granular or dissolved blood-coloring matter, actual blood-corpuscles rarely being present. Both the above conditions may exist simultaneously in some cases. (The test for coloring from blood is to be be found under hæmoglobinuria).

Transparency and Reaction of the Urine. When the urine has been recently passed it is clear and transparent, and has an acid reaction. After feeding with bread for some time it is turbid and alkaline. After feeding with fat it is alkaline. In pathological conditions when the urine is recently passed it is turbid and filled by mucus and epithelium, pus-cells, triple phosphates. An alkaline reaction generally indicates catarrh of the bladder, or we may see it in hæmaturia, in reabsorption of large exudates, and in hemorrhage into the abdomen or thorax.

Odor of the Urine. There is a slight penetrating odor in normal urine. In cases of catarrh of the bladder the urine has a strong ammoniacal odor, and when there is any amount of turpentine absorbed the urine has a faint smell of violets.

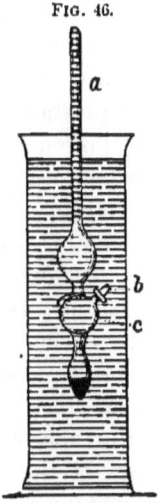

FIG. 46.

Areapikometer.

The Specific Gravity of the Urine. This varies in the dog between 1016 and 1060. It can be tested either by means of Vogel's urinometer or if we have only a small quantity we can test it readily by the areapikometer. This instrument the author has found to be very useful. It is shown in Fig. 46. Place the urine to be tested into the receptacle C. Fill it full, taking care that there are no air-bubbles in it. Close it and then sink it in water at 15° R. The specific weight of the urine will then be marked on the scale.

As a rule, it will be found that dark urine has a high specific gravity and light-colored urine has a low specific gravity. But there are exceptions to this, for in diabetes mellitus the urine is clear and high in specific gravity, while in nephritis it is dark in color and has a low specific gravity. Dark urine seen during starvation has a low specific gravity.

Foreign Substances in the Urine. The following substances appear in the urine under pathological circumstances:

Mucus. This is found in the urine under all conditions, both in health and disease, and when any of the urinary passages are inflamed it appears in larger quantities, especially in catarrh of the bladder.

Blood-corpuscles. If the blood is mixed in the urine evenly and the corpuscles are reduced in size and cylinders are present, it indicates hemorrhage from the kidneys. This condition is always present in acute nephritis, in the early stages of the disease. If the urine is bloody at irregular intervals, it indicates hemorrhage from the pelvis of the kidney, generally as a result of calculi. When the blood is not mixed with the urine, but comes down in a mass, the diseased condition must be in the bladder. This indication is not always certain, as we may see the blood evenly mixed with the urine in diseased conditions of the bladder, such as cystitis. When the blood is passed just before the urine or follows after the last of the urine has passed, it indicates hemorrhage from the prostate or urethra.

Pus or White Blood-corpuscles. When there is a considerable quantity of pus passed it indicates the opening of an abscess in the prostate. When a smaller quantity is present it indicates the presence of some inflammation on the mucous membranes of the urethra, and it is also seen in some inflammations of the kidneys. We can obtain definite information as to this condition by making a microscopical examination of the epithelium, and see whether any cylinders are present or not.

Fat may be seen in drops on the surface of the urine or shortly after it has been passed. In very fat animals this may be seen as a normal condition, and where animals have had large quantities of fat given to them it also indicates the fatty degeneration of the epithelium of the kidneys. It is also present in the various diseases of the kidneys. Do not make a mistake when you have passed a well-lubricated catheter and see oil floating on the urine to think it is a pathological condition.

Epithelium. In health there are always a few epithelial cells passed, but when they are present in large quantities it indicates some active inflammation going on in some part of the urinary tract, and a microscopical examination of the cells to ascertain their size and shape will indicate the section of the track that they come from. Large quantities of squamous epithelium indicate an irritable condition of the bladder. (Fig. 47.) Where we find

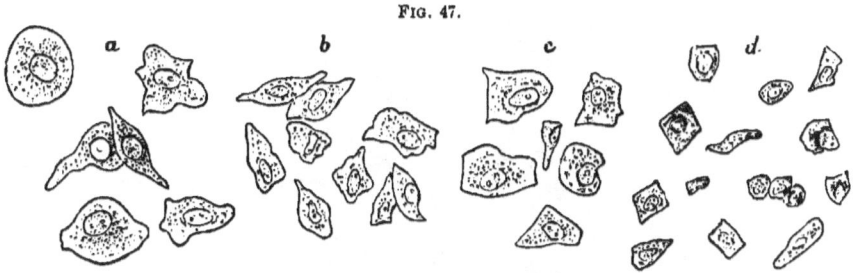

FIG. 47.

Epithelium found in the urine: *a*, from the bladder; *b*, from the ureters; *c*, from the pelvis of the kidney.

hyaline cylinders, granular cylinders, epithelial cylinders, or casts of blood, then we can feel assured that there is some disease of the kidneys. Blood-cylinders indicate hemorrhage of the kidneys. Epithelial cells in large numbers indicate great desquamation of the epithelium, as in acute parenchymatous nephritis. Hyaline or epithelial cells when mixed with pus-cells indicate nephritis. Hyaline and granular cells are present in all diseases of the kidneys and always in albuminuria. (Fig. 48.)

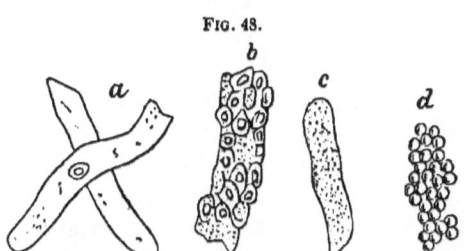

FIG. 48.

Uric cylinders: *a*, hyaline cylinders; *b*, epithelial cylinders; *d*, granular cylinders; *c*, blood-cylinders.

Crystals and Bacteria. When we find collections of precipitates in the urine and indications of alkaline fermentation, the urine being alkaline in reaction, and containing crystals of triple phosphate and in rare instances crystals of uric acid, it indicates a severe irritation of the bladder. Elongated strings of bullet-like bacteria and numerous pus-cells indicate a purulent condition of the prostate (see Fig. 49). There are a number of abnormal substances found in the urine. The principal ones are albumin, sugar, and the coloring substances of the bile.

FIG. 49.

Urine of cystitis in the dog, containing cystic epithelium, blood-corpuscles, triple phosphate crystals, and bacteria.

Albumin. The presence of albumin in the urine is always an indication of disease. The best method to indicate its presence is by Koch's test. The urine is boiled in a test-tube, having been previously rendered acid in reaction by a small quantity of acetic acid. It may become opaque from two causes: from the presence of albumin or from phosphates. We pour a small quantity of nitromuriatic acid down the side of the tube, and if there is any albumin present there will be a pronounced opaque line where the acid meets the urine.

Albumin occurs in the urine from two causes: first, in false or accidental albuminuria, and true or renal albuminuria.

The first occurs when there is free albumin in the urine from accidental causes, where the albumin is added to the urine in its passage from hemorrhage, inflammatory conditions in the passages, or from purulent inflammations. In such cases the microscope will easily make the differential diagnosis.

True albuminuria is of much greater importance, as this condition is always a symptom of pathological alterations in the epithelium covering the walls of the gland. Healthy epithelium will always retain the albumin in the blood.

We see true albuminuria in all forms of acute and chronic inflammation of the kidneys, in fatty degeneration of the kidneys, in amyloid kidneys, and in any altered condition of the circulation, such as stagnating hyperæmias as a consequence of heart-disease, chronic inflammatory conditions of the lungs, pleuritis, hydrothorax. The horizontal position of the dog does not, however, cause such a great disturbance in the posterior extremities when the smaller bloodvessels are congested as it does in man (Dieckerhoff).

Albumin will sometimes be found in the blood from anæmia, leukæmia, in acute poisoning, and from high fevers, but in the latter condition we generally find that there is more or less nephritis or a slight parenchymatous degeneration of the kidneys present.

Sugar. The grape-sugar test is generally made when an animal has loss of appetite and polyuria and becomes generally emaciated. The test is Trommer's.

Trommer's test for sugar : Put a few cc. of urine in a reagent glass, taking care to first see that there is no albumin in it, and if so coagulate it and filter it out. Take the urine and dilute it with an equal bulk of water, and render it alkaline with a small quantity of sodium hydrate, then add drop by drop a 4 per cent. solution of cupri sulphas until the liquid is clear and the sediment dissolved, then heat it until it boils, and if sugar is present we see a reddish-yellow vapor appear at the surface of the fluid.

In diabetes mellitus a large quantity of sugar is found. This disease, however, is extremely rare in the dog. It is also found when the animal has been fed on a pure sugar diet. Sinety observed it in bitches that were nursing, especially when the pups were prevented from nursing for some time. The author cannot say whether it is found in the dog as in man, in certain cases of poisoning, and from some neurotic causes.

Coloring Substances of the Bile. The coloring substances of the bile are found quite frequently in the urine of the dog.

The presence of the coloring substances in the bile indicates an obstruction in the excretion of bile. It may often be seen in catarrh of the intestines and in the gastric form of distemper. Icterus is the most common cause of this condition. (For further information, see Icterus.) Fröhner found this also in neurosis and bronchial forms of distemper, in some diseases of the kidneys, in pleuritis, and in great heart-weakness. Voigt also found it in animals that were starved. Bile acids in the urine are of no diagnostic value in the dog.

DISEASES OF THE KIDNEYS.

Inflammation of the Kidneys; Nephritis.

It is impossible to accurately separate the different inflammatory conditions of the kidneys, and as a rule it is only on post-mortem that the condition can be properly diagnosed. Consequently, the practitioner has to be satisfied if he can recognize with certainty that the animal has some affection of the kidneys, and whether it is acute or chronic. In the dog it is only in chronic nephritis that we have a general atrophy of the kidney.

The diseases of the kidneys in the dog do not possess that importance that they do in man.

Acute Inflammation of the Kidneys.
(Acute Nephritis; Nephritis Acuta.)

ETIOLOGY. The most common causes of this condition are infectious diseases and poisons. By this is meant the effect produced by the absorption of infectious noxious agents, such as the various septic diseases, or certain irritants that have originated in the body and are passed by the kidneys and cause great irritation while they are passing through these organs, and also certain micro-organisms that reach the blood and become located in the capillaries of the kidneys. Certain chemical substances that are absorbed or taken into the stomach pass through the kidneys and cause great irritation, such as phosphorus, arsenic, mercury, copper, cantharides, turpentine, carbolic and tar acids, naphthol, pyrogallic acid, and chrysarobin. Some of these preparations are absorbed by the skin from various ointments that are applied in mange, such as carbolic acid, mercury, cantharides, etc.

Acute nephritis may also originate from an extension of inflammation from neighboring organs, and also from traumatic influences, such as blows, shocks, etc., in the regions of the kidneys. There is a condition called rheumatic inflammation of the kidneys that is supposed to originate from cold, but this disease has not been observed in the dog.

PATHOLOGICAL ANATOMY. The alterations in the structure of the kidney depend on the intensity of the irritation, and the alterations are more or less distinctly marked. In slight cases the epithelium seems to be the only part affected, the connective tissue and the bloodvessels show no other pathological alteration than a reddish-gray coloration of the covering (parenchymatous degeneration). When the irritation is great there is true parenchymatous inflammation of the kidneys. The epithelium and the intermediate tissue become affected, and also the bloodvessels and all the exudation processes follow which accompany acute inflammation. The anatomical alterations that are found are as follows: The epithelium has undergone the same alteration as in parenchymatous degeneration, but more acute in its type. The capsules of the glomeruli and the small urinary canals are altered, and the connective tissue is filled with a liquid infiltration, forming numerous coagulated masses containing large numbers of leucocytes. The vessels are enlarged (hyperæmic) and partially compressed by the surrounding exudates. In the interstitial tissue and in Müller's capsule we find small circumscribed hemorrhages.

There are a number of circular-shaped inflammatory centres surrounded by liquid exudates. The inflamed kidney may present a variety of different appearances. It may be enlarged or normal in size, soft or hard, reddened or very pale, yellowish-white, and on the surface of the kidney there may be found a number of hemorrhagic spots that are slightly elevated from the surface of the gland. The capsule can easily be stripped from the body of the kidney. There are certain forms of acute nephritis and glomerulo-nephritis that present so little visible changes that they may escape the eye of the non-experienced practitioner. Concerning more accurate details the author would refer you to the various text-books on pathological anatomy.

CLINICAL SYMPTOMS AND COURSE. Slight inflammatory conditions of the kidneys are rarely recognized in the dog, as the only diagnostic points are to be found on examination of the urine. This contains a small amount of albumin, some hyaline cylinders, and a few epithelial cells and leucocytes.

In acute inflammatory conditions the animal has a peculiar stiff gait in walking, and in some cases staggering, with the hindlegs carried straight. Tenderness on pressure in the regions of the loins; a quick, full pulse; great lessening in the amount of urine secreted, and what is passed is dark in color and contains small portions of coagulated blood; the feces are dry and hard. In toxic nephritis in dogs the author has had special opportunities to make observations. The amount of urine passed in such conditions is small and contains a large amount of albumin. The urine is turbid, containing numerous tube-cylinders, epithelium, discolored blood-corpuscles, and also red blood-corpuscles, which give the urine a variable color, according to the number of corpuscles present. There is generally more or less pain in urination, which is probably due to the acrid condition of the urine. There are also more or less symptoms of uræmia present; great weakness, fatigue; temperature is generally subnormal; the pulse weak and thready; vomiting, convulsions, coma, and death. When the symptoms were milder the animal recovered, or this condition was followed by chronic nephritis.

THERAPEUTICS. Medicine, as a rule, has little or no effect on these cases. Tannin, 0.1 gm. several times daily; tinct. fol. uva ursi, 1.0, or fuschin. Iron preparations may all be used to try to eliminate the irritating substances from the kidneys.

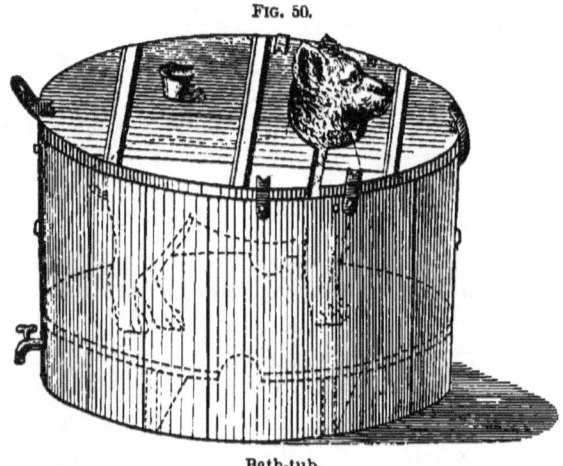

FIG. 50.

Bath-tub.

The dietetic treatment is the most successful, and consists principally of rest and food that is non-irritating to the kidneys. Milk and broth are especially useful. Meat may be given, but only lean meat, and in spare quantities, avoiding anything that is spiced. Small quantities of salt, however, are beneficial. The symptomatic treatment is to try to lessen the strain thrown on the kidneys by trying to carry the fluids out of the body by some other channel than the kidneys. (Fig. 50.) This can be accomplished to a certain extent by giving the animal hot baths or by warm bandages around the body, and by active purgatives, like senna or cascara segrada, also jalap and calomel.

    ℞.—Res. jalapæ 0.1
        Hydrarg. chlor. mite 0.05
        Sacchar. alba 0.6
    M. F. pulv. No. vi. S.—One three times daily.

We can also try pilocarpine, which produces great salivary secretion in the dog. Diuretics must not be used in nephritis, as they increase the secretion of salts, especially the alkalies. Heart-weakness must be counteracted by means of heart-tonics. General debility should be treated by general stimulants, such as brandy, whiskey, or sherry, in very small animals. Use clysters of chloral hydrate to counteract convulsions.

Chronic Inflammation of the Kidneys.
(Chronic Nephritis; Nephritis Chronica.)

ETIOLOGY. Chronic nephritis originates, as a rule, from acute nephritis, or starts in a mild form and gradually becomes chronic.

PATHOLOGICAL ANATOMY. There are two forms of chronic inflammation of the kidneys: first the large white kidney (Chronic Parenchymatous Nephritis), and the atrophic or hard kidney (Chronic Interstitial Nephritis). The first condition is generally the forerunner of the second, but, as the hard kidney is most frequently found in post-mortems, it is possible that it may develop as a primary condition. The white kidney is enlarged from the normal size, and has a smooth yellow or irregular yellow-colored surface. The cortical portion is yellowish in color, while the pyramids are red. In some cases we find the kidney large and red, or alternated red and yellow, or covered with hemorrhagic spots. The atrophic kidney (shrunken or contracted kidney) results from an increase of the interstitial substance and atrophy of the parenchymatous substance. It is hard and tough on its surface. It has small, watery-like irregularities and granulations. The capsule is thickened, and it is hard to strip from the body of the kidney. The cortical substance is lessened in diameter and striped with layers of dark colored tissue. The pyramids are smaller and deep red in color.

CLINICAL SYMPTOMS AND COURSE. As a rule, there is very little that can be recognized in the dog during life, and the author has held posts on animals that have had chronic nephritis of both kidneys that did not present the slightest symptoms of the disease during life; and even the urine may not contain any albumin, the only symptom being the amount of urine secreted. This is greatly increased in amount, the specific gravity being much lessened. In such cases there is generally hypertrophy of the left ventricle, which can be recognized by palpitation of the heart (loud pulsations and a hard, full pulse). It is presumed that this high arterial pressure tends to keep up the action on the impaired kidney and prevent any serious disturbance in the secretion of the kidney. As the disease advances we soon recognize a change: The heart becomes weaker in its action, the pulse is small and frequent, the urine is scant, dark, and very albuminous. This is followed by chronic inflammatory processes in various organs, especially the bronchia, and in the intestinal canal, and finally we have symptoms of uræmia. In the majority of cases the parenchymatous form can be recognized by the urine. This is very similar to acute nephritis. It contains much albumin, and the urine is scant in quantity, and there are certain dropsical symptoms in the dependent region. There are also loss of appetite, great fatigue on taking any exercise, hypertrophy of the heart, which finally becomes weak, and then symptoms of uræmia follow as stated above.

THERAPEUTICS. The treatment of chronic nephritis is the same as in acute, but the dropsical conditions can be treated by digitalis and strophanthus, and when there is great anæmia give iron salts.

Amyloid Kidney.

Amyloid kidney generally occurs in connection with amyloid degeneration of some other organs of the body. The kidney is contracted, and in the parenchymatous form the condition can generally be recognized by the character of the urine. This generally presents the same symptoms as acute nephritis. The urine is loaded with albumin and much lessened in quantity.

The amyloid condition is not only seen in the kidneys, but also in the liver, pancreas, and intestines. Rabe only saw one case where the kidney was the only organ affected. He observed, as a rule, the liver was also affected.

PATHOLOGICAL ANATOMY. A kidney thoroughly affected with amyloid disease is slightly enlarged, hard, smooth, and shows at the intersections a deep yellowish-white coloration, easily distinguished on section. The glomeruli are dull, glairy in color. On staining with Lugol's solution the affected parts are colored a mahogany brown, and with methyl are colored purple.

CLINICAL SYMPTOMS. Rabe made the following observations: Where the kidney was the only portion affected the animal was emaciated, the temperature 35.9°, the pulse 72. The extremities were dropsical, complete loss of appetite, coma, and death. Where the liver was affected the animal was unsteady and weak, paleness of the mucous membrane, temperature 38°, ascites, appetite good. Where the kidney and liver were affected there was great weakness, indifference, unsteady gait, temperature 39.6, pulse 96, respirations 50, appetite good, and the urine was acid and free from albumin.

With the above symptoms, which are rather meagre and liable to be very difficult to distinguish from other diseases, it still might be a guide in making a diagnosis. (In man in this disease there is always more or less albuminuria.)

THERAPEUTICS. The treatment consists in following what is described in nephritis.

Abscess of the Kidneys.
(*Suppurative Nephritis; Pyelonephritis.*)

ETIOLOGY. The direct cause of the formation of abscess of the kidney is from direct injury of the kidneys or in the region of them, causing the formation of purulent abscess in the urinary passages, the bladder, the urethra, or the pelvis of the kidney. In certain conditions it is associated with ulcerous endocarditis.

PATHOLOGICAL ANATOMY. Purulent nephritis occurs in various forms, according to its origin. When they are caused by an embolus they appear in the shape of small spots, which are easily distinguished by the naked eye. When a section is made through the kidney they are grayish-yellow in color, round or oblong in shape. They are generally surrounded by a red circle. When the spot is examined under the microscope there are swarms of micrococci in the centre of the mass, and it is reasonable to believe that these are the cause of the abscess. Only in rare cases do the abscesses become confluent, and when they do they form large pus-centres that, as a rule, cause death. When the abscess forms in the pelvis of the kidney the pus extends into the straight urinary canals—in some cases as far as the surface of the kidney—and is indicated by a protrusion or elevation of the external surface, which is yellowish in the centre and surrounded by a circle of yellowish points. When large abscesses are formed from these, becoming confluent, the whole kidney may become altered into one large abscess. The covering capsule of the kidney becomes thickened and holds the abscess with its contents (pyonephrosis). In the early stages, where the micrococci have just collected in the urinary canals, and have started to form abscess-centres, it makes a very interesting study.

Where there is a formation of a perinephritic abscess in the region of the kidney caused by traumatic causes, from purulent abscess, from purulent pyelitis, or abscess in the neighboring organs, it may lead to the formation of considerable pus.

CLINICAL SYMPTOMS AND THERAPEUTICS. The symptoms of abscess of the kidneys may not differ to any great extent from chronic nephritis. The abscess of the kidney occurring in pyæmia is only seen on post-mortem. The symptoms of pyelonephritis are also completely disguised by the preceding symptoms of purulent cystitis. Treatment is, therefore, useless.

Perinephritic abscesses may become so large that they form a tumor-like body in the lumbar region, and the pus can be detected under the skin, in some cases so large that it fluctuates. When such is the case, and we have confirmed our diagnosis by means of an exploring needle, the sac should be emptied by an aspirator, or make a fairly large opening and empty the abscess of its contents and fill it with an antiseptic dressing. If the kidney itself is not directly affected by the abscess, we may expect a quick recovery under good antiseptic conditions. (See treatment of wounds.)

Inflammation of the Pelvis of the Kidney.
(*Pyelitis.*)

ETIOLOGY. This is caused by the irritation or extension of certain inflammations from the body of the kidney, from poisonous irritants passed from the blood through the kidneys, from foreign bodies that lie in the pelvis, nephritic stones, strongylus gigas; and it is also seen in diseases that are acute in character and in hydronephrosis.

PATHOLOGICAL ANATOMY. Pyelitis occurs in a number of forms according to the intensity of the irritants. From catarrh, where it forms purulent or diphtheritic pyelitis.

CLINICAL SYMPTOMS AND THERAPEUTICS. This disease is only recognized by means of the microscope, when we detect certain forms of epithelium in the urine. There are also some symptoms of inflammation of the kidney or catarrh of the bladder.

Cysts of the Kidneys.
(*Hydronephrosis; Enlargement of the Pelvis of the Kidney.*)

ETIOLOGY AND PATHOLOGICAL ANATOMY. Whenever there is a stenosis or stricture of the urinary passages and obstruction of the urine it is dammed back and presses on all the canals back of it, and as a consequence the canals are distended and become finally enlarged. If the obstruction is in the urinary tube, the bladder, ureters, and the pelvis of the kidney become enlarged; but if one ureter only is affected, the corresponding kidney becomes enlarged; and where the pelvis is much distended the body of the kidney becomes absorbed after the condition has lasted some time. The whole kidney becomes inverted into a pouch-like mass of connective tissue, filled with liquid. This fluid at first is urine, but from the alteration soon becomes converted into mucous secretion. In one case described by Siedamgrotzky, he observed, instead of a kidney, a big bladder or cyst with walls formed of connective tissue, and filled with a slimy, brownish fluid, containing numerous cholesterin crystals.

CLINICAL SYMPTOMS AND THERAPEUTICS. The cystic kidney is generally recognized only when it is indicated by a fluctuating mass in the region of the kidney. When there is double hydronephrosis the urine is suppressed and symptoms of uræmia show very quickly. The only condition where the disease can be treated is when it is caused by obstruction of the urethra.

Nephritic Stones.
(*Nephrolithiasis.*)

Nephritic stones are formed in the pelvis of the kidney and range from the size of a mustard-seed to that of a pea. (Meguin found two stones weighing six and seven grammes each in the pelvis of a dog.) They are irregular, watery, yellowish or yellowish-brown in color. In rare cases they become very large and fill up the pelvis or greatly distend it. They are the shape of the pelvis, and on section they are found to be in layers, and consist of phosphoric acid, carbonic acid, triple phosphate, and uric acid.

The formation of these collections is not thoroughly understood, but they are probably formed by a small piece of epithelium or mass of cells becoming fastened together, and the salts are deposited on this medium in successive layers, and finally a large mass is formed.

DISEASES OF THE BLADDER.

Catarrh of the Bladder.
(*Cystitis.*)

ETIOLOGY. Catarrh of the bladder is generally caused by certain mechanical or chemical influences or by microbes which find their way into it as a result of certain infectious diseases, and are eliminated by the kidneys or by certain chemical irritants, such as oil of turpentine, cantharides, carbolic acid, and also foreign bodies. These irritate the mucous membrane. Septic instruments, such as catheters, when introduced into the bladder, may set up an irritation, and also by the extension of an irritation from the urinary ducts, the pelvis of the kidney, from the uterus, and from retention of the urine, caused by stones in the urethra, from hypertrophy of the prostate. The last two are the most frequent causes of cystitis. Where the urine becomes very alkaline from the excess of ammonia it produces an irritating effect on the kidney; continued retention of urine, especially when it is heavily charged with salts, acts as an irritant. It has been said that cold will produce cystitis, but it is not positively known.

PATHOLOGICAL ANATOMY. There are quite a number of varieties of cystitis—mucous, muscular, serous, croupal, ulcerous, diphtheritic, and gangrenous—but, as a rule, it is very seldom that we can distinguish the various forms, and it is best from a practical standpoint to distinguish the disease in its different forms by acute and chronic catarrh of the bladder. In the acute form the mucous membrane of the bladder is colored in an irregular way by dark-red spots. It is also more or less swollen and covered with mucus and detached epithelium. In the later stages of the disease the mucous membrane may be covered with detached epithelium and covered with small hemorrhagic spots. In very severe cases we find a croupous membrane covering the bladder, and it may be so acute as to cause gangrene, and mucous membrane is sloughed off and extensive abscesses are formed. In such cases the muscular and serous coats of the bladder are also greatly inflamed, and if the irritation is extensive enough we may also find evidences of peritonitis.

In the chronic form the mucous membrane becomes very much thickened and covered with enlarged mucous glands. The surface presents a peculiar greenish or slate-gray color. This is due to the hemorrhages that occur in the tissues from time to time. On the surface we often find raised papilla-like formations, and the submucous tissues and muscles are hypertrophied.

CLINICAL SYMPTOMS AND COURSE. The first symptom noticed in this disease is the passage of an increased amount of urine, the animal emptying the bladder frequently, but passes only a small quantity of urine each time, at the same time showing symptoms of pain. On making an examination of the bladder through the abdominal wall the animal shows pain on pressure of that region. An examination of the urine by the microscope will assist us in making a positive diagnosis. If there should be some disease of the kidneys present, the specific gravity of the urine is not much changed, but in the early stages of the disease it is somewhat increased in salts and contains only a normal amount of mucus, a few colorless blood-corpuscles, and epithelium of the bladder. This condition may continue for a long time. Mild cases of cystitis are not diagnosed, but as the disease continues the urine becomes thicker and turbid, and on examination of the urine microscopically we find numerous pus-cells and epithelium of the bladder; the urine rapidly loses its acid reaction, and soon becomes neutral or alkaline, and has a strong ammoniacal odor. Urine from an animal in this condition ferments very rapidly. It contains numerous crystals of triple phosphate, and in rare instances uric-acid crystals and also numerous bacteria. (Fig. 51.)

Fig. 51.

Urine of a dog with cystitis, triple phosphate crystals, red and white blood-corpuscles, and cystic epithelium. Bacteria.

Fever, as a rule, is present in this disease, but is never intense, but rather shows an intermittent character. There are also severe depression and loss of appetite. The course of the disease, generally, is rapid, and in slight cases the animal recovers in a few days, but in acute cases the case may last for a month or more, and death may finally be caused by perforation of the bladder and the animal dies of peritonitis, gangrene, or uræmia. The most frequent termination of the acute form is into the mild chronic form.

In the chronic form the symptoms are much milder, and for a long time the urine is the only guide to a diagnosis, as it is only in advanced cases that the animal will show any pain on pressure of the abdomen. The contractile power of the bladder is gradually lost, and the animal may present symptoms of incontinence of urine, passing small quantities of urine without any effort; or this is seen in well-trained house animals that pass small quantities of urine while making every effort to retain it until they are outside, or it may pass away drop by drop when they are moving about or asleep.

THERAPEUTICS. The treatment of cystitis may be dietetic, medicinal, or local, according to the symptoms presented. In slight cases it is only necessary to administer such non-irritating agents, such as tartaric acid, nitric acid, liquor potassii acetatis, infusions of juniper, and a liquid diet, such as milk or soups. This assists in increasing the urine and also in lessening its specific gravity, and by that means cleans out the bladder. In the more acute conditions we try to correct the urine by means of disinfectants, such as salicylic acid, boric acid, naphthalin, chloride of potassium, or a decoction of fol. uva ursi. The author has always obtained good results from the administration of the last two agents.

 R.—Potassii chloras 12.0
  Aqua destil. 300.0
 M. S.—One teaspoonful three times a day.
 R.—Decoc. fol. uva ursi . . . . . 15.0 : 180.0
 S. Several teaspoonfuls or tablespoonfuls daily.

In the treatment of this chronic form, besides the various alkaline salts, we should use the resinous diuretics, such as oil of juniper, oil of turpentine, or juniper water.

The local treatment of the bladder is very effectual. This consists in introducing the medicinal agents directly into the bladder by means of the catheter. The catheter is introduced into the bladder, and by means of a small hose is connected with a small funnel (see Fig. 52), and a liquid emptied into the bladder, and then the hose is placed in a dependent position and the liquid allowed to trickle out. This can be repeated several times without removing the catheter.

The author first cleans out the bladder with clean water, then allows a solution of boric acid, 2 per cent., to flow in. Creolin, 1 per cent., is also used, but is not as preferable as the former. The liquids must be tepid. In the dog, of course, it is a little harder to do than in the bitch, but with a little practice it is very easily performed and produces very satisfactory results. In the bitch a short metallic catheter can be used.

Debilitated Conditions of the Bladder.

ETIOLOGY, CLINICAL SYMPTOMS, AND PROGNOSIS. Weak bladders, due to paralysis or paresis, are generally seen in old dogs,

174 *DISEASES OF THE URINARY AND SEXUAL APPARATUS.*

and are produced from a number of reasons. One frequent cause of this condition is seen in house dogs that cannot get outside, and retain the urine for a long time, producing extreme distention of the bladder. It is also caused by obstructions of various kinds, which prevent the passage of the urine, such as hypertrophy of the prostate, strictures of the urethra, and by weakness of the muscular coat of the bladder, caused by chronic catarrh of that organ. Certain diseases of the nervous system also produce this condition.

FIG. 52.

Apparatus and method of irrigating the bladder in the dog.

There are two forms of this disease: Paralysis of the Detrusor and Paralysis of the Sphincter Vesicæ. It is quite common to find both conditions present in one animal. In the first condition the bladder becomes so distended that its elasticity is lost, and the muscular coat loses its power of contraction, and, finally, when the bladder is so distended that the connective tissue alone holds it and presses on the sphincter vesicæ and overcomes it, the urine trickles out in small quantities. This is termed overflowing of the bladder (urination by incontinence). When the sphincter is paralyzed the urine flows constantly or at very short intervals, the slightest contraction of the depressor being sufficient to expel it. In this condition the bladder is nearly always empty. In making an examination of the bladder through the abdomen, when paralysis of the detrusor is present, the bladder will be found distended, even when the animal has passed some urine a short time before that, whereas in paralysis of the sphincter the bladder will be found to be empty.

When cystitis accompanies this condition the animal shows more or less pain when he urinates. This, however, is only seen in rare instances. The prognosis is unfavorable in the majority of cases. The only case in which the author has seen a favorable termination was one of simple distention of the bladder.

THERAPEUTICS. The treatment best adapted to relieve this condition is to regulate the passage of urine, as in catarrh of the bladder, by cold injections into the bladder of tinc. nucis vomicæ, 5 to 10 drops once or twice daily; strychnia muriate, 0.001 to 0.003 subcutaneously; and fluid ext. ergotæ 0.50. We can also try faradization of the abdomen in the region of the bladder.

Cystic Cramp.
(Cramp of the Bladder.)

There can be no doubt that cramp or spasm of the bladder (cystospasmus) may occur in the dog, although we have no literature on the subject. By this condition we mean an extreme irritability of the bladder, causing an extreme contraction of the muscular coat of the bladder, and small quantities of urine, in some cases only a drop at a time, are passed with great difficulty. In some cases all the symptoms of uræmia are observed. On passing the catheter, which is extremely painful, we easily recognize it by the bladder being empty, or, if the contraction is at the neck, the urine is passed in a quick stream as soon as the catheter overcomes the contraction. Morphia hypodermatically is the best drug to insure relief; tinc. valerian is also very useful.

Stone in the Bladder.
(*Lithiasis.*)

ETIOLOGY AND PATHOLOGICAL ANATOMY. The various lithic formations that are found in the bladder may be subdivided into urates, oxalates, phosphates, and cystates.

Urates. These consist of uric acid, or uric acid salts, or both in combination. They are small, hard, yellowish or reddish-brown bodies, having a smooth surface, and on cutting through the centre are found to be in concentric layers or strata.

Oxalates are chiefly composed of oxalic acid and lime salts, and also more or less mixed with uric and phosphoric acids. They are hard, brown in color, and have an irregular mulberry surface.

Phosphates. These are composed of phosphoric acid, lime, and triple phosphate. They are gray-white in color, and, as a rule, are soft and friable.

Cystic Stones. These are soft, wax-like bodies, having a shiny, crystalline, irregular surface.

All these lithic deposits contain besides their inorganic elements numerous organic elements, such as epithelium, blood-cells, mucus, etc.

The size to which these calculi may grow is considerable. In Dresden there is a calculus taken from a German boar-hound that is 11 cm. long and 7.5 cm. wide, 6 cm. thick, and weighed 490 grammes when fresh. They are generally started in their formation in the pelvis of the kidney, and, generally, from some foreign body, such as a blood-clot, a piece of mucus, epithelium, etc., around which the sediment in the urine forms and gradually the crystalline elements accumulate. This deposit is especially favored in cases of cystitis, where the urine is undergoing alkaline fermentation and produces a copious sediment in the urine.

Paul Bert and Studensky found by experiments that the food and fluids that the animal takes may have a certain influence on the formation of stone in the bladder. The former mentions two cases in which one was fed exclusively on meat and the other on vegetables. On post-mortem of the animal fed on meat there was found a phosphatic calculus, but no trace of inflammation of the urinary organs.

Studensky placed foreign bodies in the bladder and found that when the animal was allowed to drink only water that was thoroughly impregnated with lime salts that there was soon formed over the body a thick, heavy deposit of lime salts, and differed greatly in animals fed in the usual way, with pure water and meat. In this case the calcretion was much smaller and deposited much more slowly.

CLINICAL SYMPTOMS AND COURSE. When the uric calculus lies in the bladder and has not attained any size it may stay there a long time and not produce any severe symptoms, with the exception of a slight catarrh, and that is only noticed when the animal has had a long run, the urine being voided with great difficulty, perhaps mixed with blood or mucus, and has a penetrating odor. As soon, however, as the stone gets into the neck of the bladder or passes into the urethra and lodges at the posterior end of the bone of the penis there is a series of severe symptoms. The urine is retained, which is indicated by an entire suppression, or it is passed in a thin stream or only by a drop at a time. A partial obstruction of urine is soon followed by a complete obstruction.

The symptoms presented in the dog are very striking. The animals are very restless, looking frequently towards the region of the kidney and whining. They place themselves in the position to urinate and strain violently without any result, or it may be a few drops are passed; this may be mixed with blood. The appetite is lost and the pulse is rapid and thready; they stand with an arched back or walk with a staggering gait and extended legs. The abdomen becomes distended, and we can finally feel the bladder through the abdominal walls like a hard, distended body that is very painful on examination. When the catheter is passed it goes in easily enough until the neck of the bladder is reached, when it stops and cannot be passed any further, and no urine escapes from the catheter.

Uric calculi lie on the floor of the bladder and can be felt through the abdominal walls by manipulation—that is, of course, when they have reached a good size; the small ones escape detection, but they may be suspected when the urine has a gravel or sand-like sediment.

The urine, when it is retained in the bladder, gradually accumulates, and if it is not drawn off in three days the bladder is ruptured and it may even burst in two days; when this occurs it causes death in a few hours, with the following symptoms: the animal becomes dull or comatose, with shaking or trembling of the muscles; the restlessness and pain seem to have disappeared. Pressure on the abdomen may produce slight evidence of pain, but in the majority of cases this is absent. After the first two hours the abdominal wall is covered with a cold sweat; the bladder cannot be felt on manipulation. Soon a deep coma sets in, from which the animal cannot be roused, and dies in a short time. In rare instances the animal may have convulsions, which occur with short intervals between them. Death may also occur before the bladder has ruptured, as a consequence of extensive gangrenous cystitis.

THERAPEUTICS. It has been thoroughly established that it is impossible to produce any good results from the injection into the bladder of any of the various agents that are supposed to have the property of dissolving calculi; for instance, acids for dissolving phosphatic calculi, alkalines for breaking up uric calculi, or the drinking of mineral-waters, such as Vichy, Wildung, Carlsbad. There is nothing left then but to remove the stone by means of an operation, called urethrotomy, if it is lodged in the urethra, which consists in opening the urethra in the dog at the posterior end of the bone of the penis, or cystotomy if the stone is in the bladder; this is performed by opening the urethra at the ischial arch, and by means of a small pair of forceps introduced into the bladder through the urethra the stone is grasped and crushed and afterward washed out of the bladder. In the bitch an incision is made into the short urethra and the stone is seized and crushed in a like manner.

When ischuria or stoppage of urine is present the treatment depends to a large extent on the location of the calculus—that is, whether it is in the neck of the bladder or whether it has gone into the urethra some distance and lodged there. In the first instance we can sometimes introduce the catheter, and by a gradual pressure we can push the stone into the bladder; or, if it is further in the urethra, we can push a well-lubricated catheter past the stone and allow the escape of urine and prepare for the operation, for if the stone is in the urethra this must be performed immediately.

Urethrotomy is usually performed from the posterior end of the bone of the penis, as the great majority of uric calculi pass down the urethra and lodge at the posterior end of the bone of the penis, and can be detected by the catheter; when this is passed there is a certain rough sound that resembles crepitation. Lay the animal on the side, and after having injected the skin with cocaine or administered ether—if the animal be very hard to handle, although the latter procedure is rarely necessary—make an incision about 3 cm. in length, cutting down on the urethra. The calculus can then be pushed back toward the opening in the majority of cases, and by means of a pair of small forceps the stone can be grasped and pulled out. In some cases it is necessary to enlarge the opening in the urethra; as a rule, however, do not make the opening any larger than is absolutely necessary. It is well to leave the wound open except it is a very large animal or if the stone should be exceptionally large; in that instance do not put more than one stitch in it. For two days the urine escapes out of the external opening, but soon closes up, and in about eight to ten days it has closed up completely and the urine is passed in the natural way.

Cystotomy: when the stone is located in the bladder the catheter is passed directly into it, and an incision is made into the urethra down on the catheter at the arch of the urethra, and then a well-oiled pair of forceps is introduced into the bladder and the stone grasped and crushed, if possible, and the bladder and urethra washed out with tepid water. In some cases the entire tract of the urethra is packed with small uric calculi, starting from a fairly large stone at the posterior end of the bone of the penis, and it is only necessary to remove the larger stone, when the others will be passed out by the force of the urine Friedberger mentions one case where there were forty packed in the urethra; these varied in size from a small seed to a pea, and the whole mass weighed about 28 grammes. The operator cut down on the urethra on the ischial arch and washed the stones from the end of the penis, and then by injections filled the bladder with warm water and washed out that part, assisting the emptying of the bladder by pressure on the abdominal walls. The animal made a complete recovery.

[The translator finds that quite frequently calculi accumulate in the constricture of the urethra at the posterior end of the bone, and operates in the following manner: Introduce a catheter into the penis until it reaches the obstruction, and by means of a tape looped around the free end of the penis it is drawn away from the prepuce, which is held back by an assistant, and then cut down on the end of the catheter; the catheter is pulled back a short distance, but not entirely, and the penis bent over, and by means of a small pair of blunt forceps the stone can be removed; when this is accomplished pass the catheter into the bladder, and wash out any calculi that may still remain in the bladder or urethra; by means of a small hose attach the catheter to a syringe and inject the bladder full of tepid water.

In the bitch the operation is much more simple. The urethra is opened by means of a thin tenotome introduced on a grooved director and the opening enlarged, and then the forceps passed into the opening, the stone crushed, and the bladder washed out. It is necessary to introduce one finger into the rectum to guide the stone into the forceps before it can be grasped. Great care must be taken in such an operation to avoid crushing the tissues. In the bitch there is no after-treatment necessary.]

When the bladder is so distended that it is deemed dangerous to operate before emptying the bladder of its contents, we may empty the bladder by means of a fine trocar and canula. In the bitch the trocar should be introduced on the median line at the brim of the pelvis, and in the dog either on the right or left side of the flank, low down and as near as possible to the brim of the pelvis.

Sometimes ruptures of the bladder are caused by accidents, such as being run over by wagons when the bladder is full. The animal dies, as a rule, in forty-eight hours from collapse before peritonitis has developed. On post-mortem the bladder is found to be infiltrated with blood and very much swollen at the lacerated region only. In injuries to the lumbar region where the animal is dull and comatose it is always well to consider the prognosis doubtful, and Siedamgrotzky deems it advisable to consider the prognosis doubtful in injuries to that region, even where there are no acute symptoms presented.

Indications of painful retention of urine are often presented when there is a stricture of the urethra caused by injuries to the urethra from calculi or by cicatricial contraction following the operator's knife, from intense nephritis, or by torsion following coitus. An examination with the catheter generally gives some information as to the character of the stricture; the practitioner must, however, remember that there is always more or less normal stricture at the posterior end of the bone of the penis. The sound must be passed each day and allowed to remain about twenty minutes; if the stricture will admit of it, the size of the catheters must be gradually increased; great care must be taken to thoroughly disinfect the catheters. This method has been used with success in a number of cases when it has continued for several weeks.

Hoffmann cured a case of stricture of the posterior end of the bone of the penis by opening the urethra at the spot of stricture and amputating about 2 cm. of the bone of the penis with a pair of bone forceps.

DISEASES OF THE PROSTATE.

Inflammation of the Prostate.
(*Prostatitis.*)

This disease appears in both acute and chronic forms; the causes have not been sufficiently investigated up to the present date to state positively what is the exciting cause of the disease.

The acute form is rare and causes the animal to show evidence of great pain when either urine or feces are passed. In cases where there is great enlargement of the prostate the animal may hold the feces back by not putting any pressure on the abdominal muscles or may retain the urine. On making an examination of the gland, by introducing the finger, well lubricated, into the rectum, we find it very much enlarged and hot and painful to the touch. The animal shows great pain during catheterization when the instrument passes the prostate.

The terminations of this acute condition are as follows: The prostate may break down completely and cause death, or it may assume the chronic form and ultimately form abscesses which break through into the bladder, the urethra, or the intestines, and in very rare cases into the connective tissue of the pelvis.

THERAPEUTICS. This consists in giving the animal small quantities of non-irritating food, cold clysters, and cold applications to the perineum; also the frequent passage of the catheter to prevent the stagnation of the urine in the bladder; and also the administration of saline purgatives, such as sulphate of magnesium, Carlsbad salt, etc. When pus has formed, which can be determined by a digital examination per rectum, introduce a speculum into the rectum and cut down on the fluctuation by means of a sharp-pointed bistoury. The hemorrhage which follows is very slight, and no attention should be paid to it. Where the swelling extends to the perineum and distends it the author has cut down from there and evacuated the sac.

Chronic prostatitis (Hypertrophy) is the form of the disease most frequently seen, and develops from the acute form, or in the majority of cases starts in the onset as the chronic form. It is a common disease in old dogs, and is indicated by a hypertrophy of the whole organ; as a rule, one side of the gland is larger than the other. It varies in consistency; in some cases it is very hard, in others it is soft; in the former case it is due to a hyperplasma of the fibro-muscular tissue; in the latter it is due to an infiltration of the gland with a purulent fluid as a consequence of a chronic purulent inflammation.

The symptoms of a hypertrophy of the prostate are irregular; in some cases there is difficulty in urination (dysuria, stranguria), and also cystitis, pyelitis, etc., or constipation due to the animal making no effort to evacuate feces. The best means of diagnosis is to make a digital examination per rectum of the prostate. It is distinguished from the acute form by the absence of heat and sensitiveness, but is very much larger than the normal gland.

Therapeutics are not productive of much good results. Saline laxatives, ergot, and iodide of potassium have been tried by the author. The remedy that has given the best results has been to inject into the gland a solution of iodine (iodide of potassium, 2 parts; tincture of iodine, 2 parts; and water, 60 parts) at intervals of fourteen days. The solution is injected through the rectum directly into the gland by means of a small hypodermatic syringe.

[The translator has recently tried castration, but has not had enough experience to say whether it is to be recommended. In a number of cases it has produced very good results and the animal was greatly relieved from active symptoms; but, on the other hand, in several cases the animal has steadily gone down, lost flesh, and in three or four weeks become a skeleton and died apparently from inanition.]

Cancer of the Prostate.

Cancer of the prostate is generally carcinomatous in character, causing an irregular enlargement of the gland. It is difficult to make a diagnosis, and conclusions can only be drawn from the general health of the animal, which shows a gradual want of nutrition. It is impossible to remove the prostate, and therefore treatment is useless.

DISEASES OF THE PENIS AND PREPUCE.

Phimosis and Paraphimosis.

By phimosis we mean a contraction of the prepuce over the free end of the penis. It is often of congenital origin, and is frequently caused by injuries and consequent inflammatory swellings; but as the foreskin is rarely withdrawn in the dog it is of little importance, for as soon as the penis passes through the narrow opening of the prepuce during coitus or from erection the prepuce becomes tightened behind the glans penis and causes what is termed paraphimosis; the narrow ring of the prepuce causes venous stagnation and a swelling and purple coloration of the glans, and, if this is allowed to remain some time, causes partial gangrene.

The therapeutics of paraphimosis consists in reducing the glans as soon as possible with friction and careful manipulation; this is accomplished by careful lubricating of the parts with some bland oil and putting a steady pressure on the glans, at the same time pressing forward the prepuce over the enlarged part; with a little patience it is reduced. If this is not successful, bathe the glans with cold water or alum applications. If we do not reduce it by this means, then cut the ring with a probe-pointed bistoury or a pair of scissors. The last means will reduce it immediately. It is well, however, not to resort to this until you have tried every other method.

Gonorrhœa—Gonorrhœa of the Prepuce.

By this term we mean the catarrhal inflammation of the skin of the prepuce, which is similar to mucous membrane. It is probably caused by retention of urine, dirt, uncleanliness, or masturbation; it is frequently observed in old dogs, with stagnation of the veins of the prostate (Siedamgrotzky). The symptoms consist in slight redness, swelling of the prepuce and glans, and the secretion of a thin, purulent mucus, which is generally licked off by the animal. The lymph-follicles are generally swollen, and can be felt by manipulation with the finger as small bodies about the size of a seed or pea. The treatment consists in the injection of acetate of lead water or 1 per cent. solution of zinci sulphas or argenti nitras.

In rare cases we may have an animal affected with specific gonorrhœa which has extended from the foreskin into the urethra and an enlargement of the inguinal lymphatics, forming a bubo (Siedamgrotzky and author). In one of the cases observed by Siedamgrotzky the gonorrhœa was accompanied by intense inflammation of the eyes (gonorrhœal ophthalmia).

Neoformations of the Glans and Prepuce.

Neoformations are sometimes found on the dog and bitch, and are either condyloma, carcinoma, or sarcoma. The former can be removed by the scissors or a small pair of pincers and the blood stopped by compression or a solution of alum, or, what is much better, the thermo-cautery. Carcinoma and sarcoma generally require the removal of a portion of the glans. (See chapter on Neoformations.)

DISEASES OF THE TESTICLE AND ITS COVERINGS.

We frequently see inflammatory conditions of the scrotal covering as a result of contusions; they may, however, be caused by eczema, which sometimes causes great swelling and sensitiveness. (See Diseases of the Skin.) Möller has also seen serpentine varicosis with ulceration and accompanied with profuse hemorrhage.

Inflammations of the Testicle—Orchitis.

Orchitis without any other injury is very rarely seen in the dog; it may be caused by a kick, or a blow, or from crushing. The testicle is swollen and smooth on its surface and very sensitive to the touch. In one case that the author observed the epididymis was also greatly swollen (epididymitis). The therapeutics consists of cooling applications and rest.

Injuries to the Testicles and Scrotum.

As a rule, the wounds of these parts are caused by fighting with other dogs, and are either lacerations or perforated wounds. In the majority of cases try to get drainage and keep the wound clean by antiseptics; this is best accomplished by putting a piece of absorbent cotton on the testicle, and by means of a long-tailed bandage tied around the body the cotton can be kept in place. If the testicle is injured, the gland had better be removed by castration, as it is only in favorable cases that the animal makes a good recovery and the seminal power is retained.

(For further details on the subject, consult the chapter on Hernia of the Testicles and Castration.)

[Cuterebro Emasculator.
(*Emasculating Bot Fly.*)

This parasite, which is common in rabbits and squirrels, was described by French as occurring in the scrotum of the dog, and since then the translator has observed two cases in setters where the grub has been present in the scrotum.

The scrotum swells slowly, beginning at the dependent portion, until a round, firm mass, resembling in size and shape the ordinary "warble" seen in cattle's backs, but not quite as large; it apparently gives the animal no discomfort, unless the parasite should act as an irritant and form an abscess, which is followed by great irritation of the parts, and subsequently sloughing of a portion of the scrotum and destruction of the testicle. The treatment consists in finding the opening or vent in the skin and carefully enlarging it, taking care not to penetrate the larva, when it can be pushed out and the wound cleaned with a solution of peroxide of hydrogen. If the grub is punctured and it collapses, the remaining portion of the parasite must be carefully removed, as it causes great irritation if allowed to remain.]

DISEASES OF THE VAGINA AND THE UTERUS.

Inflammation of the Vagina.

(*Vaginitis.*)

Inflammation of the vagina (catarrh of the vagina) results, as a rule, from difficult labor, and in rare cases as a result of improper copulation. The condition is indicated by a whitish,

Fig. 53. Vaginal speculum.

purulent discharge, in some cases being fetid, which is generally licked off by the animal. The examination can be made by means of a speculum in the larger animals (Fig. 53). On examination of the vagina we find it intensely red and inflamed and covered with a grayish, mucous discharge; the mucus is also grayish in color; carcinoma is often present. (See chapter on Tumors for further details.)

The therapeutic treatment consists of the daily injections of astringent and disinfectant washes: Nitrate of silver (1 per cent. solution), sulphate of zinc (1 per cent.), alum, permanganate of potassium solution, boric acid, and creolin.

Prolapsus of the Vagina and Uterus.

(*Prolapsus Vaginæ; Prolapsus Uteri.*)

Prolapsus of the vagina is more common than prolapsus of the uterus. In some instances it is accompanied by serious alterations of the vagina, especially hypertrophic alterations, and also, in rare cases, polypus formations. These alterations are generally caused by difficult whelping. As a rule, there is more or less protrusion of the vagina through the vulva, appearing in the form of pear- or flap-shaped, red, inflamed tissue covered with mucus. In very rare instances the prolapsus is so great that the os of the vagina can be seen through the external opening. When the uterus is prolapsed the protruded portion is forced out of the vulva, and we see a pear-shaped body, intensely red, with salient borders. One horn of the uterus is protruded only; the author has never heard of a case where both horns were protruded.

The prolapse of the uterus in the dog is practically impossible, for the reason that the uterus itself is merely a body in name, and really the uterus consists in the horns, the true body of the uterus being a small body from which the horns bifurcate almost at the os. (Fig. 54.)

The therapeutics of prolapsus of the vagina is practically that used in prolapsus of the anus and rectum. The retention of the vagina is much more difficult than returning it to its normal position. Hertwig advises that the vagina be returned, and for several hours it is held in position by the fingers, and if that is not sufficient, to introduce a sponge into the vagina or pack the vagina with gauze or cotton and stitch the lips of the pudenda. The author generally uses the following method: After returning the vagina to the normal position he puts two stitches in the pudenda and leaves them for three days.

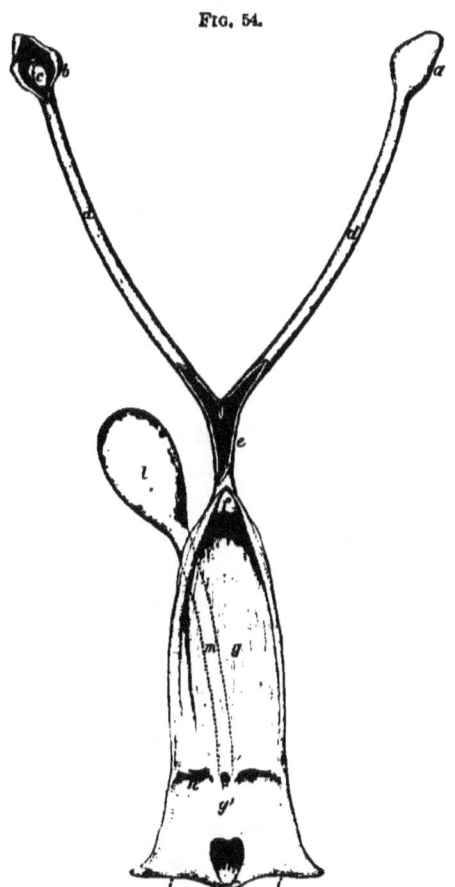

FIG. 54.

The genito-urinary organs of the bitch: *a*, ovary covered with capsule; *b*, capsule of ovary; *c*, ovary; *d*, horns of the uterus; *e*, body of the uterus; *f*, os uteri; *g*, vagina; *g'*, opening of the urethra; *h*, clitoris; *i, i*, vulva; *l*, bladder; *m*, urethra.

In one case where there was great thickening of the walls of the vagina and reduction of the prolapse was impossible, and another where the vagina prolapsed immediately after the stitches were removed after being there for several days, the author performed a partial amputation, taking out an elongated piece of mucous membrane and sewing it up by a continuous stitch of catgut, which was followed by good results.

Reduction of the uterus is much more difficult, and in the majority of cases it is impossible. The prolapsed portion should be lubricated and gradually worked back, and after the fingers cannot reach any further a tallow-candle must be inserted and the horn pushed back as far as possible. If this method is not successful, laparotomy should be performed, in the manner spoken of in hernia. An incision is made into the abdominal wall and the finger inserted until the ovary is felt, and then the animal is held up by the posterior extremities, and by gradual tension the horn of the uterus is pulled back into position and the opening in the abdomen closed up. The rules named for retaining the vagina are then to be followed. An English veterinary journal says that the uterus can be retained in position by making an opening in the median line of the abdomen and pulling the horn into position and then stitching the horn to the upper part of the abdominal wall. It is needless to say that the stitch must be of catgut.

Amputation of the uterus by ligating or crushing the prolapsed portion is done in the following manner: Ligate tightly the base of the protruded portion and amputate the free portion of the uterus—not too close to the ligated portion, as the ligature might slip and push the stump back into the pelvic cavity. Another method is to remove the ligated portion by means of an écraseur; this latter operation is by far the best.

Inflammation of the Uterus.

(*Metritis.*)

It is a common occurrence to have inflammation of the uterus after protracted labor, and the disease can be subdivided into the following varieties, according to the exciting causes:

Catarrhal Metritis. In this condition the disease is limited to the mucous membrane, and presents the same symptoms as are seen in all catarrhal inflammations of mucous membranes; the causes are mechanical injuries which the uterus may be subjected to during labor or immediately after.

The clinical symptoms are as follows: The vulva is slightly

reddened and swollen, and there is a copious discharge from the vulva, which is purulent, sometimes bloody or slightly putrid, and is much increased in quantity after the passage of feces or urine; but the animal licks it off so soon that the observer must look immediately after each evacuation or it may escape his notice. Some bitches carry their tails in a curved position when suffering from this condition; some animals have complete loss of appetite, and in some cases slight fever is present.

Fig. 55.

The therapeutics consist in tepid injections of non-poisonous antiseptic fluids, such as permanganate of potassium (1 per cent. solution), boric acid (2 per cent.), and creolin (1 per cent.). In using these solutions it is best to use the irrigator with the two catheters that have been already mentioned (Fig. 55). In the chronic form (dysmenorrhœa) we should use injections of ergot.

℞.—Ext. ergotæ 2.0
Spts. vini dil. }
Glycerinum } . . . . āā 6.0
M. S.—Inject a small portion several times daily.

Double catheter for washing out the uterus.

Septic Metritis (*Puerperal Fever*). Septic inflammation of the uterus should be considered a disease of wound-infection in which we find intense irritation of the uterus and vagina, accompanied by violent constitutional disturbances. During and after labor septic materials find their way into the uterus, and, owing to the condition of the uterus at that time when it is practically in the same condition as an open wound, the septic materials are taken up very quickly and every condition is favorable for their propagation. Collections of blood, decidual tissue, etc., exposed to the air decay very quickly, and where there is any erosion of the vagina or the cervix, or even the uterus at the points of placental attachment, the poison is taken up. The eroded portion that has taken up any of the septic material soon presents an ulcerated surface which is covered by a necrotic or diphtheritic coating, and in some cases the vagina becomes intensely swollen, dark brown or reddish-brown in color, and covered with spots of diphtheritic ulcerations.

The inflammatory process rapidly extends from the mucous membrane into the deeper tissues, affecting the muscular and the pelvic cellular tissues and the lips of the pudenda, and from the internal surface of the uterus it extends to the uterine muscles and the broad ligament, and in acute cases to the serous covering of the uterus and the peritoneum. When the acute symptoms are present ptomaïnes and septic substances enter the circulation and cause acute septic fever. (For further information, see chapter on Wound Infection.) The prognosis is generally unfavorable.

CLINICAL SYMPTOMS. The vulva and the mucous membrane of the vagina are swollen and livid red, and discharges copious masses of discolored, fetid pus. In the earlier stages the animal shows great pain on pressure to the abdomen; the pulse is thready and finally becomes imperceptible and very fast. The respirations increase in number. The temperature in the early stages is increased, but soon falls to normal and frequently becomes subnormal toward the end. The mucous membranes of the mouth and conjunctiva are livid.

When the animal presents the acute symptoms early and does not eat or drink from the onset, it soon becomes comatose and dies in from twelve to twenty-four hours.

THERAPEUTICS. In such cases treatment must be prompt and energetic to get any favorable results. The uterus and the vagina must be thoroughly irrigated with antiseptic fluids, and also the general treatment indicated in septicæmia. For antiseptic irrigating fluids we use creolin, 2 per cent. solution; corrosive sublimate, 1 to 2000 solution. First irrigate the uterus with warm water, and clean it thoroughly until there is no discoloration in the escaping fluids; then inject the medicated solution into the uterus several times; repeat this several times daily. As a stimulant use camphor, either internally or hypodermatically; the latter is the best, as you are apt to get quicker results and you also avoid the danger of the animal vomiting it, which it is very apt to do. Ergot and salicylic acid are also used with some success (Letzerich).

R.—Camphor pulv. 0.2
Gummi acacia 0.6
F. chart. No. xii. S.—One powder every two hours.

Obstetrics and Castration of the Bitch.

As a rule, the bitch has her pups without any difficulty. The period after conception varies from fifty-eight to sixty-two days [Dun kept a record of 189 bitches and found the average period was 63.28 days, the maximum being 71 days, and the minimum being 53 days], when she generally seeks a quiet place and drops from one to eight blind pups, the period of whelping being from one to six hours (quite frequently lasts ten or twelve hours). The labor-pains generally come on from three to ten hours before birth, and are indicated by the bitch being very restless and going into dark corners or scratching as if to make a bed, and on putting the hand on the abdominal walls the fœtuses are found to be very lively.

Immediately after the birth of each pup the placenta is passed out and is eaten by the bitch.

The retention of the whole or a portion of the placenta is very rare in the bitch, and must not be mistaken for a dead fœtus. Violet has seen three such cases, and describes them as follows: Great depression; no milk in the mammæ; the bitch pays no attention to the pups; frequent contraction of the uterus similar to labor-pains; entire loss of appetite; pain on pressure of the abdomen. The temperature was normal at first, but gradually increased; the pulse was quick and hard; and a fetid discharge from the vulva.

The treatment consists in constant irrigations of antiseptic solutions, ergot, warm poultices around the abdomen, and stimulants.

After the birth of the pups there is slight lochial discharge, bloody in the onset and finally purulent. The short but strong umbilical cord is torn during labor or bitten off by the bitch immediately after birth, and the entire mass of placenta and amnion is eaten by the mother.

The normal course of birth may be changed in some instances by certain circumstances. 1. The labor-pains may not be strong enough; there may be a narrow, contracted pelvis; the vagina may be lessened in diameter by cicatricial contractions, tumors, etc. The fœtus may be very large or may be presented in an irregular position. Extract of ergot is the best preparation to increase the contractions of the uterus. [Several writers have recently spoken

192 DISEASES OF THE URINARY AND SEXUAL APPARATUS.

very highly of glycerine as an agent to encourage the contraction of the uterus. In cases of difficult parturition it is injected directly into the uterus; in 1 to 10 solution with warm water the translator has had very good results from it.] If the animal is depressed and weak, administer stimulants, such as whiskey, wine, or alcohol; and if these fail to produce the birth of the fœtus, it may have to be removed by forceps, hooks, or the fœtus may be noosed by means of a copper wire held in a tube (see Fig. 56).

FIG. 56.

Apparatus for the extraction of the fœtus and method of extraction : *a*, Brulet's apparatus ; *b*, method of application. ; *c*, Defay's apparatus.

Fluid extract of ergot 1.0 to 2.0 every half-hour; or if the animal vomits, give 0.50 to 0.75 of ergot hypodermatically every half-hour.

When the fœtus is in an irregular position, and after failing to remove it by means of forceps, etc., or if the fœtus is so very large that it is impossible to get it through the pelvic opening, or if it cannot be reached so that it can be cut into sections, or if the pelvis is contracted or a tumor present, we must perform the Cæsarean operation (gastro-hysterotomy). This is not a very dangerous operation, provided it is performed before the animal is in a state of collapse or the fœtus is not dead and commencing to decay. Empty the bladder and the lower bowel, and having washed out the genital passages with an antiseptic solution, the bitch is laid on her back, the legs are held by an assistant, the forelegs together and the hindlegs wide apart. The region where the incision is to be made should be thoroughly washed and the hair removed from the part. Make an incision on the median line of the linea alba from the umbilicus with a sharp-pointed bistoury, and cut into the abdominal cavity, taking care not to injure the intestines or uterus; then insert a probe-pointed bistoury and make the opening larger, cutting toward the pubis; then cut through the omentum; the uterus is now visible and can be lifted out and the fœtuses can be felt in the uterus, separated by a constriction in the body of the horn. Pull the uterus out of the opening as far as possible and have an assistant keep the opening of the abdominal wall closed, so as not to allow the intestines to escape, and also to avoid any of the fluids from the uterus falling into the cavity; and by means of a bistoury open the uterus by making an incision through its wall; the opening should not be any larger than is necessary to get the fœtus and the membranes out. It is not necessary to make an incision in the horn over each fœtus, but after one fœtus is removed the others can be pushed toward the opening and removed through it, taking care to take the membranes also. The uterus is now thoroughly disinfected with corrosive sublimate solution (1 to 5000) or boric acid, 2 per cent., and by means of a continuous suture, (using the stitch illustrated in Fig. 19, page 70), using catgut ligature, then sew up the abdominal muscles by an interrupted suture, using silk. The abdomen is covered with a piece of absorbent cotton soaked in a mild solution of corrosive sublimate, and held in position by an eight-tailed bandage of muslin tied over the back. This has to be dressed daily. The animal must have absolute rest, and be fed on food that is easily digested and not apt to constipate or ferment. Meat-juice or extract is the best, but not vegetables.

Castration of the Bitch (*Ovariotomy*). This operation is generally performed to avoid the trouble that owners have when a bitch is in "heat," and also that they make good house dogs. The operation is a very simple one and not attended by any great danger if the proper antiseptic rules are followed and the animal is not too fat or in "heat." The bitch is given a narcotic or ether and placed on a table on her back and an incision made in the linea alba at the umbilicus with a sharp-pointed bistoury, and then the opening is made larger by means of a probe-pointed bistoury, cutting toward the diaphragm. The operator can find the uterus easier by putting a sound into the uterus previous to the operation. The finger is introduced into the abdomen close against the wall and the horn of the uterus is felt and drawn toward the opening, and by careful traction the ovary is drawn toward the opening and cut off with the scissors; the same procedure is followed in the other ovary and the wound closed with an interrupted silk stitch.

The ovaries of the dog are small, round, elongated bodies located at the posterior edge of the kidneys and are imbedded in a deep fatty covering or pocket (see Fig. 54).

Hoffmann cuts through the broad ligament and ligates the ovary both above and below and cuts off the ovary with a blunt pair of scissors.

The abdominal wound should be stitched with a double row of stitches. We first sew the muscular coat with a continuous catgut suture, and then sew the skin with an interrupted suture of silk; an antiseptic dressing is useful, but not absolutely necessary. The animals should be muzzled.

Many operators perform castration in very young and old dogs by opening the abdominal cavity at the linea alba and ligating the uterus by two catgut ligatures about an inch apart on the body of the uterus, and cut through between the ligatures. This method has the advantage of being very simple, and there is little or no danger connected with it, but the author has tried a number of cases for experiment and found in a short time a great collection of cream-like matter gathered at the ligated end of the uterus, and distended that portion very much, which was noticeable in the animal.

Many operators advise castration through the flank, and proceed in the following manner: Make an incision in the flank about 4 cm. long, midway between the last false rib and the thigh, in an anterior direction, cutting through the skin and muscular layer; then tear the peritoneum by means of the finger and pull the ovaries through the opening and cut them off with the scissors, and sew up the wound as described in the other operation. Friedberger has operated on hundreds of bitches in the above-described manner; he removes both ovaries through the one opening in the left flank. Gunther makes an opening in both flanks, taking the ovary out of each. The subsequent treatment consists of feeding the animal on small quantities of easily digested food, treating the wound in the regular antiseptic way.

DISEASES OF THE NERVOUS SYSTEM.

EXAMINATION OF THE NERVOUS SYSTEM.

DISTURBANCES of the nervous system are marked by impairment of consciousness, sensitiveness, and motility. Besides these there are complications in the functions of the eyes, ears, and the digestive system.

1. **The Disturbances of Consciousness** are variously defined according to their intensity. Dulness (indifference to any external influences), somnolence (drowsiness, sleepiness, the patient may be awakened easily), stupor (deep sleep, difficult to arouse the patient), coma (entire unconsciousness, the animal is not disturbed by external influences). In extreme cases of unconsciousness all sphincters of the body become relapsed. Such cases are found in the various diseases of the brain and its coverings and in cases of injury and concussions of the brain; it is also seen in poisoning by narcotics, in uræmia, in acute anæmia, and in all diseases accompanied by intense fever and pain. Short attacks of unconsciousness may occur in the form of dizziness, and are seen occasionally as the result of great excitement or pain (in operations); and also idiotism, which occurs in rare instances as a result of distemper, when it assumes the nervous form.

2. **Disturbance of Sensitiveness.** This is not easily recognized in the dog. In all instances it is advisable to cover the patient's eyes, and compare the sensitiveness of the affected side with that of the healthy one. In cases of hæmaphraic diseases we test the sensitiveness of the skin by pricking it slightly with a needle or letting cold water drop upon it so as to produce some irritation or symptom of pain. A test may also be made by means of a battery; still this method has failed to be as reliable and practical as the needle and cold-water test have been to the author.

Total anæsthesia occurs, as a rule, from poisoning, and must not be mistaken for a want of reaction when in a comatose condition. *Local anæsthesia*—that is to say, a more or less circumscribed or disturbed zone of sensibility—may be found in any part of the body. In such a case, if anæsthesia corresponds with a region of a special nerve or a mixed nerve, or if it is extended upon several nervous regions, or if it is even double-sided, we can distinguish peripheric anæsthesia. Peripheric anæsthesia indicates an injury of the end organs of the sensitive nerves and originates through local influences—intense cold, acids (especially carbolic), also alcohol and certain narcotics (especially cocaine). Peripheric anæsthesia may be caused by some traumatism, compression, malformation, or inflammatory exudates; also through inflammations, such as degenerating processes, etc., of the peripheric nerves. Special anæsthesia is seen and, as a rule, is double-sided; due to compression of the nerve or the spinal cord. Cases of cerebral anæsthesia are caused by hemorrhages, tumors, inflammations, etc., in the zone of the sensitive nerves. It may also be caused by the effects of various poisons—chloroform, ether, alcohol, morphia, and bromine.

Hyperæsthesia. This is an increased sensitiveness of the cutaneous nerves, and is, as a rule, found in the early stages of certain diseases of the spinal cord. It is very rarely seen in the later stages of such diseases. Siedamgrotzky observed in one dog with lameness in the hind-quarters such intense hyperæsthesia in the paralyzed centres that the animal gnawed his hindlegs to the bone, notwithstanding all the precautions that were taken to prevent him.

3. **Disturbances of Motility** appear in paralysis and convulsions of the affected muscular system.

Paralysis. We generally make a distinction between paralysis and lameness—that is to say, an entire loss of movement—and paresis or weakness, which is simply due to debility. In the first case there is not the slightest movement performed in a muscle or a whole group of muscles. In some cases there are slight muscular movements, but they are weak, without strength, and do not last very long. In order to determine the origin of paralysis it is necessary to have some knowledge of the psychomotor centres. These centres are located in the cerebrum, and are called the cortico-muscular leading tracks. Up to the present time they have definitely located the following motor centres in the external surface of the cerebrum, the position of which is indicated in Fig. 57: 1 is the centre for the movements of the muscles of the neck; 2 is that of the extensors and adductors of the anterior limb; 3 is

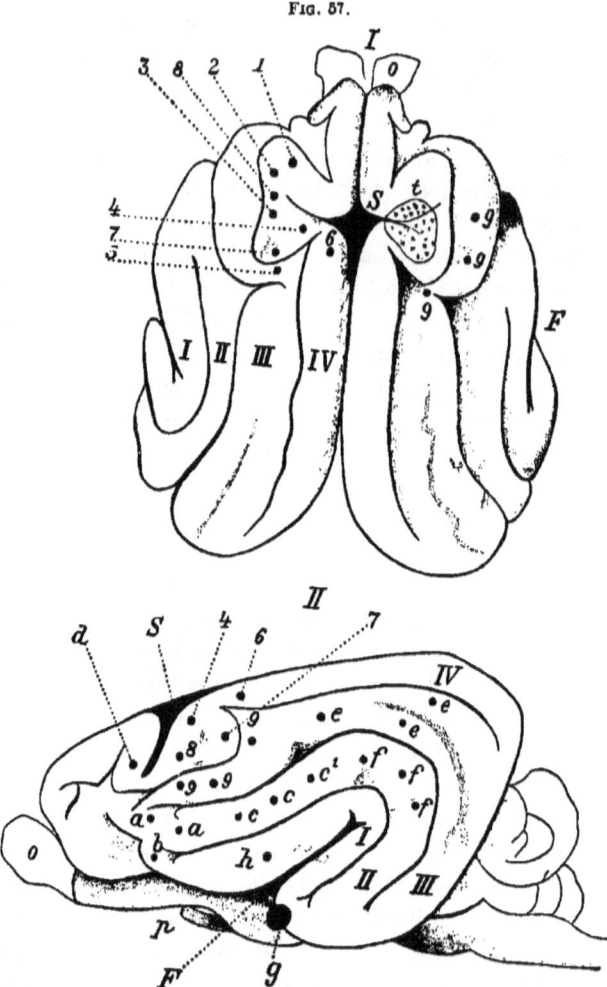

Fig. 57, *I.*, shows superior portion of the cerebrum; *II.*, the lateral surface; and *I., II., III., IV.* are the four convolutions.; *S*, is the sulcus cruciatus; *F*, the fissure of Sylvius; *o*, the bulbus olfactorius; *p*, is the optic nerve. The motor centres are: 1, for the muscles of the neck; 2, for the extensors and adductors of the anterior limbs; 3, for the flexors and rotators of the anterior limbs; 4, for the muscles of the posterior limbs; 5, for the facial muscles; 6, for the lateral movements of the tail; 7, for the retraction and adduction of the anterior limbs; 8, for the lifting of the shoulder and extension of the front limb (walking); 9, 9, for the orbicularis palpebrarum, zygomaticus, and closing of the eyelid; *I., t*, the heat-centre of Eulenberg and Landois. (LANDOIS.)

Fig. 57, *II.*, *a, a*, retraction and elevation of the corners of the mouth; *b*, opening of the mouth and movements of the tongue; *d*, the opening of the eyelids.

for extending and turning the anterior limbs; 4 controls the movement of the posterior limbs; 5 the facial muscles; and 6 the lateral movement of the tail; 7 for retraction and adduction of the anterior limbs; 8 for elevating the shoulders and stretching the front legs (walking); 9 for dilating and contracting the orbicularis palpebrarum and zygomaticus muscles. In the front of 9 we also find the centre for the movements of the tongue. Between the anterior and middle portion of 9 is for closing the jaw. On irritating 9 we have a retraction and elevation of the corners of the mouth. By irritating 6 the mouth is opened and the tongue is moved. c, c, causes a retraction of the corners of the mouth; c' lifts the corners of the mouth and half of the facial muscles as far as the closing point of the eyelids. The middle e (on irritation) opens the eye and dilates the pupil.

Any disease which becomes located in any portion of this cortico-muscular brain centre and inflames or stops the power of these centres must lead to paralysis of the centre which it controls. We therefore can locate any disturbance in the motor centres of the brain by the paralysis which occurs in certain parts of the body. A diseased condition of the covering of the brain, if not very extensive, generally causes the paralysis of one part of the body, as the single motor centres are separated and very distinct from one another. Diseases of the brain, when they occur in the inner surface between the capsules and the pyramids, where all the motor fibres are close together, cause a more or less complete paralysis of one side of the body. That is to say, a hemiplegia (affecting one side of the brain) causes the paralysis of the muscles of the other side of the body. For instance, if the disease is located on the left side of the brain, the muscles of the right side become paralyzed. In diseases of the spinal cord the muscles affected are on the same side, except in the case of diseases of the cervical portion of the spine, when, as a rule, paralysis is seen in all the extremities, and in disease of the lumbar region paralysis of the posterior extremities is seen. We therefore summarize in a general way that hemiplegia is usually a form of cerebral paralysis (of the controlling centres); paraplegia indicates a diseased condition of the spine; and monoplegia is due to a paralysis of the brain as well as the spine. This description gives only the fundamental theories on this subject. Concerning more precise details we would direct our readers to some one of the various physiological text-books.

The most important peripheric paralyses which have been observed in the dog (by traumatism, compression, or exudation, inflammatory or degenerating processes of the affected nerves) are as follows:

1. *Motor Trigeminal Paralysis.* (Paralysis of the lower jaw.) The lower jaw hangs down; mastication is impossible; saliva runs out of the mouth. This condition occurs very frequently as a symptom of rabies. In rare instances it has been observed as a result of some other disease.

2. *Paralysis of the Anterior Limbs.* The front legs hang inert and all the joints flex very easily.

3. *Paralysis of the Posterior Limbs.* The hindlegs are dragged along the ground, the paws being flexed and drawn backward. If the paws are drawn forward and this flexion overcome, the animal is able to stand on its legs if the body is held.

4. *Paralysis of the Cruralis.* In this condition the animal does not use the posterior limb. All the joints become flexed abnormally, and the thigh bends backward. This condition may also be due to some disease of the spine.

The most important test of paralyzed muscles is their size. In all cases of prolonged paralysis the muscles atrophy quickly. The muscle gradually becomes smaller and smaller until it resembles a cord or tendon. In cerebral paralysis this does not occur, while in spinal paralysis it is always present. Of course, in some instances an inactive muscle will atrophy without any actual disease being present. The amount of atrophy which may occur in certain cases is indicated by a communication given to the author by Goubaux. In this instance the paralyzed anterior limb of a dog weighed 103 grammes, while the perfect limb weighed 148 grammes.

Convulsions. Convulsion of the controlling muscles is the very opposite of paralysis. Convulsions are diseased contractions of the muscles which are independent of the will. There are several varieties of them. Clonic convulsions are short muscular contractions that occur at intervals, and between the intervals the affected portion of the body quivers constantly. Tonic convulsions are muscular contractions in which the muscle remains constantly contracted. It may occur for a minute or two, or may last several days. Tonic clonic convulsions are the medium form of the two conditions before described. A mild form of clonic contractions is noticed in the original muscular twitchings. Trembling and shaking convulsions seen in chills, fear, or sudden cooling after heat. Epileptiform convulsions, or eclamptic convulsions, are seen and extend over the whole body. In very rare instances they may be restricted to one portion, such as the head or neck. These generally come on suddenly and disappear in a few minutes. They are generally seen in the early stages of distemper, in teething, in irritated conditions of the bowels, or from noxious and poisonous food and from parasites; in cases of pentastomum in the nasal cavities, in encephalitis, meningitis, uræmia, and occasionally in acute anæmia; they may also occur from some injury or irritation of the peripheric centres, and are very prominent in epilepsy. Rhythmic twitchings are seen in some muscular regions where the affected part of the body makes regular motions; for instance, in the muscles of mastication, in the muscles of the chest during sleep, and also in the twitching of certain limbs. They are very often mistaken for chorea, and appear as a result of distemper or some disease of the brain. They may also occur from disorder of the spine. These so-called cataleptic attacks consist of a rigid and contracted condition of all the muscles of the body, but are subject to passive movements. Nothing is known concerning their etiology. Tetanic convulsions are tonic convulsions of the whole muscular system of the body. They appear in tetanus and in some cases of poisoning (strychnine, brucine, caffeine, etc.). A variety of these tetanic convulsions is observed in the so-called cases of eclampsia in bitches who are nursing a litter. Forced irregular actions of the body, such as walking backward or in a circle, or the animal rotating on its own axis, are seen as a rule in diseases of the cerebellum and in some cases of poisoning (cocaine). In rare instances we see, in the above-mentioned, symptoms of "epileptiform attacks," which we will refer to further on.

Ataxia is due to disturbance of motility or an interference in the coördination of muscular action. Animals are unsteady on their legs, stagger from one side to another, and their action in walking is irregular. Ataxia is undoubtedly found in some diseases of the cerebellum, and may also be seen in disease of the pons and the fore ventricles, and, in very rare instances, of the spinal cord. Ataxia occurs very often as a result of distemper, and it occurs without any previous brain or spinal symptoms.

Concerning disturbances of vision, hearing, and the action of the sphincters, they will be described under their special chapters.

DISEASES OF THE BRAIN AND ITS COVERINGS.

Hyperæmia of the Brain.

ETIOLOGY. An active congestion of the brain is caused by an increase of the circulation as the result of increased heart-action. This occurs in hypertrophy of the left ventricle, from excitement, from heat (sunstroke), in great bodily exertion, in teething, and high temperature.

Passive hyperæmia (stagnation) occurs in compression of the jugular veins by tumors, such as large goitres, by obstructed respiration in acute bronchitis, and in compressed conditions of the lungs, extended indurations of the lungs, defects in the venous openings of the heart. Hyperæmia of the brain accompanies various acute internal diseases, and as a secondary symptom of a number of disorders; it is also seen as a result of various poisons, such as alcohol, certain narcotics, etc.

PATHOLOGICAL ANATOMY. As a rule, hyperæmia of the brain occurs in connection with congestion of the coverings of the brain, especially the pia mater. When hyperæmia is very intense, or where it has existed for a long time, we cannot definitely separate the conditions. We find the dura mater distended, but very little changed. The vessels of the pia mater are much injected, the torsions of the vessel are flattened, and the sulci are perfectly flat as if pressed out of shape. We find the gray matter is darker red than usual, while the white brain-substance is dull gray or yellowish-red, and presents numerous bloody spots which may be easily removed. In chronic conditions of this disease we find venous hyperæmia. The brain appears in such cases pale and anæmic, very moist and soft, and on section has a brilliant, mirror-like lustre. It is lessened in size, and the subarachnoidal fluid is increased.

In a dog which had died suddenly from sunstroke Siedamgrotzky found all through the entire muscular system a number of small hemorrhages. Inside the skull was hyperæmic. Between the dura mater and the arachnoid he found considerable accumulations of bloody serous liquid. The surface of the brain was greatly injected and covered with hemorrhages, and here and there small hemorrhages in the brain and medulla. The chambers were normally filled with fluid. The lungs were congested and œdematous. The heart was collapsed, flabby, and filled with dark, clotted blood.

CLINICAL SYMPTOMS. The symptoms of hyperæmia of the brain are characterized by a sudden development of excitable symptoms. These consist in restlessness, running around, frequent changes of position, irritability, a tendency to biting and attacks of delirium, partial or general convulsions, and an increased activity of the action of the heart. The pulse is quick and irregular; the respiration is short. There is congestion of the mucous membrane of the head, and the upper section of the head is warm to the touch. There is contraction of the pupils and occasional vomiting. These symptoms of excitement rarely last long; they generally disappear quickly, although in rare instances they may last some time without leaving any trace on the general system. They may, however, alternate with periods of apparent rest to recur again in a short time. We have observed this in cases of apoplexy of the brain. In this condition we have dulness, unsteady gait, and if there is entire stupor we have stertorous respiration with this last symptom. It is doubtful in such cases if we have to deal with actual hyperæmia; more likely a more or less serious alteration in the brain.

THERAPEUTICS. Bleeding, as a rule, is contraindicated on account of the debilitated condition of most dogs. We would, however, recommend enemas (soap and water) and purgatives with quick action, such as sulphate of magnesium in large doses, senna-leaves, or castor oil. Cold compresses around the head are also useful, while violent purgatives such as croton oil, are not advisable, as they excite the animal and do more harm than good. The animal should be put in a cool room and kept as quiet as possible, avoiding excitement, heat, and also feed the animal very little. In cases where marked symptoms of excitement show themselves an injection of morphine is generally indicated.

Anæmia of the Brain.

ETIOLOGY. The most common cause of anæmia of the brain is from impoverished blood, acute hemorrhage, prolonged and debilitating disease, or from some obstruction of the arterial system, such as tumors, hemorrhages, or inflammatory exudations within the skull; compression of the carotid arteries by emphysema, and in some instances from contraction of the small arteries of the brain caused by excitement.

PATHOLOGICAL ANATOMY. The white substance in rare instances has a few bloody points. As a rule, the brain appears on section dull white, the gray matter being unusually bright, without any trace of coloration. The meninges and coverings of the brain may possess their normal quantity of blood even in intense anæmia.

CLINICAL SYMPTOMS. Acute anæmia, especially when it has been caused by hemorrhages, is indicated by a small, weak pulse, distention of the pupils and a coldness of the extremities, attacks of dizziness, and loss of consciousness. Convulsions are rarely present in chronic anæmia of the brain, and very often stupidity, quivering of the muscles, great fatigue on the slightest exertion, loss of appetite, and a tendency to vomiting are noticed.

THERAPEUTICS. The therapeutic treatment consists in stimulants, such as wine, ether, camphor, etc. In the chronic form nutritive diet, blood-producing food, tonics.

Cerebral Hemorrhage.
(*Apoplexia Sanguinæ; Hæmorrhagia Cerebri.*)

ETIOLOGY. The chief cause of cerebral hemorrhage is an increased pressure on the vessels containing the blood, and where the walls of these vessels present some abnormal condition by which they are debilitated or weakened. This condition of the walls of the vessels may be caused by atheromatous degeneration, or by some disturbances in the nutritive process of those parts, as in serious diseases, except specific diseases, such as distemper, leukæmia, and in certain forms of poisoning.

PATHOLOGICAL ANATOMY. Hemorrhages appear, as a rule, on the cerebrum, and occur from a capillary hemorrhage, and are indicated by a slight red coloration which cannot be wiped off; but in the most serious forms you may find a distinct number of spots which become confluent. In some cases there is a considerable bloody discharge, indicating the breaking down of some large bloodvessel. If the bloodvessel is located in the hemisphere near the surface, the dura mater appears distended at the affected location; the convolutions of the brain are flattened and the furrows depressed. The substance of the brain is always more or less destroyed, and, if the animal does not die quickly, the discharged blood forms clots very rapidly. Its fluid parts become absorbed, fibrinous substances are formed, and the blood-corpuscles destroyed. The blood-substance is altered into a chocolate-colored emulsion and finally becomes absorbed. The coloring matter of the blood remains on the brain as a rose-colored pigmentation. The centre becomes smaller and smaller until we see the development of numerous connective-tissue adhesions uniting it to the wall, or an apoplectic cyst is formed which has a smooth inner wall filled with serum. This cyst takes the shape of the surrounding parts.

CLINICAL SYMPTOMS. Without any premonitory symptoms we suddenly see serious cerebral symptoms—that is to say, apoplexy. The animals drop, and immediately, or in a short time afterward, walk unsteadily for a distance, and then lose entire consciousness. The pulse becomes weak or irregular, or rapid and very small. The respirations are deep, stertorous, and irregular. The mucous membranes of the head are intensely reddened, and in the early stages of the attack convulsions are very frequently noticed. This is followed by partial or complete paralysis which is due to a direct destruction of the brain-substance, by the blood pressing on the brain. This paralysis may affect the extremities, both anterior and posterior, that half of the body which is opposite to the extravasation in the brain being the one affected. The animal may also become blind. This disease may result: 1, in death, which occurs either in a few moments or may take days; 2, in complete recovery—this, however, only occurs where there is a small hemorrhage, and in the centre of the hemisphere; 3, in complete recovery with partial or complete paralysis, according to the amount of hemorrhage. The treatment of hemorrhage of the brain is connected closely with congestion of the brain, and it consists of applications of cold compresses around the head, of enemas, and, when there is a weak, irregular pulse present, of cardiac stimulants.

Great hemorrhages of the cerebral membranes are marked by the same symptoms as apoplexy of the brain. Apoplexia meningia occurs generally in connection with violent traumatisms of the skull, such as shocks, concussions, fractures, etc. The blood is generally found in the cerebral membrane between the dura mater and the skull. It may also be observed in the subarachnoidal chamber and in the brain-cavities. The symptoms are similar to those of apoplexy of the brain, but, as a rule, convulsions appear earlier, and the animal, while he may present symptoms of coma, makes a much quicker recovery. The treatment is similar to that of cerebral apoplexy.

Inflammation of the Brain.

From a pathological standpoint we have to make a distinction between inflammation of the hard cerebral substance (pachymeningitis) and that of the soft cerebral membrane (leptomeningitis). However, this classification need not be used in a clinical way, because in the dog the described forms run their course with the same symptoms.

ETIOLOGY. Inflammation of the brain is primarily a result of traumatism, such as sunstroke, great psychical excitement, overexertion, etc. This occurs secondarily from disease, such as distemper and pyæmia, also with suppuration in the skull, in inflammation of the frontal cavities from parasites, and purulent inflammation of the ear (in connection with external otitis).

1. *Inflammation of the Dura Mater. Pachymeningitis.* The dura mater is covered with a number of small hemorrhages. It is loose and easy to tear, and over the surface is a collection of bloody purulent masses of exudation. In the later stages of the disease we see a circumscribed or extended thickening and adhesion of the covering to the base of the skull or to the soft cerebromembrane.

2. *Inflammation of the Cerebral Membrane. Leptomeningitis.* The arachnoid is loosened and dull. The subarachnoid chambers are filled with more or less torpid fluid. The pia mater is hyper-

æmic, loosened, and covered by fibrinous exudation. The coverings of the brain are almost always infiltrated and detached from the pia mater with difficulty and according to the amount of inflammation and purulent fluid that may be found in the ventricle. In a chronic case we have a circumscribed thickening of the cerebral membranes and adhesions uniting the coverings with the brain, etc.

3. *Inflammation of the Brain Mass. Encephalitis.* This disease, as a rule, involves single centres and causes a general irritation of the healthy tissue without any distinctly marked limit. In the affected regions the substance of the brain is swollen, hyperæmic, and frequently filled with small hemorrhagic centres. In the course of time the inflamed cerebral substance becomes softened and pulpy. This condition may be present without any hemorrhage, but as a rule the brain matter becomes red and finally yellowish. This latter color is due to metamorphosis of the coloring substance of the blood or to fatty degeneration. These conditions are divided into white, red, or yellow—softening of the brain. Finally cicatrices and cysts are formed, as in apoplexy, or an abscess may be developed which is filled with thick yellow or greenish pus, and becomes encysted and sometimes solidified (calcareous). In some cases small encephalitic centres may heal without leaving any trace. In some cases we see the development of a (non-inflammatory) softening of the brain with thrombosis and embolus of the arteries; and, as a general rule, we find symptoms which resemble apoplexy very much.

CLINICAL SYMPTOMS. The symptoms of inflammation of the brain in its early stages resemble those of hyperæmia. The animals are excited; they run aimlessly from one side to the other, and are fretful and irritable. They whine and howl constantly. The head is hot; the conjunctiva is more or less reddened, the pupils are contracted, and the reflex action is very slight. The appetite is lost; constipation is generally present, and more or less vomiting. The patient is indifferent to the impressions of external objects, being sleepy and apathetic. Soon the disease changes in its character. We see acute convulsions, especially those of the jaw, or eclamptic convulsions. The animals cry and howl. At the same time the sphincters are relapsed, the animal apparently having no control of them. Then there is an interval of quietness, in which the animal falls back into a deep semicomatose condition, and between these periods of quietness we very often see automatic movements, such as quivering or twitching of one or two of the legs; also the corners of the mouth may be retracted. Many cases either howl constantly, and at the same time seem to be semicomatose, or they may bark hoarsely (delirium). As a rule, the temperature is a little above normal. Within a short time the animal becomes gradually paralyzed, losing all power of the muscles. The patient is dull and unconscious of external influences. The breathing is rattling and stertorous. The pulse is increased a number of beats, but is almost imperceptible to the touch. The temperature now begins to rise. In some cases the temperature may remain normal, and in rare instances has fallen below. As a rule, the animals die shortly after the convulsions make their appearance. Complete recovery is very rare, and slight attacks terminate as a rule either with paralysis (partial or complete), idiotism, or blindness.

Very similar symptoms to those already described appear in cases of cysticercus cellulosæ in the brain or its membranes. Siedamgrotzky found in the dura mater of both hemispheres of a dog, which had suddenly developed symptoms of encephalitis and which died in twenty-four hours, twenty-three sacs the size of a pea. This is peculiar from the fact that the animal had been perfectly healthy up to twenty-four hours before its death, and had not shown the slightest loss of intelligence or in muscular movement.

THERAPEUTICS. The treatment of inflammation of the brain corresponds with that of hyperæmia of the brain. Rest, cold applications to the head, clysters, laxatives, especially calomel. In cases of great excitement sedatives (morphine, sulphate 0.02 subcutaneously, chloral hydrate 2.0 to 4.0 by the mouth or per rectum in the form of clysters). The violent irritants which were formerly used on the skin, such as croton oil rubbed on the inner fascia of the thighs and along the spine, or cantharidal ointments, are of no particular benefit.

The course of this disease varies greatly in affections of the cerebellum. If the hemispheres are affected, we may have extensive alterations of the brain, which may run their course without any decided symptoms being shown; but as soon as the cerebellum and one or both hemispheres become affected we then see the various symptoms peculiar to this disease, and a diagnosis can be made with almost absolute certainty. In diagnosing disease of the cerebellum there is generally an unsteadiness of the gait in walking. There are peculiar movements, such as walking around in a circle and rolling on the ground, when both hemispheres are involved. We may have paralysis of the posterior extremities. In rare instances, however, these symptoms may be presented in cases of poisoning (by cocaine or apomorphia).

The therapeutic treatment of this disease is not very definite. In cases of simple unsteadiness of the gait the author has been able to secure good results by means of laxatives and collodium of cantharides applied to the neck. Where the animal turns in a ring constantly, or rolls on the ground, such agents as morphia, chloral, and bromide are often used.

DISEASES OF THE SPINAL CORD AND ITS MEMBRANES.

Cerebro-spinal Meningitis.
(*Meningitis Cerebro-spinalis.*)

ETIOLOGY. Nothing is definitely known of the causes of this disease. It is extremely rare in the dog. Renner and Kempen have made several observations on the subject, and the author had one case of his own. In this the disease seemed to be related, in some way, with a wound on the anterior extremity.

PATHOLOGICAL ANATOMY. The anatomical foundation of the disease seems to be an acute suppurating inflammation of the brain and spinal membranes, for Renner, as well as the author, found purulent exudation in the arachnoid, especially on the hemispheres and the base of the brain, which was infiltrated by a quantity of serous fluid. The same condition was also found in the spine.

CLINICAL SYMPTOMS AND THERAPEUTICS. The symptoms which were observed by Renner and the author were disturbances of the sensitory nerves, in some cases the animal becoming unconscious. There were loss of appetite, fever, and on the fifth day a marked unsteadiness of the gait, beginning with a slow, dragging walk, and becoming complicated with tonic convulsions which become finally epileptic, and, lastly, stupor, coma, and death. Renner treated two cases with calomel, opium, and purgatives. The author did not have good results, although he treated a case in the same way.

Inflammation of the Spinal Cord and its Membranes.
(*Myelitis and Spinal Meningitis.*)

ETIOLOGY. A common cause of myelitis and spinal meningitis is traumatisms of some kind causing direct injuries to the spine. It may also be caused by simple contusions, violent blows, shocks, falling out of a window, etc., and further by concussions of the spinal cord. Violent muscular exertions frequently bring it on. In very rare instances the disease may follow the presence of an abscess on the outside of the spinal canal (for instance, in one case which was observed by the author, in the long muscle of the back), by extension of the suppurating process through the orifice of the vertebra, and occasionally you see it originate in connection with some infectious disease (distemper, rabies, pyæmia). It may also be caused by cold.

PATHOLOGICAL ANATOMY. The inflamed pia mater appears thickened, infiltrated, and injected in some places, and, as a rule, adherent by means of the exudation to the spine itself. It is covered on its upper surface by a serous, fibrinous, or purulent exudation. The arachnoid exudation is covered by a milky, false membrane and greatly thickened. The dura mater is rarely involved, but when such is the case it becomes thickened and loosened, and covered with a thin serum. The spine itself shows the inflammatory process either extended over large surfaces or else confined to small centres. In the early part of the disease the spine is slightly swollen; the gray substance is somewhat reddened, dark, and soft. Later the spine becomes a yellowish-red, breaks down and undergoes white, yellow, or red degeneration. In the chronic course we see atrophy of the nerves as a consequence of malformations of the connective tissue.

CLINICAL SYMPTOMS. The symptoms of alteration of the spinal cord appear gradually, and become more intense as the disease progresses, where the disease is due to violent traumatisms, producing a direct destruction or laceration of the nervous centres, or pressure, which is caused by the blood being discharged and pressing upon the spine. In all diseases of the spinal cord it is very important to recognize the fact that consciousness is present. As a rule, the symptoms appear either slowly or quickly, according to the amount of irritation present on the spine itself, and in cases where the spinal cord is very much involved and compressed by masses of exudated serum we find complete paralysis. We will take up all these symptoms in the following description, which may be observed in affections of the spinal cord :

1. *Motor Symptoms of Paralysis.* These are, as a rule, the first symptoms presented. The patients have a heavy, dull look; staggering gait, but not irregular (in this it differs from disease of the cerebellum). Finally, they drag their hindlegs; as a rule, these extremities are the parts paralyzed. When they are placed on their legs they stand with them spread apart, or they may simply drop sideways on their hind-quarters. In rarer cases, not only the posterior extremities but also the anterior are paralyzed, and it is evident that in cases of paralysis of all the members the spinal substance of the neck must be affected, while paralysis of the posterior extremities must occur no matter what part of the spine becomes affected; it may be in any part of the spinal column. In these cases we always have the double-sided paralysis; and in very rare cases paralysis is marked more intensely on one side than the other; but, as a rule, it is very rarely present, and we can only suppose that in one-half of the spinal cord the disease is more advanced than in the other.

2. *Motor Symptoms of Irritation.* These appear in the shape of slight, irregular twitchings, rarely of any great consequence, and seldom leading to convulsions. They are generally noticed in the early stages of the disease upon the extremities.

3. *Disturbances of Sensitiveness.* We observe more rarely disturbances of sensitiveness in the shape of hyperæsthesia than in the form of anæsthesia. In the former it may invariably be observed in the early stages of the disease that patients show intense pain, especially when touched, lifted, or pressed upon the spinal cord. (This they indicate by biting, howling, etc.) In the latter case they do not show the slightest reaction in the

affected regions even when subjected to serious irritations of the skin.

4. *Disturbances of the Sphincters.* In mild stages of this disease the sphincters, such as the bladder, appear slightly affected. In the serious stage we observe complete paralysis, loss of control of the sphincters, and complete paralysis of the sphincter vesicæ. More details will be introduced on this subject under Diseases of the Bladder. Such paralytic conditions of the bladder may occur in all diseases of the spine. There is difficulty in the passage of fecal matter, as a consequence, producing constipation and paralysis of the intestines, caused to a certain extent by the loss of abdominal pressure. This is evinced by a gaping rectum and escape of fecal matter which accumulates in the lower bowel.

5. *Nutritive Disorders.* Through want of active exercise the muscular system of paralyzed animals, especially the extremities, becomes flabby, soft, and atrophied. The temperature is reduced in the paralyzed portion, the extremities being cold and anæmic. In cases where there is paralysis of the spinal cord caused by compression, and in cases of atrophy due to hemorrhage on the spinal cord, and also in certain luxations or fractures of the vertebræ, we see the same symptoms.

(*a*) Paralysis of the spinal cord caused by compression may result from thickening of the membranes and pressure on the spine itself. It may also occur in some diseases of the vertebra, for instance, in exostosis, but both of these are very rare. In such cases the symptoms come on very slowly and gradually increase in intensity.

(*b*) Apoplexy may occur, due to the presence of some blood escaping on the spine and causing pressure. In these cases the paralysis appears very suddenly, but may gradually disappear after some time.

(*c*) Luxations of the spinal cord only happen in the vertebra of the neck, and cause a peculiar oblique position of the head, as if it were twisted to one side. This is due to displacement of the ligaments. At the same time there is present a series of what might be called "special symptoms," which are not very pronounced in any of their characters.

(*d*) Fractures of the spine: These are generally recognized by some change in the position of the region in which they are located (bending inward, flattened depressions, and in rare instances slight distortions of the spinal cord), and also by the extensive sensitiveness to pressure in this location. In certain instances there may be an abnormal mobility of the part. Crepitation, as a rule, is absent. In fractures of the cervical vertebræ we generally notice an oblique position of the head. If the symptoms just described are absent, when an animal has had a severe fall on the spine, unless paralyzed or remains so without loss of consciousness, it is always doubtful if there is a fracture of the vertebræ or a hemorrhage within the vertical canal. In such cases we simply have to await developments, or if paralysis does not immediately follow the injury, but comes some time afterward, it is due to compression of the spine from a gradually increasing hemorrhage. We must remember, however, that a fall, shock, or blow upon the back, or ordinary irritations of the spinal substance may occur, like a concussion of the brain, in which there is not the slightest alteration to be found in the spinal substance, or its membranes. In many cases we may expect a recovery as long as there is no myelitic complications.

THERAPEUTIC TREATMENT OF THE DISEASES OF THE SPINAL CORD. In the early stages of the disease when fever, hyperæmia, and accompanying convulsions give pronounced evidence of the disease, it is advisable to give antiphlogistic treatment, consisting of compresses upon the spinal cord, and vigorous purgatives (calomel), and lastly enemas. In cases where the paralytic symptoms predominate we use irritants along the spinal cord, such as cantharides, croton oil, or biniodide of mercury. Sometimes in mild cases mustard oil. If we succeed in lessening the convulsions, or if the paralytic symptoms predominate, we must use stimulants, such as strychnia and electricity.

The first should be used internally in the form of tincture of nux vomica, from five to twelve drops, or subcutaneously in a strychnia solution; the latter method is the better. We must remember that one daily injection is sufficient, and that a medical pause of from thirty-six to thirty-eight hours ought to be made every four or five days, in order to prevent the cumulative influence of this drug.

℞.—Strychnia muriate 0.005
Aqua 5.0

Electricity is applied in the following method: One pole of the battery is placed on the spine and the other at the termination of the paralyzed limb. For instance, one is put on the foot and the other in the middle or side of the spine, gradually increasing the current after having previously dampened the region with a concentrated saline solution. In such cases, besides administering a purgative and cleansing the bowels, we must also see that the bladder is emptied by means of a catheter. Electricity is also a useful agent in peripheral paralysis, which has been mentioned. The faradic current is preferable. Place one of the poles as close as possible to the point of the central location of the affected nerves and rub the paralyzed muscles with the other pole. This treatment should be renewed every day for ten or fifteen minutes. Alcoholic frictions, which are so popular among the general public, are of slight value and only to be recommended when connected with true massage (pinching, friction, and massage of the paralyzed muscle in its proper direction).

Epilepsy.

Epilepsy is a disease which is rare in the dog. Its chief symptoms are irregular attacks of unconsciousness accompanied by acute convulsions in older cases.

ETIOLOGY AND PATHOLOGICAL ANATOMY. The causes of epilepsy are unknown, but at the same time there is no doubt that certain diseases of the brain and its membranes, especially chronic diseases, very frequently cause epileptiform seizures which are similar to true epilepsy, and we may also observe in some cases a reflex epilepsy, which does not resemble true epilepsy in any way except in some general symptoms. These will happen after traumatic lesions of the peripheral nerves, in intestinal parasites, in poisonous substances in the intestines (for further particulars, see page 201). We may also observe epileptiform convulsions in distemper.

In true epilepsy there are no anatomical alterations to be found in the brain. Wherever they are found they cause epileptiform convulsions. It is, therefore, certain that in a case of epilepsy it is only due to some temporary irritating condition, and that the membranes of the brain are the starting-point of the irritation.

The experiments which have been made upon dogs in connection with this disease by Ferrier, Eulenberg, Landois, and others are interesting. They found that with great irritation of the motor regions of the large brain (the cerebrum) a complete attack could be produced. This begins with twitching of the muscles which belong to that centre. It then becomes extended over the corresponding group of muscles on the other side, producing shocks and twitching of the whole muscular system of the body from tonic and, later, clonic convulsions. The convulsions extend from centre to centre, and they never miss any region, but run consecutively from one to the other. If the chief centre is cut out, the convulsions will not be present in that region during the epileptiform attacks. Irritation of the subcortical white substance of the brain also causes epilepsy. This begins, however, in the muscles of the same side. Bromide of sodium administered for some time has been found very valuable in preventing epilepsy caused by membranous irritation.

From the above experiments it can be readily understood that the membranes of the cerebrum are the original centres of epileptic attacks. It is hard to explain, however, the actual cause of this irritation. Epilepsy can hardly be caused by over-stimulation or feeding, for, as a rule, the largest number of true epileptic subjects are weak, delicate, and anæmic; but at the same time we often see vigorous, well-fed dogs of all ages suffering from this disease. There are many cases in anæmic animals which, under treatment, gradually improve, at the same time the epileptiform attacks becoming less and less as the animal improves. It is doubtful if these cases can be called true epilepsy.

[The translator is inclined to think that quite a number of these cases should be classed under the head of hysteria; in two cases in particular where he advised to have them castrated (ovariotomy), he found in one case a large cyst attached to the ovary, and in the other intense hyperæmia of the ovary (the left). After the operation both animals made good recoveries; one, however, had slight attacks for three months afterward. A third was operated on that had been affected for two years, and the ovaries were found to be hypertrophied and congested. In this case the attacks were lessened, but not entirely cured.]

CLINICAL SYMPTOMS AND COURSE OF THE DISEASE. In acute attacks of epilepsy the symptoms begin suddenly, or they may start with slight premonitory symptoms. In the later stages the animals run in a circle, are restless, have a staring look out of their eyes, or remain standing with outstretched legs, and shake their heads from side to side. We soon see clonic convulsions followed by loss of consciousness, and in some cases a rapid change into clonic tonic convulsions. The muscles of mastication are especially affected. Single muscle-contractions follow one another with astonishing rapidity, so that the saliva which lies in the mouth is turned into foam. The convulsions, which are now tonic, extend over the whole muscular system. The body and neck are drawn backward or sideways; the legs are stretched; the respirations seem to cease. This tonic form of convulsion lasts but a short time. A few seconds after its appearance it has altered into clonic cramps of the muscles, especially noticed in the legs, which are frequently twitched. After a few minutes these twitchings stop; the animal lies on the ground for some time; it finally rises and recovers very quickly. The pulse and temperature during an attack of this kind present no alteration of any consequence. The mucous membranes of the head are reddened and congested. This is noticed at the termination of an attack, and is probably due to the interruption of perspiration and the slight respiratory movements. In very rare instances an involuntary passing of feces and urine is noted during these convulsions.

There are also certain forms in which the animal is restless, running from side to side, or having fainting spells (dropping on one side), slight muscular twitchings of the head or extremities, and occasionally, in mild attacks, a very slight twitching of the jaw. The duration of these attacks varies, as a rule, not lasting very long, generally only a few minutes, although severe attacks have been known to last for five or six hours. Their frequency is very uncertain; some animals have had several attacks daily, while in others they have appeared at intervals of months. A peculiar feature of some cases of true epilepsy was the frequent attacks on the slightest excitement.

THERAPEUTICS. No agent seems to have any decided effect upon epilepsy. The author has tried a number of remedies, one after another, without result. Bromide of sodium seems to be the best (this is preferable to bromide of potassium, as it has no detrimental effect upon the appetite), provided it is given in substantial doses. With this drug it is always possible to prolong the intervals between attacks; they are also shortened, and relatively less serious. Other agents, such as oxide of zinc, arsenic, nitrate of silver, belladonna, hyoscyamus, valerian, bromo-hydrate, cold water, and electricity.

  R.—Bromide of sodium 15.0
   Aqua 150.0
  S.—One tablespoonful three times daily.

In connection with this disease we must devote a few words to convulsions of young animals. We very often see weak, debilitated animals which are backward or poorly fed, but which have rickets as a consequence of reflex irritability during the course of catarrhal diseases of the digestive tract or of the nasal cavities. We also notice them after the absorption of large quantities of fermenting, indigestible food, in constipation, and in cases of intestinal parasites, at the time of teething, and also as a consequence of great psychical excitement. We often see spontaneous convulsions; these are very similar to epilepsy, and are probably of reflex origin. In some of these cases we may have to deal with true epilepsy, but, as a rule, they may be ascribed to an undeveloped form of distemper. In some cases it may be due to some brain affection, such as congestion of the membranes. It cannot be denied, however, that there are a great number of convulsive attacks for which the cause remains obscure.

We may, therefore, conclude that we can only obtain an approximative insight into these convulsions by the symptoms which are presented. Frequent occurrence of eclamptic attacks with a short interval between must be considered as a very serious symptom.

The therapeutic treatment of convulsions consists in the use of applications of cold water to the head; large doses of bromide of sodium, morphia, and similar sedative agents. We must also take into consideration the causes of the disease and keep the animals as quiet as possible.

Chorea.
(*St. Vitus's Dance.*)

We define this disease as a persistent clonic convulsion of some muscular group in certain parts of the body. For instance, shaking of the head, twitching movements with one or two legs, regular, rhythmic contractions of the mouth, and also an automatic opening and closing of that part; regular movements of the tongue, and an undulating action or movement of the whole body. If the patients are left to themselves, the twitching action is generally less marked, and under physical excitement becomes much more aggravated. For instance, when eating, if any pain is present, and during catarrhal conditions of the air-passages, or the intestines, stomach, etc. The choreic movements lessen during sleep and under the influence of ether, chloroform, and bromo-ether, but morphia and chloral have little or no influence upon them. Sensitiveness and consciousness are not disturbed in any way whatever, but are perfectly normal. The course of this disease is slow, and may extend for months and years; but, as a rule, the symptoms lessen, and in rare instances may disappear entirely. A fatal termination is only to be feared when complications arise.

ETIOLOGY. Under the name of chorea there are a great many complications of the dog which should really be classed under another head; for instance, nervous distemper, or obscure cerebral diseases, also myelitis, and some cases of symptomatic chorea.

In true chorea of man we do not see any pathological alterations of the brain, and in the few cases which the author had to consider as true chorea on account of the anæmia, absence of any symptoms of distemper, or other diseases of the brain and spine, the convulsions were restricted to certain special muscular groups, and not, as in human chorea, to irregular regions—that is to say, in the various muscular centres of the body. In some of these cases the animals were destroyed, and their post-mortems gave an entirely negative result, there being no apparent pathological change in the central nervous system. As a rule, the affected animals are in an anæmic condition and show all the effects of bad nutrition, and, after some observation, we are convinced that with improvement in the general system the choreic symptoms become very much lessened.

THERAPEUTICS. The author has tried all the various agents recommended in this disease, but without any decided results. Arsenic, either in the form of Donovan's or Fowler's solution, or alternated with some preparation of iron, has given the best results, but these drugs must be given for some time, and it is only after prolonged administration that any favorable result is observed. The author thinks that more benefit is derived from a nutritive diet than anything else.

Antipyrine, which is used in man, is of not much service in the dog. Bromide of potassium, chloral hydrate, oxide of zinc, nitrate of silver, electricity, and hydropathy can all be used.

Catalepsy.

Catalepsy, or "cataleptic rigidity," is understood to be a peculiar rigidity of the muscles in which the animals may be placed in certain positions and will remain so. Consciousness and sensitiveness seem to be suppressed entirely. Such an attack lasts for hours and days, and (according to Hertwig) for weeks. In many cases they finally relapse and die in a short time. If this is really a disease, or merely a symptom of some brain complication, the author has not been able to positively determine.

Hertwig mentions as causes of catalepsy cold, fright, overloading the stomach with indigestible food, and metastases in various diseases, while Fröhner considers this disease as a purely functional neurosis of the brain and spine. He found it impossible to recognize any definite alterations in the central organs, either in catalepsy, eclampsia, or tetanus, but he found occasionally certain secondary alterations in the muscles, namely, hemorrhages, dark venous swellings, and fatty degeneration of the muscles, also waxy degeneration of the fibres of the heart.

No practical therapeutic treatment is known. Fröhner advises electricity and cold douches as a means of restoring the disturbed reflex irritability of the nervous system.

Tetanus.

(*Lockjaw.*)

This very rarely occurs in the dog. The symptoms consist (according to Hertwig and Siedamgrotzky) in a stiff, stilt-like gait, the head and neck being distended and drawn, the eyes fixed, the ears more or less retracted and stiffened; prolapsus of the nictitating membrane; wrinkling of the skin of the forehead; convulsive closing of the mouth, making the animal utterly unable to eat, bark or drink; great fretfulness, and hardness of the muscles, which when touched no symptoms of pain are shown by the animal. Consciousness is not affected, and the temperature is generally normal. [The translator has observed two cases in which the temperature rose to 43°.]

The therapeutic treatment consists in lessening the irritation by narcotics, especially morphia, clysters, chloral; and if there is any wound present, it must be treated with poultices or anything to lessen the irritation. It is almost certain that a great majority of cases are due to diseased wound-infection and the presence of microbes (tetanus bacilli). These bacilli remain in the wound or in the neighborhood of it. It is generally advisable, therefore, to cauterize, or, better still, to excise the wound with its entire surroundings. The author does not consider it impossible for the bacillus of tetanus to enter the organism in other ways than directly through the skin.

Eclampsia.

Eclampsia, which is not a very good definition, is a tonic-clonic convulsive spasm which is observed in bitches, and, as a rule, during the attacks the animal is perfectly conscious.

ETIOLOGY. The causes of this disease are very little known. According to Hertwig, it may be caused by cold, stagnation of the milk in the udder, taking away the young, and sometimes by worry. In one-third of the cases of true eclampsia which were observed by the author, all the young were still with the mother. [The translator has observed a large number of cases of this disease, and invariably found the animal weak, inclined to be delicate, light in bone, but to be excellent mothers, and the litters were generally strong, healthy pups. They laid on flesh very quickly while the mother lost it. The onset of the disease was generally at the end of the second or third week.] In the rest of the cases, either one or more had been taken away from the mother. In the onset of the disease the mammary glands contain very much milk. The animals are generally small, delicate (house dogs and pet animals), and, as a rule, have a light coat. Friedberger and Fröhner are of the opinion that the disease may originate from anæmia of the spinal cord, or in a reflex way from the lacteal glands. With this last theory the author is inclined to agree. According to the statements of authors, deep anatomical disturbances of the brain may be caused directly from the mammary glands. Friedberger has observed two bitches that had eclampsia without having puppies.

CLINICAL SYMPTOMS. The disease may appear in from forty-eight hours to thirty days after whelping; very rarely later than this time; in the majority of cases appearing at or about four weeks. In one case of Friedberger's fifty days elapsed. It comes on suddenly without any marked symptoms. The animals become restless and anxious; they have a staring expression of the eye, short, rapid respiration, reddened mucous membranes; they show no pain from pressure on the walls of the chest, neck, or abdomen. After a short time (about a quarter of an hour after the appearance of increased respiration) they become paralyzed, are no longer able to stand on their feet, and remain for some time with their legs stretched from them. A slight increase of temperature has been observed in several instances at the onset of the disease. The dog lies on her side with her legs firm and tense; the muscles of the body hard and quivering to the touch; the joints are stiff and hard to bend; and at intervals we see clonic convulsions of all the muscles, especially those of the extremities, and the respiratory muscles are especially involved. The respirations become more rapid as a consequence of this, and finally the mouth is opened and the tongue protrudes, while the animal breathes with great difficulty. The pulse is small, hard, and sometimes irregular, and always quick; the eyes are staring and protruded, and there is an anxious look in the face. All the visible mucous membranes are cyanosed. The saliva which accumulates in the mouth is either swallowed convulsively at certain intervals, or, as is generally the case, it dribbles out of the corners of the mouth. As a rule, consciousness is not disturbed. The pupilla are normal in size; reflex action is present. The animal seems to notice external objects or impressions, such as calling the patient, or noticing one it knows coming into the room. The appetite is lost; the normal discharges are entirely suppressed; the urine, after such an attack, gives an albuminous reaction. The attack may last for twenty-four hours, but generally varies a little in intensity. If the attack is very acute, the animal falls into a deep comatose condition and dies in about forty-eight hours after the onset of the disease from apoplexy and paralysis.

THERAPEUTICS. Any of the narcotics can be used, and, as a rule, produce good results. Here they use injections of morphia, which were first recommended by Siedamgrotzky; the quantity is 0.002 to 0.005 gm. of muriate of morphia diluted with water. As a rule, a few minutes after the hypodermatic is administered, the animal becomes quiet and rests easily. Inhalations of chloroform, chloral hydrate, bromide of potassium, etc., are also recommended. Warm baths and friction produce relaxation of the tense muscles. Valerianate of zinc in 0.5 gm. dose every two hours.

DISEASES OF TRUE INFECTION.

Distemper and Contagious Catarrhal Fever.

The definition of the word "distemper" means a disease which is peculiar to the canine race, and it is caused by specific poison which finds its way into the system, as a rule, through the lungs and air-passages. It generally attacks young animals and runs its course as a catarrhal fever, affecting all the mucous membranes of the body, and almost invariably accompanied with certain nervous symptoms, also skin eruptions.

Etiology. Distemper is a disease which is contagious in the highest degree, and is only communicated by infection. An animal affected with distemper can remain but a short time in any locality and affect every animal there. As a rule, few young animals escape distemper, generally contracting it before they are a year old, and dogs over that age very rarely take the disease. That, however, may be accounted for from the fact that dogs having arrived at that age have either come in contact with the disease previous to that and they have had it in a mild form, or the system was in such a condition that they did not contract it. The disease affects animals but once during life, although a few exceptions are presented where animals have contracted it the second time. As a rule, delicate, weak, poorly-fed animals (vegetable diet), or animals which have been affected by some catarrhal disorder of the respiratory mucous membranes, contract the disease in its acutest form; while, on the other hand, dogs which have lots of exercise, especially animals in the country or small cities, are mildly affected with the disease.

Distemper exists in all countries of the world. In the large cities it is found at any season of the year, while in the country it is generally present during the warm weather. The specific poison of distemper is not definitely known. It is undoubtedly a fixed and volatile poison which enters the system by the mouth and nose, and it exerts its first influence on the respiratory passages. Vaccination of young animals by means of the secretory fluid from animals affected with this disease has been tried, and often, as a rule, produces the disease artificially.

Semmer believes that he has definitely defined the contagious germ in the blood, and also found it in the lungs, liver, and spleen, in the form of small, dagger-shaped microbes, which he calls the "bacilli of distemper." Rabe has found in the secretion of the nose and connective tissue, also in the blood, small cocci which accumulate in heaps, or are generally together in small groups of three or four in a superficial sac-like manner, or they may hang together like a string of beads. In some cases they take the form of a light, thin membrane, which is easily colored by methyl-violet. He considers these as the specific infecting agent of distemper, but this theory is one that Friedberger does not agree with. Mathis found in the mucus contained in a pustule a diplococcus which could be colored with fuchsine. He used bouillon cultures of this for the inoculation of dogs. These were affected by symptoms which resembled very closely those of distemper. Marcone and Meloni found a micrococcus in the dog which was affected by distemper, and considered that this agent was the true pathogenic fluid, as it produced the skin eruptions, broncho-pneumonia, and gastro-enteritis in dogs which had been inoculated with pure cultures. Legrain and Jaquot obtained pure cultures of micrococci, when held in certain mediums, from fluid obtained from the bladder in the exanthematic form of distemper. These were gathered together and in the form of diplococci and short chains. In dogs vaccinated with these cultures the skin eruption, with the development of pustules, was seen only, but the subjects so treated seemed to enjoy immunity from the disease. Millais made cultures from the nasal excretion of the dogs affected by distemper upon gelatinous cocci of two various bacilli, which, on inoculation, produced distemper. [Galli-Valerio has isolated ovoid bacilli two micro-millimetres in length which grow freely in gelatin. These he found in abundance in the lungs and central nervous system, but did not find them in the blood. The inoculation of the cultivations produces characteristic distemper in puppies, but did not give the same results in adult dogs. This he accounts for in that they may have had previous attacks of the disease, and were thus protected.]

Direct vaccinating methods have been practised by various practitioners. For instance, Trasbot placed secretions from the nose and bladder of animals affected with the disease in the abdominal wall of healthy young animals. The disease appeared after eight days.

Krajewski vaccinated numerous young animals with secretions of the nose and pustule, these inoculations being on the mucous membrane and under the skin, and arrived at the following conclusions:

1. The contagious germ of distemper sticks to the secretion of the nose and eyes, and the blood is also contagious.

2. The germ does not lose its virulent properties in any degree when dried at a normal temperature, or frozen at 18° to 20° of cold. However, its virulence becomes attenuated when kept for any length of time in a dry place.

3. The disease, which is produced by vaccinating, runs a very mild course, and kills, as a rule, from 10 to 15 per cent., while the ordinary disease kills from 32 to 70 per cent. Laosson has obtained the same results after vaccinating ninety-eight animals, and found also that the contents of these pustules are generally inactive, and that the nasal secretion loses its virulence after eight days. Friedberger's observations are diametrically opposite, for he contends that he has caused infection by means of the contents of the pustules. He also recognized in one case that the disease originated from vaccination passed through a short intervening stage, and, as a rule, was much less in intensity, ran a very rapid course, and that the group of pustules was confined to the region of vaccination.

Schantyr has lately published certain observations concerning the microbes of distemper. He agrees with Pütz that distemper of the dog resembles distemper in horses to a remarkable degree, and his theory of the subject is that distemper may be classified into three diseases, according to the presence of three micro-organisms of different characters. These diseases are: Abdominal typhus, true distemper of the dog, and canine typhoid. Their clinical as well as their pathological symptoms have a great similarity with one another, and it is only with a careful microscopical examination that the specific micro-organisms can be separated. The bacilli of typhoid (small, short bacilli, which are almost exactly like man's bacilli) are generally found separate in the blood, while the bacilli of distemper (small, somewhat bead-shaped) and the bacilli of typhoid (typhoid are very small and thin) are generally arranged in groups. The bacilli are hard to color with fuchsine, and become colorless with Graham's test. This is not the case with the bacillus of typhoid. Typhus and typhoid bacilli give characteristic cultures upon gelatin and potato, while the bacillus of distemper is extremely hard to culture under any circumstances.

CLINICAL SYMPTOMS AND COURSE. The stage of incubation of distemper is generally from four to seven days. In rare cases it may linger, after contact with the diseased animal, until eight or twelve days, and Krajewski states that cases of infection through cohabitation may sometimes take from two to two and a half weeks to develop. The first actual symptom is an increase of temperature. In the initial stage it rises to 40°, and some cases 41° and over.

An increase in temperature has been observed by the author in all cases of distemper, when the examination was made early in the disease. Later on the temperature falls slightly, but in some cases very rapidly, and it may even go to the normal point, according to the condition of the animal. In cases developed by inoculation we occasionally find a marked increase in temperature. The next symptom is the disturbance of the general condition. The animal is depressed, restless, has little or no appetite, seeks heat, becomes easily fatigued, is chilly and shivering, the nose is hot and dry, the skin is hard, and the hair becomes harsh and dry. In some instances vomiting occurs, but that can hardly be called a characteristic, initial symptom of the disease. This stage of the disease is short; the symptoms increase rapidly, and have many characteristic points, which are as follows:

1. *Symptoms on the External Membranes.* These appear in the majority of cases and are of great importance. We see a number of small red spots upon the inner fascia of the thighs, the abdomen, and in rare instances the mouth and eyes, and still more rarely covering the entire body. They are generally scattered, very rarely confluent. They rapidly form small bladder-like blisters filled with serum, and later on this serum changes to pus. They are about the size of a lentil or small bean, and soon dry up, forming yellowish scabs and crusts. After these scabs fall off (generally in about one week), they leave on the skin a red, cir-

cular spot which disappears slowly. In other cases we find more or less depth to the cicatrix, leaving pit-like ulcerations. They are probably due to the animal scratching or gnawing the sore. This is the only skin eruption that characterizes this disease, and it dries up very quickly, so that in from eight to fourteen days we see no other marks except those light, granulating spots (exanthema of distemper, distemper-pox). Hertwig and Friedberger have observed some cases in which this eruption made its appearance without any other symptom of distemper.

2. *Symptoms Indicated by the Eyes.* There is generally more or less purulent catarrhal conjunctivitis. The animal avoids the light. There are redness and swelling of the conjunctiva. In the early stages the secretion is serous and very fluid. Later on it becomes a muco-purulent secretion, either light gray or yellowish in color. This sometimes occurs in large masses (blennorrhœa of the eyes). This fluid collects in the corner of the lower eyelid or trickles down over the face, drying in yellowish crusts in the edges and borders of the eyelids, frequently gluing them together. The corrosive action of these secretions and also the inflammation of the surrounding membranes may cause lesions of the cornea, sometimes from the animal scratching and rubbing the eye, especially in animals with prominent eyes (such as pugs and king charles spaniels). In some cases it may be due to deficient nutrition of the cornea. This ulceration starts with a slight swelling on the external surface of the cornea and subsequent formation of an ulceration. (Other details will be found in the chapter on Diseases of the Eye.)

We see in rare cases keratitis parenchymatosa by extension of the inflammation of the cornea. This may be complicated with a permanent opacity of the sclerotic membrane, and in rare cases the whole eye becomes acutely inflamed and breaks down (see Diseases of the Eye).

3. *Symptoms of the Respiratory Apparatus.* These are generally a catarrhal inflammation of the mucous membranes of the upper air-passages, and, if the disease is acute, the finer sections of the bronchi become inflamed. The first symptom is a catarrh of the nose, which is marked by sneezing and the animal rubbing or wiping his nose with his front paws. This discharge increases. In the early stages it is simply serous; later it becomes mucous,

grayish-white or grayish-yellow, sometimes bloody, and in some cases even purulent, with more or less odor. We also see a "sniffling" respiration. This is particularly noticeable in short-headed dogs (such as pugs or bulldogs). In all cases there is catarrh of the larynx, bronchi, and bronchioles. Catarrh of the larynx is generally marked by a loud, hoarse, dry cough, which is particularly distressing to the animal, especially at night. As the disease advances it becomes moist and looser, and is easily produced by a slight pressure on the larynx. Where there is simple laryngitis, we do not generally see any visible increase or difficulty in respiration. This is changed, however, as soon as the large bronchial tubes become involved. In such cases we see a marked increase in respiration, which gradually becomes more intense as the inflammatory process goes downward into the finer bronchi. Any pressure on the sides or tapping upon the walls of the chest causes a very distinct, painful, distressing cough. On auscultation we hear an increased vesicular breathing, as well as dry and moist rattling bruits, which are of various forms and intensity.

If the inflammatory process has extended to the fine bronchi, it is not rare to see the formation of lobular pneumonic centres—that is to say, catarrhal pneumonia. Difficulty in respiration now appears more pronounced; respiration is superficial but laborious, as is proved by the inflation of the cheeks. The number of respirations may increase from 60 to 80, and even more. The cough is very painful, dull, and weak; the pulse is greatly increased, and the temperature may increase to a marked degree, but it is remittent. On auscultating we hear in the lungs snoring, groaning, and wheezing sounds and rattling bruits (these last are moist and numerous), also more or less blowing sounds in different regions. We notice an increased vesicular respiration with sharp, prolonged, expiratory bruits, and alternating bruits of a mixed character. In the same region we may notice bronchial respiration. Percussion, as a rule, is not very instructive.

4. *Symptoms of the Digestive Tract.* The chief of these is catarrh of the stomach, which may vary in intensity. There is entire loss of appetite, vomiting of a thin turbid liquid, shiny or muco-purulent, which is frothy. There are frequent discharges from the bowels of a thin, muco-purulent fluid, occasionally streaked with

blood, and always accompanied by a painful tenesmus. We may also find the abdomen very painful on pressure, and, as a rule, contracted and tense.

5. *Symptoms of the Nervous System.* The animal is very dull, especially its senses. There is a marked apathy and depression, and in some cases deep coma. In a great many cases this condition may be accompanied by periods of excitement, nervousness, great restlessness, and even true delirium. These periods, however, are not of any great length, as a rule, the animal sooner or later showing signs of marked depression. Motor disturbances, such as twitching of various groups of muscles, mostly the head and extremities, are noticed, and, in some cases, convulsions or true eclamptic attacks. These follow one another at long intervals, or keep the animal irritated for days. Clonic convulsions of the maxillary muscles are very frequently seen. They consist of a rapid and regular twitching of the muscles of the lower jaw, sometimes confined only to chattering of the teeth, and occasionally sufficiently strong to make a foam of the saliva. Beside this, we may see symptoms of motor paralysis. The patients are unsteady and irregular in their actions. In some instances they drag their legs, or occasionally their posterior extremities lose their power, and the animal is unable to stand; in rare instances, due to paralysis of the sympathetic, the bladder and the lower bowel lose their nervous control, and urine and feces are evacuated involuntarily.

The anatomical alterations produced by this disease of the nervous system, which are shown in the section of the brain, are sometimes very slight, and it is rather remarkable to find such acute nervous symptoms with so little pathological alterations. The microscopical examination showed little change, or what alterations you might expect from many of the infectious diseases of other animals. We must, therefore, admit that the microbes of distemper are not as yet well known. Like all other pathogenic micro-organisms, they produce " ptomaïnes." It has been proven that the severity of the nervous symptoms depends to a certain extent upon the natural disposition of the animals, and also on their bodily health. When they take the disease, as weak, anæmic, poorly-fed animals, they are very apt to be severely attacked with a nervous form of the disease. Occasional symptoms appear in this disease which should be mentioned, such as serious weakness of the heart. This may be due to a parenchymatous degeneration of the heart-muscle. It is generally fatal, as it produces œdema of the lungs. Albuminuria is produced by parenchymatous degeneration of the kidneys, and in rare instances from true nephritis; decubitus is seen occasionally in severe cases in the elbow- and knee-joints, also at the femoro-tibial articulation. This sometimes causes septicæmia and produces death in this way.

The large number of the above-described symptoms shows how completely the whole body may be affected with this disease. We also observe in some instances peculiarities and symptoms which may to a large extent come from a general want of nutrition, or want of resistance in some cases, while in others, and especially in the terrier classes, they seem to be able to throw off the disease and stand more acute attacks than other animals. There are some forms of the disease which may be said to deviate from the regular course. These are as follows:

1. *Distemper with a Mild Termination.* In such cases we have a mild exanthema which may be difficult to recognize. A slight respiratory or intestinal catarrh. The duration of this mild form of the disease may be from half to one week.

2. *Distemper with Severe Termination.* In these cases we have for a long time separated the disease under the following divisions: "pulmonal," "nervous," "gastric," according to the acuteness with which the symptoms may appear in the respiratory tract, the nervous system, or the digestive apparatus.

3. *Acute Distemper with a Protracted Course.* Distemper lasts generally for two to three weeks, although we occasionally see cases where the disease is prolonged for a much longer period. In such case this prolongation is not due to the influence of the disease directly, but rather with secondary complications. We may count among these certain nervous diseases which frequently remain or appear after the disease has run its course. For instance, paralysis of some of the muscles, of the hind-quarters, or of all the extremities, and rhythmic movements resembling St. Vitus's dance; in some of the muscular groups, especially the muscles of the face or of the legs, and indicated by constant twitching, clonic in character, sometimes severer at one time than another, but more especially after excitement. Amaurosis (deafness) may occur in some cases.

PROGNOSIS. The prognosis of distemper, as a rule, should be regarded as unfavorable even in those cases which are apparently mild. Of course, the danger of the disease increases with the intensity of the symptoms, and especially if the symptoms are prolonged and with them a persistent high temperature, and even in cases where we have a subnormal temperature. Another series of cases which must be regarded as unfavorable are those which are in their course complicated by serious nervous symptoms, or by symptoms of catarrhal pneumonia. Young dogs which are delicate (especially when not fed on meat), anæmic, or rhachitic, will succumb to the disease sooner, and, as a rule, present severer symptoms than those which have been fed with meat and have had plenty of open-air exercise. A marked decrease of the temperature, without a similar improvement in the general condition, is always to be looked upon as an extremely serious symptom. Death may occur in two ways: through paralysis of the brain or œdema of the lungs, and occasionally from septicæmia or from general exhaustion. From the experience of the author, the death-rate is from 20 to 30 per cent. [The translator's experience does not admit of such a favorable percentage; he would say about 50 to 60 per cent.] It depends to a great extent whether there are a number of cases together or solitary cases—in the former the percentage is much higher; but at the same time it is impossible to give any positive statistics, because in cities the death-rate is much higher, and in small towns and in the country, where distemper runs a comparatively mild course, the death-rate is much smaller. The author finds that in a large city the death-rate amounts to 60 to 70 per cent.

PATHOLOGICAL ANATOMY. The most prominent and constant anatomical alterations found on the post-mortem are those in the respiratory and digestive organs. The lesions of the respiratory tract are as follows: The pituitary membrane is injected, infiltrated, and covered with a muco-purulent exudate; numerous ecchymosed spots are found on the membrane. The mucous membrane of the larynx, trachea, and bronchi shows various degrees of inflammatory alterations—the large bronchi are filled with bloody mucus, the smaller bronchi are filled with a thick, tenacious exudate; with this condition we frequently have evidence of lobular pneumonia; the tissue is firm, and gangrenous masses are found in the centre of the lobules. The pleura is covered with a rose or citron-colored exudate. The bronchial lymphatics are infiltrated and tumefied, and in rare cases purulent.

The lesions of the digestive tract are principally confined to the small intestine; the mucous membranes are red, and numerous ecchymosed spots are found, and decided hemorrhages in the submucous tissue. The follicles of the patches and solitary glands of Payer are tumefied, sunken in the inflamed mucous membrane, and superficial ulcerated spots are found over the entire length of the intestine (Nocard and Leclainche).

We find also more or less pathological alteration in the central nervous system, such as hyperæmia and small hemorrhages in the coverings of the brain; œdema of the brain is sometimes present, and serous infiltration into the subarachnoids. In the ventricles and base of the skull we have more or less marked venous hyperæmia, and in rare cases purulent meningitis. As a rule, the spinal cord shows nothing abnormal except that it is pale and seems soft and bloody in consistence.

Under the microscope decided changes have been noticed in the brain. Kolesnikoff detected an infiltration of brain-matter and walls of the brain-vessels with lymphoid cells, as well as a distention of the capillaries and arteries. These were filled with red and white blood-corpuscles. In the infiltrated walls of the vessels of the brain were found dark-colored, brittle, homogeneous granulations and accumulations. Krajewski found also the perivascular spaces and the ganglionic cells filled with lymphoid corpuscles, and he mentions particularly that those cases had died without showing any prominent nervous symptoms. Another observer found inflammation of the spinal cord in acute nervous distemper, in which there was marked hyperæmia. He also found alterations in the walls of the vessels, and an albuminous exudation in the upper third part of the spinal cord along the bloodvessels, as well as in the interstitial tissue of the gray substance. In "chronic" distemper we have found an interstitial myelitis with partial atrophy of the spinal cord. [The translator questions very much whether there is a condition that can truly be termed "chronic" distemper; if so, he has failed to observe it. The conditions that the author speaks of should more properly be called sequences of the disease.]

Other abnormal conditions are found in distemper, such as

anæmia, parenchymatous or fatty degeneration of the heart, liver, kidneys, and an abnormal swelling of the lymphatic glands

THERAPEUTICS. No special therapeutic treatment can be given for distemper—that is, no agent has been found up to this time which has the property of destroying or rendering harmless the specific micro-organisms present in this disease. Certain antiseptic and antibacterial remedies, like quinine, salicylic acid, antipyrine, etc., may generally reduce the fever, but they produce no influence on the general course of the disease. The use of agents for reducing the temperature is objectionable, as they deprive us of the symptom of temperature, which is of greatest importance during the course of the disease. According to Fröhner's experiments, calomel is supposed to have a slight claim as a universal agent, on the same order as black coffee, which was formerly advocated by Trasbot. Common salt has been recommended by Zippelius, and ergotin was highly recommended and frequently used a few years ago. All of these remedies, while they prove beneficial in some cases, are not to be laid down as a specific for the treatment of the disease, therefore we must continue to treat it in a purely symptomatic manner until it is possible to discover some specific which may be ultimately found in the altered products of the bacilli. Antipyrine, which has lately been advocated as an absolute specific, does not in the least deserve this recommendation. The diet must be easily digested food, but at the same time as nutritious as possible. Milk, bouillon, soup, and scraped raw meat (which is generally taken with a relish) have much to commend them. In grave cases where there is entire loss of appetite, we must use concentrated food, such as peptonized meat, extract of beef, and clear broth. This may be given with some mild alcoholic stimulant, wine, etc. There are some forms of extract of beef which are not to be recommended on account of their slight nutritive value, and containing a large proportion of sodium salts. When the temperature rises above 40° we must try to reduce it by means of cold compresses and mild antiseptics. It is best, however, not to try to reduce a normal increase of temperature, as this is necessary, as a rule, to restrict the growth of bacilli, or even impair their vitality, and in this way lessen or destroy their virulence. The nutritive medium upon which the bacteria have developed may possibly undergo some alteration, so that they can no longer multiply.

The "antipyretic" treatment can only be used in rare instances in the dog. The chief medicinal agents are quinine, salicylate of sodium, antifebrine, and antipyrine. The older remedies (digitalis, veratrum) have been abandoned for some time on account of their direct action on the heart. This is also the case with kairin, thallin, and phenacetin. The author, as a rule, does not advise the use of quinine on account of its action upon the heart. [The translator cannot agree with this.]

   R.—Antipyrine 1.0
   F. chart. No. v. S.—One powder in a little water twice daily.

   R.—Antifebrine 0.5
    Sacchar. alb. 1.0
   F. pulv. No. v. S.—One powder twice daily.

   R.—Ferri. et quininæ citratis 15.0
    Elixir simplex. 96.0
   S.—One teaspoonful three times daily.

Good, nutritive food and slight alcoholic stimulants, as a rule, produce good results. These assist in stimulating the digestive powers, preventing loss of tissue, and assist in reducing the temperature. Other therapeutic measures will have to be treated as the symptoms arise, and we would refer you to the Diseases of the Nose, Larynx, Bronchia, and Air-passages, also to those of the Stomach and Intestine, and lastly Diseases of Brain, Spinal Cord, and Eyes. As a rule, no treatment should be used for the skin eruption in distemper. If any irregularity arise, however, this may be treated according to the methods recommended under Diseases of the Skin.

Conjunctivitis is generally treated by a solution of sulphate of zinc (1 to 100), or painting the diseased membranes with a solution of nitrate of silver (1 to 70). This must be followed afterward by a 1 per cent. solution of chloride of sodium. "Blennorrhœa of the eyes" should be treated by bathing the parts with some antiseptic solution, such as creolin (1 to 100); corrosive sublimate (1 to 2000), or boric acid (1 to 40), or by painting the mucous membrane by means of a camel's-hair pencil with a 2 per cent. solution of sulphate of copper. Ulceration of the cornea should be treated with a 3 or 4 per cent. solution of boric acid. Parenchymatous keratitis may be treated with a few drops of a 1 to 100 solution of atropine. After the inflammatory symptoms of the eye have subsided blowing calomel directly on the cornea produces good results. [The translator finds it also useful in the early stages, when the ulcer is acutely inflamed.] In catarrh of the upper air-passages make the animal inhale vaporized solutions of creolin, carbolic acid, or infusions of calomel and tar-water. In catarrh of the lungs and lobular pneumonia we use expectorants, such as have been described under Diseases of the Lungs. Catarrh of the stomach is to be treated with opium, tannic acid, and creosote. In the acute nervous form of the disease we may produce good results with bromide of potassium, chloral hydrate, or subcutaneous injections of morphia, while motor paralytic symptoms should be treated with strychnia and electricity. In severe depression stimulants, such as ether and hypodermatic injections of camphor, may be used.

[Infectious Bronchial Catarrh.
(*False or Bench-show Distemper.*)

Within the last ten years bench shows have become a regular institution, and also where large kennels have increased in number the translator has frequently observed a disease that resembled canine distemper in a great many of its characters, but the general symptoms and course were such as to lead the observer to think that it is not the true contagious distemper, although it is decidedly infectious, and for a better name has called it "bench-show distemper" or "kennel distemper." Since making the translation he has noticed that the author has also felt that there may possibly be such a condition, and has intimated that fact under the head of Catarrh of the Bronchia (page 120).

ETIOLOGY. It is generally seen in large kennels, attacking one after another or several at once. It may also be observed where several dogs have been sent to a bench show, developing shortly after they return. The period of incubation is three to five days. Another peculiarity is that one attack does not insure immunity from another. The writer has observed several dogs that have developed this disease, and the next year repeat the attack after returning from a show.

PATHOLOGICAL ANATOMY. The lesions found are very similar

to those of true distemper, but milder in character. The alterations in the lungs are those of catarrhal pneumonia. The most frequent condition observed is great irritation of the mucous membrane of the intestines, with more or less swelling of the whole intestinal tract. The follicles and glands of the intestines may be swollen or enlarged, and in rare instances ulcerated, but not to the marked degree seen in distemper.

CLINICAL SYMPTOMS. The animal is dull and listless for two days, when the temperature will be found to be 39° or 40°; slight running from the eyes; and invariably diarrhœa. This last symptom is generally observed from the first, the stools being liquid the first few days, and later filled with gelatinous mucus. At the end of a week there may be some blood passed in the stools, but this is not commonly seen.

The appetite may be very poor or even lost, but generally in three or four days the animal will commence to eat, but stop again if the diarrhœa should be severe or eat very small quantities. Vomiting is rarely seen except at the onset.

The discharge from the nose and eyes is difficult to distinguish from distemper, except that it is thinner and muco-purulent. The cough is stronger, and not the soft, shallow cough observed in distemper. There is no rash on the skin, but the hair is dry and harsh, and frequently the hair falls out very rapidly in the long-coated dogs, especially collies.

The mouth very frequently becomes sore and the gums may ulcerate. In rare cases a series of aphthous ulcers are seen on the lips and around the free end of the tongue. This condition rarely causes death unless the diarrhœa is persistent and the animal will not eat; and any attempt at forced feeding is followed by vomiting.

In some cases shortly after the acute symptoms commence there may be evidences of congestion of the brain, accompanied by severe and continued convulsions, which frequently cause death.

The treatment is practically the same as in distemper. Keep the animals warm and dry, give easily digested food, lean meat, carefully removing all fat, and quinine, iron, and some of the pepsin preparations, and allow them to run if they are not too weak. Penning them up closely does harm.

℞.—Ferri et quininæ citras 12.0
　　Elixir simplex 96.0
S.—One teaspoonful three times daily.

If the diarrhœa is severe, give

℞.—Bismuth subgallate 0.75
F. charta No. xii. S.—One powder three times daily.]

Rabies.
(*Hydrophobia.*)

This is an acute disease of the entire nervous system caused by a specific poison, and distinguished by a variable period of incubation, as well as by an absence of any marked anatomical alteration.

ETIOLOGY. Rabies is a true infectious disease, and never occurs spontaneously, but is only transmitted by direct infection through the bite of affected animals. This disease, as a rule, is confined to the canine race (dog, wolf, fox, hyena, and prairie dog). It is seen in rare instances in the cat, horse, cattle, sheep, goat, deer, guinea-pig, rabbit, rat, mouse, chicken, pigeon, and in man. The dog is the animal that contracts the disease quicker than any other. Country, climate, care, nursing, age, and sex do not seem to have any influence upon it. The disease is more frequently seen in central Europe and the New England and Middle States than anywhere else. This may be accounted for by the fact that dogs in larger numbers run at large, and also to the fact that the owners do not conform to the rules of the sanitary police. Rabies seems to be influenced, to a certain extent, by the seasons of the year, as cases are more frequently seen in the spring and summer than in the fall and winter. The poison of rabies is as yet unknown, or at least it has not been definitely described. It is reproduced in the body of the animal only; never outside of it. It is mixed with blood, saliva in the salivary glands, and in the secretions of the lachrymal glands. It is also said to occur in the mammary glands. From direct inoculations, this disease appears in its most concentrated form in the brain and spine.

This poison is virulent in the spine and brain during the incubative period, and retains its full strength for several days after the death of the affected animal. Pasteur has demonstrated that a rabid brain loses its infectious virulence only when that part has become partially decomposed—that is to say, after four or five days; while it remains virulent in air-tight tubes or in moistened carbolic gauze. Neustube found that the brain of a rabid dog retained its virulent properties when kept under a slightly elevated temperature for ten or twelve days. Mergel found the virulence as strong as ever in the putrid brain of a rabid wolf fourteen days after the animal had been killed. Galtier noticed the same conditions in the decayed brain-substance of a rabid dog, when kept under a low temperature (12° Celsius). An affected brain was not rendered harmless even when exposed for three weeks at a time, but its virulence was attenuated when kept some time at 61° Celsius. Blumberg found that an affected brain is rendered harmless when it has undergone a freezing process at 20° or 30°. Galtier was able to destroy the virulence of affected cerebral matter in four to twenty days by placing it upon plates and allowing it to become dry. Saliva and blood are much less resistant than brain-matter. Both substances, as a rule, lose their harmful property twenty-four hours after leaving the animal.

As a rule, it is necessary to make a natural or artificial inoculation in order to obtain any successful transmission of the rabid poison, as no infection will take place if the inoculation is simply rubbed on the cutaneous or mucous membranes. The most common method, of course, is the bite of the rabid animals; more rarely, licking of a wound. In many cases the bite may not be severe enough to cause its development in dogs or in man. Deep bites, however, are certainly the most dangerous, especially when made on the unprotected parts of the body (hands and face in man). Wounds which bleed much are less dangerous, as the poison may be washed out of the wound by the flowing blood. Bites of dogs which have bitten numerous others are less dangerous than the first or second bite made by a rabid animal.

Infectious wounds which were made by biting or inoculation, according to Hertwig's observations, showed only 37 per cent. of positive results, and Renault's 67 per cent. Of 137 animals which were bitten by rabid dogs under observation for the last five years at the Veterinary College of Berlin, six only ultimately developed the disease. Zundel finds that about 25 per cent. of inoculated animals become affected, while Haubner found 40 per cent. At Alfort they have found the proportion to be about 33 per cent., and at Lyons 26 per cent. In man 50 per cent. of the bitten subjects develop the disease, but if we sum together the cases of true rabid and "suspected" dogs, the proportion is reduced to about 8 per cent.

It has not up to the present time been definitely determined that the disease can be transmitted through the medium of milk and meat, or by any other intermediate agents. The period of incubation between the time of the actual bite and the appearance of the disease is not as yet definitely fixed. This peculiar fact may be explained in different ways. Some have contended that there is a form of encysting of the poison in the inoculated region which takes place.

This is supported by the following facts: 1. That by a rapid destruction of the inoculated region, and even when this is performed some time after the bite, the disease may be prevented. 2. In animals and man there are a peculiar itching and swelling of the bitten cicatrix before the appearance of the true disease. This "encysting theory," however, is opposed by the observations of Galtier upon rabbits. These he inoculated in the ear with a rabic virus, and they afterward became affected with the disease, notwithstanding the fact that the ear was amputated three or four hours after inoculation.

Another explanation of the various lengths of the period of inoculation is the theory that a small amount of poison enters the body, and that this has to be reproduced according to the quantity inoculated until there is sufficient virus in the body to develop the disease. Pasteur has positively demonstrated that the period of inoculation is much longer when the amount inoculated is in very small quantities, and also in cases where the poison is very much weakened. The disease may not be developed at all. This theory, however, does not thoroughly explain the varying length of the period of incubation, and some observer may yet be able to give us a more thorough and reliable explanation.

The character of the rabic poison is as yet unknown. We have to accept the theory that it is a micro-organism, for Paul Bert was able to render the infectious material innocuous by filtering it through tablets of gypsum. Hallier claims to have found a micrococcus in the blood of rabid dogs and horses. Zürn, Frank, and

Bollinger obtained negative results. Pasteur has found fine granulations in the brains of rabid animals, which could be colored with aniline, and he is inclined to consider this as a specific organism of rabies, but he was not able to make any cultures from them. Chamberland and Roux noticed micro-organisms in the blood of rabid animals, which were shaped like fine network. Rabbits which had been inoculated with such cultures became very sick, but did not show any symptoms of rabies. Babes noticed in the brain and spinal cord of rabid subjects microbes which were crowded together, forming shiny granulations. These were colonies of diplococci or egg-shaped corpuscles which could be cultivated in blood-serum at 37°. Dodeswell found in the spine and medulla a coccus, and Rivolta noticed a "coccobacterium lyssæ." Aurep produced a very poisonous alkaloid with the brains of 100 rabbits (affected by furious rabies).

Notes on Pasteur's Methods of Vaccination. (Preventive Inoculation.) Within the last ten years Pasteur has made a series of very remarkable observations which have led him to recommend a special method of prophylactic inoculation of rabid virus. The observations which he made were as follows:

1. The rabid poison is most concentrated and purest in the brain and spine.

2. If the brain is the particular seat of the rabid poisoning, the affected animal has furious rabies. If the spine is affected the most, we see the quiet (or dumb) form of rabies.

3. After direct inoculation of rabic poison on the brain-surface, under the dura mater (intracranial inoculation), the disease appears much more rapidly than it does from cutaneous or subcutaneous inoculations. With direct brain inoculation the disease may appear in from six to ten days.

4. After cutaneous or subcutaneous inoculation of the poison the rabid symptoms appear after a much longer time, and seem to depend on the fact that the further the inoculated region is from the brain the longer it takes to develop the disease.

5. The disease appears more rapidly if the virus has been introduced directly into the circulation than cutaneously or subcutaneously. In the latter case it generally takes the form of quiet or dumb rabies.

6. A spontaneous cure of rabid inoculation may occur after the

appearance of the first symptoms of the disease, provided the first symptoms are extremely mild. We can never expect any good termination when the symptoms are very violent in the early stages of the disease. An injection of blood or saliva of a rabid animal into the veins does not, as a rule, terminate fatally, but at the same time it does not appear to protect an animal, in the future especially, if it is inoculated again under the dura mater with rabid virus.

7. The intensity of the poison may become very much modified by inoculation through the medium of other animals. The rabid poison loses its intensity if it is inoculated into monkeys. After a series of generations of inoculation through different monkeys, it is much weakened and does not produce rabies in dogs, either by subcutaneous or intracranial inoculation, but this " weakened " virus, if injected into the dog, renders the animal proof against further inoculations of the most active virus. On the other hand, rabid virus increases in intensity if it is inoculated from one rabbit to another, and the period of incubation is lessened until the disease shows itself positively in seven days. By experimental transmission over forty to fifty generations, Pasteur has obtained a fixed virus which has a constant and regular virulence. This he obtained from the rabbit's spine, and is even more intense than the rabic poisoning of a furious dog, and he was able to produce the disease from eight to ten days after inoculation.

8. If the brain and spinal cord are cut into small portions and mixed with fixed virus, and subjected to a careful and slow drying process under 20° Celsius, the infectious substance gradually loses its activity and becomes perfectly harmless at the end of fourteen days. We may thus obtain an inoculating substance which possesses varying degrees of intensity, and it is possible to inoculate animals with weakened virus, rendering them proof against direct inoculation from a rabid dog. This inoculation is made by means of a hypodermatic syringe directly under the abdominal muscles. After twelve or thirteen mild inoculations, each inoculation being increased in intensity, the subjects become proof against the inoculation of the disease in any form whatever. When Pasteur first made these inoculations, using the material in varying degrees of strength, and at periods which took at least ten days, he was able later on to make all the inoculations within twenty-four hours, making each inoculation two hours apart.

These observations within the last year or two have been proved correct by scientists in different parts of the world. Pasteur concludes from his observations that man may be protected against rabies by inoculation, and this is even possible when infection has already taken place. As is well known, Pasteur, before his death, applied this theory for some years upon inoculated people, and he stated that he reduced the mortality, which varied from 16 to 60 per cent., down to $\frac{1}{2}$ to 1 per cent. Similar results have been obtained in other institutions established in different parts of the world by following the same methods ordinarily practised by Pasteur. In the year 1888 they had 454 cases of patients inoculated by rabid animals, which were afterward treated with weakened virus, only 1 to $1\frac{1}{2}$ per cent. of which died.

Pasteur's system has been opposed by several authors. For instance, Frisch claims that it is impossible to prevent the development of rabies after infection by means of Pasteur's preventive inoculation, as the poison has reached the cranium, and it is too late to do anything. This opinion is indorsed by Amoroso and de Renzi; and Babes, after numerous experiments, arrived at the conclusion that it is very difficult to protect dogs from intracranial infection, even after following Pasteur's method. Nevertheless, we cannot but admit that there is great value in the experimental observations made by Pasteur; but, on the other hand, they still require a great deal of improvement to make them perfect. The method of obtaining the lymph is yet very primitive, and it has not been accepted by other countries as a method for general adoption. Pasteur's observations, however, have shown the way, and there is no doubt that in the future, with improved appliances and close observation, the disease may be prevented or cured with success, as we know that vaccination of splenic fever and tuberculosis belong to the same class, and they are still very incomplete.

Other vaccinating methods, like, for instance, Högyes's, who uses a virus which was weakened with 1 per cent. of a saturated solution of chloride of sodium, have been very little used.

PATHOLOGICAL ANATOMY. The post-mortem results are generally negative and vary in different animals, but, as rule, specific alterations are noticed. These are as follows:

Great emaciation with very distinct muscular rigidity and a rapid tendency to decay; collections of mucus upon all the natural orifices, such as the mouth, nose, and the prepuce; prominence of the cutaneous veins, which are found to be filled with thick, imperfectly clotted blood; redness and swelling of the mouth and mucous membranes. The throat is covered with a whitish-gray mucous exudation; intense inflammation of the glands of the pharynx; in some cases slight swelling and hyperæmia of the salivary glands. In the cavity of the throat and mouth we find foreign bodies, such as hair, straw, coal, wood, etc.; they may also be found in the œsophagus, which is frequently very red and covered with clammy, gray mucus. This condition is seen in the stomach which contains little or no food, but, as a rule, numerous indigestible objects of various kinds and sizes—straw, hair, wood, stones, or pieces of leather or rags. The mucous membrane is reddened and swollen, especially on the surface of its folds, and marked with hemorrhagic erosions. The intestine may be empty, or it may contain some of the foreign bodies. The mucous membrane of the pharynx is always very red, swollen, and covered with mucus in its anterior portions. These alterations are also seen in the trachea and the large bronchia. The lungs are, as a rule, filled with blood, but otherwise normal. In rare instances we find circumscribed centres or irritation due to foreign bodies being inhaled through the bronchial tubes. The heart and its envelope are generally normal. The inner surface of the pericardium may show hemorrhagic spots. The chambers of the heart, as well as the large bloodvessels, are filled with dark, imperfectly clotted blood. The liver and kidneys are hyperæmic. The spleen is always filled with blood, swollen, and occasionally streaked with hemorrhagic spots.

The condition of the brain and spine was formerly supposed to present some reliable indications of the disease, but, according to the investigations of the last few years, it cannot be said that they present any constant pathological alterations. They vary greatly, and in some cases may present nothing at all. We frequently find hyperæmia of the covering of the brain and spinal cord, accompanied by slight hemorrhages, and the brain and spinal matter itself contains more blood than usual and is in a more or less œdematous condition.

Kolesnikoff found on microscopic examination of the walls and neighboring vessels of the brain (of dogs which have died with rabies) an accumulation of lymphoid cells and extravasated red blood-corpuscles. Wassilieff observed also dull masses which were considered by Weller as peculiar fatty bodies present in rabies, while Czokor and others have demonstrated that these corpuscles are products of involution which are found in other animals in the normal state. He also found that these were entirely absent in the early stages of rabies. The accumulation of discolored cells and red corpuscles in the walls and perivascular chambers of the small bloodvessels indicates to a certain extent a condition which in rabies is of pathological importance. They are undoubtedly symptoms of inflammation. These changes vary in different cases. According to Czokor, it was noticed to a very slight degree in dogs affected with the furious form of rabies, but it was noticed to a marked degree as soon as the disease developed the dumb form (the perivascular spaces and their neighborhood were filled with leucocytes). Similar alterations have been noticed in other diseased conditions, such as chorea, tetanus, and meningitis.

CLINICAL SYMPTOMS AND COURSE. The period of incubation lasts in the majority of cases from three to five weeks. In very rare instances the disease may appear in one week. According to Haubner's observations upon nearly 200 dogs, in 83 per cent. of the cases the disease developed in two months; in 16 per cent. of the cases within three months; and in 1 per cent. four months, or even later. Zündel has calculated that in 264 dogs 1 per cent. became affected within twenty-four hours after being bitten; 11 per cent. between the second and third day; 33 per cent. between the fifteenth and thirtieth day; 19 per cent. between the thirtieth and forty-fifth day; 10 per cent. between the forty-fifth and sixtieth day; 16, 18, and 10 per cent. over three months. The longest period of incubation was observed by Leblanc; this case developed in 364 days. In the human race it is generally admitted that the average period of incubation is seventy-two days (this average covers over 510 cases).

During the period of incubation nothing abnormal may be observed in the affected animal, but Högyes, Babes, Ferré, and others have observed in rabbits which were inoculated with virus a slight increase of temperature on the fourth or fifth day, and Babes has noted that the time this fever is observed there are no nervous symptoms presented, the animals remaining healthy for weeks until finally the disease appears.

There are two forms of rabies—a furious and quiet (or dumb) form. Both forms are fatal.

Furious Rabies. This comprises three distinct stages, namely, the melancholic, the irritating, and the paralytic stage.

In the melancholic stage the dogs seem to change in their disposition. They are capricious, and at other times irritable or depressed. They show symptoms of anger, are easily excited, fretful, and rarely very affectionate. They soon show a tendency to gnaw or swallow indigestible substances. They refuse their usual food, or they may take such food as they have a special taste for. They will lick and gnaw in a greedy manner various objects, such as wood, coal, furniture, and eat straw, earth, stones, wood, blankets, and even their own feces. The sexual excitement is very much increased, and we see in the first stage an uncertainty in the gait and a weakness in the hind-quarters. After a short space of time, generally from one to three days, the second stage appears. This is the irritable or maniacal stage. This is characterized: 1. By a tendency to escape and run away; 2. By a great irritation and an inclination to bite animals, objects, or man; 3. By a strange alteration in the voice, or bark.

The inclination to run off is very marked. As soon as they get their liberty they will run about aimlessly, covering very much ground in a short space of time, and return in one or two days, showing every indication of great excitement or of having travelled long distances. During this condition they bite any object that comes in their way. Soon the delirium increases and they run around in an insane way, attacking and biting anything that is within their reach, snarling or biting all the time. As a rule, these cases do not tear or mutilate their own bodies, and, if they do, they generally bite the region of the wound where they were formerly bitten. In the first stage of the disease we have often noticed that they will lick and bite places where they have had wounds before. The patients snap frequently, as if they were catching flies, and, as a rule, will bite any animal or man that will come within their reach.

The biting and delirium are not constant, but appear after alternate periods of rest, followed by uncontrollable delirious attacks, especially if another dog should come near. These attacks may occur at intervals varying from one to four hours. The peculiar change in the voice is due to a paralysis of the vocal cords, and the sound of the bark is prolonged into a higher vocal sound, so that it makes a combination between a howl and a bark, which has been described by different authors as a "howling" bark. This is harsh and raw. Repugnance to water does not exist in the dog as in man, but toward the end of the second stage, from paralysis of the muscles of deglutition, we see great difficulty in swallowing, and very often see an animal pick up some indigestible object, attempt to swallow it, and, not succeeding, drop it from its mouth. Vomiting sometimes occurs. There is great difficulty in defecation, which seems to produce evident pain. There is very little alteration in respiration, but it may be slightly increased. The pulse is increased; the temperature also rises, but falls toward the end of the disease.

The duration of the second stage, which does not always present all of the characteristic symptoms, may last from two to four days. After the paroxysms have increased in intensity and the intervals between them grow shorter the paralytic, or last, stage begins. The animals rapidly become emaciated; the eyes are staring, dull, and the eyeball is retracted into the skull. The conjunctiva is generally hyperæmic; the hair is erect; and we begin to see symptoms of paralysis. As a rule, the first sign of this is a paralysis of the muscles that close or raise the lower jaw. This allows the saliva to run out of the corners of the mouth and form threads which hang down, and we easily recognize the fact that the tongue and lower jaw have lost their power. The tongue becomes lead-colored and hangs out of the mouth. Soon we see paralysis of the posterior extremities. This begins with a staggering, unsteady gait, and finally total inability to use the posterior half of the body. Then the animals stretch themselves out and become completely paralyzed, or in the last stage we may see convulsions, but that is very rare. Death, as a rule, occurs in the fifth to the seventh day after the onset of the disease. In rare instances it may last ten days.

The **quiet or dumb form of rabies**, according to Bollinger, comprises about 15 to 20 per cent. of all cases. [The translator thinks that the average given of this form of rabies is entirely too small, and should be at least 60 per cent., the great majority of cases observed being the dumb form.] This is distinguished from furious rabies by the fact that the irritating or nervous symptoms are less marked, and in very rare cases entirely absent, also that the paralytic symptoms appear rarely in the disease. First we see paralysis of the muscles of the lower jaw. The mucus or saliva runs out of the opened mouth, and an inclination to bite is entirely absent, although under certain conditions when the mouth is forcibly opened the animal will be able to bite. The voice is also changed, but it is very rarely heard. We see a loss of appetite, the animal being unable to seize or swallow foreign bodies. In this quiet form the three stages follow very closely on each other, the course of the disease being very rapid, and death, as a rule, appears in two or three days, never over five.

The diagnosis of rabies may be complicated by certain conditions present, due to other diseases. This is especially noticed in the mild form and in well-trained, affectionate animals which obey their masters to the last. [The translator knows of two instances in which the English setter was under complete control; hunted in the field, obeying whistle and call instantly, and at the same time had every symptom of dumb rabies.] Often we see cases where the history is either insufficient or the owner can give none at all. On the other hand, in the furious form, a history, as a rule, is not required, as the disease can be constantly recognized from the appearance of the animal. Great excitement and restlessness, a tendency to escape, biting and delirious actions, rapid emaciation, and debility are characteristics of the furious form of this disease, while great depression and paralysis of the lower jaw are characteristic of the dumb form. In both forms there is a great inclination to gnaw objects. Sexual desire, in the early stage, is prominent. A depraved appetite and altered bark; more or less rapid symptoms of paralysis, and the cases being invariably fatal. The post-mortem confirms the disease when we find acute hyperæmia of the throat, pharynx, and mucous membrane, hemorrhagic erosions, and foreign bodies, etc., in the stomach. In doubtful cases the disease can only be accurately diagnosed by vaccination—that is to say, by the injection of small quantities of brain or spinal substance which have been diluted with distilled water. This should be injected into the dura mater of a dog or rabbit after it has been trephined. The operation is easily performed, and is especially valuable when the suspected animal may have bitten not only other dogs, but man. As this inoculation from the spinal matter of a suspected dog takes at least two or three weeks, the persons bitten should not delay, while waiting for development, but all measures should be taken as soon as possible.

Another method of vaccination for diagnostic purposes is recommended by Nocard and others, and is used at Alfort at the present time. This consists of making a solution of the spinal matter of the suspected animal in distilled water. The emulsion which is thus obtained is filtered through a piece of linen and brought in contact with the anterior chamber of the eye of the animal which is to be inoculated. They do this by means of a small hypodermatic syringe, having first placed cocaine on the cornea, and then inject the solution directly into the anterior chamber. If the suspected animal was rabid, we will see the development of the disease in from fourteen to seventeen days, even if the chamber should suppurate from the irritation of the injected solution. Gal opposes this procedure by pointing out the fact that the stage of incubation may be greatly delayed. According to Di Vestæ and Zagari, the inoculation of the rabbit is more reliable than dogs or guinea-pigs, and it is much more certain when a direct inoculation is made on the dura mater. He also proposes that a small cutaneous wound can be made, exposing a nerve-trunk, and the rabic poison placed in contact with the cut end of the nerve.

The following diseases are sometimes mistaken for rabies: Certain affections of the brain, teething, distemper, angina, intestinal parasites, inflammation of the intestines, pentastoma in the nose and frontal cavities, foreign bodies in the mouth (between the teeth) or in the throat, paralysis of the lower jaw, luxation of the lower jaw, intense excitement in bitches that have had their young taken from them, and poisoning. The course of the disease, however, and the after-symptoms always enable one to make a differential diagnosis. Concerning the prophylactic measures, which are of great importance, relating to the prevention of the spread of this disease (that is, muzzling, taxing, etc.), we must limit ourselves to the publication of the German law on the subject, as follows:

Dogs or any domestic animals which are suspected of rabies must be killed immediately by their owners or keepers, or kept safely locked up until the arrival of the police.

No attempts at medication of suspected animals may be made before obtaining the consent of the police officials.

It is forbidden to sell or use any portion of a suspected animal, or, if it is a cow, to consume its milk.

If the existence of rabies is established in a dog, the animal must be destroyed at once, as well as all dogs, cats, or other animals which are suspected of being bitten. If any other domestic animals are suspected, they must immediately be placed under police observation.

If they show any symptoms of rabies, they have to be destroyed at once.

In exceptional cases suspected dogs may remain under observation and confinement for a period of three months. This, however, is left to the judgment of the police officials, provided the owner of the animal is willing to bear the expense.

If a rabid animal has been running loose, the police authorities of that district must see that all dogs therein shall be muzzled, or held by a leash, for at least three months. If any dogs are allowed to run about loose during that period, the police have instructions to kill them at sight.

The cadavers of dead, or killed rabid subjects, must immediately be burned, and no animal suspected of this disease shall be skinned, or any portion of its hide retained.

Instructions of the Veterinary Congress of February 24, 1881. The stables and other premises in which rabid animals have been kept, as well as the utensils and other objects with which the animals may have come in contact, must be disinfected according to rules and regulations. Vehicles and other means of transportation which have been used for the removal of dead animals must undergo the same cleansing. Straw and the kennels of dogs must be burnt.

Disinfection must be made according to the direction of the official veterinarian and under police supervision.

The owner or keeper of the premises must satisfy the authorities that these orders are obeyed without delay.

The official veterinarian must send his report to the police department certifying that the above orders were executed to the letter.

Tuberculosis.

Under this name we class all affections which owe their origin to a peculiar specific bacteria known as "tubercle bacilli." These are found in all tubercular deposits in man or in animals, whether they occur spontaneously or are inoculated. Under the microscope they appear in the shape of very thin tube-like casts, showing a certain activity of movement. They multiply by means of transverse sections, and under certain conditions oval-shaped spores form in the body, which ultimately develop new bacilli. The tubercle bacilli should be considered as true parasites which multiply and live in the body only, but they also seem to possess the property of living outside of the body for a certain length of time, as the excretions of consumptives can be used successfully in inoculating animals, after having been dried for several weeks. We therefore conclude that tuberculosis is only produced by infection, or a better term would be transmission of tubercle bacilli from one subject to another.

While it is well known that tuberculosis of man and of certain domestic animals, such as cattle, is very common, it is rather rare in dogs. They seem to possess more power of resistance and are able to throw off the disease. [In the last three years the translator has seen a great number of cases of tuberculosis, and has been surprised to find such a large number, especially in fine-bred animals, and in a number of instances could trace the cause of the disease directly to women that were affected with tuberculosis, and had the animals as pets; in one instance a woman had three dogs; one after the other died with symptoms of the disease, which was confirmed on the post-mortem of two of them.]

Certain experiments by inoculation and inhalation have demonstrated the fact that one-third of the cases develop the disease, and the feeding of tubercular matter in the food invariably produced negative results. Considering the rarity of this disease in the dog, we will not give any detailed explanation of any length concerning its etiology, pathological anatomy, etc.

ETIOLOGY AND PATHOLOGICAL ANATOMY. A number of observers agree in the fact that, as a rule, an animal affected with tuberculosis has been at some time near or in the vicinity of some person who was in an advanced stage of consumption. In one case, particularly, which was observed by the author, the affected dog had been an inseparable companion of a woman who had died of phthisis. In another, the dog had frequently licked the expectorations of a man in the last stages of consumption. In such cases the bacilli may be introduced in the form of fine dust and be respired into the lungs, or they may be taken up by the intestines, finding their way into the bowels mixed with food. In one case which the author observed there were tuberculous ulcers in the parotid region, and also tubercular deposits in the lymphatic glands of the neck. It is demonstrated that it is possible to absorb the poison through the skin. The disease appears in the dog in the form of an acute or local tuberculosis. The disease may be found in the lungs, the mesenteric glands, the intestines, liver, kidneys, and peritoneum, and in rare instances affecting the entire body. This has been shown by post-mortems made by a number of observers, and especially by Jensen. He has made post-mortems of twenty-eight tuberculous dogs, and in nine cases he found the lungs involved. In the same cases he found accumulations of miliary tubercles. These masses were scattered and were of a cheesy character. The tubercular mass varied in size between that of a millet-seed and a bean. In two cases he found collections as big as an egg which had undergone slight degeneration in their centres. In some cases tuberculosis has taken the form of lobular pneumonia, separating certain sections in the lungs. In these cases cheesy masses of tubercular matter were generally found. The hepatized tissue of the lungs often breaks down, and large sections of the lungs remain, while the broken-down portion is coughed up, leaving a series of irregular, cavernous spaces, frequently hollow and at other times filled with pus-like masses. In one case they were directly against the large bronchia, although this condition, as a rule, is rare. In nearly 50 per cent. of all cases the lymphatic glands of the thorax, especially the bronchial glands and the glands which are located above and behind the mediastinum, are invariably infected to a marked degree with tubercular deposits, and are found to be very often enlarged, forming large tumor-like masses. These consist of a lardaceous tissue and generally contain a centre cavity filled with a cheese-like mass. True cheesy tuberculosis is rather rare in the dog, but, on the other hand, we have a peculiar process of absorption of the tissues, forming white masses, which on examination are found to be tuberculous deposits, or have undergone fatty degeneration.

When the process of breaking down, or disintegration, has gone on to any marked degree, the tuberculous mass forms a tumor-like body containing in its centre a whitish fluid held in fibrinous tissue. This was noticed in 50 per cent. of the cases observed in the dog where the lymphatic glands had undergone this degeneration. In the other half of the cases the serous membranes of the abdominal cavities were covered with tubercular masses, the pleura being the most common seat of the disease. In the majority of cases of pleural tuberculosis it takes the form of what is known as the "pearl" tubercular masses. These are known to be deposits of soft connective tissue, of numerous conglomerating granulations, or in large round tumors. In some cases there is extensive exudative inflammation present (sero-fibrinous and purulent pleuritis). Two cases of tubercular inflammation were found in the pericardium, and a very peculiar alteration of the mediastinum has been observed in several cases. This part was changed into a large, thick, partially folded, or twisted leaf-like body. This consisted of tubercular tissue with tubercular masses in enormous quantities lying on its surface. The heart, as a rule, rarely presents any tubercular formations. In the digestive organs the lymphatic glands of the head and neck are rarely invaded; also the submaxillary and retro-pharyngeal were only noticed to be affected in one case. On the other hand, the mesenteric glands were particularly affected, some cases presenting large tumor-like masses containing broken-down centres.

Tuberculosis of the Intestines. Tuberculosis of the intestines is rare, and is restricted to slight ulcerations or abscesses. The liver, as a rule, is generally involved to a marked degree, its substance being filled with small knots, also large granular masses which are milky white in color. In the centre of these is found a broken-down opaque fluid, the result of fatty degeneration. The spleen was only noticed to be tubercular in two cases, and that only to a slight degree. The kidneys are frequently the seat of more or less tubercular deposits, and in twelve cases scattered granulations were found in the spinal and membranous substance, but cheesy abscesses and centres were also found. These were accompanied by chronic indurative nephritis. Ulceration of the pelvis of the kidney was observed in one case. One dog showed but a slightly tubercular ureter and bladder. The sexual organs are, as a rule, found healthy and very rarely attacked by the disease. In rare instances a tubercular testicle is noticed.

Tuberculosis of the prostate has been observed in two cases by Cramer. The same author observed a tubercular ovary in one case.

CLINICAL SYMPTOMS AND COURSE. On account of the various ways in which tuberculosis appears, no positive line of symptoms can be made. Tuberculosis of the lungs only will show marked symptoms, especially if it has made considerable progress, and is very similar to chronic catarrh of the lungs or chronic lobular pneumonia (see this disease). There are rapid emaciation, notwithstanding a good appetite, and a quick loss of strength, to suspicion tuberculosis of the lungs. We can only be positive of our diagnosis by recognizing tubercle bacilli within the secretions, although it is very difficult to obtain such.

Ehrlich advises that the observer place the secreted matter in a very thin layer upon a covered plate, and allow it to dry in the open air. When this is done pass the glass three times slowly over the flame of a gas- or alcohol-lamp. Then place it in a watch-glass which contains a colored solution of sputa. This can be prepared previously in a small reagent-glass, in which we mix six parts of water and one part of aniline, then filter. The filtered liquid is placed in the watch-glass and diluted with six or eight drops of concentrated alcoholic solution of fuchsine. The covered glass with the dried sputa must be left as long as possible, say twenty-four hours, in this coloring solution, or it may be heated, but not to the boiling-point. Then it has to be left standing ten or fifteen minutes, and after that the covering should be removed. This is then quickly washed in water and placed for a short time (six or seven seconds) in a solution of one part of nitrate of sodium to three parts of water, and the agent again thoroughly washed. This preparation is now ready for examination.

The tubercle bacilli will be found to be colored intensely red, and the rest of the material is either colorless or a very dull red. Another method is to place, for a short time (one or two minutes), some sputum in a watery solution of Bismarck brown. This renders the bacilli still more distinct. Other coloring methods are known, but the reader is advised to follow the above method, as it is the best.

M. Tempel, of Dresden, injected Koch's tuberculin into two apparently healthy dogs, and in one dog which was affected with the pulmonal form of distemper, doses from 0.006 to 0.1, without observing any rise of temperature. The post-mortem of the dogs, which were killed some time later, showed no tuberculosis present.

[There have been a number of suspected animals inoculated at the University of Pennsylvania, and in all the cases that afterward proved to be affected with the disease the reaction was most pronounced, rising to 40° and 41°.]

Tuberculosis of any of the abdominal organs is very difficult to recognize. The only way we might succeed is by pressure, or manipulation, of the abdominal cavity, recognizing swollen lymphatic glands or some external manifestation of this in this region. We find, however, great emaciation and symptoms of chronic catarrh of the intestinal tract. These last two symptoms would be sufficient to make us suspect intestinal tuberculosis. In one case of tubercular ulceration of the intestines which was observed by the author, the dog was very thin and had shown this for some time. There were also present symptoms of catarrh of the lungs upon the upper portion of the neck and a deep abscess was formed. This was quite large and contained numerous masses of thin pus. In the region of the neck near the abscess we observed a granular mass, the size of a chestnut. This could be pushed under the cutaneous membrane and moved about freely. There were also present a few enlarged lymphatic glands in the upper portion of the neck.

THERAPEUTIC TREATMENT. When you have once established the fact that the animal is affected with the disease, it is the duty of the veterinarian to warn the owner of a tubercular or suspected dog of the danger of infection, and advise him to destroy the animal. The successful treatment of this disease is as yet unknown. It may be that Koch's inoculating method will produce favorable results, but up to the present date nothing positive has been done. Koch's lymph or tuberculin has been tried thoroughly, and while it has no apparent value in curing the disease, it has fairly established itself as a reliable diagnostic agent.

Anthrax.

Anthrax is quite rare in the dog, and when it occurs it is generally caused by the animal eating portions of cadavers of animals that have had this affection. All forms of anthrax have been observed in the dog, but generally the seat of the disease is in the mouth and throat and in the intestines. Therapeutic treatment is useless on account of the rapid progress of the disease. Concerning sanitary laws, the following apply to this disease:

Animals which suffer from or are suspected of anthrax cannot be slaughtered for consumption.

Any operation that will cause bleeding in an animal suspected of anthrax can only be performed under the supervision of the official veterinarian.

All cadavers of animals which are affected or suspected of having anthrax must be rendered harmless by burning the cadavers. Skinning the animal is strictly forbidden.

CONSTITUTIONAL DISEASES.

Anæmia; Chlorosis.

By anæmia we mean a lessening or thinning of the blood. This is especially noticeable after great hemorrhages. At the same time much greater importance must be placed on that condition of the blood where it contains a very small quantity of albumin, and where the number of red blood-corpuscles is very much decreased. This is the most important form of anæmia.

Etiology. The disease occurs frequently in young, delicate animals of the improved or closely bred classes. It seems to be hereditary in some of these animals, and may depend to a certain extent on the defective development of the arterial system and an abnormally small heart. Anæmia occurs most frequently from the lessening in quantity of the vital fluids, such as the albuminous, or after a large or long-continued slight hemorrhage; from prolonged suppuration in chronic, persistent diarrhœa; chronic inflammation of the kidneys; and lastly a want of proper nutrition—for instance, young animals in a poor condition should be fed on meat. Very often impaired digestion prevents an absorption of certain nutritive substances in chronic disease, in fever, etc.

Clinical Symptoms. The symptoms of the disease consist in a reduction of the coloring elements of the blood and a general condition of debility, showing every indication of loss of blood. The skin and visible mucous membranes are very pale in color. The animals are easily fatigued and have a draggy way of walking; the pulse is often small and generally rapid. The temperature in many cases is below normal, in other cases it may be normal or even higher. The respiration is increased with the pulse, and especially after very slight physical exercise. Reflex excitability of the brain in anæmic subjects is increased to such an extent that the animal will go into convulsions at the slightest provocation. Impaired digestion is a frequent symptom and naturally assists in complicating the disease. It is generally chronic, but proper treatment will often produce very good results.

THERAPEUTIC TREATMENT. The treatment must all tend to one object—that is, the formation of more blood. This may be obtained by proper hygienic measures, feeding with light, easily digested substances, especially meat (not milk, which does not agree with the animals for any length of time), as well as medicinal substances—that is to say, ferruginous preparations. Among the latter, carbonate of iron, saccharated oxide of iron, and lactate of iron. These should be given in 0.4 to 0.5 gramme three times daily. Tincture chloride of iron, 10 to 20 drops daily. In many cases these iron preparations do not agree well with the patients, as the drug irritates the stomach and their appetite becomes impaired. These preparations should have some vegetable tonic added to them, the bitter principle stimulating digestion and counteracting the irritant effect of the iron. A very useful preparation in this disease is citrate of quinine and iron. This preparation is valuable not only for the iron it contains, but the tonic properties of the quinine, and also the very slight tendency it has to disorder the stomach. Frequently arsenic is useful as a general tonic.

Leukæmia.

This disease is one that is characterized by an alteration of the blood, due to the presence of an increased quantity of white blood-corpuscles which must be due to some disorder of the lymphatic organs. The pathological anatomist distinguishes two conditions in the affected lymphatic—a lienal and myelogenic form—according to the origin of the disease: the spleen or the marrow of the bones. This, however, is of no special value to the practitioner, as both of these forms, as a rule, are combined in the dog, as in other domestic animals. The myelogenic form has never been observed alone (Siedamgrotzky and others).

ETIOLOGY. The causes of this disease are not definitely known at present. In the human race we find that middle-aged men are mostly affected with this disease; in the dog, the middle or advanced period of age seems to show the greatest tendency, but young animals frequently show very acute cases. This disease was observed in 1878 by Siedamgrotzky. From his own statistics with those of many physicians he was inclined to consider leukæmia an infectious disease. Attempts to produce the disease by transfusion of leukæmic blood in healthy animals always gave negative results. The same observer saw two cases of secondary leukæmia. In both there was a virulent catarrh of the prepuce. This soon produced a swelling of the glans and of the lymphatic glands in its immediate neighborhood. This is accompanied by a marked increase in the white blood-corpuscles.

PATHOLOGICAL ANATOMY. The most important alteration always observed in this disease is an increase of white blood-corpuscles in the blood. This may become so great (in the dog) that we find the proportion of white to red blood-corpuscles is 1 to 5 (Bollinger). We find in this "leucocythæmia" the blood possesses a much lighter color than it does normally. We also notice a great tendency to emaciation and a characteristic alteration of the spleen, lymphatic glands, and the marrow. This alteration is especially found in the spleen, which is very much enlarged in all directions, and is also increased proportionately in weight. It is not rare to find it weighing at least 1000 grammes, and in among the sections marks of true hyperplasia. We also see at times circumscribed hyperplasia of the spleen in dogs. As a rule, the lymphatic glands are enlarged, and in other cases very slightly. This is caused by a hyperplasia of the glandular tissues. The marrow of the bones is occasionally involved and appears dark red. In serious cases the color is yellowish-gray, becoming soft and plastic. In very rare cases hyperplasia is seen in other organs, such as the tonsils, liver, and lungs.

CLINICAL SYMPTOMS AND COURSE. The symptoms of the disease are similar to those of intense anæmia. First, there is a characteristic alteration of the blood, and, second, the symptoms presented by the spleen and lymphatic glands. In mild cases a microscopic examination and counting the number of blood-corpuscles will insure a diagnosis. The best way to obtain a small quantity of blood for the purpose of making an examination is to make a slight slit in the upper surface of the outside of the ear. Place it under the microscope without adding any other substance to it, and we will recognize not only an enormous increase in the number of white blood-corpuscles, but a difference in their normal size.

While we may be able to correctly diagnose the disease from the condition of the blood during life, we may also notice certain alterations in the size of the spleen and lymphatic glands. In the glands of the head and neck we may find considerable enlargement, as is also the case with the testicles. It is somewhat hard to really detect an abnormal enlargement of the mesenteric lymphatic glands; while tumors of the spleen may occasionally be detected by manipulation, it is only when they have reached a very much enlarged condition (Fig. 58). Various observers have mentioned other symptoms, such as increase of the pulse (130 to 140 per minute); loss of appetite; the buccal mucous membrane is red and inflamed, and the tongue is coated. In rare instances, diarrhœa and dropsical symptoms may be present. The disease is generally chronic, and death may occur after several months as the result of total exhaustion.

FIG. 58.

The blood in leucocythæmia.

THERAPEUTIC TREATMENT. The agents generally used by physicians in the treatment of this affection are iron, quinine, iodine, and bromine, but, as a rule, none of these produce favorable results. Arsenic seems to have answered better than any of the others, and is, therefore, to be recommended for dogs. Besides the disease just described, we have a condition which is very rarely seen in a dog—"pseudo-leukæmia." In this condition we see exactly the same hyperplasia of the lymphatic glands as in true leukæmia, but there is no increase in the white blood-corpuscles (Fröhner). One case which was observed by the author was that of an old setter dog which showed considerable hyperplasia of the lymphatic glands of the neck and trunk; also acute anæmia. There was not any enlargement of the spleen or the lymphatic glands of the abdominal cavity.

Diabetes Mellitus.

ETIOLOGY. By diabetes mellitus we understand a peculiar abnormal condition of the urine which contains a large quantity of sugar. The true cause of this peculiar disease is not exactly known, but from observations which have been made on dogs and other animals it is supposed to be due to a partial paralysis of the vasomotor nerves going to the liver—"glycosuria." The same results may be produced by certain poisons—coal-gas, amyl nitrite, prussic acid, and in some cases it is produced by morphia and chloral hydrate. Another peculiar condition is also seen in cases of concussion of the brain, fracture of the skull, and epilepsy, in which sugar may be found in large quantities in the urine as a result of this disease. Some observers have noticed it in true infectious diseases, such as distemper.

CLINICAL SYMPTOMS AND COURSE. The author has not been able to find any sugar (grape-sugar) in the urine of dogs, notwithstanding the fact that he has made a large number of tests. According to our text-books, the symptoms of diabetes are as follows: Depression, dulness, great emaciation, in spite of the fact that the animal has an enormous appetite; there is increased thirst, and the animal passes an ordinary amount of urine with a high specific gravity, containing from 7 to 12 per cent. of sugar. (The method used for the detection of sugar in urine will be found under Examination of Urine.) In many cases cataract may develop in both eyes, causing total blindness. In other cases the hair falls out; chronic bronchial catarrh, phthisis of the lungs, persistent diarrhœa, and some have noticed an ulceration of the skin and cornea.

The course of the disease is gradual; emaciation and debility increase until finally the animal sinks into a deep coma, accompanied, as a rule, with convulsions, and finally death. The prognosis in all cases should be unfavorable.

THERAPEUTICS. The treatment of diabetes consists of feeding the animal on food which does not contain any carbon, or as little as possible. This may be accomplished to a certain extent by a meat-diet, and even this diet cannot be followed up for any great length of time.

Diabetes Insipidus.

This form of diabetes is extremely rare in the dog [the translator has been fortunate enough to have observed six cases in the last ten years], as we find but one case of this disease described in veterinary literature (Holzmann). In this disease we have an abnormal increase of the urine without the presence of any sugar. It is more frequently found in young than in old animals, and may be ascribed to be due to some disease of the nervous system. Claude Bernard has demonstrated that simple polyuria (without sugar) may be produced on a certain location on the left side of the brain, immediately in front of the diabetic centre. Peyrani was able to obtain the same effect by intersection of the splanchnic nerve, and by an irritation of the sympathetic nerve of the neck. Kahler produced polyuria in rabbits by injecting a solution of nitrate of silver into the medulla oblongata. In man this disease occurs very frequently in those cases where brain-tumors, meningitis, encephalitis, and concussion or injury of the brain is present. This disease is frequently seen in man without any apparent cause, and may be frequently found in the dog, and should be observed, as was proved in Holzmann's case. The dog shown to him was three years old, having a pale mucous membrane and rectal temperature of 38°. This animal drank 12.76 c.c. of water daily, and passed about 12.760 c.c. of urine. The urine was yellowish, had a weak acid reaction, its specific gravity was 1.006, and contained nothing abnormal. On post-mortem nothing of any great consequence was found, except a myxoma hyalinum, which appeared in the shape of a yellowish, transparent, coagulated mass between the periosteum and the dura mater, entirely surrounding the spine with the exception of a small portion of the neck. There was also some hyperæmia and slight bleeding in the gray substance of the lumbar region. Five elongated osteoid sarcoma masses were found pressing on the dura mater. Holzmann could not decide which of these conditions was the true cause of the disease. [Of the translator's cases the disease followed recovery from distemper in three of them, two had no definite history, and one had an enormously enlarged thyroid gland. All the cases passed large quantities of urine so pale that it could only be said to be tinted with yellow; the reaction was not taken; the mucous membranes were pale and blanched, especially the inside of the lips and tongue, which was yellowish-white. The appetite was good, and it was noticed that bread and rice aggravated the condition, whereas meat seemed to lessen the amount. They drank large quantities of water, and gradually became thin, with the exception of one which kept in fairly good condition. One recovered and two died; three were lost sight of. On holding a post-mortem in two there was nothing particular found, except the mucous membranes of the body were very pale and anæmic; the liver was enlarged in both cases, and in one there was a greatly enlarged thyroid gland, which was a sarcoma. The treatment consisted of belladonna and iodide of potassium.]

The therapeutic treatment of diabetes in man consists of a meat-diet, open-air exercise, suppression of all physical or nervous excitement, small doses of opium, belladonna, valerian, and ergotin.

Obesity.

ETIOLOGY. This disease is due to the absorption of large quantities of hydrate of carbon, and also to a lack of proper exercise, and in some cases as a consequence of improper oxidizing processes in the body. It may also be hereditary in some cases. This disease is especially seen in lap-dogs or pet animals, and is also noticed in bitches after ovariotomy and in dogs that have been castrated.

CLINICAL SYMPTOMS. The common location of fatty deposits is in the panniculus adiposus, around the region of the abdomen, and surrounding the internal organs—for instance, in the mediastinum, the pericardium, and the capsule of the kidneys. The circumference and weight of the body increase very much, and round prominences form in different parts of the body, especially the neck, shoulders, back, and hips. The abdomen is round and distended. The animals are lazy, dull, awkward, and tired on the slightest physical exertion. When this condition becomes very marked, and there is a large deposit of fat in different parts of the body, especially when it has accumulated in the thorax and neighborhood of the heart, we have a lessened heart-action and more or less difficulty in respiration, sometimes from the pressure of quantities of fat on certain bloodvessels, decreasing their size and thus requiring greater effort of the heart's action, until finally the heart becomes overtaxed, and we have symptoms of heart-failure, bronchitis, chronic catarrh of the stomach, and œdema.

THERAPEUTIC TREATMENT. The following causes which produce fat in the body must be understood, so that we may be able to properly treat the animal:

1. The source of fatty deposits may be due to albuminous or carbonaceous substances, or to fat itself. The nutritive fat, if not taken up, is deposited in the fat-cells of the body.

2. Albumin is a factor in the formation of fat in the animal, while carbonaceous substances are very easily digested, and prevent a disintegration of reabsorbed fat which comes directly out of the food and favors its accumulation.

3. Hydrate of carbon and fat may act as substitutes, so that an animal eating albumin and fat, or albumin and carbon hydrate, may become fat.

4. A purely fat or hydrate of carbon diet cannot sustain the body for any length of time. In the first case it gains fat but loses flesh; in the latter it loses flesh and also fat. A pure lime-diet is also insufficient, although it has been demonstrated that lime may replace to a certain extent albuminous substances in the food.

5. A dog can be kept in this abnormal fat condition when fed on lean meat or when he is given large quantities of fat (one-twentieth to one-twenty-fifth of his own weight daily); but if a fat dog receives less meat than the quantity mentioned above, he will lose flesh.

From the above indications it will be seen that, besides medical treatment, we have two ways of reducing obesity:

1. By reducing the quantity of fat. 2. By feeding with lean meat. The choice of the method employed is left to the practitioner. The author's experience has been that both are practicable, and must be applied according to circumstances. As a rule, the first method should be tried, as it generally corresponds with the owner's ideas. The animal should be weighed from time to time, as this is the only way in which we may ascertain whether the treatment is producing the desired effect.

The animal must also be exercised regularly, as muscular exercise increases the destruction and use of fat in the body. It also increases the heart-action, the heart-muscles thus becoming strengthened and the circulation improved.

A method employed by a number of practitioners is similar to that followed in man, viz., suppressing as much as possible the use of all fluids. This, however, is hardly practicable in dogs, as the only fluid they drink, as a rule, is water, and, if this treatment is carried to any extent, it is actual cruelty. The pilocarpine treatment might be useful. According to experiments made by various authors, subcutaneous injections of pilocarpine were found to produce good effects (0.006 of pilocarpine daily); but this must be used very carefully, as in old, fat dogs we frequently find a chronic bronchitis, and from the increased respiration and amount of fluids thrown out by the lungs it may produce death by suffocation. Sulphate of magnesium and sulphate of sodium are useful to increase the action of the intestines and to carry away a certain quantity of fluid out of the body. They should be given on an empty stomach, a teaspoonful at a dose, diluted in a small quantity of warm water.

Hæmoglobinæmia and Hæmoglobinuria.

When there is any decomposition of red blood-corpuscles in the body (hæmoglobinæmia) the coloring substance is eliminated through the kidneys, staining the urine and producing hæmoglobinuria. These conditions occur as the result of the action of certain chemical poisons, such as large doses of naphthol, chloride of potassium, carbolic acid, and by certain infectious, poisonous substances, transfusion of blood, and sterilized water. Influences of extremes in temperature also produce it. In this condition the urine is characterized by a dark red, brownish, or brick-red coloration, and when examined through the spectroscope shows streaks, α and β, of the hæmoglobin in yellow and green (Fig. 59), and

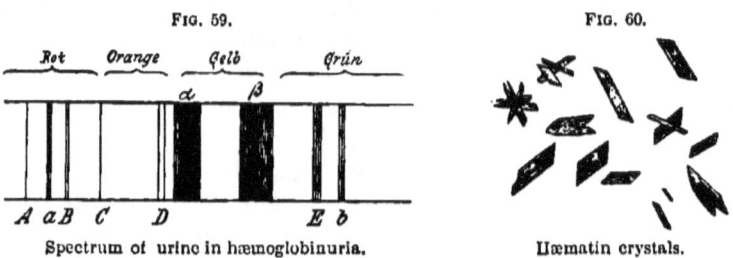

Fig. 59.
Spectrum of urine in hæmoglobinuria.

Fig. 60.
Hæmatin crystals.

close to it is a narrow methæmoglobin streak in orange. If we cannot examine it by means of a spectroscope, we may use the following tests : First, by means of the guaiac treatment or Teichmann's hæminprobe. The first method consists in placing a small portion of a mixture composed of equal parts of tincture of guaiac and oil of turpentine in a reagent-glass and covering it with the urine which is to be tested. If any coloring substance of the blood is present, we immediately notice the formation of a dirty white segment surrounded by an indigo-blue ring; and if the test-tube is agitated, the whole solution becomes a light blue opaque fluid (Fig. 60).

The hæmin-test consists of drying a large drop of urine in a small saucer, and with the dry mass we mix a small quantity of finely pulverized chloride of sodium, placing it on a plate. Then add two drops of cold glacial acetic acid. Now slowly heat the cup over an alcohol-lamp and allow it to cool. As it does so, you will see a quantity of dark-brown crystals. If these are not easily distinguished by the eye, they are with a magnifying glass. While we cannot distinguish the presence of the coloring matter of the blood in the urine with the aid of the microscope, we may detect the presence of blood-corpuscles in the fluid. We may also find by this means uric casts and epithelium of the kidneys, and small red granulations. These may be considered hæmoglobin.

The therapeutic treatment of hæmoglobinuria consists of the use of various diuretics, and an attempt must be made, as soon as possible, to remove the coloring matter from the blood and the kidneys.

Uræmia.

As a consequence of disease and impaired activity of the kidneys certain substances that should be thrown out in the urine remain in the blood, also the watery excretions of the body, producing a condition known as "uræmia." Certain experiments have been made on the dog to produce these uræmic symptoms artificially—for instance, when both kidneys are removed or the ureters ligated. Voit observed that when healthy animals were fed on food containing uric acid, and at the same time deprived of water, these conditions produced the disease. Grehant and Quinquaud produced death in dogs when urea was injected into them subcutaneously to the amount of 1 per cent. of the whole weight of the body. This produces convulsions, apparently from suppression of respiration. Feltz and Ritter produced uræmic symptoms in the dog with injections of salts of ammonium. It is of practical interest to know that uræmia may also occur in acute nephritis, in cases of enlargement of the prostate and obstruction of the passage of urine, or from uric stones filling up the urethra or the neck of the bladder.

The clinical symptoms have been described by Roll and others as high temperature alternating with chills, constant vomiting, convulsions, paralysis, coma, decrease in the temperature, and death within a few days. Roll also states that dogs which have suffered with hypertrophy of the prostate showed the same symptoms of this disease, but they were produced gradually and the symptoms were not so acute. In such cases we find dulness, disturbance of the intestinal canal, and convulsions.

Scurvy.

It is doubtful if true scurvy occurs in the dog—that is to say, a hemorrhagic diathesis marked by a spontaneous bleeding of the cutaneous and mucous membranes, and also from the muscles, joints, etc. Siedamgrotzky described a case of a two-year-old dog which died suddenly with symptoms of hemorrhage of the brain after being under treatment for four days. Numerous hemorrhagic centres were found in the skin and cellular tissues. The buccal mucous membrane was somewhat swollen and filled with hemorrhagic spots. The gums were also in the same condition. The intestinal canal was filled with spots of hemorrhage from one end to the other, the mucous membrane of the pylorus being especially affected. It was much swollen by a bloody infiltration. The mesenteric glands were filled with blood; the spleen was very much enlarged and weighed 107 grammes. On section it contained apparently a normal amount of blood. The liver and kidneys were healthy and normal. The lungs showed small hemorrhagic spots under the serous membrane and were slightly œdematous. The heart was flabby, light in color, and contained a quantity of non-coagulated blood. The frontal cavities were filled with blood-clots. The dura and arachnoid upon the left side also contained small hemorrhages. On the brain itself there were numerous flea-like spots, especially on the base of the brain. The blood on chemical examination was very deficient in salts of potassium.

Friedberger and Fröhner observed a case of scurvy in which there was bleeding of the gums and nasal mucous membrane, also in the retina of the eye. Friedberger found numerous hemorrhages in the cutaneous membrane of the hunting dog, in the neighborhood of the joints, in the serous membrane, and in the mucous membranes of the various organs, and an enlargement of the spleen to twice its normal size. He was of the opinion that this condition very much resembled the morbus maculosus Werlhofii of man (a variety of scurvy). The treatment consists in nutritive feeding, stimulants, and in following out the treatment given under the head of Ulcerative Stomatitis.

[Priessnitz's Compress.

This compress is mentioned a number of times in the work, and as it has special advantages in the treatment of dogs, the translator will attempt to describe it, as the author has not done so, probably due to the fact that it is so very well known in German therapeutics that it needed no explanation, but to English-speaking veterinarians this is the reverse.

The object of the compress or bandage is to keep up a continual heat, either dry or moist, to certain parts of the animal's body. We first apply against the part affected a piece of absorbent cotton, thick wool, or dry felt; or if moist heat is required, it is soaked in warm water or a medicated solution and wrung out to remove the excess of fluid; this is then held in position by a covering of some light material—a wide bandage of cheese-cloth is the best—and next a layer of oiled silk or rubber cloth (the object of this is to retain the heat and, in case of a wet compress, the moisture), and finally over this is placed a compress or bandage of flannel. This last is to prevent loss of heat by radiation. Sometimes the inner layer of cheese-cloth is omitted, or else it is put on the outside of all.

The above procedure may seem to the hurried practitioner a rather long and unnecessary method, but after one has tried it and found the great advantages it has in the retention of heat, especially in diseases of the lungs, in hastening the maturing of an abscess, or in the lessening of a tumefaction by the constant and direct application of heat and moisture, he will realize its benefits.]

DISEASES OF THE BONES AND ARTICULATIONS.

Rhachitis.
(*Rickets.*)

ETIOLOGY. The different theories which have been advanced concerning the origin of rhachitis do not seem to answer in some cases (a deficiency of lime-salts as a consequence of disturbances of digestion; excessive formation of carbonic or lactic acid, which would dissolve the lime-salts; an alteration of the general nutritive condition on account of abnormal influences in young animals; inflammatory hyperæmia and an increase in the number and size of bloodvessels in the osteogenic tissues, so that the lime-salts continue to circulate in the blood instead of being deposited in the bones). We therefore do not know positively anything relating to the character and origin of rhachitis. It is, perhaps, better to admit that it is a specific disorder (which has not as yet become positively known). We know positively, however, that rickets can be developed in the dog by deficient, improper food, by want of meat, and especially bones, as it has been demonstrated that animals with this disease if given these articles of diet seem to improve immediately. A proper amount of exercise is specially important for puppies kept in a small place.

Rickets generally appears in young animals in the first few months of their life. It is often hereditary. The symptoms appear relatively in proportion to their growth. If the animal grows quickly, rickets appears quickly; if it grows slowly, the disease comes on gradually.

PATHOLOGICAL ANATOMY. Rickets consists of a peculiar disturbance of the bones of the whole system. It seems to be due to a deficiency of lime-salts in the bones, making them soft and flexible. At the same time the nutritive process in the periosteum seems to be changed. The bones are light and soft enough to cut with a knife, and the epiphyses of the long bones are very much thickened; the marrow and periosteum are reddened. When the latter is removed from the bones of an animal in this condition certain portions of the bony tissue come away and remain attached to the membrane. This is especially noticeable between the epiphyses of the vertebræ. The inner layer of the periosteum is thickened and the diseased tissue seems to have undergone a spongy degeneration. Inside of the bone we find it soft and cavernous.

CLINICAL SYMPTOMS AND COURSE. The first appearance of rickets is gradual, and generally the veterinarian is not consulted in the early stages, but only when the skeleton shows marked alterations of form, especially in the bones of the extremities. We find periosteal inflations in the frontal bone and bones of the temple, so that the head shows a peculiar marked alteration. Schütz has found that in rhachitic animals the bones of the skull are extremely thin and the sutures separated. In the thorax there is a weakening of the walls of the chest, and the animals present that one-sided or "chicken-chest" condition. There is a peculiar knot-like swelling of the ribs both at their upper extremities where they unite with the vertebræ, and in their inferior extremities where they unite with the sternum and false ribs.

In this latter condition there forms a series of small, round nodules known as "rhachitic bead-string." In acute forms of this disease the spinal cord is twisted or bent in different directions. The most striking alterations are observed in the extremities. The long bones are thickened at both ends and bent on account of the softness of the bone and pressure of the weight of the body when standing. The upper portion of the front legs bends inward, rarely outward, and the animals have a peculiar, unsteady, awkward gait. They stand on the hind legs with the leg twisted under them, and in aggravated cases the bones are bent in a circle, the bend of the astragalus coming down on the ground. As a consequence of the altered position of the bones the ligaments become distended and stretched, causing an inflammation of the joints, consequently more or less enlargement of them. At the same time we observe emaciation, loss of appetite, and in some cases catarrh of the stomach and air-passages. The disease, as a rule, is chronic and the prognosis is unfavorable. If the disease is taken early, it may be checked by means of proper feeding; but when the deformity is once formed, it is only in extremely rare cases that it does not show as the animal grows to an adult age; either in the form of a peculiar bending or bow-legged appearance of the front legs, or a twisting, or show halt-shape in the hind legs.

THERAPEUTIC TREATMENT. The treatment of rhachitis consists of improving all the nutritive conditions and encouraging digestion as much as possible. Give the animal plenty of meat and bones, adding to them a certain amount of phosphate of calcium, egg-shells, and lime-water to drink. Improve the digestion as much as possible by tonics.

Canine literature does not show that osteomalacia exists in dogs, and it is not likely that they are affected by this disease, which affects the middle-aged or old animals. It is a progressive disintegration of the phosphates and softening of the bones. Kitt described, in 1890, a peculiar diseased condition of a German bulldog, and compared it with myositis ossificans progressiva. The head of the affected dog was disfigured by enormous osteophytes on the lower jaw and by prominences of the frontal bones. The bones of the forearm and thigh were covered with large osteophytes which had accumulated, particularly around the muscular centres, while, on the other hand, around the joints there was very slight indication of the disease. The whole spinal vertebræ, as far as the last one in the tail, as well as the ribs, chest, and shoulder-blades, were normal and well formed, abnormalities being confined entirely to the bones before mentioned. During life the animal seemed lively and free from any fever, had a good appetite, but walked in a peculiar, undulating way, giving it a very awkward and unsteady appearance.

Multiple periostitis has been observed by Siedamgrotzky in a dog. This was very different from the case described above. The animal during life showed marked symptoms of general muscular rheumatism, the disease affecting the periosteum of the entire body, especially the joints.

DISEASES OF THE JOINTS.

Inflammation of the Joints.

GENERAL PATHOLOGICAL ANATOMY OF INFLAMMATION OF THE JOINTS. The most common affection of the joints is synovitis. In a simple case of inflammation of the joints we see an increase of blood, an infiltration of the small cells, and even disintegration of the endothelial cartilage, the tissue under it becoming granular. We find quite frequently an accumulation of fibrinous or "croup-like" membranes, followed by a cicatrization of the synovial membrane. In all acute forms of synovitis we see hemorrhages in the form of small, tick-like bodies. Inflammation of the joints, when it takes a chronic form, makes the synovial membrane thick, tougher, with marked indentations which present a tree-like form. The synovia appears in large quantities, is yellowish, clear, or slightly turbid, and dulled by cells or fibrinous flakes. It is very rarely thick. If this synovia is gathered in a large quantity, we see a distention of the capsule, producing a hernia-like protrusion in the parts of the joint where there is the least resistance. Occasionally we find the synovial membrane covered with thick masses of clotted fibres. These occur from the excessive formation of secretion of synovia in the joints. Sometimes small bodies appear in the joints due to some parts of the hard cartilage becoming loose, and in rare instances by a breaking off of small pieces of bone, and, finally, we may see the development of a peculiar cicatricial contraction of the synovial membrane. This is due to an acute or chronic inflammation of the joints, or when for any cause (for instance, dressing of fractures) a healthy joint is rendered immovable for some time. This condition may produce a temporary stiffening of the joint, but this, as a rule, is overcome in a short time.

The fibrous capsule of the joint is occasionally inflamed, but, as a rule, in acute and chronic inflammation of the joint it remains unaffected. Where there is suppuration present it may become detached from the periosteum with the bone, and also perforated by the pus. The ligaments are also impregnated with the pus from a purulent inflammation, but they are rarely destroyed. Occasionally, however, we may see in chronic inflammation of the joints a cicatricial contraction where the joints become firm and united, immobility being lost. Sometimes from traumatisms we find only the soft parts which surround the joint, such as the external ligaments, and the neighboring tendons become involved in the inflammatory process, while the inner joint seems to be very little affected.

The cartilage of the end of the joints is very little affected in all conditions. In acute cases of suppuration of the joints the cartilage may be softened, perforated, or partially destroyed, so that the bone is bare in some places. In many chronic cases of inflammation of the joints the cartilage becomes macerated and dissolved into fibres, or it may be overgrown with abnormal synovial extensions. As soon as the bone proper becomes involved in the inflammatory process extensive granulations form, causing a peculiar spongy growth. These crowd and perforate the bone here and there, and also affect a cartilage of the opposing bone, leading to a cicatricial growth on the end of the joint. In some cases we also see the fibres and cells of the cartilage becoming soft and finally growing up with numerous raised cartilaginous cells, and an acute inflammation of the ends of the joints. From these periodical conditions we may have a marked alteration in the form of the joint. Edges of the joint protrude, the inner surface being hollowed and grooved. A peculiarity of deforming inflammation of the joints is an inflammation of the synovial membrane, with a normal excretion of synovia and a great enlargement of the free or loose portion of the membrane which may develop into papilla-shaped masses.

The bone, as a rule, does not become affected in acute inflammation of the joint; but if it should become uncovered from suppuration of the cartilage, the inflammation extends to the spongiosa, and we see occasionally the formation of purulent or granular centres on the surface. In rare cases the periosteum becomes covered with osteophytes.

In tubercular diseases the joints of the dog may become diseased, but as yet such cases have not been demonstrated in veterinary literature.

Acute Synovial Inflammation of the Joints.

(Synovitis Acuta Serosa.)

The joint is swollen and hot, and the animal shows pain on pressure or movement of it. These symptoms indicate an inflammation of the synovial membrane and a lessening of the secretion of synovial fluid into the joint. It is very rare that we see intense fibrinous excretions (synovitis sero-fibrinosa), and still more rare are those cases of colorless blood-cells mixed with detached epithelia. The patients are lame when the joint is moved, especially at the beginning and toward the end of any movement of the joint. Very frequently small dogs will only walk on three feet, carrying the inflamed member.

ETIOLOGY. The following may cause synovitis: Crushing or concussion of the joint, blows, sprains (such as falling from a height). In cases of injuries of the joints we may expect only a simple synovitis when the injuring object is clean and the wound is cleansed immediately after the injury (by blood-clots or an antiseptic dressing). According to the observations of the author, acute synovitis occurs most frequently in the carpal joint, joints of the toes, in the knees, and hip-joints.

Its course is, as a rule, rapid. If the patient receives proper treatment, in a short time we see an improvement (especially if the animal gets complete rest). In other cases the disease takes a chronic form—that is, it may form one of the following conditions:

Chronic Serous Inflammation of the Joints.
(Synovitis Chronica Serosa.)

In this the joint is slightly swollen and painful, also very feverish. In some cases we may see a fluctuating swelling as a result of enlargement of the capsule by serous secretion. If the disease is still more acute, we may have a thickening of the fibrous capsules, and very frequently quite an enlargement starting from the edge of the joint.

This chronic synovitis may appear in the onset of the disease, but, as a rule, it results as a consequence of the acute form. The author has seen these cases in the carpus and knee-joint. The lameness is not especially marked, but any active movements increase it very much.

Purulent Inflammation of the Joints; Suppuration of the Joints.
(Pyarthrosis.)

While the two forms which have before been described are rarely accompanied by fever, it is quite different in suppuration of the joint. In this there is great fever from the beginning, which is ushered in by a chill. We may see a more or less rapid development of a swelling of the joint, which is extremely painful. The joint is kept in a bent or flexed position, and the patient walks on three feet. We may also see an œdematous swelling extending both above and below in the neighborhood of the joint. The temperature is considerably increased in some cases; the skin appears normal or reddened, sometimes even bluish-red. The pus may eventually break through the skin in the neighborhood of the joint, or it may lie in the joints, become absorbed, and cause pyæmia.

This termination will perhaps occur even when the pus has broken out externally, and in some cases where the inflammation has been very acute we may have a subsequent adhesion of the joint (ankylosis).

ETIOLOGY. Suppuration of the joints is frequently produced by infected wounds at or near the joint. In rare instances it may be the result of a phlegmonous inflammation in the neighborhood of the joint; concussion or crushing may also cause it, or it may occur in a metastatic way. Such inflammations of the joints may also occur as a purely suppurating inflammation; but, as a rule, they are sero-fibrinous or sero-purulent, and with it we may see purulent centres of abscesses, or pyæmia, abscesses forming in the glands, or the development of the disease in several joints at the same time, or at short intervals. The author saw metastatic suppuration of the joints of the knee, carpus, and toes.

Rheumatic Inflammation of the Joints.
(*Rheumatic Arthritis.*)

This form of disease of the joints seems to be caused by cold, especially in shooting dogs, if used in cold weather or during winter, when they become very wet and lie around in a draught. It has also been ascribed to be due to a specific infectious substance, and this is brought out in animals that take cold. There are two forms of this disease: an acute and chronic form. The former appears in a serous, but more rarely sero-purulent synovitis, accompanied by great pain and high fever. The lameness is much greater than in any other form of joint-irritation. Very often several joints become diseased at one time, or the disease may go from one part to another. As a rule, if the animal is kept in a warm place, the disease abates in severity in a few days. When the disease takes a chronic form, either from the onset, or merges into the chronic from the acute stage, it resembles very much chronic sero-synovitis. There is great thickening of the capsule, a formation of adhesions between the surface of the joints and the connective tissue, and in rare instances we may have ankylosis of the joint. The most common seat of this disease is in the knee-joint, and still more rarely in the ankle and hip. While the diagnosis is rather difficult where the disease in confined to one joint, it is easily distinguished when you see it appear in several joints at once, and also from the fact that it may move from one joint to another.

Disease Producing Malformation of the Joints.
(*Arthritis Deformans.*)

The cause of this disease is very little known. It is very probably due to a chronic rheumatism, or to some inflammation of the joint. It may also be due to great exertion, and is especially seen in Holland, where animals are used to pull carts and vehicles. The first symptom of this disease is a slight lameness in the diseased joint. This lameness may be overlooked, as it is generally very slight, and after the animal has taken a little exercise it gradually disappears, although in some rare cases the lameness may continue, or even with exercise become aggravated. In the early stages of the disease there is no indication of pain on movement or pressure of the joint, but later on pain on pressure and motion begins to show itself. At the same time there are a gradual swelling and thickening of the capsule of the joint, with apparently a loss of the normal amount of synovia. Sometimes we notice slight heat. A peculiar symptom of this disease, which is noticed from the very onset, is a peculiar creaking or crepitating sound when the joint is moved. After a time stiffness of the joints becomes more marked. There are hard swellings on the cartilaginous borders, also a tendency of the ends of the joint to enlarge, and finally marked alteration in the form of the joint. By these changes we are enabled to distinguish between arthritis deformans and chronic serous inflammation of the joints.

The anatomical alterations have already been mentioned. Arthritis deformans, as a rule, occurs in the knee-joint, the elbow, and shoulder. The prognosis of this disease is always to be unfavorable, because it seems to defy medical treatment, going on until finally the joint becomes a large unsightly mass.

THERAPEUTIC TREATMENT OF INFLAMMATION OF THE JOINTS. In all cases, except those of slight synovitis, the joint must be kept as quiet as possible. In simple cases the animal should be kept in a kennel or in a room for several days. In serious cases where no operation seems to be required, and there is no danger of poison breaking through the joints, and where the inflammatory swelling is not very great, it is best to apply the bandage of cotton and dress over that with a plaster or silicate of sodium bandage, treating it the same as a fracture. The author has obtained very good results with this method in the carpal, tarsal, and toe-joints. Albrecht advises that the joints should be rubbed with a thick layer of citrine ointment before applying the dressing. (For further details, see under head of Dressings, etc.)

It is well, however, to take into consideration one point: that the dressing must be in such a position as not to interfere with the use of the leg. With the above treatment we generally obtain good results in a short time. In the serious forms of the disease, and where the dressing cannot be used on account of the position of the joint, we must apply such local applications as will abate the inflammation. As a rule, the best treatment is cold-water applications containing lead or arnica. In cases where there are great pain and acute rheumatic inflammation of the joint, it is better not to apply too much cold water, but use instead Priessnitz's compress. Wrap the joint in a piece of linen which has been folded several times, similar to a handkerchief, and then cover it with some impervious object, such as oil-cloth, silk, rubber, or a woollen cover. If, for some reason, neither the cold nor the moist treatment is practicable, we must paint the part with tincture of iodine once or twice daily, and the fluid must be rubbed into the skin by means of a rag. The author has never had very good results from this method of treatment, but painting with iodine produces better results than any of the liniments, such as camphor or soap liniment. Massage has been found to produce good results in many diseases of the joints in dogs, although it has not been used very extensively among canine practitioners. In chronic cases where there are great thickening and a large quantity of secretion of the capsule, as in cases of acute inflammation of the joint, or in purulent arthritis, massage with cocoanut oil is particularly adapted. In cases of rheumatic inflammation of the joint, which have been recognized as such, we must use internal remedies, such as recommended in muscular rheumatism.

In many traumatic and purulent inflammations of the joint we can only get good results by an operation which varies according to the condition. The general procedure is as follows:

Puncturing. This method of treatment is indicated in all chronic serous secretions of the joint. As soon as we find that the measures which encourage reabsorption, such as tight dressing and massage, do not produce good results, and where the secretion causes great distention of the capsule, and where there are great lameness and indications of suppuration, we proceed in the following manner:

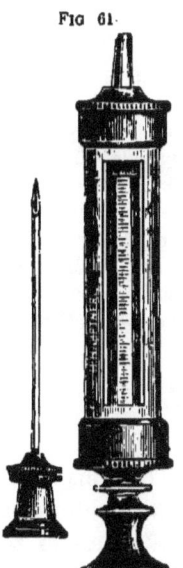

Fig 61.

A large hypodermatic syringe for puncturing enlarged joints.

a. The part to be punctured must be rendered strictly aseptic; *b*, the part must have a particularly tight dressing over it for a few days after the operation.

If this latter method is not practicable on account of the position of the joint or some other circumstance, puncturing the joint will not give favorable results and may even lead to very serious conditions (suppuration, etc.). The method of operation is very simple.

After having removed the hair from the region of the joint and washing with sublimated soap, disinfecting it with a ½ per cent. solution of carbolic acid and 2 per cent. of creolin or 1 per cent. of corrosive sublimate, we then puncture the part with a good-sized hypodermatic needle and slowly evacuate the sac by drawing it into the syringe. If the syringe becomes filled and the joint is not entirely emptied, the syringe must be detached from the needle and the opening closed at once by means of the finger, as any air that may find its way into the joint will produce bad results. Empty the syringe and proceed as before.

This method, as a rule, is absolutely harmless, evacuating the sac in cases of serous secretions. If, however, we find in the fluid withdrawn from the joint many cellular elements—that is to say, if it possesses a marked purulent character—we must use at the same time an injection of antiseptic fluid directly into the joint, so as to make it aseptic. For that purpose we use a slightly warm solution of 1 to 1000 solution of corrosive sublimate or a 2 per cent. solution of carbolic acid and a Lugol solution of iodine (1 per cent. tincture of iodine, 2 per cent. of iodide of potassium, and 50 per cent. of water). Either of these solutions may be injected through the needle into the joint; then, by manipulation, try to work this solution inside of the capsule by means of careful pressure, allowing it to flow out through the needle in one or two minutes. The needle is then withdrawn and the perforated opening is closed at once by means of an iodoform-tampon, and over that an antiseptic dressing is placed. This should be allowed to remain on the wound for a few days.

(For further particulars, see the chapter on Treatment of Wounds.)

In chronic inflammations or great secretions we may also use simple injections of disinfecting solutions, such as iodide of potassium, as a means of reducing the inflammation or destroying its products. We perforate directly into the cavity of the joint by means of a hypodermatic needle and with a syringe inject a quantity of fluid in proportion to the size of the joint. This operation has to be repeated every three or four days, following the same procedure before and after the operation as has been already described.

The joint may be opened by means of a puncture with a lancet. This is advisable where there is extensive suppuration going on in the joint and where the diseased part shows every indication of a septic condition. The joint to be opened should be punctured by means of a lancet or bistoury, making a wound just sufficient to empty it freely. It must then be cleansed with an antiseptic solution and any clots or detached portions of tissue washed out; then close the wound by means of sutures. In some cases it is well to leave one corner open for drainage, that, of course, being the lower one. We then place an antiseptic dressing over the whole part.

Injuries of the Joints.

These may be divided into several groups—true wounds of the joints, contusions, distortions, and luxations.

Wounds of the Joints. Wounds of the joints—that is to say, injuries which expose the joint proper to the atmosphere—are divided into perforating or cutting wounds, being produced by laceration, contusion, and shot.

CLINICAL SYMPTOMS AND COURSE. The first symptom of injury to the joint, as a rule, is a discharge of synovia from the wound. This, however, may be absent in cases where the wound is very fine, or where the puncture runs in an oblique direction;

the amount of discharged synovia, as a rule, is very slight at the beginning and of normal consistency. If the wound is not closed immediately, it increases in amount and becomes thinner. In some cases it is difficult to tell positively whether the synovia comes from the joint or from the sheath of a tendon. In the latter case, however, the amount of synovia is generally very slight. Blood may accumulate in the cavity of the joint and develop a hæmarthros. In some cases where there is hemorrhage, the wound may be very small and close up quickly, or it may lie in an oblique direction and prevent the escape of blood. This flows into the joint and fills it up. Hæmarthros is distinguished from serous or purulent secretions by appearing shortly after the injury, and the absence of all inflammatory symptoms—that is, at the onset of the disease.

The other symptoms of wounds of the joints are acute sensitiveness, the animal limping and showing great pain, holding its leg in a flexed condition. Generally the external opening of the wound can also be distinguished.

The course of this disease differs greatly according to the character of the wound and whether the object that caused it was clean or not. Small perforating wounds heal rapidly, and the animals limp only for a few days. In serious wounds where the joint has been exposed, and dirt or other foreign bodies have obtained entrance into the joint, the prognosis is less favorable. In such cases we notice a great discharge of synovia. This is clear in the early stage of the disease, but soon becomes turbid by the addition of pus-corpuscles and fibrinous clots. It then becomes flaky and finally purulent. At the same time there is great fever around the joint, which is swollen very much, and the neighboring tissues become œdematous, extending in all directions. We may see numerous abscesses forming all around the joint or in the intermuscular connective tissue, and finally the animal dies from general exhaustion or pyæmia.

According to the circumstances and condition of the wound, the course may be much more rapid. The synovia becomes purulent in a short time; septic fever shows itself quickly; there is a rapid pulse; the animal sinks into a coma, and dies from septicæmia. This may even occur in slight wounds, if they have not been treated properly, and where thorough disinfection has not been followed.

THERAPEUTIC TREATMENT. The first thing to do after an injury has occurred is to thoroughly disinfect the wound and its immediate neighborhood. Clip the hair from all around the part, then wash it with a solution of corrosive sublimate, and, in cases where the puncture is very narrow, clean it out by means of a syringe with a 2 per cent. solution of creolin and 5 per cent. solution of carbolic acid, or a 1 per cent. of corrosive sublimate. If you find the object which caused the puncture was very dirty, the wound must be enlarged and thoroughly washed with any of the above-named solutions. The wound should then be closed by means of sutures, taking care when stitching it up not to include the synovial membrane or any part of the joint in the sutures. It is well, however, in some cases, to place a small piece of catgut or silk in the lower surface of the wound in order to assist in emptying the joint. We then place the joint in an antiseptic dressing and cover it up.

If we have to deal with a wound that has been neglected and where suppuration has been going on for some time, and the owner does not wish to destroy the animal, we must enlarge the wound at once, and all pockets, or sacs, in the joint must be emptied and washed with a solution of corrosive sublimate. Any clots, masses, or pieces of tissue must be removed, and the operation finished as before described. In all these cases the animal must have absolute rest, and the dressing be renewed frequently.

Contusions of the Joints. Under this head we class injuries to the joints which have been caused by compression of the soft parts against the bones or from shocks, such as jumping or leaping from a height, kicks, and where the extremities have been run over by vehicles. In this we may have a series of results, such as crushing or laceration of the capsule of the joint, with formation of hæmarthros, or a concussion or crushing of the bone with little escape of blood. In rare instances we may see a laceration of the cartilage.

CLINICAL SYMPTOMS. The animal shows great sensitiveness and pain on manipulation of the joint, and, as a rule, carries it in the air. There is a rapid swelling of the joint and œdema of the surrounding parts, also a high temperature.

THERAPEUTIC TREATMENT. The treatment consists in cold-water applications, if the position of the joint admits, renewed constantly. The best method is to soak a piece of absorbent cotton in water, lay it on the joint and bandage it up lightly, moistening it in cold water from time to time. In old cases use friction (massage) of the joint in a circular direction (twice daily for ten or fifteen minutes), or use a tight bandage. Any stimulating liniments, such as camphor, soap, or arnica, may be used, but it is questionable whether the good effects are not due more to the massage than to the drugs themselves.

Distortions of the Joint (*Sprains*). By this is meant a twisting or temporary displacement of the joint, as a rule, in a lateral direction. The capsule and the ligaments may be partially torn and in some cases entirely ruptured on one side. The round ligament of the hip-joint is sometimes torn, as are also the tendons of the knee-joint.

CLINICAL SYMPTOMS. When the sprain occurs there is violent pain. The animals use the joint irregularly, or may carry the member. The lameness increases, and in the region of the joint swelling soon appears. Any manipulation of the joint produces great pain, and we may be able to recognize a laceration of some of the ligaments, and the joint shows greater mobility on one side than the other. Where there is tearing of the broad ligaments of the hip-joint there is nothing indicated beyond the lameness and symptoms of pain when the joint is turned or twisted.

THERAPEUTICS. The treatment of distortions, or sprains, is the same as that for contusions. It is well, however, to be careful to put the joint, by means of the bandage, as near as possible to its original lines.

Luxations of the Joint (*Dislocations*). While distortions of the joints disappear in a short time in cases of luxation, if it is not reduced it is lasting. If both surfaces of the joint are no longer in contact, it is called an entire dislocation. If they are partially in contact, it is called an incomplete luxation (subluxation).

The causes of dislocation are, as a rule, mechanical, falling out of windows, jumping from high objects, getting the foot caught, and hanging, as in jumping over a fence; concussions and blows by being run over by vehicles, etc. In all dislocations there is invariably laceration of the capsular ligament. This membrane only remains intact in dislocations of the lower jaw. As a rule, the accessory ligaments are seldom torn except in such cases where a portion of the bone is torn with them. The cartilage of the joint may be torn or detached in some cases by the subsequent inflammation. The ends of the bones may be unaffected and in some cases broken. Other alterations are seen in the muscles and tendons in the neighborhood of the joint. They are abnormally extended on one side and flabby on the other side. They may be torn, lacerated, or even crushed. It is only in rare instances that the large bloodvessels and nerves are lacerated. The joints which are dislocated are surrounded by a large quantity of blood which infiltrates the tissues and is gradually reabsorbed.

When reduction is not performed quickly—that is to say, the displaced end of the joint remains in its abnormal position—we have what is called nearthrosis as a consequence of the irritation which it produces in the immediate neighborhood of the joint. In such a case there is slight immobility due to partial adhesions of the affected part, and also due to a certain extent to atrophy of the muscles surrounding it. In some cases motion of the joint is entirely lost.

CLINICAL SYMPTOMS AND PROGNOSIS. When a dislocation has just occurred, and when it has been there for some time, the symptoms are more marked than they are in the intermediate stage, for the reason that the hemorrhage produces so much swelling as to render obscure, to a certain extent, the position and character of the luxation. In some cases the condition can be very easily recognized by comparing it with the perfect joint on the other side; at other times, it is only by careful manipulation in the region of the joint that the alteration can be felt. We may find a projection of bone at one place and depression in another, where they do not occur in the healthy side. We may even feel the luxated end of the joint. In some cases where the deformity has been concealed by the rapid swelling of the surrounding tissues, the leg may be shorter, or it may be on a longitudinal axis with the other leg. Another characteristic symptom is the loss of movement in the luxated joint, especially when the case is seen early, although in some cases where the ligaments have been so lacerated or torn, or where a piece of bone has broken, there is abnormal flexion in that part. This is especially important, as it enables us to locate a fracture of the bone that is in the neighborhood of the joint.

There is also a slight crepitation. This, however, is soft, and not the hard, rough crepitation that we find in fractures.

Luxations are not dangerous to life except those of the vertebræ, but they are very troublesome, and, as a rule, make slow recoveries. Dislocations can be reduced quickly where the animal is seen a short time after the injury; but in rare cases, on account of the lacerated condition of the capsule and ligament, it is rather difficult to hold the injured joint in position after it has been reduced.

THERAPEUTIC TREATMENT. The treatment consists of: 1. Reduction of the dislocation. 2. In holding the joint in position after the reduction has been made.

It is rather hard to lay down any rule to be followed in all cases, but try if possible to return the joint in the same position as it was before, comparing it with the joint of the opposite leg, following, as a rule, the same procedure as that followed in fractures of the bone. As soon as the reduction is made the joint must be dressed and allowed to remain if possible for a period of three weeks (further particulars will be found in the chapter relating to fractures of the bones and wounds), so that the soft parts which are lacerated—the capsule and the ligaments—may have an opportunity to grow together and return the joint to its normal position. If the dressing cannot be applied in cases of dislocation of the hip, the animal must be kept in a cage or in a small room, in order to keep it as quiet as possible. We may find more or less stiffness of the joint when the dressing is removed. This can be assisted to a certain extent by means of massage.

The following dislocations appear more frequently in the dog and require especial mention:

Dislocation of the Lower Jaw. This is extremely rare, and may occur in some instances where a setter or retriever endeavors to carry a very large bird, opens his mouth, and distends it in such a way that it is dislocated. In some cases this luxation is confined to one side, and in others both articulations are out of joint. The lower jaw projects forward, the incisors project beyond the upper incisors, giving the animal an "undershot" position, while in a lateral direction the jaw is pushed to one side, the mouth remains wide open, and cannot be closed except with great exertion. In many cases, on account of the pressure which is caused by the coronoid process pressing on the posterior portion of the eye, it is bulged, causing what might be termed an incomplete prolapsus of that organ. Other symptoms are salivation, great pain, restlessness, blue coloration of the tongue. (For differential diagnosis of paralysis of the lower jaw, see Diseases of the Mouth.)

THERAPEUTIC TREATMENT. According to Stockfleth, the animal must be held by an assistant. The best method is to hold him between the legs and steady his head while the operator by means of a lever-like action upon the lower jaw endeavors to reduce the dislocation. To accomplish this, wrap a cloth around the hand, place the thumbs on both teeth of the lower jaw, and by means of external pressure attempt to reduce the bone into its normal condition. Another method which the author finds is not as reliable consists in placing a strong stick between the jaws, as far back as possible, then by pressure on the anterior portion of the jaws, allowing the stick to act as a fulcrum, the jaw will very often fly into position. In order to prevent a recurrence of this, the dog for some time should wear a particularly (Fig. 62) tight-fitting muzzle and should receive nothing but soft food.

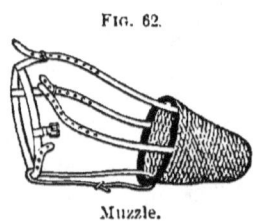

FIG. 62.

Muzzle.

Dislocation of the Elbow. In the dog the bone of the forearm forms with the elbow a pivot joint. Each of these joints has a capsular ligament. The upper is fitted with a ring-like band, and in the lower portion the radius is kept in position by means of transverse ligaments. A slight rotation of the radius may occur independent of the elbow-joint itself. A dislocation of this articulation may occur from jumping from tables, chairs, falling from some height. In the former case the bone of the forearm is dislocated backward and outward. In dislocation of the lower pivot joint the bone of the forearm may project forward as well as backward. If dislocation of the upper joint occurs in the dog, the forearm is kept flexed; it becomes immobile in the elbow-joint, the animal using three legs and carrying one in the air. The joint is wider, and the dislocated portion of the forearm may be felt distinctly, also may see more or less marked sensitiveness or swelling. If, on the other hand, we have a certain amount of movement on extension of the elbow-joint and great elasticity in the joint, too much for the normal condition, the animal evinces great pain on movement. This dislocation is easily corrected. The joint may be moved freely, but as soon as the animal stands upon its feet again the displacement recurs. This is due to the annular ligament, which holds the joint to the forearm in place, being torn. If this dislocation is not reduced and left for some time, the leg will be held constantly in a flexed position, and the animal will not use it.

In cases of lower dislocation of the joint the animal walks upon three legs, and on examination we find that the lower end of the bone of the forearm is displaced in a posterior direction, and more rarely in an anterior direction. This dislocation is easily reduced, but on the slightest movement reappears again. The prognosis is not favorable, as it is a rather difficult condition to treat. The weak ligaments (the annular ligament and transverse ligaments) do not heal quickly, and the dislocation has a tendency to become chronic, especially in the upper joint.

TREATMENT. In the treatment of the upper joint the forearm becomes extended and the legs should be crossed and an attempt made to push the forearm backward and outward into its normal position. It must then be held there by means of a tight bandage. This bandage must be changed once a day, as it is apt to produce tenderness of the skin from being so tight. If the dislocation affects the lower joint, the bone of the forearm will have to be pushed into its normal condition with more or less force and a silicate of sodium bandage applied.

Dislocation of the Patella. Stockfleth states that the patella may become dislocated on both sides, but not upward, and that the dislocation is generally on the inner side, on account of the forced extension of a very much flexed tarsus and a tendency of the muscles to turn inward. This is seen occasionally in circus dogs (grayhounds) making high jumps. In cases of inside dislocation the patella lies on the inner side of the joint where it moves on the tibia, and in external dislocation it lies on the outside of the external condyle.

Inner Dislocation of the Patella. In the early stages, shortly after the dislocation occurs, the animal holds its leg in a very flexed position. The hock is flexed and the heel turned outward. At the joint the patella may be found lying sideways, and is easily moved laterally. If we take hold of the knee and flex or extend it, the animal evinces great pain. The leg must be bent backward and straightened as much as possible, then by means of manipulation of the fingers the patella can be made to slip into position This is very easily performed, and the animal walks away as if nothing has occurred. This dislocation, however, may recur when the animal jumps any distance. When the disease becomes chronic and dislocation occurs often, the animal runs on three legs, or walks lame on the affected leg. The stifle-joint is uneven, thick, and the patella can be dislocated, or put into position simply by pressure of the fingers. If the dislocation affects both legs, these are kept in a flexed position, the animal making peculiar jumping movements, using both legs at the same time when he attempts to walk. If he lies down, the hind legs are extended backward and crossed. The prognosis is favorable in new cases, but unfavorable in old ones.

TREATMENT. The tarsus must be extended in order to overcome the tension in the straight ligaments and extensors, and the patella may be easily shoved into position. If the animal is then kept quiet for several days, as a rule, no after-treatment is required. If the dislocation of the patella is old, treatment is useless.

Stockfleth has used a dressing in this disease which he describes as follows:

He attached a broad linen bandage around the tibia, and fastened a wide girth around the abdomen, and a breast-piece to prevent it from slipping backward. The bandage was then fastened to the tibia, close to the girth around the abdomen. The affected leg was then pulled up close to the abdomen, so that the animal must stand on three legs. The dressing remained on for twenty days, and when it was removed the animal was entirely cured. In another case he had a double-sized dislocation of the knee. After returning the patellæ to their position, the knee- and ankle-joint were covered with thick wadding, and a capsule of gutta-percha, which had previously been soaked in hot water, was applied to each leg, surrounding the leg from the knee to the toes. In order to prevent bending of the gutta-percha before it was sufficiently hardened, a wooden support was fastened to the outside. The dog, which had formerly crept upon its hind legs, walked upright as if on stilts. The dressing was left on the animal for two weeks, and on removal of the dressing the dislocation did not recur.

External Dislocation of the Patella. This accident is very rare. Stockfleth saw but one chronic case in both legs in a small dog. The subject was lively, walked rapidly, but had very flexed ankle-joints, giving him very much the appearance of a weasel. The tarsus appeared thick and uneven; the patella, which was located in the muscles of the outside, could easily be pushed back into its normal position; but if left, it immediately slipped out of position, and became dislocated again. This was due to the fact that the crest of the joint had disappeared, offering no resistance to dislocation.

Möller states he has seen external dislocation of the patella quite often, especially in Skye-terriers, while Hoffmann believes that an external luxation of the patella in dogs is impossible for anatomical reasons, because of the straight ligaments. The middle one is the only one of any consequence, and for another reason the patella is extremely small.

Other luxations occur in the dog—for instance, in the hip-joint. In this the head of the femur becomes pushed upward after laceration of the capsular ligament, and the joints of the phalanges sometimes become dislocated. These do not possess any special symptoms that may not be easily recognized by the indications stated under Clinical Symptoms of Luxations.

DISEASE OF THE BURSA MUCOSA.

Diseases of the mucous capsules which lie under the skin—for instance, in the acromion, olecranon, and at the ankle. These are not of any special importance in the dog, although we occasionally see them affected.

These diseases are developed in the form of circumscribed, fluctuating swellings, either caused by hemorrhage, sero-fibrinous or purulent inflammation of the mucous surfaces. These may be caused by blows, jars, or by some other traumatism. The purulent form is generally caused by some injury produced externally. It is easy to recognize these enlarged bursæ. We find a large fluctuating swelling, accompanied by acute inflammatory symptoms. There is much pain on pressure, and the fever, when it has been caused by active inflammation and not through hemorrhage, is very acute. Purulent secretions, as a rule, perforate the skin and escape.

Serous or sero-fibrinous secretions are rarely entirely absorbed, but leave a slight, fluctuating tumor with thickened walls, which is to be termed a "cystic abscess."

When the condition comes on gradually, continuing to swell and increase, taking a chronic form from the first, the walls of the pouch become very much thickened. There is a gradual accumulation of a mucus-like fluid. As a rule, true inflammatory symptoms are not present; but if they are, only very slightly.

TREATMENT. In cases of large fluid secretions (blood or serum) it is best to puncture, following the antiseptic rules. Purulent secretions may be removed by opening the pouch, making a particularly large opening, and using a draining-tube. Cystic abscesses may be removed by means of tincture of iodine injected in them, or by cutting them open, but best of all by excising them. The author has found good results from first opening them, using the drainage-tube, and applying such stimulating agents as tincture of cantharides, creosote, solution of nitrate of silver 1 to 10.

Diseases of the tendons or sheaths are of no importance in the dog, and need not be discussed.

MUSCULAR RHEUMATISM.

Muscular rheumatism is a primary infection with more or less complication of the muscular system. In some cases there is little or no inflammation present, no fever, and the only indication of rheumatism being present is stiffness of gait and pain on pressure.

ETIOLOGY. The cause of rheumatism, which has been described as a certain poisonous substance, may also be due to cold, atmospheric influences, etc., or dampness, animals lying in kennels that do not get the sun, or being kept in the cellar. We have, undoubtedly, a number of diseases of the muscular system which do not develop from rheumatism, for instance, abnormal muscular exertion and consequent laceration of some of the muscular fibres; also from disturbances of the circulation, from chronic toxic influences, etc. It would be much better to discard the name "muscular rheumatism" and simply call it "muscular pain." Experience has taught the author that muscular rheumatism is seen frequently in old, delicate, or fat dogs, and is oftener observed in winter than in summer.

PATHOLOGICAL ANATOMY. It is very difficult to make any definite statement as to the cause of rheumatism. We speak of rheumatic muscular inflammation, but at the same time we do not, as a rule, find any different muscular alterations on post-mortem from animals which have suffered from muscular rheumatism. We may find slight alterations which have occurred from other causes, such as hyperæmia, slight exudation in the muscles, tendons, and fascia. It is well known that slight inflammations of the mucous membrane are not generally recognized during life. On the other hand, we find cases in veterinary literature where very distinct alterations have been observed in the affected muscles. Deposits occur in the connective tissue (rheumatic callosities). These occur in a man who has suffered for a long time from muscular rheumatism, and in old rheumatic dogs we may also observe characteristic alterations in acute or chronic inflammations.

CLINICAL SYMPTOMS AND COURSE. Muscular pain is a most marked symptom. This is observed in slight cases by the animal having a contracted appearance of the muscles, or when by pressure upon them they are found hard and tense. We also observe that dogs affected with this disease move with fear, showing great disinclination for any movement, and occasionally they cry out with pain when touched or lifted in certain parts of the body, or if any portion of a particular muscle is touched. If compelled to rise, they do so in a slow, fatigued way. Their movements are stiff and strained, and when fæces are passed the animals do so with pain, frequently crying or howling, or it may be they make no effort, producing obstinate constipation.

As rheumatism is generally located in the joint regions, these symptoms become modified in certain parts of the body and intensified in others. We very often see rheumatism of the back and loins. Rising and stretching of the extremities and all movements of the trunk are very painful. The region of the back and loins is very sensitive, so that the animals cry at the slightest movement. The muscles in the neck are also subject to this disease. Animals show great pain while eating on account of being compelled to bend their neck in stooping down to reach their food. The muscles are distended and painful to the touch. If the head is bent, the animal shows great pain. In rare cases we see rheumatism in the masseters (a great difficulty in mastication). Only in very severe cases is any fever noticed.

The course of the disease is sometimes acute and occasionally chronic. In the former case the disease runs its course very quickly, and may disappear without any special treatment, but there is always a tendency to relapse. In the latter form the disease may be prolonged for months, varying in degrees of intensity, also showing a tendency for the pain to move from one part of the body to another. This peculiarity is noticeable in chronic rheumatic conditions.

THERAPEUTICS. The agents recommended for the dog are salicylic acid, antipyrine, tincture of colchici, morphia, friction, massage, and electricity. The first three drugs produce the most favorable results:

R.—Salicylic acid 5.0
Aqua destillata 50.0
S.—One tablespoonful three times daily.

R.—Antipyrine 5.0
Syrup. simplex 25.0
Aqua destillata 50.0
S.—One teaspoonful three times daily.

R.—Tincture of colchici, 10 to 20 drops several times daily.

R.—Salicin 2.0
Potassii iodidi 1.0
Fiat divid. charta No. viii. S.—One powder twice daily.

In the chronic form of the disease various cutaneous stimulants have been used, such as spirit of camphor, opodeldoc, spirit of mustard, but we must remember that their influence is more due to the massage than to anything else. It is advisable to rub the stimulating embrocation into the skin, either by the hand or with a woollen rag. Albrecht has found that this therapeutic treatment may be greatly improved by putting the patient into a bath of 28°, rubbing it dry and wrapping it in hot blankets. (Fig. 63.) The opinion concerning electricity is much divided. The author has never been able to obtain any very marked results by using this form of treatment.

Muscular rheumatism in some cases may be confounded with those of cysticercus cellulosus. In the latter case parasites should appear in very large numbers. Pauli found, for instance, in one dog a peculiar, stiff, flexed condition of the head, a surface one inch square in the psoas muscles which was filled with cysticercus cellulosus the size of a pea; and Trasbot found, at the post-mortem

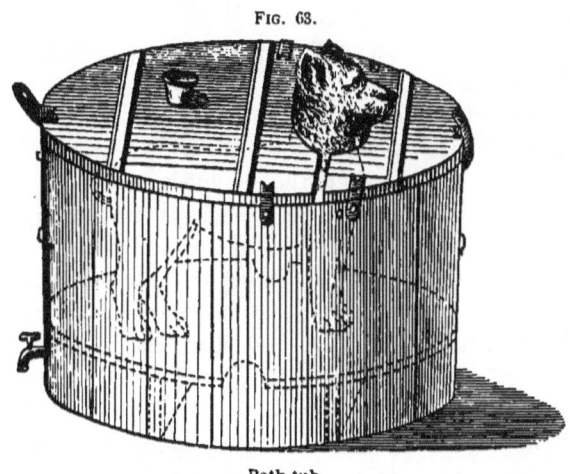

Fig. 63.

Bath-tub.

of a dog which had shown great pain during life, especially when touched or moved, all the muscles filled with cysticercus of tænia solium.

(For further details concerning cysticercus, see Internal Parasites.)

FRACTURES OF THE BONES.

ETIOLOGY. By a "fracture of the bone" we mean a breaking or disunion of a bone or a bony cartilage. Most fractures are caused by external forces, and the bone fractured is at the region where the force or shock has expended most of its force—for instance, from blows or being run over; or in some instances a fracture may be some distance from the region where the greatest amount of force has been made, such as falling for some distance, or concussions. We also see fractures of small projections of bones caused by great muscular exertion. The author saw a fracture of the olecranon in a hunting dog, which could not have originated in any way than by enormous muscular strain. Very old and young dogs have a predisposition to fractures and rickets, or a tendency that way may also produce fractures from a weakened or softened condition of the bone.

General Classification of Fractures. We separate fractures under different names according to their position, severity, and the complications accompanying them.

General Classification of Complete and Incomplete Fractures. In the first class belong infractions, splits or cracks, impressions or depressions.

In the second class belong oblique, transverse, longitudinal, and fissure fractures; in pups where the epiphysis and diaphysis would sometimes have fractured through the symphysis due to traumatic influences. This fracture, which is rather common, especially in the humerus and radius, is always confined to the immediate neighborhood of the symphysis. The general course of these fractures is the same as ordinary fractures, and no special mention is necessary regarding fractures of the soft parts.

The condition of the soft tissues in the neighborhood of the fractures and the amount of injury that they have had are of great importance in the prognosis. All fractures in which the soft tissues are not very much injured, and where the skin has not been torn, heal very much quicker than those where there is an open wound extending into the fractured end of the bone. The first are termed simple fractures, and the latter compound fractures. Where the fracture has involved a joint, it is called an intra-articular fracture. They are very slow and difficult to treat, and present such symptoms as synovitis, either with or without serous or purulent inflammations. In such fractures, even when we have union of the broken ends of the bone, we may have either a stiff joint or ankylosis from complications in the joint.

CLINICAL SYMPTOMS. The symptoms of fracture are generally indicated by partial or complete loss of the use of the whole or part of a limb. There is pain on pressure, deformity in the symmetry of the broken bones of that part of the body, and on moving the fractured ends there is a rubbing sound (crepitation) similar to rubbing two hard, rough surfaces against each other. The amount of loss of power in a broken bone depends to a great extent on the amount and severity of the fracture. This is very marked in fractures of the extremities; great pain on pressure, especially on the line of the fractured bones. This may also be of especial diagnostic importance in case of cracks or fissures of the bone. In such a case, while the symptoms are all present, the ends of the bones are not displaced. This is generally seen in the longitudinal form and in very young animals where the bone pivots on the fractured epiphysis. Crepitation and an abnormal movement are easily recognized by taking hold of the part above and below the fracture and moving it in different directions. Both of these symptoms are absent in incomplete fractures and in such fractures where the bones will close together with very little displacement. This is especially seen in longitudinal fractures of the short compact bones. We occasionally find a mild, rubbing bruit or sound produced by dry blood-extravasations or fibrinous coagulations between the surfaces of joints. In cases of fracture where the periosteum has not been torn, we will have a certain amount of swelling in the fractured region, pain on pressure, loss of appetite, and a certain amount of fever. This last symptom, however, is rarely noticed.

Where there is an external wound which becomes rapidly closed by the blood and the purulent agents cannot penetrate between the fractured ends of the bone, we have a form of fracture that is not so difficult to treat; but if any septic materials should have penetrated into the wound and found their way between the ends of the bones, the condition is generally indicated in the following manner: There is a marked inflammatory swelling in the neighborhood of the wound. At first the discharge from the wound is blood-colored, then rapidly becomes pus-like, and finally purulent in character. If the discharge becomes obstructed in any way, we quickly notice a purulent, œdematous swelling all around the part, which is always a very grave symptom. If the course is favorable, the injured part becomes rapidly filled with red, granulating tissue, which finally dries, becomes hard, and forms a scab. By means of strict antiseptic treatment this is possible, and we can reduce the danger and time of an open fracture by strictly following the usual antiseptic forms of treatment. In the dog, however, this is always rather difficult to accomplish, as the animals are hard to confine, moving about constantly and pulling or tearing the bandages.

The Phenomena of Union in Fractures. The healing and

union of the fractured ends of a bone are very similar to those of wounds, either by first intention (primum intentionem) or by second intention (secundum intentionem). In simple fractures we generally get union by first intention, and in compound fractures, unless the union be extremely small, we get union by second intention. (Fig. 64.) In both cases the union is accomplished by means of a callus growing around the ends of the bone—that is to say, a soft cellular tissue which forms an envelope surrounding the bone and gradually becoming hard through the ossific action of the periosteum and the marrow of the bones. The ring-shaped or external callus surrounds the fractured parts. This cellular tissue is formed of osteoblasts. The inner callus is formed by the marrow, forming a peculiar plug-shaped body and filling up the open ends. The periosteum is the true factor in making union between broken ends of bones. This is especially noticed in fractures where the periosteum is exposed, and where that envelope is torn or injured union is almost twice as long as where the periosteum is preserved. The extravasation of blood found in the early stages of a fracture which lies in the surrounding parts does not in any way assist in the actual union, but helps to a certain extent in holding the bones together until the callus is formed. The callus beginning is a spongy mass, especially in bones containing a large quantity of marrow. This gradually changes into a bony cicatrix or callosity. This becomes thinner and denser, lessening in diameter, and finally becomes smooth on its surface, forming what is known as "final callus." Reabsorption commences at the same time until the bony masses, which are useless after the bone is united, finally disappear, but there is always a certain amount of enlargement around the fractured ends of a bone at the point of union. Cracks and fissures undergo the same process.

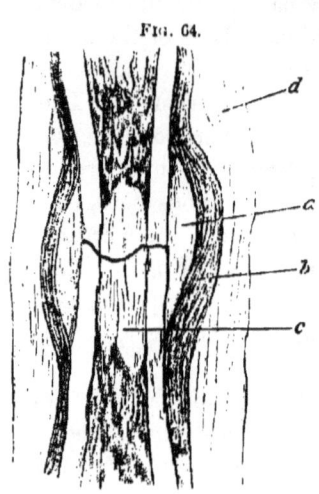

Fig. 64.

Diagram of union of fracture in the tibia of the dog: *a*, outer callus; *b*, periosteum; *c*, inner callus; *d*, inflammatory deposit.

Period of the Process of Union in Fractured Bones. The time required to obtain complete union of a fracture—that is to say, until the animal can use the part without any pain or difficulty—depends largely on the size and position of the bone, the age of the animal, and the amount of use the patient makes of it. According to the observations of the author and others, in fractures in which the periosteum is not torn, or simple fractures of the large bones containing marrow, the time is from eighteen to twenty-four days in adult healthy animals. Fractures of the ribs unite in from ten to fifteen days; in metacarpal and metatarsal bones, ten to eighteen days. In young animals the process is a few days shorter; in very old animals it is much longer. After the union of the fracture, as a rule, the affected leg is not used with as great freedom as it was before. This is especially noticeable in young animals that are growing. Very often there is a subsequent atrophy and impaired development of the muscles of that part. While this may be due to a certain extent to the inactivity of the muscles when tied up in the splint, and also to pressure of the dressing, it is often noticed after the dressing is removed, and sometimes for weeks afterward the animal walks stiff or is even lame.

Therapeutic Treatment. In simple fractures the treatment consists of returning the broken ends of the bone to their proper anatomical position, and holding them in position.

The bringing together of the fractured ends of the bones must be done as soon as possible, and it is accomplished by pulling or extending them in a longitudinal direction until the fractured ends fit together. In some instances where the tissue is loose they have to be pressed back in their normal position. The animal should be held by an assistant while the operator manipulates the ends into position. In cases where there is extreme pain and in order to keep the animal from struggling, it is advisable to etherize. In such cases as fractures of the metacarpal bones, bones of the face, etc., a reduction can be made without an assistant. When the bones have been placed in position as near as possible to their normal shape, we must then apply a dressing which will keep the fractured ends in their proper position until they have united.

The best dressing for fractures in dogs are those which dry rapidly, such as plaster and silicate of sodium solution. In some cases it becomes necessary to apply a temporary splint apparatus for a few days. This splint apparatus must be used where there is great swelling or where the condition of the wound or part would lead you to expect much swelling. The author finds the best thing for these dressings is a broad pasteboard splint. This should be dipped in water and kneaded by the hand until flexible. There are various other materials for making splints—gutta-percha, wire gauze, etc. In some cases where there is an open wound wire gauze may be used, fastened above and below the fractured ends, leaving the wound exposed. This gives it sufficient support, and proper antiseptic methods can be followed. A plaster-of-Paris or silicate of sodium dressing may be applied immediately after the fracture, provided there are no wounds. Where there are wounds or swellings we must wait until the swelling is absorbed.

We apply a permanent dressing, or a temporary dressing may be put on in the following manner: Cover it thoroughly with cotton wadding and apply the ordinary bandage, taking care not to make it too tight. In plaster-of-Paris dressings the ordinary gauze, crinoline, or cheesecloth may be used, and the plaster, in powder form, rubbed into the part. Then oil the point of the fracture to prevent the bandage sticking. At the same time place the plaster bandage in water for a few minutes and then wrap it carefully around the part, following the methods adopted in ordinary bandage rolling, being careful not to place it too tight. Smooth the water out of the part, making the bandage as level as possible. In some cases where you want a very stiff bandage, it is advisable to put a certain amount of plaster between the folds of the bandage and finally give a good coating over the entire bandage. After the dressing has been applied the animal must be kept perfectly quiet for at least ten to twenty minutes to allow the dressing to become hard. A plaster dressing will dry and harden a little

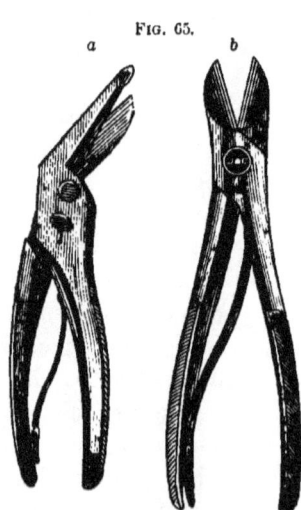

Fig. 65.
a. Bandage-cutting scissors.
b. Bone forceps.

quicker by the addition of a small quantity of alum or common salt. The scissors shown in Fig. 65 (a) are the most practicable for the removal of this dressing. Tripolith dressing (a mixture of plaster-of-Paris and soot) can be applied in the same manner as the plaster. Its composition is said to be much lighter and it dries much more rapidly. Silicate of sodium dressing has the advantage of lightness, durability, and of being removed easily, but it has one disadvantage, and that is it dries slowly, sometimes taking a couple of hours. The author likes this form of dressing best, and to overcome the drawback of slow hardening has placed thin layers of wire gauze between the dressings. Flannel may be used as an under layer. Another dressing is a mixture of benzoate of sodium and silicate of sodium. The dressing may be left in place until we feel sure that union has taken place. In cases where the dressing has been too tight, or if the patient shows restlessness, whining, crying, loss of appetite, or fever, indicating that something is wrong in the fractured region, the dressing must be removed at once. (Fig. 66.)

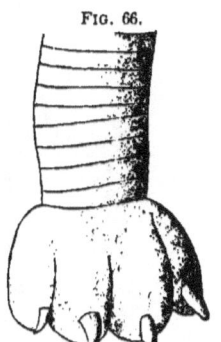

FIG. 66.

Effects of tight bandaging of a splint.

In complete fractures we follow the same rules as in the subcutaneous forms—that is to say, we endeavor in one way or another to hold the broken ends of the bone together while the wound is healing, and at the same time to dry up the wound antiseptically. This is rather difficult to do in the dog, but it may be accomplished by making a "window" or hole in the dressing. The wound must first be made thoroughly clean, dressed antiseptically, and then we apply a plaster dressing according to the usual method, and place a piece of wadding upon the wound. When the dressing becomes hardened we cut a hole over the wound by means of a probe-pointed bistoury, coating the edges of the opening with a small quantity of plaster-of-Paris or collodion in order to prevent the discharge of pus, etc., from running under the dressing. The rest of the operation is performed according to the general rules followed in the treatment of wounds. In cases where the fracture is fresh and the wound is very small we cover it with an antiseptic dressing (for instance, tincture of iodine and several

298 DISEASES OF THE BONES AND ARTICULATIONS.

layers of corrosive sublimate gauze). Then apply the closed dressing of plaster-of-Paris entirely over it. If the wound is slight, as a rule, you do not require to remove the bandage. Care must be taken, however, to take the temperature and watch the leg to see if it swells, and if the animal is restless and uneasy. In cases where there is a wound and several broken bones, making a compound comminuted fracture, the patients can only be saved by amputating the leg. Amputation of the leg, as well as exarticulation, has been performed a number of times in the dog, and generally successfully, the animals soon becoming accustomed to the loss of the leg, using the other three with almost as much ease as they did with four.

Amputation. Before the operation clean the affected leg with soap and a brush; then disinfect with powerful antiseptics (5 per cent. solution of carbolic acid, 1 to 1000 solution of corrosive sublimate, and 2 per cent. solution of creolin). In operating do so with as little loss of blood as possible. To accomplish this use Esmarch's rubber bandage. All of the rules

FIG. 67.

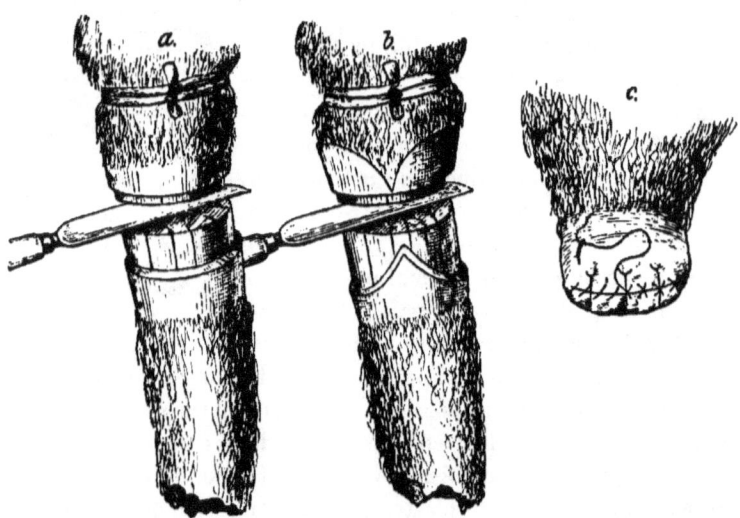

Different methods of amputation: *a*, straight section; *b*, flap operation; *c*, method of sewing the wound.

of antisepsis must be strictly adhered to, and at short intervals during the operation the wound must be irrigated with some antiseptic. Avoid any serious manipulation or compression of the soft parts. The skin must always be cut in such a manner as to cover the stump when the two ends or flaps are united. All the vessels, arteries as well as veins, which have been cut must be taken up separately with the forceps and ligated with catgut or silk. All stumps of nerves which lie loose upon the wound are to be drawn out with the forceps and cut off as close as possible. The bandage must not be removed until all the bloodvessels have been ligated (Fig. 67). The wound and its neighborhood are then thoroughly irrigated with an antiseptic solution and closed with stitches; the skin is also stitched at the same time. The different forms of stitching are illustrated on page 314. The whole wound is to be covered with a permanent antiseptic dressing. (For further details, see Treatment of Wounds.)

Amputation by means of a Circular Section. Cut through the skin of the affected extremity to the fascia, making a complete circle around the member. Pull this back and have it held by an assistant, he pulling the skin toward the body as far as possible. It may be necessary to dissect the skin and the cellular tissue from the under layer of the skin. After that make a sharp, clean cut, entirely circular, close to the edge of the skin which is pulled back, amputating all the muscles, and finally cut with bone forceps (Fig. 65, *b*, page 296), or saw through the bone. While cutting through the bone it is necessary for the assistant to pull back the soft tissues as far as he possibly can toward the body, either with his hands or by means of a linen compress which has been dipped into an antiseptic solution. In cases where amputation of the extremities has to be performed, where there are two bones, as in the forearm, it is necessary to cut the soft tissues which are located between the bones.

Flap Amputation. We cut two half-moon-shaped flaps of the skin and separate them from the fasciæ in which they are located as far as their base, turning them upward and backward. The muscles are cut close to the flaps, the tissues pulled back, and the bones sawed through.

FIG. 68.

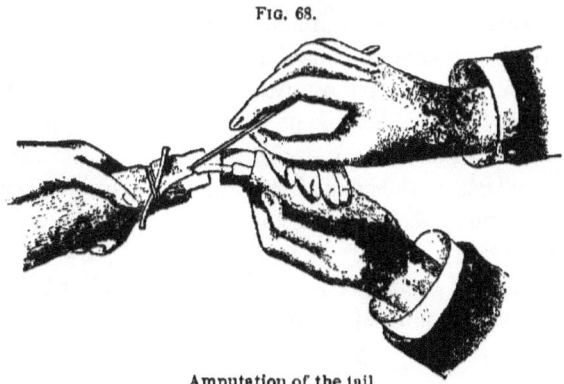

Amputation of the tail.

Exarticulation. Separate the soft parts exactly as in amputation by means of a circular or flap cut. We then open the affected joint by bending it, producing a tension of the ligaments which are located in front of it; then cut through them with a bistoury. Exarticulation is finished by separating the other ligaments and the capsule of the joint; then proceed exactly as we do in ordinary amputation.

Amputation of the tail is one form of exarticulation: This operation, which is comparatively harmless, is sometimes required in cases of necrosis of the bones of the tail after serious injuries to the soft parts or from fracture of the caudal appendage. An amputation between two of the vertebræ is much better than cutting through the bones. The operator must distinguish the slightly enlarged point (Fig. 68) where the articulation lies; then proceed by means of the "flap" or "round" operation, whichever is preferred. As the vessels are slight they can easily be stopped by means of a thermo-cautery. The author generally uses the circular operation, cutting posterior to the bony protuberances of the articulation. Pull the skin back, cutting through the muscles and tendons just below the articulation; then, with the help of an assistant, pull up the tissues and cut between the cartilaginous disk. In cases where there is much hemorrhage the artery may be taken up by means of a catgut ligature. The edges of the skin are united by an interrupted suture and an antiseptic dressing is applied, taking care not to make it too tight.

When the average period of union of fracture has passed remove the dressing carefully and see that the fragments are united. If we recognize any mobility in the fractured region, we then understand that we have a slow, callous formation, and nothing else is to be done but to renew the dressing as soon as possible, having first rendered the parts antiseptic by means of sublimate soap and water. Put on the bandage again and let it remain for two or three weeks more. If we do not obtain a cure at the end of that time we may conclude that we have a false joint (pseudoarthrosis).

The methods pursued in man of introducing ivory pins into the bone or screwing it together by means of clamps or resecting the ends with a saw are hardly practicable in the dog. If, however, we discover that there is any danger of the formation of a false joint, we may irritate the ends of the wound by rubbing the broken ends together and applying a dressing, giving the animal phosphate of lime or phosphoric acid.

Other diseases of the bones in the dog are of so slight importance that the author has omitted them.

WOUNDS AND THEIR TREATMENT.

By a wound we mean any injury which lacerates or punctures the skin, no matter what is the depth. Wounds are classified according to various authors in the following manner:

1. Their location, whether they are in the head, neck, chest, or extremities.

2. According to their depth into the muscles or bones, they are called penetrating or non-penetrating. Those that injure the skin slightly are called lacerations or excoriations.

3. They are also termed longitudinal, transverse, or oblique, according to their direction or length. Regular or irregular—that is, indented or flap wounds.

4. Their cause is also considered, whether produced by cuts, blows, lacerations, concussions, bites, or gunshot. These causes, however, are of no special importance.

CLINICAL SYMPTOMS. All wounds are accompanied by three symptoms: the open, gaping condition of the edges of the wound, hemorrhage, and pain. As a rule, the wider the wound the deeper it is. If the wound is long but does not gape, it corresponds with the direction of the muscle or the tissues beneath it. On the other hand, wounds across muscles are much wider and gape more, this being due to the retraction of the muscles.

The bleeding is either arterial, venous, or capillary. The former may be recognized by the fact of blood being mixed with more or less light-colored arterial blood. The danger of such arterial bleeding depends on the size of the arteries and how severely they have been injured. In small arteries the bleeding generally stops of its own accord, due to contraction of the severed bloodvessels; but in large arteries the animal will frequently bleed to death unless surgical interference stops it. In cases where the artery is cut in a transverse wound the hemorrhage is more severe than when it is in a longitudinal wound. There is more bleeding in cleanly cut wounds than there is in those produced by laceration or concussion, but the latter present more complications than the former, due to consecutive hemorrhages. In venous bleeding dark-red, even colored, blood flows out of the wound. Hemorrhages in small and medium-sized veins generally stop without any surgical interference, but the large veins, especially those in the neighborhood of the heart, are dangerous and should be taken up quickly. Capillary bleeding consists in a slow trickling of blood, which, as a rule, lasts for a very short time and is of no great importance.

A serious hemorrhage endangers the animal's life, and the more rapid it is the greater the danger. The following symptoms are presented: general coldness of the skin and extremities; paleness of the mucous membranes, especially the mouth and eye; great prostration; staggering gait; and often from weakness inability to rise. In some cases we have unconsciousness, dyspnœa, enlargement of the pupils, uncontrollable evacuation of urine and feces, finally slight convulsions, and death. This conclusion is to be expected if about half the blood contained in the body is lost in a very short time.

Many experiments have been made upon the dog in order to find what are the consequences of slight hemorrhages. One-fourth of a dog's blood may be withdrawn without causing any appreciable lessening of the blood-pressure in the arteries. The pulse may become very indistinct while the blood is withdrawn, but it is soon restored to its ordinary pressure if the hemorrhage is stopped, from the fact that the arteries contract in proportion to the smaller quantity of blood. The rapidity of the current and the number of contractions of the heart remain the same as before the hemorrhage. Any loss of blood amounting to more than one-third of the blood-mass reduces the blood-pressure very much. The current becomes slow and contractions of the heart are much less. At the same time the composition of the blood is changed. At first we observe a compensation of the water of the blood, and the salts which are thereby being reabsorbed from the tissues when this is exhausted; then albumin is drawn into the blood. It requires a much longer time to form new blood-cells after the animal has been bled of one-fourth of the weight of the body. The red blood-corpuscles become normal and return to their original number in from seven to thirty-four days.

The hemorrhage is stopped by the closing of the bloodvessel by a clot or thrombus. The blood within the walls of the bloodvessels is only kept in a liquid condition as a result of its contact with the endothelium, and if from any diseased condition the endothelium is changed, or if the blood runs off through another opening, or if the circulation is obstructed by a ligature, the blood becomes coagulated, and we quickly have the formation of a thrombus. This not only closes the bloodvessel externally, but it is more or less extended into the bloodvessel until it reaches the first branch where there is an active current of the blood. These useless vessels soon become converted into solid cellular connective tissue. We shall refer later to the puriform, pussy, and purulent degeneration of the thrombus.

It is readily understood that the formation of a thrombus may occur rapidly when the ends of bloodvessels which have been detached have their opening reduced by contraction or twisting of the coats (media and intima), as in the case of crushing or lacerating, especially in the capillaries or small veins. In partial injuries of the bloodvessels the bleeding may be stopped without complete obstruction of the bloodvessel. In favorable conditions the lacerated wall of the bloodvessel becomes coated with a solid coagula. This becomes organic, so that the only result is a slight thickening of the wall.

The pain of a wound is indicated in the dog by howling and crying when the injury occurs, or later when the wound is examined. The pain evinced by the patient also depends upon the individuality of the animal. Some dogs are great cowards and show great sensitiveness to the slightest pain, while others will stand any amount of it; and we must, therefore, always carefully examine a wound, seeing its depth, situation, and character, and not in any way be guided in making a diagnosis by the symptom of pain indicated by an affected animal. Wounds of the lips, lower extremities, external genitals, and of the bones are the most painful. In the dog we see occasionally a series of symptoms which are identical with what is known in man as " shock." This, as a rule, occurs immediately after any painful injury, such as extensive crushing of tissues or bone, and during or after operations. The visible mucous membranes in the skin become pale, then cold; the eyes are fixed, the pupils dilated; the pulse becomes irregular, reduced in volume; and the respiration weak and irregular. The animal appears indifferent or unconscious. These symptoms may disappear very rapidly or in some cases go on until the animal dies without rallying in spite of any form of treatment that may be tried.

Symptoms of a very similar character, as a result of extensive hemorrhage, are sometimes presented, and must not be mistaken for "shock." The same may be said to occur occasionally in the dog when under the influence of chloroform. It is believed that the symptoms of "shock" presented are due to an irritation or concussion of the sensitive nerves, producing reflex paralysis of the vasomotor or centre of the medulla oblongata.

In connection with the above symptoms we occasionally see disturbance of a function—that is, when certain muscles are injured and their nerves are separated, or when any of the joints or cavities of the body are opened. The symptom which appears when the muscles are divided or cut is a loss of power in that region covered by the affected muscle. The symptoms after the separation of peripheric nerves consist in the loss of movement and a partial loss of sensation. The latter is extremely hard to recognize in the dog on account of the numerous anastomoses which occur between the branches of the fine nerves of the skin and also of the injured nerves in the immediate vicinity. We also observe a marked decrease in temperature in the paralyzed or partially paralyzed part.

The Course of the Healing Process in a Wound.

The healing of a wound depends to such a large extent on its form, condition, location, and treatment, that from a practical standpoint we may generally separate the processes into, first, healing by temporary union; second, healing by second intention or suppuration; third, healing under a dry scab; fourth, healing under a moist scab.

Healing by First Intention. This may only be expected when the edges of the wound are smooth and sharp, due to cuts with sharp objects that are clean or surgical wounds which can be easily closed with stitches and covered by dressings. The microscopical examination shows that the healing of such wounds often occurs within twenty-four hours, and the adhesions form so quickly that the edges of the wound can only be separated by exerting a certain amount of strength. The wound is covered by a narrow, thin blood-scab; its edges appear normal or only slightly swollen or inflamed. The scab drops off after a period of five or six days, leaving a somewhat depressed, pale-red cicatrix. This gradually loses its color, and in a short time it is difficult to distinguish it from the surrounding tissues.

Healing by Suppuration or Second Intention. This appears when the wound is left to itself, and, if the animal does not lick it, it becomes quickly covered with dry blood and lymph, also a thick crust, which varies in color between red and dark-brown, covering over the edges of the wound. If the wound is licked from time to time, we have a discharge of bloody, watery fluid. After this the wound becomes covered with a veil-like gray covering, the secretion becoming more and more copious and thicker, then yellowish-gray, and finally pure yellow (pus). The edges of the wound become swollen and red, the gray covering of the edges drops off in pieces, carried away by the pus or licked off by the animal. From the second to the fourth day we see the appearance of small red granulations from the wound. These increase in number and finally fill up the spaces in the surface of the skin. Now the active secretion of pus begins to stop. The skin gradually contracts around the wound, the neighboring epithelial border rises above the edges, and eventually forms a cicatrix. The granulating surfaces, as a rule, shrink, contracting and drawing together the cutaneous borders from all directions, finally leaving a whitish somewhat depressed cicatrix. This is more irregular, broader, and thicker than the cicatrix formed in wounds healing by first intention.

Healing under a dry scab occurs, as a rule, in small wounds which are not exposed to infection or have not been licked. Under this head we may class excoriations, cauterizations, various small incised or superficial wounds which have been covered in their early stages by antiseptic powders, such as boric acid, iodoform, or antiseptic collodion. The same effect is seen after the use of the thermo-cautery. Dried blood, tissue fluid, etc., form a scab which becomes adherent, and only when this scab is removed by force does it produce bleeding. If it is not interfered with, it drops off in from eight to fifteen days, according to the size of the wound, and as a result we see a reddened, non-resistant cicatrix which soon becomes pale and hard. If the scab drops off at an early period from some other cause, we generally see distended, red, irritable granulations, surrounded by a cicatricial wall.

Healing under a Moist Scab. This may be produced by following the antiseptic method of healing wounds. In closing an entirely clean wound with a strictly antiseptic dressing, the wound having been produced as a result of an operation, and which is no longer bleeding, after having been closed it becomes filled with blood which coagulates. This coagulation, if perfectly antiseptic, fills in the cavity for a short time, when it is soon crowded out by the quick formation of granulations, and soon undergoes a change, becoming yellowish, due to an alteration of the coloring matter in the blood. This healing process is distinguished from that which occurs with the formation of pus by the fact that the constant loss of cells used in building up the tissues is not required, and that the cellular elements which are destroyed as a consequence of the injury are not detached to any great extent by the cleansing process of the wound, but they undergo a quick molecular destruction, and are then as quickly reabsorbed.

Notwithstanding the fact that under the microscope the healing processes of wounds seem to differ greatly, still the histological process is the same in all. The formation of a deficient vascular cicatrix is the main point in all forms of wound treatment. This is accomplished by neoformation of bloodvessels, by the appearance of numerous wandering cells, and by alteration of these cells into fixed bodies of connective tissue with a rigid interlaying substance. The various modes of healing already described depend on the degree of irritation that the wound has been exposed to. The most marked symptom of acute irritation under the usual conditions is granulation with suppuration, and we must also point out that it may be well, from a practical standpoint, to consider suppuration as an abnormal condition due to infection. We must also state that the regenerative power of the disconnected tissue varies. The skin and mucous membrane are always closed by a cicatrix, and it usually heals by first intention because the epithelium unites quickly. Compensation tissues which fill up wounds that have been accompanied with a loss of a certain amount of tissue, it either being cut out or destroyed, especially when they contain few or no bloodvessels, seem to fill up very rapidly.

Diseases Resulting from Septic Infection of Wounds.

There are a number of conditions which appear in wounds that are due to microbes and germs, producing certain irritations of the tissues surrounding the wounds, especially the bloodvessels and the lymphatics.

Phlegmone. By this we mean the inflammation of the soft tissues which has a tendency to formation of pus, especially in the loose subcutaneous connective tissue between the muscles and under the fasciæ. There are two forms of this condition—a circumscribed and a diffused phlegmone.

Circumscribed phlegmone. The symptoms are very prominent, especially when it is near the skin. We find in a certain circumscribed region a hot, painful, very red swelling, firm and tense in the early stages, but soon becoming soft, doughy, and finally fluctuating, due to the tissue breaking up and forming a purulent liquid. From the pressure of the pus the skin becomes gradually thinner and thinner, until it finally makes its exit through the skin and escapes. If, for some reason, the skin is too tough, or if the pus has not been allowed to escape by means of an incision, it may cause a purulent infiltration of the surrounding tissues, which is very serious and ends with necrosis of the parts, especially of the fasciæ, tendons, muscles, bones, and it may be taken up in the blood, and portions of the diseased tissues are carried in the circulation to different parts of the body.

Diffused phlegmone is generally a very serious condition. The local symptoms are the same as the circumscribed, but the fever is much higher, and the purulent pus rapidly extends in all directions in the loose connective tissue, undermining and frequently causing extensive necrosis of the skin, fasciæ, muscles, tendons, etc. Death occurs, as a rule, from septicæmia or pyæmia.

The treatment of diffused phlegmone consists of scarification and incisions. Numerous slight incisions are made to reduce the inflammatory tension of the tissues and to encourage the pus to escape, also to prevent it from burrowing in different directions, and to make an opening into the parts so that they can be disinfected by means of injections or irrigations of 1 to 1000 solution of corrosive sublimate, 3 to 5 per cent. of carbolic acid, or 2 per cent. of creolin. In circumscribed phlegmone it is better, as a rule, to wait until the abscess is in that condition known as "ripe," or "points." This can be distinguished from the fact that the swelling fluctuates or is soft in the centre. In a light skin it may be even yellow. As soon as the incision is made it should be emptied and irrigated and injected with an antiseptic solution, afterward treated as an ordinary wound.

Inflammation of the Lymphatics (*Lymphangitis*). This is caused by poison absorbed from an unclean, unhealthy wound, although in some instances it may be caused by a high nitrogenous condition of the blood due to over-feeding. The author has observed several cases in dogs where one or more of the legs was hot, painful, and swollen, and there were also lameness and an increase of temperature. On examining the subcutaneous lymphatics they were found to be enlarged, presenting a peculiar corded appearance and running in the direction of certain of the lymphatics. These were enlarged and very tender to the touch. In cases of this kind we may see two terminations: first, a rapid recovery; second, the formation of an abscess containing a large amount of purulent pus in the swollen lymphatic glands, producing extensive inflammation, blood-poisoning, and the animal eventually dying from septicæmia.

The therapeutic treatment consists first in the irrigation of the parts with cooling applications, and, if the glands show indications of forming abscesses, apply hot poultices and open as soon as possible.

Inflammation of the Walls of the Bloodvessels (*Phlebitis*). This is especially interesting to the veterinarian, as it is quite frequently seen in the dog. Purulent inflammations of the bloodvessels are seen in connection with infectious purulent wounds, and originate as a secondary symptom by extension of the suppurating process from the surrounding tissues. This is especially noticeable where the wall of the vessel is crushed, forming a thrombus, and this thrombus, lying in the bloodvessel, becoming infected from the wound, produces suppuration and breaks down, and is carried into the general circulation and deposited in some part or organ of the body, setting up an irritation, and a consequent formation of an abscess. This condition is termed "metastatic abscess."

The therapeutics are the same as those of lymphangitis. Open the wound as soon as possible and thoroughly disinfect the abscess.

Fever. Concerning the clinical symptoms of fever, we have given all necessary details on page 23. The fever which accompanies wounds varies greatly in intensity according to the cause. The following are the different varieties of wound fever:

1. *Aseptic Wound Fever.* This is produced by entrance into the circulation of the blood of harmless substances (water, irrigating fluids, non-decomposed wound secretions, and fibrinous ferments). This occurs in the majority of cases shortly after the animal receives the wound, and causes very slight disorder in the general condition. The rise of temperature is generally the only visible symptom in the dog. There is no alteration in the appetite, and the temperature is reduced within a few hours; in very rare cases it may be slightly increased for two or even three days.

2. *Septic Wound Fever and Septicæmia.* As soon as putrid or decayed substances find their way into the system by means of a wound the symptoms of fever appear rapidly. If they are mild in character, it is called "septic wound fever;" if they are acute, presenting symptoms which may endanger the life of the animal, it is called "septicæmia." Septic wound fever and septicæmia are only separated by their degree of intensity, otherwise they are similar. They are both produced by ptomaïnes which are developed in putrid wounds finding their way into the circulation. There is one difference that we will point out between septic poisoning and septic infection, and that is, in the first form, the micro-organisms which produce putrefaction are to be found only in the centre of infection and not in the blood, while in the second form the centre of infection is in the blood and in the tissues.

Septicæmia appears, as a rule, thirty-six to forty-eight hours after the injury with an increase of temperature as high as 40.5°, rarely above, and showing a remittent character marked by depression, fatigue, and loss of appetite, the last being very rare. If the wound is treated quickly and rendered thoroughly antiseptic, the symptoms rapidly disappear. The most dangerous forms of septicæmia which occur most frequently in the dog appear two to four days after the injury, showing a general disturbance of the system, and frequently without presenting any unusual symptoms in the wound itself. In many cases, however, we may then distinguish symptoms of putrefaction. The animal suddenly refuses food, becomes weak, somnolent, the mucous membranes become livid, and death occurs in a few hours, or more rarely after some days. The temperature is rarely increased to any extent. More often it is normal or subnormal. We are not able, therefore, to place any dependence on the temperature as far as prognosis is concerned, the only value being when the normal temperature is presented and the acute symptoms already described begin to abate.

We sometimes see very peculiar cases—for instance, the author has observed a case of septicæmia with normal temperature the first day accompanied by weakness, depression, loss of appetite, etc. In the next few days the temperature gradually increases; sleepiness, fatigue, and rapid emaciation; the symptoms increase in intensity; the pulse becomes weak, rapid, and much slower, until it falls below the normal rate, and finally ends in the death of the animal. In many cases diarrhœa is present, and in rare cases convulsions.

THERAPEUTICS. Antiseptic solutions must be used vigorously and the wound irrigated frequently. If there is any dead tissue that is hard to loosen, the thermo-cautery should be used to render it aseptic. The animal must be stimulated by means of ether, alcohol, and camphor. The author finds subcutaneous injections (4.0 to 6.0 doses) of spirit of camphor or camphorated ether, 1 to 10, of great value in such cases. This drug he is inclined to call a specific agent in septicæmia. It must be injected every two or three hours under the skin until the alarming symptoms have disappeared. Slight muscular contractions which sometimes follow the use of camphor are not to be regarded as anything especially serious.

3. *Purulent Fever and Pyæmia.* When a suppurating wound becomes very much inflamed and infects the surrounding tissues, it is generally followed by the entrance into the blood of some micro-organisms. If the symptoms of fever are slight, the patients may recover, with only a chill and a slight increase of temperature. If the fever is very serious and the temperature rises high, it is called pyæmia. In this disease you will find that the majority of cases are followed by metastatic suppuration in various organs of the body. This is due to the fact that the thrombus undergoes purulent destruction in the bloodvessels, breaks down, and the infectious matter is carried into the circulation, and from there it finds its way to different organs or locations in the body. The symptoms of pyæmia in the dog are not very easily distinguished from those of septicæmia, and it is very hard in the majority of cases to make a positive diagnosis. Very frequently we see symptoms of septicæmia and pyæmia combined, forming what is known

as septico-pyæmia. In this case the animal dies before any deposit of the suppurating poison has produced abscesses. In pyæmia the symptoms are marked by chills in the early stages, and by intermittent fever. The appetite is often good, and, as a rule, rarely entirely absent, as in septicæmia. Later the disease presents much more serious symptoms: the fever loses its intermittent character, the temperature remaining high; the appetite disappears; fatigue and weakness may occur; the patients become rapidly emaciated and finally die. With these symptoms we see metastatic suppuration in the internal organs.

The therapeutic treatment of pyæmia is similar to that of septicæmia.

Treatment of Wounds. In the treatment of wounds we must pursue the following directions to obtain good results: 1. That the edges of the wound must be brought together as soon as possible to encourage union. 2. That in the treatment of wounds we must protect them from all kinds of irritation, and especially from the invasion of micro-organisms.

A wound may be infected with microbes through the hair, or by direct infection from unclean hands, instruments, dressing materials, or septic fluids. It is also possible to infect a wound from the blood. The main point in the treatment of wounds should be to prevent the direct entrance of microbes into it, or to destroy the infectious substances which have entered the wound, and finally to put it in such a condition as to prevent the further development of any microbes that may still remain there. The first is rather difficult in the dog even under ordinary circumstances; the last can be followed out to a certain extent, as the treatment of wounds is greatly influenced in the dog by two facts: first, many dogs will not allow a dressing to remain in place; and, second, a wound is interfered with to a certain extent by the tendency that all dogs have to lick the injured part. For this reason we frequently have to modify the treatment of wounds in the dog. We must, however, apply a dressing in all cases where we can keep the patient quiet and prevent him from removing it. The veterinarian has two powerful agents at his disposal for the treatment of wounds: the first is, primary disinfection of the wound and its neighborhood; second, keeping the wound as dry as possible.

1. *The First Disinfection of Wounds.* This is of special impor-

tance, and especially during and after operations where there is much blood lost. The wound and everything coming in contact with it, also the tissues surrounding it, should be carefully rendered antiseptic. The hair has to be shaved or cut very close, the skin washed with ether and benzoin in order to remove all the fatty matter lying in the skin. Follow this by washing with antiseptic fluids (1 per cent. solution of sublimate, 3 per cent. carbolic acid, 2 per cent. creolin). Any existing wound has to be treated in the same manner. If there is a wound the shape of which forms a cavity, an antiseptic solution must be injected into it and come in contact with all parts. The irrigator shown in Fig. 69 is especially adapted to that purpose. For cleansing wounds do not use sponges unless they are thoroughly aseptic, also disinfect the gauze and dressings (tampons). Instruments and the operator's hands must also be carefully attended to. The former should be placed in an antiseptic solution of carbolic acid, 5 per cent., or a 2 per cent. solution of creolin. Do not use corrosive sublimate solution for instruments, as it leaves an insoluble coating of mercury on the steel. The hands and nails have to be brushed and washed with carbolic solution, or sublimate soap. During the operation the wound should be disinfected from time to time—that is to say, it should be washed or wiped with the solutions referred to above.

Fig. 69.

Apparatus for the antiseptic irrigation of wounds.

2. *Future Treatment of the Wound.* This consists of various measures, according to whether there is hemorrhage and the condition of the wound.

Stopping all Hemorrhage. If the blood which runs into a wound is left there, it has a bad effect, preventing an adhesion of the surfaces of the wound, and also being a favorable ground for the development of microbes.

Drainage of the Wound. By this we mean the removal of wound secretions, especially pus, by means of drainage-tubes. The regular drainage-tubes are made of rubber, having numerous holes cut in them. These are placed in the deepest part of the wound, and fastened by means of a stitch in the skin, or the wound closed around it. In small wounds we use instead of this small pieces of silk thread or catgut, which have been twisted together in the shape of a cord. Wounds which are not deep, but cavernous, and where it is difficult to get quick adhesion in order to insure proper drainage, it is best to leave the wound open, covered with antiseptic powder, such as iodoform, sulphonal, boric acid, naphthalin, salicylic acid, etc. The first-named agents possess special properties for the treatment of surgical wounds, drying them rapidly and depriving the microbes of a proper medium to develop in, and thus rendering it impossible for them to extend.

It is advisable to use some material that will take up the secretions of the wound quickly, and assist in drying them. For this purpose, we use iodoform, salicylic-, or carbolic-acid gauze. Cover the wound with the gauze, and in wounds with cavities fill them with a tampon of the same material. In a wound where there is a deep cavity it may be well to fill it in with a tampon of iodoform for twenty-four to forty-eight hours after the operation, then, having cleaned it, by means of sutures bring it together and cover it with iodoform-gauze.

The following is the ordinary treatment of wounds:

(1) *Controlling the Hemorrhage.* This may be accomplished in various ways. The best method is by means of a ligature. As a rule, this is performed by carefully ligating the bleeding bloodvessel, either directly on the vein or artery, or taking up a certain portion of the tissue with a pair of forceps, including the bloodvessels, and tying it behind the point of the instrument with catgut or silk. When the bleeding end of a bloodvessel is located in very firm tissue, out of which it cannot be drawn far enough to ligate, we pick up the bloodvessel with the end of the forceps, draw it out as far as possible, and twist it in a spiral direction; by this means we usually succeed in controlling the hemorrhage. If, however, the above does not answer, we pass a thread through the tissue underneath the bloodvessel and tie it tightly, and by this means close the opening.

Compression is sometimes used as a means of stopping hemorrhage. This we can accomplish by pressure of the finger above the bleeding region, or, if it is an extremity, ligate the member above the part by means of a rubber band or tube, or even a handkerchief. Esmarch's rubber bandage is the best. If there is a cavity, we may also fill the wound with a tampon of aseptic wadding of gauze or oakum. Another means of stopping a hemorrhage is by using a cauterizing iron (thermo-cautery), a solution of chloride of iron, vinegar, alum, and tannin. These, however, should only be used in wounds where you do not expect healing by first intention. All agents which have the property of stopping hemorrhages, as a rule, coagulate or draw the tissues in such a way as to prevent healing by first intention. Oil of turpentine is sometimes used, and is a particularly reliable styptic.

Capillary or slight subcutaneous hemorrhages can be stopped by pressure or irrigation with cold water. Hot water is also used to control hemorrhage.

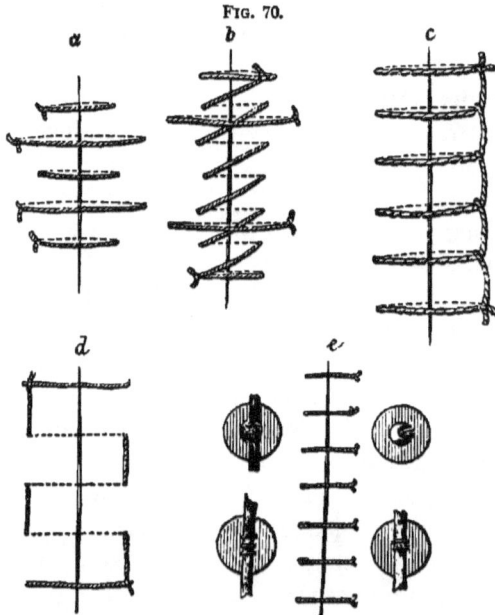

Fig. 70.

Different forms of stitches used in the dog and method of tying: *a*, head-stitch; *b*, continuous oblique stitch with cross-stitch; *c*, deep continuous cross stitch; *d*, mattress-stitch; *e*, button and interrupted stitch.

Wounds which can heal by first intention, such as all operative wounds which have been thoroughly disinfected according to the method described above, and where the hemorrhage has been stopped, we bring the wound together by stitches or ligatures (Fig. 70). As a rule, the ordinary knot-stitch with antiseptic silk is used, although we may connect it with other forms, such as the extension-stitch (Fig. 70). Small wounds do not, as a rule, require drains. The wound should be compressed for several minutes by means of an antiseptic sponge, and after that covered with iodoform-collodion. If the position of the wound allows, we must apply a firm, compact dressing over every wound that is stitched; if it is a simple one, the dressing may remain until it is entirely healed—that is, for about one week. If we have a large wound, however, with flaps, caverns, etc., it is advisable to place drains in the wound and change the dressing after three or four days. Instead of collodion dressing in such wounds, use antiseptic powders, such as sulphonal, iodoform, and boric acid. These should be dusted on the wound itself, directly on the line of the severed skin.

Lister's dressing in its original form is very rarely used at the present time. The author has been in the habit of covering ordinary sewed wounds with a thin layer of salicylic or carbolic gauze, and over it a dry, aseptic muslin bandage, and over this a damp starched gauze bandage. The latter has the advantage of forming a stiff envelope, becoming dry on account of its starchy contents, and exerting a certain hold on the injured member. If a serious rise of temperature takes place, the dressing must be immediately removed and the directions followed which are given under the head of "Wound Fever." When the bandage has been displaced, and when it has been moistened by the wound secretion, it must also be changed.

Wounds which heal under a dry scab are generally superficial. These do not require to be closed by means of stitches, and they seldom are licked or irritated by animals. We use in these cases the following method of treatment:

After thoroughly disinfecting the wound and its neighborhood, by means of caustic agents (nitrate of silver, chloride of iron, burnt alum, or with a thermo-cautery), we produce an artificial scab, or we cover the wound surface with collodion. The latter is recommended in common lacerations. As a rule, no dressing is used. The scab loosens after some time and falls off. When we are obliged under certain circumstances to leave a wound open it is advisable to muzzle the animal (Fig. 71), not only to prevent the patient from licking the wound, but in order to properly apply the sprinkling powder, which is less dangerous than iodoform. The best powder to use is boric-creolin (1 part of creolin to 40 or 50 parts of boric acid), naphthalin or sulphonal (1 part to 5 parts of starch). An open wound generally requires antiseptic washings daily. It frequently happens that granulating wounds, especially when they have been subjected to exposure to air, may at some period lose their power of healing and become converted into ulcers.

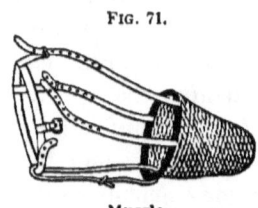

FIG. 71.

Muzzle.

Ulcers or Ulcerations. By this we understand a granulating surface which does not heal on account of the purulent destruction of the granular tissue. Wounds are changed into ulcers when they are continually irritated by some mechanical or chemical irritant, or as a consequence of the skin becoming inflamed or necrosed from pressure (muzzling, etc.). Callous ulcers and fistulous ulcers are the most difficult to treat. The former are superficial ulcers with hard callus, having raised edges, and a whitish, hard, baconlike surface. This is covered with a thin unhealthy secretion. They may form sinuses or canals, which very often contain at the bottom a foreign body or ulcerated tissue. They may also lead to some of the glands. These pipes are called fistulæ or fistular canals.

The treatment of ulcers is, to a certain extent, the same as that of wounds—that is, to follow all the antiseptic rules. The use of iodoform, salicylic acid, naphthalin, powdered camphor, or boric-acid ointment is advisable. We may also remove callous ulcers by surgical means and convert them into fresh wounds by taking a knife, paring the tissue at the bottom of the ulcers, and treat them as indicated in cases of fresh wounds. Caustic agents, such as nitrate of silver, tincture of iodine, etc., as a rule, produce little or no good effects. If the tissue surrounding the ulcers is hard and rigid, preventing contraction of the ulcerated area and the healing process, we must perform circumcision of the part, as transplantation is not practicable in the dog. We cut about 1 cm. from the border of the ulcer over its entire thickness, keeping the wound open by means of vaseline. When the location of the fistulous sinus admits of it we split open the fistulous passage and convert it into an open wound. When the fistulous canal is not very deep we may also try to produce healthy granulations by means of actual cautery, or the injection of caustic fluids and introduction of crayons of caustic (nitrate of silver or caustic potash). Always try to slit open the canal, if possible, as it produces the best effects. Nitrate of silver or any of the mineral acids, and in obstinate cases a small piece of corrosive sublimate, is pushed down into the bottom of the wound; these caustics produce more or less irritation and consequent sloughing of the wall of the canal and allow the growth of healthy granulations.

Contusions. In subcutaneous wounds of the soft tissues (bruises and contusions) we find a different condition of the tissues. These injuries are generally caused by some blunt object—for instance, a blow, kick, shock, or fall. The soft parts are bruised and injured according to the intensity of traumatism; very slight resistance is offered by the loose connective tissue; small bloodvessels are ruptured from crushing or bruising of the soft parts, and the hemorrhage that follows percolates all through the torn tissues. The greatest amount of resistance is found in the skin, face, sinews, and large bloodvessels.

CLINICAL SYMPTOMS OF CONTUSIONS. One of the first symptoms of a subcutaneous bruise is a swelling in the region of the injury. This appears, as a rule, immediately after the injury, and is due to the blood running out of the torn vessels. The fluids in the enlargement always contain lymphatic substances on account of the laceration of certain lymphatic glands. In rare cases we see a lymphatic secretion only, which is distinguished from the blood secretion by being very slowly absorbed. The fluid which appears lies either in the loose connective tissue under the skin or between the muscles, and, as a rule, is irregularly divided, or we may find the condition presented in a number of ways, so that we may have a "doughy" swelling in one case, or it is accumulated in centres in another, and we see a fluctuating swelling or a "bloodboil" (hæmatin), or it may run into a cavity, and we have a bloody secretion of the joint (hæmarthrosis), or we find a bloody secretion in the cavity of the chest (hæmatothorax). The swellings, as a rule, occur shortly after a contusion, and in the early stages rarely show any inflammatory symptoms. Later the inflammatory symptoms may appear.

Beside the swollen condition, the animal may present symptoms of pain, especially at the time of the injury, and later on we find the injured region very tender to the touch. We may also find a crushed muscle which will no longer contract, or a torn nerve that does not convey sensation or motion.

The further course of the wound depends to a great extent on the amount of the injury. If the skin is crushed in such a manner that all the vessels are torn, it will become necrosed from deficient nutrition, and, as a result, we see a putrid process going on as indicated in the discharge, which contains septic blood and broken-down tissue. The same is to be expected if the skin is deprived of nutrition, caused by the destruction of the bloodvessel supplying it.

This condition is materially different from a contusion where the skin has been removed; but if the integrity of the skin is maintained, the subcutaneous secretions under it are generally absorbed very rapidly. The soft parts which are lacking in vitality are absorbed, and are gradually replaced by a new connective tissue in exactly the same way as healing under a moist scab. Exceptions to this termination occur occasionally, and we may sometimes find a cyst, which is a hollow cavity filled with a yellowish-red liquid and enclosed in a capsule of connective tissue. In very rare instances this may be filled with calcareous concretions. This, however, is only seen in rare instances and is the result of a chronic irritation of the tissues at that particular locality.

In the treatment of contusions, to get good results we must have one object in mind—that is, the rapid reabsorption of the secretion. For that purpose we use cooling compresses soaked in lead-water (Goulard's extract), or arnica-water, or we may try to get absorption by means of massage—that is to say, make a centrifugal friction with the thumbs, fingers, or hand for fifteen or twenty minutes at a time. We may also squeeze the excreted blood into the tissues and lymphatic passages, and apply a tight bandage immediately afterward to prevent any recurrence of subcutaneous bleeding. This latter treatment is not to be practised unless the swelling is very small and there is very little fluid in it.

The therapeutic treatment is not simple in all contusions. In large "fluid-boils" we rarely can wait for an absorption of the secretion, but are compelled to open the swelling at the point where it is soft, and where the skin is thinnest. In animals we must always try to make an opening in the dependent part of the enlargement, so as to get perfect drainage. After having opened the tumor clean it out, removing all clots, etc., and treat the inner surface of the wound according to the usual method applied in such cases. If the location of the wound prevents such a procedure, the fluid may be emptied by means of a hypodermatic syringe, and an antiseptic solution injected in its place, and, if possible, this should be followed up afterward by a compress-dressing.

In all cases where the skin is very much injured, or where extensive destruction of the soft parts has taken place, or even fracture of the bone has occurred, we cannot use massage, but instead compressing antiseptic dressings must be applied. As a rule, treat the slightest injuries of the skin according to the best antiseptic methods.

Inflammatory symptoms are observed as soon as fever appears. The skin becomes hot and painful; finally fluctuation is found in some parts. Then we must immediately remove the secretion, clean out the wound, and by drainage keep the cavity empty, at the same time inject into it a 1 to 1000 solution of corrosive sublimate or a 5 per cent. solution of carbolic acid, and use an antiseptic bandage.

ABDOMINAL HERNIA.

Hernial Rupture.

By the word "hernia" we understand a protrusion of a certain portion of the abdominal contents through a normal or abnormal opening in its wall, and where the displaced portion is covered, or partially covered, by the peritoneum. In the majority of cases hernia appears under the external skin, although we may find it in other parts, such as hernia of the diaphragm. There are several different forms of hernia.

We distinguish the following parts in a hernia: first, the intestines or contents which protrude from the abdominal cavity; second, the hernial pouch; third, the envelope, or covering of the rupture; and, fourth, the entrance or constricted portion of the rupture, or where the intestine passes through the abdominal wall. By "hernial pouch" we mean that part of the peritoneum which is around the part protruding from the abdominal cavity, and we distinguish it where it is near the constricted portion by forming at the neck. The portion which lies in the hernial sac is the body and lower portion. The hernial pouch is absent in some cases—for instance, in a hernia which has occurred in a traumatic way, as a result of some injury, and the injury has been severe enough to tear the peritoneum; or where the hernial pouch collapses or draws together. Hernial coverings of the pouch are the names given to that portion of the skin and subcutaneous cellular tissues which cover that part; in some instances we also include the muscles and aponeuroses. The contents of the hernia consist of some portion of the abdominal organs enclosed in the hernial pouch. As a rule, it is the intestines, in most cases the duodenum, and in some cases the jejunum. Very frequently the duodenum may be found lying in the hernia with some portion of the large intestine or uterus, and more rarely the bladder or stomach. Under certain conditions we find a certain quantity of fluid lying in the sac. This is generally serum, and originates from venous stagnation.

According to the location of the hernial orifice we distinguish umbilical, ventral, inguinal, scrotal, and hernia of the diaphragm.

The causes of hernia are generally described as direct and indirect. In the former we have a certain number of abnormalities which are due to diseased conditions—for instance, an umbilical hernia is due to an imperfect closure of the opening of the umbilical ring. The latter may occur from the abdominal walls being flaccid from cicatricial contractions after operations, and occasionally from great abdominal pressure in prolonged straining, vomiting, etc., the muscular wall is ruptured, or from kicks or blows on the abdomen.

In traumatic hernia which has been caused by blows the hernial pouch is sometimes absent, and its contents are surrounded by a hernial envelope; in most cases by the skin; and in rare instances certain muscles are included in the sac.

CLINICAL SYMPTOMS AND COURSE. The symptoms as well as the course show a marked difference, according to the character of the hernia, and it depends to a large extent on the " possibilities "—that is to say, if the hernia can be reduced and replaced in the abdominal cavity or not.

Reducible Hernia. This is generally seen in the region of the wall of the abdomen. We find a swelling which does not present any inflammatory symptoms, and is especially prominent when the animal is walking or standing. It is also seen during abdominal pressure, especially after the dog has eaten a hearty meal. If the animal is turned in such a way that the hernia occupies a superior position, as a rule, it immediately disappears, as the contents fall back into the abdominal cavity, or they may do so on a slight pressure of the hand. If we examine the abdominal walls the orifice of the hernia can be distinctly felt, and we may even be able to penetrate the abdominal cavity with the finger.

Further symptoms depend upon the nature of the prolapsed intestine; this intestine will be recognized as a soft, elastic swelling, having to a certain extent the round or tubular form of an ordinary intestine. It may also be further distinguished by a slight distention which is generally due to gas or air. The omentum is soft and doughy to the touch, having an uneven surface and dull on percussion. Ruptures of the bladder may be distinguished by the acute symptoms of hernia and also by the entire absence of urination. Hernias of the horns of the uterus are only distinguished from a loop of intestine after conception and during whelping.

Mechanical influences, such as bites, blows, contusions, etc., may cause an inflammation of the hernia with a thickening of the pouch, and an adhesion between it and the contents of the hernia. If the injury is severe enough, we may have suppuration in the pouch. In such cases we may have a subsequent mechanical contraction and reduction of the hernia, especially when the pouches are small, or in some cases the hernia has only been large enough to admit a fold of the omentum.

Irreducible Hernia. 1. This may be due to an adhesion of the intestinal contents with the hernial pouch.

2. The union of the intestinal contents with each other (for instance, adhesion of the intestines).

3. From thickening of the omentum, which lies in the hernial pouch.

4. From strangulation of the hernia. This is especially important, as it may occur in all cases of abdominal hernia and at any time.

Concerning the causes of strangulation there are three important groups:

1. Strangulation by extreme distention of an intestinal tube by fecal matter.

2. A distention of the opening of the hernia, which subsequently closes on the intestine and strangulates it.

3. By the intestines becoming twisted in the sac. Invagination is very frequently seen in young animals.

In many cases we distinguish three stages of hernia, according to the anatomical alterations produced as a consequence of strangulation in the prolapsed parts. First, we have a venous hyperæmia, then inflammation, and lastly suppuration. In the first stage the veins and capillaries are gorged with blood, and serum is exuded in different directions. In the second stage we observe inflammation of a septic character, which extends from the mucous membrane to the serous membrane, as a consequence of the noxious or poisonous contents of the intestines. In the third stage the prolapsed parts become necrosed, due to the stricture of blood-circulation. The intestinal portion becomes black, easily torn, dull in color, and covered with gray or greenish spots on its surface, the hernial fluid becomes purulent, and the inflammatory processes in the intestine above the strangulation cause septic peritonitis.

The clinical symptoms of strangulated hernia are very marked in most cases. The hernia can no longer be reduced or pushed back into the cavity, or a swelling suddenly appears after any traumatism, or after great abdominal pressure, and cannot be reduced even with careful manipulation. The hernia is distended, harder and fuller than usual, becoming very sensitive to pressure, and especially so as the inflammation becomes more intense. The skin covering the hernia is normal in the beginning, but later becomes red, swollen, and warm to the touch. Another symptom which is generally present is vomiting. This may be so constant and violent toward the later stages that the animal will vomit feces. At that period symptoms of severe intestinal obstruction present themselves. The hernial swelling becomes cold, insensible to pressure, and symptoms of collapse appear, and death occurs from twenty-four to forty-eight hours after strangulation first appears. The temperature can hardly be said to have any diagnostic value, as we very often find it normal or even subnormal up to the time of death.

In rare instances we have the formation of a fecal abscess; this is caused by the sloughing of a certain portion of the intestine, allowing the contents of the intestine to escape into the sac; this is due to the circulation being cut off and subsequent mortification of the part; this is quickly followed by purulent inflammation of the hernial covering. If an incision is made in the hernial swelling, fecal matter and pus flow off externally without being followed by any grave symptoms, except that it may subsequently form a false anus in the cavity.

Fecal fistule, intestinal fistule, or preternatural rectum is seen in very rare instances. The expression "fecal fistule" or "intestinal fistule" is used where there is an external intestinal orifice, but the greater mass of fecal matter is passed through the rectum. The term "preternatural rectum" (anus præternaturalis) is used when all the fecal matter passes through this opening. Such an opening may also be produced by penetrating wounds or the entrance of foreign bodies.

In strangulation of the omentum the symptoms are less marked, but there is great pain on pressure. We frequently find adhesions between the omentum and the orifice of the hernia. This inflammation produces a complete immobility of the hernia and gangrene, followed by the formation of an abscess, and finally the escape of pus externally. Death is rare in such conditions, and if it should occur it is caused by septicæmia.

The prognosis of irreducible hernia depends greatly on the length of time that the strangulation has been present, and also on the character of the contents of the hernia. In cases where a loop of intestine is strangulated and is gorged with fecal matter the results are generally serious; but, on the other hand, strangulation of the omentum is not serious.

THERAPEUTICS OF HERNIA. In cases of reducible hernia we cannot use a truss, which is the favorite mode of treatment in man, it being impossible to keep a hernial bandage steady in any position for any length of time on the dog. When hernia has been caused in a traumatic way, and followed by a subcutaneous rupture of the abdominal wall, or in umbilical hernia of very young animals, we may close the orifice in such cases by means of a dressing, and the hernia may be entirely removed by the following method:

Place the animal on its back or in such a position that the hernia is placed as high as possible. Then reduce the sac by working the contents back into the abdomen. In some cases this is accomplished very easily, but in others it requires a certain amount of careful and patient manipulation. Then place a tampon of wadding or a small piece of cardboard upon the hernial orifice. This will have to extend over the borders of the hernia far enough to entirely cover the opening. Now fix small pieces of adhesive plaster across the cardboard and attach them in a circle around the piece of cardboard. These will adhere easily if the skin has been cleansed and any fat or other material has been removed by means of ether or benzine. [The translator finds that the plaster adheres a great deal better than the ordinary adhesive plasters sold, if, after the hair has been shaved off, ordinary shoemakers' wax made liquid is put on the end of the plaster strips.] We now place a gauze bandage around the adhesive-plaster dressing and the whole posterior part of the body, in order to protect the dressing from being torn or shifted by the animal. The dog should be fed on light, easily digested food, avoiding any that has a tendency to flatulency or constipation, at the same time assisting defecation by means of laxatives. The safest and most certain method, however, of removing hernia is the operation of herniotomy, or hernial section, which will be discussed later.

Where we have a strangulated hernia we must attempt to reduce it by pushing the contents of the hernia back into the abdominal cavity. This may be accomplished either by means of taxis or by hernial section. The former method is only to be used when the strangulated intestines have not yet undergone any serious alterations, namely, when they are not affected by gangrene, and when there are no serious symptoms of a local or general character. In the operation of taxis the patient must be placed in such a position that the hernia occupies the highest region in the abdomen and assists the relaxation of the abdominal covering and the orifice of the hernia as much as possible. We first try by manipulation upon the orifice of the hernia with one hand, and by pressure of the flat of the other upon the periphery of the swelling to push the contents of the hernia back into the abdominal cavity. When the animals are under the influence of ether or a narcotic, the reduction is easier. Taxis must be considered successful when the swelling of the hernia has disappeared and when the aperture of the hernia can be felt, and also when the symptoms of distention have gone. If the latter still continue, notwithstanding the fact that the contents of the hernia seem to have disappeared, we have a false reduction—that is to say, the hernial contents and pouch have been shoved entirely through the orifice into the abdominal cavity, or we have to deal with a volvulus or invagination of the intestinal portion in the cavity; or it may be that the hernial contents are crowded between layers of the abdominal muscles. In the first instance the orifice of the hernia seems free, and in the latter instance it is closed.

If the attempts at taxis to produce reduction fail, or if the above-mentioned contraindications are present—that is, where the hernia has been left too long—we must proceed at once to perform herniotomy, which must be done under the strictest antiseptic rules.

Herniotomy is, as a rule, a rather easy operation in the dog. It may be performed in two ways: with or without opening the hernial pouch. The former is especially used in fresh cases of hernia with wide orifices and in old cases of hernia with extended adherences of the hernial contents, where the whole mass is firmly fastened together. The latter method of operation is used in cases of hernia which are not complicated with a hernial pouch, in strangulated hernia with considerable alteration of the contents, or with a very narrow hernial opening. These conditions, however, are only distinguished during the course of the operation, and we are then forced to change from the first to the second method of operation. In both methods the skin of the operated region must be shaved and carefully disinfected. We then lift up a fold of the skin corresponding with the axis and the length of the hernia and split it open with a longitudinal incision. This must be made very carefully until we reach the hernial pouch. This is recognized by its irregular surface, which is of a grayish-yellow color; also by the fact that it is impossible to get an ordinary sound directly into the abdominal cavity.

Having opened the sac, taking care not to injure the contents, we follow one of the two methods before spoken of—that is, not opening or opening the hernial pouch.

In the former case we introduce by means of the index-finger a probe-pointed bistoury, or herniotome, between the neck of the hernia and its orifice, turning the cutting edge of the knife toward the neck or restricted portion, the dull side of the knife being toward the strangulated portion of the intestine. By means of a small incision the tension becomes greatly relaxed, and reduction is very easily accomplished. If the opening of the hernial pouch is required, we hold up one of its folds with a hooked-shape forceps and split it by means of a knife held flat or a pair of scissors. After the discharge of the fluids in the hernial sac a notch is cut in the hernial pouch by means of the herniotome. The exposed loop of intestines, which is intensely red and inflamed, must be cleaned by means of warm boric-acid water (4 per cent.) or creolin (2 per cent.), taking care not to allow the cleansing fluid to get into the abdominal cavity. This exposed piece of intestine is reduced by the method just described by cutting through the constricted portion and working the intestine back in such a way that the portion of the intestine which was prolapsed last must be reduced first.

If the intestine is much distended by gas, it may be emptied by means of a puncture of a very fine trocar (or the canula of a large hypodermatic syringe). Any degenerated portions of the epiploon must be amputated after being ligated. If the intestine is intensely inflamed or gangrenous, we must either resect it or make an artificial anus. Such operations, however, are extremely rare in the dog. We therefore will not enter into minute details on the subject.

After reducing the hernia we must close the hernial orifice. For that purpose we place a tight catgut ligature around the entire hernial pouch, which, if necessary, must be isolated, or, better still, we close the pouch and orifice by means of a continuous stitch after having amputated the superfluous portions of the hernial sac. In cases where no hernial pouch is presented or it has been shoved back into the abdominal cavity it is advisable to freshen the borders of the orifice by means of a blunt knife or curette; then stitch it up by a continuous suture of catgut. After thoroughly disinfecting it for the second time the external wound is to be stitched and covered with an antiseptic dressing, held in position by means of a bandage (eight-tailed) around the body.

Inguinal and Scrotal Hernia.
(*Hernia Inguinalis and Scrotalis*).

The inguinal canal of the dog is located in the abdominal muscles with the seminal cord, and runs from the testicles into the abdominal cavity. In the bitch we find a round ligament from the end of Fallopian tube toward the subcutis. Inguinal hernia may be produced by a portion of the intestine passing from the abdominal cavity into the inguinal canal. If this is the case in the dog, and the loop of the intestine goes as far as the scrotum, we call it scrotal hernia. If it simply lies in the canal, it is called inguinal hernia.

CLINICAL SYMPTOMS OF INGUINAL AND SCROTAL HERNIA IN THE DOG. According to Hertwig, from the external abdominal ring as far as the scrotum the canal is almost cylindrical, and we find this filling up with an abnormally warm swelling, which has a peculiar elastic softness and "doughy" feel under the skin. In large hernias we may reduce this partially or altogether by placing the animal on its back, holding up the hind-quarters, and gently pressing or rubbing with the finger upon the hernial swelling. If the intestine has entered the scrotum, the affected side appears full and large, and may be reduced by the manipulations indicated above. In cases of strangulation the symptoms which have been described before become apparent, and, if the symptoms are very acute and all attempts at reduction are futile, we must perform the operation of castration.

Castration. In normal conditions—that is to say, when no hernia is present—castration of the dog must be performed by laying the animal on his side, rendering all the parts aseptic, and holding the skin tightly over the testicle, compressing it between the finger and thumb. Then make an incision the entire length of the scrotum, cutting through the scrotum, the tunica dartos, and tunica vaginalis, so that the testicle, which is covered by the tunica vaginalis, is exposed (compare with Fig. 72).

This must be removed, and after that the common intersecting membrane is opened up as far as possible by means of a pair of scissors; then place a strong silk suture around the seminal cord, close up to the inguinal ring and ligate it. When this is done, the seminal cord, with all the superfluous portions of the interstitial membrane, is amputated about 1 cm. below the ligature. The other testicle must be removed in the same manner. After carefully closing the wound with a strong non-irritating disinfectant, the

328 ABDOMINAL HERNIA.

wound of the testicle has to be closed with an ordinary head-stitch, and it is advisable to place a small drain, like a silk thread, into one of the corners of the wound. No dressing is required, provided the animal is muzzled. Healing occurs generally within a few days. If, however, we have

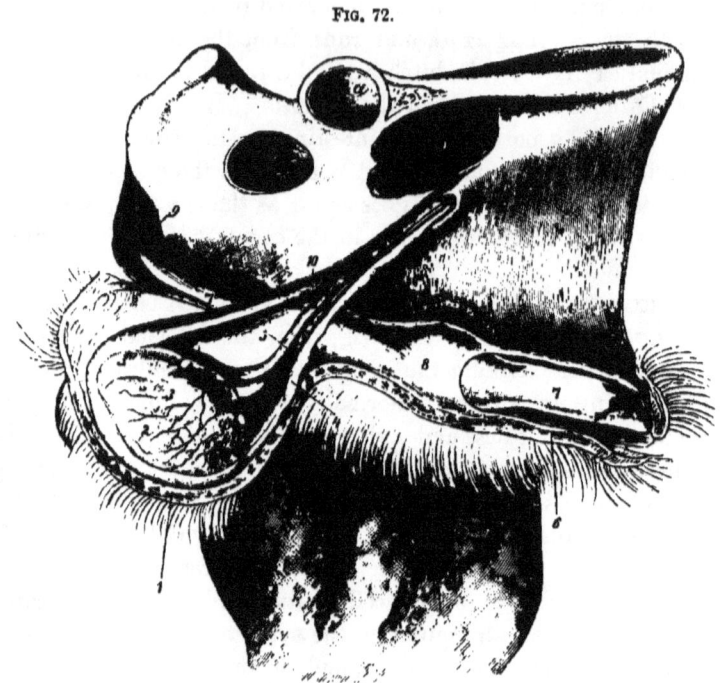

FIG. 72.

Genital organs of the dog: 1, scrotum opened; 2, right testicle; 3, body of the epididymis; 3', globus major and, 3'', globus minor; 4, spermatic cord; 5, vas deferens; 6, prepuce (partially dissected); 7, free portion of the penis; 7', posterior attachment of the penis; 8, erectile masses (bulbous bodies); 8', size of erectile masses when distended by blood.

a case in which we wish to operate for inguinal or scrotal hernia, we deviate from the above described method of castration by ligating the intersecting membrane externally and as close as possible to the external inguinal ring. In valuable breeding animals the testicle of the affected side only is removed.

Sarcocele. This is a collective name for all kinds of tumors of the testicles, especially for sarcoma, carcinoma, enchondroma, and cysts. The testicles are swollen, the swelling, as a rule, being hard, tough, and sometimes fluctuating; never warm or very painful. The condition can only be remedied by castration.

INGUINAL AND SCROTAL HERNIA. 329

Hydrocele. By this we define an accumulation of serum in the scrotum. The affection is often associated with œdema of the lower extremities and of the scrotum. It is frequently seen with ascites, hydrothorax, etc., appearing in the shape of a fluctuating swelling of the testicular pouch, which disappears when the animals lie on their back.

THERAPEUTIC TREATMENT. This consists of puncture and emptying of the sac, also injection with any of the following stimulating fluids: alcohol, Lugol's solution, carbolic acid (1 to 40), etc. Of course, these are only to be used when castration is not performed.

A variety of hydrocele is seen where we have œdema of the spermatic cord. This appears as a fluctuating swelling which may be easily moved from one side to the other. It occupies the whole length of the spermatic cord, and, as a rule, is never interfered with. When the fluid of the hydrocele, which is discharged by puncture, consists of bloody serum, we call it hemorrhagic hernia, or hæmatocele. Any other complications of the testicles and their membranes may be found on page 184.

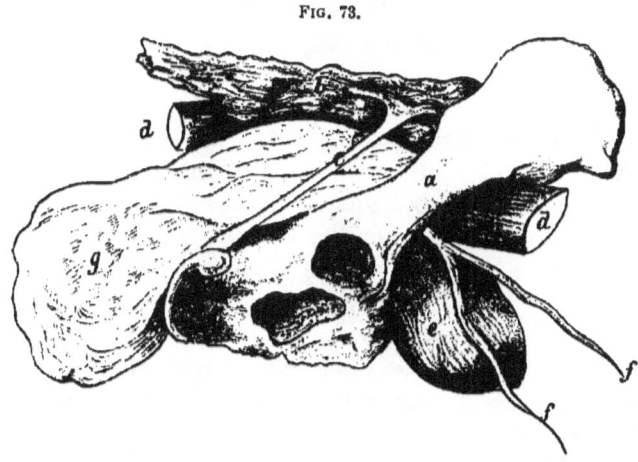

FIG. 73.

Middle section through the pelvis, showing the organs: *a*, pelvis; *b*, coccygeal vertebra; *c*, broad pelvic ligament; *d*, anterior and, *d'*, posterior portions of the rectum; *e*, bladder; *f,f*, seminal vesicles; *g*, fold of the peritoneum.

CLINICAL SYMPTOMS OF INGUINAL HERNIA IN THE BITCH. The contents of the hernial pouch are generally the uterus, and it may either be one or both horns; in some cases the gravid uterus may form the hernia.

Cadéac saw a great accumulation in a bitch which was affected by double-sided inguinal hernia. Each pouch had attained the size of a child's head; the right side contained the whole intestinal tube; the left side contained the epiploon, spleen, uterus, and bladder. The hernial covering was formed by one-half of the mammary glands and the external membrane.

This condition is easily distinguished. In the posterior sections of the mammary glands we find an elastic, painless swelling which disappears generally after manipulation, when the animal is placed on its back; provided, of course, that we find the uterus which is located in the hernia is not gravid. In that case the progeny may be distinguished by manipulation externally. It is hardly possible to confound this form of hernia with hypertrophic conditions of the round ligaments, or the so-called false inguinal hernia. A radical operation of double-sided hernia is to be performed according to the general rules already described.

Umbilical Hernia.

(*Hernia Umbilicalis.*)

The hernial ring is formed by the umbilical ring. The contents may consist of the omentum, duodenum, and in rare cases part of the large intestine. In the hereditary form the intestines are located in the umbilical cord, and are not covered by the abdominal membrane (hernia of the umbilical cord). In accidental hernia of the umbilicus we always have a hernial pouch, originating from the peritoneum. As a rule, umbilical hernia occurs a few days after birth. It may increase gradually and become eventually strangulated, but it often disappears without any surgical interference. Hernia of the omentum we see occasionally, but, generally, it cures itself by an adhesion between the hernial pouch and the hernial ring. Umbilical hernia is easily recognized. We find a swelling under the umbilical ring, which may vary in size from a hazelnut to a walnut. Treatment consists, as a rule, in replacing the contents of the umbilicus into the abdominal cavity and ligating the umbilical cord.

Femoral Hernia.
(*Hernia Cruralis.*)

Femoral hernia is extremely rare in the dog. The ring is formed by the upper end of the so-called femoral canal, and is formed of the crural fascia, the external membrane forming the hernial covering. The femoral canal of the dog is a long, three-cornered cavity in the median surface of the upper part of the leg, which is surrounded front and back by the inverted muscles of the upper thigh—that is to say, in the front by the sartorius muscle, and back by the long adductor, the large and short adductor, and on its upper surface by the ileo-psoas, while the floor of the cavity is formed by a portion of the muscles of the thighs and by the crural fascia. Below the borders of the sartorius the adductors run together at an acute angle. This canal, as a rule, is filled with masses of fat, nerves, and bloodvessels. In cases of fracture of the pelvis the intestines which leave the abdominal cavity, after having followed the direction of the large bloodvessels, locate themselves in this cavity and are covered by the peritoneum, the crural fascia, and external membrane; but they may also under certain conditions penetrate directly under the skin through an opening of the crural fascia.

In the inner fascia of the thigh we find a soft swelling which has more or less pain when the condition is examined before the disease has been of recent origin, and in cases of strangulation. In the latter cases, however, we see also a peculiar dragging motion of the thighs, with lameness and symptoms of intestinal obstruction, such as vomiting, etc. Herniotomy has to be performed according to the rules mentioned before, but must only be done in extreme cases. In making incisions into this region great care must be taken to avoid the large bloodvessels which pass into and through the femoral canal.

Perineal Hernia.

Perineal hernia occurs in both dogs and bitches. In the former it is recognized by a peculiar bulging or lifting of the recto-vesicalis, and in the latter by a bulging of the vesico-uterina. In both cases we observe a prolapse of the duodenum or lower bowel, and sometimes in the dog we observe a prolapse of the bladder.

In the dog we recognize perineal hernia by a soft swelling the size of an egg or the size of a hand. This appears in the side and above the anus, between the root of the tail and the tuber ischii. In the bitch this hernial swelling is seen under the vulva and on the peritoneum. This hernia can only be removed by means of an operation.

TUMORS.

A THOROUGH description of tumors with the different varieties and forms cannot be discussed here as explicitly as the author would like, and he therefore will confine himself to such tumors as are met with in general practice, and for further details would direct the reader to books on general pathology and morbid anatomy. The following tumors have been found in the dog:

Tumors of the Connective Tissue.

Soft and Hard Fibroma. A soft fibroma consists of connective tissue containing bloodvessels and cavities. These are filled with a serous or mucous fluid. They are generally found lying in the skin, and form round, soft, inelastic bodies, not especially circumscribed, flabby in consistency, and generally with a broad base. A hard fibroma consists of a very firm body made up of closely united fibrinous tissue, and forms rounded or oblong, distinctly circumscribed hard tumors, which originate, as a rule, in the skin or subcutis.

Fibromas belong to the class called "mild tumors," and are easily removed.

Lipoma (*Fatty Tumor*). A lipoma is formed exactly like normal fatty tissue, but possesses larger fat cells. It is also flabby and soft, but no fluctuation is present. As a rule, it is very distinctly circumscribed, being separated from the neighboring tissues by a layer of connective tissue. Very rarely do we find it diffused in different directions. As a rule, it is found in the dog around the synovial folds of the joints, in tendons and their sheaths, as well as in the internal organs.

Lipomas occur in the lower cellular cutaneous tissue, and, as a rule, can be easily removed by an operation. After the removal of fatty tumors which had not been distinctly circumscribed the author saw several recurrences of the tumors; also septic inflammation in the neighboring tissues as a result of the wound.

Enchondroma (*Cartilaginous Tumor*). Enchondroma consists of cartilaginous tissue, either hyaline or mucous. We find it in a normal condition in the bony system and quite frequently in the lacteal glands.

True enchondroma is considered as a very mild form of tumor, and may be recognized by its round or nodulated body, distinctly circumscribed, hard and cartilaginous character.

Osteoma (*Tumor of the Bones*). Osteoma is a compact or spongy bony tissue, consisting of a tumor generally developed on the body of a bone. As a rule, it occurs on the periosteum; more rarely in the muscles, fasciæ, tendons, and still more rarely in the thyroid glands. (This last condition was described by Siedamgrotzky, and may be generally recognized by its location and bony consistency.) The author has seen an old dog in which he found osteomata nearly as large as a hen's egg. These were remarkable for their extremely irregular surface, and were attached by distended tendinous tissue to the left of the transverse prolongation of the fifth cervical vertebra, but were removed without any bad results. As a rule, osteomas are removed only when they are closely connected with the bone, and when they are likely to cause a great deal of trouble.

Sarcoma. By sarcoma we mean a tumor which originates in the connective tissue, which is developed from a certain type of embryonal connective tissue, and formed with numerous cells. It originates in various parts of the body, such as cartilages, bones, periosteum, connective tissue, fatty tissue, etc. We may also observe it in the form of mild tumors. Their histological formation and their different varieties are better described in text-books of pathological anatomy.

Sarcomas are generally considered as malignant tumors: 1, because they possess a great tendency to become large; 2, because they are apt to reappear after removal; and, 3, because under certain conditions they are apt to form in other parts of the body. Their malignant character is generally much greater in proportion to the size of their cells and the softer their intercellular substance.

The external anatomical appearance of a sarcoma does not always present characteristic symptoms. In most cases these tumors are round, distinctly circumscribed, and sometimes they form encysted knots, which are of different consistency and color. We may recognize fibrin and even bone in sarcomas, and some that are soft as gelatine or mucus. Their color depends, as a rule, on their vascular condition, and any blood extravasations which may have occurred also produce certain alterations, so that on section a sarcoma may appear white, yellow, brown, gray, dark red, and even entirely black (melanotic sarcoma).

The metamorphoses which occur in the sarcoma are of some diagnostic value, especially the mucous softening, which leads to the formation of cysts, and sometimes to bony deposits. This is frequently noticed in sarcoma, and the ulceration in sarcoma of the skin and mucous membranes occurs without producing any active disintegration of the tumor.

There are very rare forms of osteosarcoma, or myeloid tumors, which occur in the marrow cavity of bones. They have been noticed in the forearm, also in the shoulder-blade, the bone of the arm, and femur (Siedamgrotzky and others). Circumscribed nodules are developed in the medullary cavity which gradually crowd out the bone by their growth, and, when new bone is formed from the periosteum, filling up the entire cavity. In this manner we find enormous lumps, or masses, possessing the hardness and firmness of bone, and in the centre is found a soft tumor surrounded by a bony cyst. Sooner or later the soft parts penetrate the bony envelope and certain of the fluid escapes.

The treatment of sarcoma consists in removing it as soon as possible, and always endeavor to remove the entire tumor, as a small portion allowed to remain may form a nidus for the commencement of a new growth. There is a group of tumors of the connective tissue which we see occasionally, called **angioma**. These are mostly in the form of fibro-angioma, small, ball-like, tough, cutaneous tumors, which on section are generally colored bluish-black.

Epithelial Tumors.

Papilloma. Papilloma originates by hyperplasia of the covering epithelioma of the cutaneous and mucous membrane, with a proportionate formation of connective tissue. These are separated as follows:

(a) *Warts.* A wart is a neoformation of the papillæ of the skin and of the epidermis. Warts vary very much in size, from a lentil to the size of a pea. The external covering of a wart is very often hard and firmer than that of the connective tissue, so that the surface is surrounded by a firm, hard, horny covering (horny warts). The reverse is found in the case of soft, fleshy warts. These little formations are found on the skin of dogs of all ages, as a rule, on the head and back, but also in other regions, and they often disappear without any treatment. Now and then these horny warts grow to a very large size and form what are called "cutaneous horns." Such are found on the forehead, the ear, and flanks; they are generally seen in old dogs. Enormous numbers of warts are sometimes seen in the mouth on the buccal membrane.

(b) *Flat Condyloma.* By this we mean certain marked malformations which have the shape of a papilla, but, as a rule, are ramified and divided, forming coxcomb-like collections. They also appear in some cases as true papilloma, particularly as a sarcomatous formation. As a rule, they appear upon other regions than the skin, such as the lips, cheeks, and prepuce, also upon the mucous membranes in the buccal cavity. They are generally salient and easily made to bleed. This is due to the large number of bloodvessels they contain, their softness, and very thin epithelial covering. The author has noticed that dogs affected with condyloma of the vulva or penis also show these formations quite frequently on the edges of the lips. Gratin has often seen the obscure transmission of condyloma from one dog to another. This would tend to establish the fact that this disease is contagious.

All varieties of papilloma may be removed by a curette or a pair of scissors. The use of caustics, ligatures, or amputations is also recommended.

Palm recommends the following:

R.—Acid. salicylicum . . . 1 part
    Acid. lactic.   } āā 2 parts
    Collodion-ether }
S.—Apply twice daily.

Adenomata. These are malformations of the true glandular tissue, which always originate in some gland and can be distinguished from simple glandular hypertrophy by the fact that they stand out from their surroundings, are knotty, tough, or sometimes soft tissue. Their growth is slow; their metamorphoses consist, as a rule, in the formation of cysts; and in those cases that are superficial we may have ulcerations externally somewhat resembling carcinoma. While adenoma is not malignant, it may become so in certain cases and change into a carcinoma. We have observed adenoma in most of the various glandular organs, upon the skin, in the mucous membranes, in the mammary glands, in the salivary glands, and thyroid gland. Tumors of the anus and stomach deserve special mention.

(*a*) *Tumors of the Anal Glands.* The rectum of the dog has beside the ordinary cutaneous glands: 1. Glands of the anal pouches. These are glands having a branch tube-shaped form, located in the walls of the anus. 2. Acinous glands, which are formed in the so-called anal protuberance. 3. Anal glands, which are small, grape-like bodies located between the lower bowel and the anal mucous membrane.

All these glands may become the seat of adenoma, but the latter is mostly developed in the circum-anal glands. Sarcoma and carcinoma occur quite frequently in the rectum of the dog.

Tumors of the circum-anal glands, which are generally found in old dogs, have been carefully studied by Siedamgrotzky. They appear as round or irregular, firm tumors which are connected closely with the skin, and produce more or less enlargement of that part; otherwise they are connected with their neighborhood by a loose connective tissue. In the transverse section they appear to be formed of yellowish-white or yellowish-red tissue, which is similar to the circum-anal glands. As a rule, they are easily removed.

In some cases we have acute inflammation of the circum-anal glands with a formation of abscess. The tumors may be easily distinguished by the presence of pain, heat, and later fluctuation. We also see on these occasions an inflammation of the anal pouches. The anal pouches represent the cæcal pouches, which vary in size from a hazelnut to a walnut, and lie between the mucous membrane and the muscular membrane. They contain within their walls the above-mentioned glands and have only an external exit by means of a very narrow canal. Inside we have a yellowish-brown, thick fluid, which, as a rule is fetid. Various influences, generally of a traumatic character, may cause inflammation of these pouches and a retention of their contents. The anus becomes swollen considerably on one or both sides. The membrane over the swelling is red, feverish, and painful to pressure. The animal makes frequent attempts to defecate without any result. A local examination shows the presence of a discharge of purulent matter from the orifice. This condition is soon relieved by means of cooling applications and frequent emptying of the pouch.

(b) *Goitre; Struma.* Goitre is a non-inflammatory swelling of the thyroid gland, and is frequently seen in the dog as a simple hyperæmia and enlargement. In some cases we find an adenoma of the thyroid gland (true goitre). In very rare cases we find a sarcomatous or carcinomatous deposit of the thyroid gland (false, malignant goitre). It has been observed that in 30 or 40 per cent. of tumors in old dogs the disease is a cancerous degeneration of the thyroid gland.

The thyroid gland in the dog consists of two portions, lying on each side of the trachea, separated by the median line, a short distance below the larynx, and connected in the larger animals by a narrow isthmus. In small dogs this connection may be absent. We generally speak of two thyroid glands in the dog, and more so because we occasionally find only one side diseased, and very frequently find one portion more affected than the other.

We divide goitre into three varieties: the hard, soft, and cystic forms. A tumor of the neck is the symptom of all three varieties, which may sink downward as far as the entrance of the chest. As soon as goitres reach any development they may cause alarming symptoms, such as difficulty in respiration by pressure on the trachea, and, in rare cases, dysphagia. Leisering saw a goitre in a poodle dog which extended from the larynx to the sternum, and covered almost the whole lower surface. It was about 16 cm. long, 10 cm. wide, and 3 cm. thick.

The hard goitre (struma fibrosa) is a fibrous hypertrophy of the gland and a disappearance of the glandular substance. The swelling is hard and firm. In the soft form of goitre (struma mollis) there is more or less hyperplasia of the glandular tissue. In the cystic goitre (struma cystica) the gland is altered into one or more fluctuating cavities, which, as a rule, are filled with a colloid fluid. There are other varieties of this tumor, but the writer refers you to the text-books on pathological anatomy.

Carcinoma and sarcoma of the thyroid gland are distinguished from true goitre by the fact that the swelling does not possess the smooth surface seen in the ordinary form, but is uneven and irregular, becoming developed into a goitrous degeneration of the gland. The etiology of the mild form of goitre is very obscure, notwithstanding numerous researches. In man, as well as in horses and cattle, the appearance of goitre has been found to be due to their existence in certain districts, especially in mountainous ranges, and on that account its cause has been looked for in local conditions of the soil and water, especially where they contain large quantities of lime. In the dog no such reason can possibly be ascribed, as in the regions where man, horses, etc., are rarely affected, many affected dogs of various ages and different nutritive conditions are found. The observation made by Maumeni of feeding fluor calcium to dogs was of no especial value. The fact has been pointed out by Schrauz that goitre is due to or may accompany certain affections of the heart; this is a much more important cause, according to the author's opinion. Schrauz has found that in a goitre district of the Tyrol in 66 per cent. of cases of heart-disease the people were affected with goitre. It is advisable therefore to make an examination of dogs affected with this trouble, following the same procedure as is described under Diseases of the Heart. We do not know if this affection is hereditary, but we question it, although some authors claim that it is.

THERAPEUTIC TREATMENT. The treatment of goitre may be medicinal or operative. As soon as the enlargement occurs, or signs of development appear, we obtain satisfactory results with preparations of iodine. Use iodine internally in the form of iodide of potassium in small doses, and externally in the shape of ointment of iodide of potassium, tincture of iodine, or ointment of iodoform (Siedamgrotzky). Also injections into the gland of tincture of iodine, or alcohol and iodine, equal parts, are very successful, but are sometimes dangerous from subsequent fever in cases of parenchymatous goitres. These injections must be strictly aseptic in order to avoid suppuration. After thoroughly disinfecting the cutaneous region, we thrust a hypodermatic needle into the goitre, and first see if any bloodvessel has been injured. With this syringe inject into the gland equal parts of tincture of iodine and pure alcohol. In large goitres the injections must be repeated at intervals of several days. In all cystic and fibrinous goitres the parenchymatous injections are generally useless, as is also the internal treatment with iodine. We must treat these forms like any other cystic tumor—that is to say, by puncture, opening it freely, tamponing with iodoform-gauze or wadding, and encouraging the formation of true granulations to fill up the cavity.

The removal of a thyroid gland which is affected by goitrous degeneration is performed in the same manner in the dog as the removal of any other tumor. We must, however, consider three very important things during the operation:

1. The large number of bloodvessels in the immediate vicinity requiring careful incision and subsequent ligation.

2. The fact that after removal of both parts of the thyroid gland we often have the appearance of serious constitutional symptoms and death.

3. Any uncleanliness during or after the operation always produces severe septic irritation in the remaining portion of the gland and its surroundings.

We have found from the observations made on a number of these cases that removal of one part of the gland does not affect the animal materially; but if both are removed, or the whole gland, we might say, the dog dies within three or four days, with symptoms resembling those of acute poisoning, or it becomes affected by marasmus, becoming depressed, will not eat, emaciation follows, the number of white blood-corpuscles in the blood increases to an enormous extent, the animal becomes unsteady and uncertain in walking, there are muscular twitchings and convulsions, and finally general paralysis, and death occurs in three or four days after the acute symptoms make their appearance.

It is only in rare cases that the dog survives removal of the whole gland. We can, therefore, conclude that if the dog is affected on both sides we should remove the one that is affected the most. In rare cases we see a goitrous degeneration and enlargement of the thyroid gland. The symptoms of this inflammation invariably occur in young animals, and may be due to traumatic influences. In these cases we find a traumatic swelling over the region of the gland, sensitiveness to pressure, increased temperature, slight fever, generally followed by the formation of an abscess. The treatment is to be that advised under the treatment of abscesses.

Cysts (*Cutaneous Tumors*). A cutaneous tumor generally consists of a closed sac or pouch, which is lined with epithelial cells, and contains more or less liquid. Cysts are divided into several varieties:

Dermoid Cysts. These consist of cutaneous tissue, sebaceous glands, sweat-glands, and hair-follicles forming in the centre a pulpy-like sebaceous mass. Esser found dermoid cysts in the ovaries.

Retention Cysts. These are described as accumulations of sweat in the glandular passages or follicles, as a consequence of an obstruction of the canal at its exit. Atheroma originates as a result of these accumulations in the sebaceous glands. They are generally small, round cysts, lying in the skin, and filled with a grayish-white, fatty, or pasty mass. Secretory accumulations in the salivary glands cause mucous cysts or mucous polypi. These are small formations having a soft, elastic feel externally, and filled with watery or mucous secretions. In the large secretory glands, when the canals of exit have become plugged up, we have the formation of true retention cysts. There are two forms, called the "honey-pouch" cyst and "glandular." These have already been described (page 51).

Extravasation Cysts. These cysts are developed in all loose tissue, especially the cellular tissue under the skin; and in cases where the inflammation is acute and the secretion becomes encysted we generally find an accumulation of bloody, lymphatic fluid.

The therapeutic treatment of cysts varies greatly, and depends to a certain extent on their formation and location. Entire removal is, of course, the best method, and this is generally adopted in cases where the pouch or sac has been uninjured, while in cases where the fluid has been allowed to escape it is almost impossible to remove the follicle entirely. There are some cases where a simple puncture with a scalpel is effective. The puncture must be followed by an injection of tincture of iodine for the destruction of the cyst wall. Where we simply make an incision and evacuate the sac, we clean it out and follow it up by applications of creosote solution, oil of turpentine, tincture of cantharides, or nitrate of silver solution (1 to 10), or we may "touch it up" with the thermo-cautery. This, however, as a rule, takes a long time to heal.

Carcinoma, or Cancerous Tumor. We call "carcinoma" a neoformation which has originated by an accumulation of epithelial cells. These cells possess the peculiar property of forming metastases through the various lymphatic glands, and producing a general cancerous infection of the body, and are, therefore, considered malignant. Almost all the cancerous forms are distinguished by their tendency to regressive metamorphoses. These are mucous, colloid, and fatty degeneration with cystic formation, calcification, cicatricial contraction, and in superficial carcinoma of the skin and mucous membranes ulcerous disintegrations with formation of a purulent centre are called "phagedenic" tumors.

We recognize the following forms of carcinoma:

Squamous Cancer, or Cellular Epithelioma. This occurs in the cutaneous membrane and in all the mucous membranes containing squamous epithelium, as the mouth, throat, larynx, external genitals, bladder, and urethra.

This affection in the cutaneous membrane, cutaneous cancer or cancroid, is very often seen in old animals, and occurs in any part of the body. It originates as diffused, thickened, or warty growth of the skin, becoming rapidly extended over its surface, and finally altered into cancerous tumor (ulcus rodens). It is a peculiar fact that this cancerous growth may accumulate rapidly for a short time, and then remain stationary without increasing any more.

Squamous cancer or cellular epithelioma, which appears in the mucous membranes, especially in the vagina, which deserves special mention, has a great tendency to extend superficially, followed by a cancerous disintegration, also by a constant, bloody, purulent discharge.

Cylindrical-cell Cancer. We observe this in the mucous membrane of the digestive tract and the uterus. Cancer of the stomach is of some importance, as it has been recognized in a number of post-mortems. Its existence during life can only be guessed at by frequent vomiting of more or less blood.

Cancer of the Glandular Tissue. This is found in all glandular organs and especially in the mammaries of old bitches. This cancer of the mammaries is marked by the following characteristics:

It is of slow growth, is particularly hard and firm, and has a tendency to remain stationary for a long time. In some regions of the glands we may see a small, hard knot developed, which is not sensitive to pressure, and shows no signs of inflammatory action. This enlargement gains slowly and may be accompanied by other knots in the immediate neighborhood, which finally unite and form one mass. The carcinoma at this stage is found to be a hard, irregular, circumscribed tumor, and united, as a rule, with smaller masses by a thin, cord-like enlargement that lies in the integument. When this enlargement is located very near the skin it shows a peculiar cicatricial contraction, and especially if it is near the teat this may be drawn entirely into the skin. This is quite common. We also observe great distention of the cutaneous veins, which may even be varicosed. As a rule, the enlargement is rarely confined to one, but we may find scattered through the gland numerous lumps or knots of various sizes. The author has counted twenty scattered through a gland. We also see in the mammaries of the dog fibromas, chondromas, adenomas, sarcomas, and cysts, but these are much rarer than carcinoma.

It is hardly possible to confound these tumors of the mammaries with inflammation of the lacteal gland. True acute mammitis occurs very rarely in the bitch, and is indicated by a circumscribed, painful, very sensitive reddened swelling of a definite glandular section. The section may undergo complete disintegration, forming an abscess and sloughing, or we see chronic inflammation with a formation of knotty lumps, and a peculiar cicatricial contraction. A rapid improvement generally results from the use of acetate of lead solution. True mammitis must not be confounded with inflammation of the lacteal glands, which may appear in bitches that are nursing and deprived of their young. The swelling disappears in a few days by itself, but it may be hastened by a light diet and saline purgatives. In very rare instances there is a peculiar condition of the lacteal glands that is seen in bitches that have had several litters of pups; about forty-five days after they have been in "heat" we may find a general enlargement and filling up of the entire glands, also the appearance of a thin milk or colostrum in the glands, and every appearance of active lactation. This might lead the practitioner to believe that the bitch was in whelp.

The tendency of carcinoma to become malignant and cause a general infection of the whole body is especially marked in the soft forms of cancer, particularly those having a tendency to ulcerative degeneration, while the hard forms, such as above described in cancer of the mammaries, may remain months and even years after producing no other effect than a gradual enlargement. The process is generally developed in the lymphatic glands, but we may see the appearance of secondary tumor centres which swell up without being accompanied by any pain or inflammation. A large part of the body may become affected in this manner— that is to say, the gradual development of the process through the entire body, these various tumors being supplied from the primary tumors, or carried into the circulation and scattered in all directions, forming new centres of development. We may see this occur in cancerous masses in the liver, kidneys, and lungs, producing very little irritation of the surrounding tissues beyond the centre tumor, but we find the animal falling away quickly, becomes emaciated, has weak heart-action, and presents all the symptoms of what is known as cancerous cachexia.

The prognosis is always unfavorable. Removal of a cancerous tumor may only be made when the neighboring lymphatic glands have not become affected, and where the animal is in good nutritive condition. Cases of ulcerated carcinoma must always be considered unfavorable, except in the form of cancroid, which has been already described. The treatment of cancer consists of speedy removal and keeping the animal in as healthy condition as possible.

GENERAL THERAPEUTICS OF TUMORS. The internal medicinal treatment by preparations of iodine may be used in cases of goitre. In carcinoma and sarcoma we may give arsenic in the form of a solution of mercury, iodine, and arsenic (Donovan's solution), and the treatment advised under Chorea (page 218).

Surgical Treatment. This is generally palliative in cases where the tumor is difficult to reach, being restricted to the prevention of hemorrhage, suppuration, and a fetid odor. The therapeutic measures used by Fricker and Hertwig are as follows:

Tampons of tow which have been saturated in a solution of chloride of iron and injections (where there is an opening) of subsulphate of iron, 1 to 90.

This palliative method is only indicated where a radical operation cannot be performed from some cause or location of the tumor and where the owner wishes to keep the animal alive as long as possible without surgical interference. The methods of radical removal of tumor are as follows (these do not include torsion or twisting):

Ligation. This method may be applied in all cases where the base of the tumor is not too broad, and if it has not penetrated deeply into the tissues. It is useful in many forms of warts, fibromas, and sarcomas; but, as a rule, it is objectionable because it acts slowly, is extremely painful, produces great inflammation with suppuration, and the tumor has a tendency to return. Ligate the base of the tumor with a strong silk thread or a rubber band. Another method which is more rapid is the use of the écraseur, either by chain or wire. The chain of the écraseur is put around the base of the tumor, and greatly tightened by means of the instrument, when the tissues are gradually crushed. The author

FIG. 74.

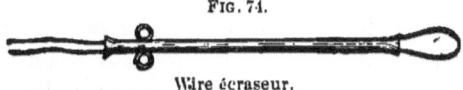

Wire écraseur.

has used the wire-loop, shown in its simplest form in Fig. 74, for the removal of epulides. The bleeding, as a rule, is very slight if the crushing is done slowly, but there is always a danger of recurrence of this condition. We must, therefore, touch the open space left after the removal of the tumor with a thermo-cautery.

Cauterization. We may destroy tumors of the cutaneous or mucous membrane, flat warts, etc., by means of Paquelin's thermo-cautery, or we may use some of the various cauterizing substances. The best form of using this treatment is by the instrument illustrated in Fig. 75 (page 346). This instrument is based on the fact that platinum, under certain conditions, very readily takes a red-heat at a low temperature. The instrument is made in the form of a pipe or cylinder, with different forms of platinum fitted on the end. By means of an ordinary blowpipe or hand-bulb a fine spray of benzine or rhigolene is thrown on the heated platinum end, causing constant combustion, and if the flame is kept steady it reaches a white heat. This instrument has the advantage of being kept at an even heat for a long time, and on account of this steadiness is especially valuable in controlling hemorrhages.

The caustic chemical substances, such as burnt alum, caustic potash, blue-stone, chromic acid, chloride of zinc, and nitric acid, are not especially valuable in the therapeutic treatment of tumors.

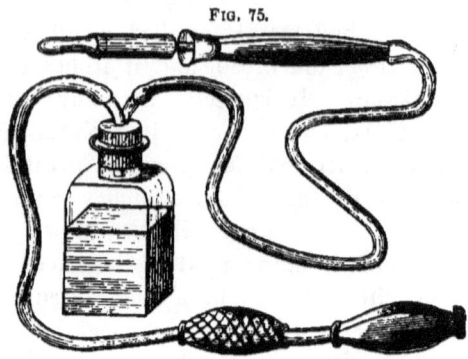

Fig. 75.

Paquelin's thermo-cautery.

Removal—Extirpation. This method is the best one to follow in all large tumors which are easily reached. Various modifications are possible, according to the form and location of the tumor, but the following is the general mode of procedure:

1. The incision: The cut should be made by an ordinary scalpel between the tumor and soft parts; making the incision, if possible, in the direction of the hair and of the large bloodvessels.

2. After the extirpation of the tumor the cavity should be cleared of all loose tissue by means of a pair of scissors or scraped with a curette.

3. Ligate all the bloodvessels.

4. Tie up, or bring together by means of sutures, the edges of the wound.

5. Place over the wound an antiseptic dressing.

Anæsthesia. We have already given information as regards the last three points of the operation. We must confine the animal, in all operations, in such a way as to prevent him from biting or from moving that part of the body which is operated upon. It is best to place a leather strap or bandage around the mouth (see Fig. 76), and have an assistant hold it. This method is preferable to strapping with cord, etc. Berdez, Arnold, and others have constructed special operating-tables which are to be used in hospitals.

In very serious operations, accompanied by great pain, it is advisable to place the animal under the influence of some anæsthetic (except in slight operations of the eye, in which "local" anæsthesia with cocaine is sufficient). We generally use chloral, ether, chloroform, or bromo-ether. It is advisable to give chloral

FIG. 76.

Manner of tying the mouth.

in the form of a clyster. We inject the following solution in the rectum of a medium-sized dog, fifteen minutes before the operation:

Chloral hydrate	8.0
Aqua	100.0
Mucilage	25.0

The other agents are inhaled by means of an anæsthetic covering—a flannel mask. The mask is made of wire netting shaped like a muzzle, covered with flannel, and held under the animal's nose (Fig. 77, *a*). We must take care that a certain amount of air is inhaled with the vapor of the anæsthetic. The pulse, respiration, and reaction of the eyelids must be watched at the same time. After a few inhalations we notice a period of excitement which is marked by great restlessness, howling, groaning, and, in rare cases, delirium. This is followed in a short time by a period of depression, and after that the narcotic condition is completely established. The cornea has now become insensible—that is to say, there is no reflex action or closing of the eyelid when touched. The muscles are now entirely relaxed, feces and

FIG. 77.

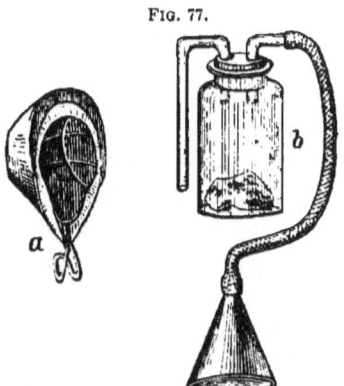

a, inhalation mask; *b*, inhalation bottle.

urine are discharged involuntarily. This result is not always even or regular, but depends to a large extent on which of the above-mentioned remedies is used. For instance, in using ether the stage of excitement is usually prolonged (twenty to forty minutes) [this is not the translator's experience with a good assistant—ten minutes at the most], and in the stage of depression reflex excitement does not disappear immediately. Chloroform produces much quicker results, and, as a rule, answers fairly well, but it has one disadvantage: the attendant or administrator must be very careful not to push it too far, or it is apt to produce paralysis of the lungs or stop the action of the heart, or perhaps act on both parts at the same time, causing death. We prefer to use a combined narcotic in the form of an injection about ten minutes before the operation. This injection consists of 0.03 to 0.06 of morphia muriate dissolved in water. Afterward administer a mixture of equal parts of ether and chloroform. The narcotic stage is mild, the period of excitement short, and death is very rare.

But even by this method, if there is any acute disease of the heart, it is apt to be dangerous. For this reason the author has lately used bromo-ether after having repeatedly tested its reliability. The author uses an inhalation of bromo-ether by means of an apparatus shown in Fig. 77 (b), which, of course, may be used to administer any anæsthetic. The funnel is placed under the animal's nose so that he is compelled to breathe through the bottle. The sponge in the bottle is impregnated with bromo-ether; a double curved tube serves to supply the requisite amount of atmospheric air. The amount of bromo-ether necessary varies from 10 to 40; the stage of excitement is short but very marked; the narcotic effect is deep but lasts a few moments only, so that it is not advisable to discontinue the inhalation at any time during the operation. The stage of excitement may be reduced to a minimum by means of morphia injections. As a rule, the temperature of the rectum drops from 1° to 3° after this narcosis. The lowest the author ever observed was 35.5°.

[The translator has recently used an inhaler suggested by Professor Hobday, of the London school, that has a number of advantages over the methods suggested by the author, but at the same time it must be admitted that it is really an improved modification of the apparatus suggested in the author's work, the mask and the bottle being greatly improved in "Hobday's" apparatus.

It consists of a mask that has the form of an elongated blunt cone, having a stopcock at one end where the tube enters that carries the anæsthetic into the apparatus. This is fixed on the head by means of a collar, and a circular continuation of the cone made of soft cloth, which is adjustable, is fitted over the face. A container with a broad base to prevent any chance of it being overturned contains the anæsthetic. This container has two openings— one to connect the tube and the other to allow the admission of air to mix with the vapor of the anæsthetic. Connecting the container and the mask is a bulb apparatus usually seen on the thermo-cautery.

The muzzle apparatus is fixed on the animal's head, and by means of the bulb the mixed vapor is blown into the muzzle and directly on the animal's nose, thus preventing the irritation of the direct contact of the ether or chloroform. By means of the stopcock the supply of vapor can be stopped instantly, or, if need be, the whole apparatus can be slipped over the animal's head or the rubber tube can be pulled from the container and a supply of pure air blown directly on the animal's nostrils.]

The most important requirement, after the use of the anæsthetic, is controlling the hemorrhage in large operations. In operations on the extremities we may use for that purpose the bandage recommended by Esmarch. The member must be held high and the blood removed by frictions made by the hand from the periphery toward the proximal end, then place a rubber bandage around the limb above the part that has to be operated upon. This method not only gives us a clean field for operation, but it enables us to find numerous little arteries which may have been overlooked, and which begin to bleed as soon as the bandage is removed. We find, as a consequence, fewer consecutive hemorrhages than were formerly noticed. This method must not be practised under any circumstances where there is any risk of introducing pus or purulent matter into the blood. For instance, in purulent cellular inflammation of the tissues, gangrene, etc. In such cases we avoid any manipulation of the part. Place a simple compressing bandage above the operating region in order to prevent hemorrhage during operation. We must not use friction in order to carry or empty the blood from the affected member.

DISEASES OF THE EYES.

AFFECTIONS OF THE EYELIDS.

Closure of the Eyelids.

It is a well-known fact that puppies are born blind—that is to say, the palpebral fissure is closed at birth. This is not a simple agglutination of the eyelids, but a true adhesion of membranes. This has been proven from the fact that if they are forcibly separated after birth the cornea has an opaque look and the edges of the eyelids bleed. As a rule, the fissure opens itself in from seven to twelve days. It is very rare that we have an obstinate closure of the eyelids. If this should be the case, we try to produce separation by means of emollients, tepid water, and normal tension upon the eyelids. If these are not successful, the eyelids must be separated by means of a pair of scissors; then we rub the edges of the wound with vaseline, or, if they persist in uniting, with caustics in order to prevent an adhesion.

Entropion—Turning in of the Eyelid.

By this term we understand a turning or wrinkling of the eyelid in such a manner that the edge of the lid is directed toward the eyeball, and the eyelashes come in contact with the conjunctival tissues and cornea. Entropion occurs quite frequently, especially in bulldogs, Newfoundlands, and setters, although it may be present in all breeds. In some cases it is present at birth, or it may be developed by constant convulsive closing of the fissure of the eye, due to some irritating conditions of the cornea or conjunctiva. It is occasionally caused by cicatricial contraction of the conjunctiva of the lid, after injuries, caustic substances in the eyes, burns, or some chronic inflammatory condition. The looser the cutaneous tissue may be in the neighborhood of the eyelid, the more obstinate the diseased condition is to treatment. Haltanhoff considers that the tendency to entropion is hereditary.

CLINICAL SYMPTOMS. As a rule, the inversion of the lid occurs more frequently in the upper than the lower eyelid, but we may also see both affected at the same time. Sometimes we see a lateral inversion of the eyelid. This is extremely rare, however. A symptom observed is constant irritation, which is caused by the hair of the lashes being directed toward the cornea. We also see a marked lachrymal secretion, a twitching and convulsive compressing of the eyelids, and a thick, gray mucus accumulates in the corners of the eyes. The hairs of the eyelashes become adherent, and the eyelids may become completely glued together. Besides this we see an intense inflammatory condition of the connective tissue, and in some cases inflammation of the cornea, and in extremely bad cases suppuration.

PROGNOSIS AND THERAPEUTICS. The prognosis may be favorable when we operate at the proper time, but relapses are not rare, especially in dogs which show a peculiar wrinkled condition of the facial membrane. We may expect a relapse in such cases where we do not entirely remove the conjunctivitis (primary or secondary) at the same time as the entropion.

It is only in fresh and very mild forms of the disease that we obtain any favorable results by means of medicinal treatment, and this must be directed toward removing the conjunctivitis which exists in conjunction with entropion, otherwise an operation alone will answer.

The following methods of operation are suggested:

1. *Simple removal of the turned-up eyelid by means of scissors.* This is undoubtedly the simplest method, but it is very evident that the appearance of the animal is very much impaired by it, and that the eyeball may be affected in some manner on account of the insufficient closure of the lid.

2. *Incision of the eyelid in the neighborhood of the internal corner of the eye.* This method, which was formerly described by Stellway and recently by Zirin, is not thought by the author to be advisable. This operation consists in taking a wedge-shaped piece from the lid through its whole thickness. We cannot advise this, however, as we doubt if the lid will become thoroughly united.

3. *Ligation of small portions of cutaneous membrane in different parts of the lid.* Stockfleth describes this method in the following manner: We introduce a number of needles through the fold of the skin in the eyelid, drawing the portion of skin together by means of a thread in the form of a figure-of-eight. This will act as a ligature. The points of the needle must be cut short, and a small piece of wax put on the ends to prevent

either slipping or puncturing the skin. After the ligated portion of the skin has become inflamed and detached we see a series of round, cutaneous wounds near the eyelid, which heal by granulation. The eyelids turn out of their normal position by means of a contraction of the cicatricial tissue.

4. *Excision of a portion of the cutaneous membrane from the eyelid.* This is the best and most common mode of operation. It may be performed in two different ways:

a. Take up a horizontal fold of about 0.5 to 1.0 cm. by means of a strong pair of pincers (Fig. 78, *a*), or what are known as entropion forceps, about

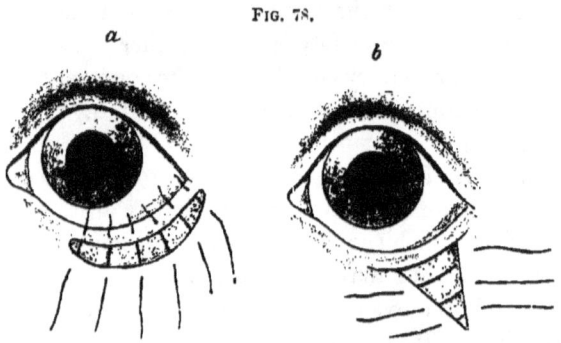

FIG. 78.

Operation for entropion by means of excision: *a*, elliptical incision; *b*, triangular incision.

5 to 8 mm. from the edge of the eyelid, cutting it off closely by means of a pair of scissors (Fig. 78, *a*); and

b. Take up and cut out a triangular or heart-shaped piece, instead of an elliptical one (Fig. 78, *b*). We then close the wound by a united or continuous suture, and paint over this suture with collodium. While we do not, as a rule, obtain union by first intention, the wound closes very quickly and gives satisfactory results.

Ectropion—Turning Out of the Eyelid.

This condition is, as a rule, in the lower lid, the free edge of the lid being turned out from the eyeball toward the external side of the eyelid. This is generally noticed in bulldogs, St. Bernards, and setters, especially so in the animals that have sunken eyeballs. It may be due to an alteration or partial paralysis of the palpebral muscles. Sometimes it may occur from the shape of the cartilage, which does not consist of a firm disk, but of bunches of connective tissue mixed with elastic fibres. In some cases it may be caused by a contraction of the membranes of the face, especially cicatricial contraction, such as results from wounds or burns. It may also be due to a loosening or softening of the tarsal cartilage as a result of prolonged conjunctivitis.

CLINICAL SYMPTOMS. The affected eyelid is turned up and out, so as to show the conjunctiva. The latter is inflamed from the action of the air and is more or less reddened, and at the same time there is considerable secretion of mucus and tears along the checks (lachrymal eyes).

THERAPEUTIC TREATMENT. We must first endeavor to reduce by "touching" the connective tissue of the eyelid with a pencil of nitrate of silver or sulphate of copper, or by removing a portion of the eyelid. This, however, is extremely hard to do, and, as a rule, it is not advisable. If these measures are useless, or if they seem doubtful from the onset, Möller recommends to excise from the external half of the affected lid an arch-shaped piece of skin, 0.5 to 1 cm. broad, the arched edge standing from the edge of the lid. Placing a few stitches is advisable, but is really not necessary.

Concerning other diseases of the eyelids, we would refer you to text-books on ophthalmology.

DISEASES OF THE CONJUNCTIVA.

Inflammation of the Conjunctiva—Conjunctivitis.
(Conjunctivitis; Syndesmitis.)

Inflammatory conditions of the conjunctiva are the most frequent affections of the eye in the dog, and appear in various ways according to their cause. Under ordinary circumstances we see the development of a simple catarrh of the conjunctiva, which, like all catarrhs of the mucous membrane, causes swelling, great redness, and formation of loose folds of tissue. The redness may vary from a slight injection to a dark or bluish-red coloration. This is, as a rule, regular and rarely spotted with blood extravasations. The secretion of the mucous membrane is sero-mucous in the beginning, but later on becomes muco-purulent, and in some cases there is a peculiar grayish secretion. This secretion becomes agglutinated to the interstices and corners of the eyelids, producing a gluing together of the lashes, and during the night, when the animal is asleep, it dries up, forming a grayish-yellow adhesive mass. The inflammation is usually restricted to the conjunctiva of the lid, the transition fold and the bulb of the conjunctiva being very rarely affected. The follicles of the connective tissue are generally swollen in all prolonged forms of catarrh of the eyes. Sometimes they protrude here and there from the reddened connective tissue in the shape of a millet-seed or a sago granule.

In cases where the irritation is due to the influence of some infectious substance we notice a marked cellular infiltration of the tissues of the mucous membrane, with proportional swelling of the connective tissue, and the production of a copious, thick, yellowish-green secretion. Under the influence of chemical irritants we have the formation of grayish-white or transparent membranous accumulations upon the surface of the mucous membranes, and sometimes we have ulcers which may lead to trichiasis (turning in of the hair of the lashes toward the bulbs; the mildest form of entropion). In some cases it may cause a natural entropion or symblepharon adherence between the lid and bulbs of the conjunctiva).

The following forms of conjunctivitis are noticed in the dog:

Catarrhal Ophthalmia (Conjunctivitis). By this we mean an acute catarrh with intense redness and loosening of the conjunctiva, also copious mucous or muco-purulent secretion. The local disturbances do not seem to be very marked, but we see in rare cases irritation and itching, the patients attempting to rub their eyes with their paws. The course may be acute or chronic.

Conjunctivitis follicularis is a variety of this disease (catarrh of the eyes). Fröhner says that this is indicated by the appearance of large quantities of lymphatic follicles upon the internal surface of the membrana nictitans. These stand out distinctly in the form of rounded millet-seed bodies upon the surface of the mucous membranes. They are dark-red and transparent, consisting of ball-shaped accumulations of lymphoid cells. Soon they appear in numerous masses, giving the membrane the appearance of a granulating wound surface, and in such cases the membrana nictitans is detached from the bulbus and extended over the cornea. The question, is follicular conjunctivitis to be accepted as a disease *sui generis* or not, we have not been able to determine fully, but we know that the presence of numerous lymphatic follicles prolongs indefinitely the course of conjunctivitis. We ought, therefore, to always expose the membrana nictitans by means of a pair of forceps, especially in catarrh of the connective tissue. According to Fröhner, 40 per cent. of all dogs are affected more or less by conjunctivitis follicularis.

ETIOLOGY. Catarrh of the eyes may occur at any period of the animal's life, and, as a rule, affects both eyes; in very rare instances only one. It is generally the result of exposure to cold or the influence of sharp, cold winds. It is, therefore, apparent why it appears at certain seasons of the year more than at others—that is, in the spring and fall. Mechanical and chemical influences also produce a certain effect, such as foreign bodies (dust, hair, etc.), eyelashes turned in, smoke of soft coal, etc.

Catarrh of the conjunctiva is intimately connected with catarrh of the respiratory organs, especially cold in the head, distemper, and all serious internal diseases which have a prolonged course.

Purulent Ophthalmia (Purulent Conjunctivitis; Blennorrhœa). This form of conjunctivitis is marked by considerable swelling of the membrane. This is sometimes spotted red by hemorrhages, sensitiveness to light, and photophobia, the animal constantly winking or convulsively closing the eye. The secretion of the eye is changed into a muco-purulent mass, becoming filled with a thick, yellowish-green fluid with pus, and in this condition complications of the cornea are generally present. The latter becomes dull in the centre, showing erosions in some cases. This opacity of the cornea gradually increases, becoming darker, more opaque, and then taking a yellowish-gray coloration. We may see in some cases ulceration of the cornea.

This blennorrhœa of the conjunctiva is a rare and dangerous disease, causing extensive inflammation and ulceration of the cornea, the condition being prolonged in some cases from four to eight weeks, and in extremely bad cases the eye is lost.

ETIOLOGY. It is admitted that this disease is due to a specific infectious substance in the course of some epizootic disease. This may or may not be present. It is possible to produce the same form of the affection by inoculating the conjunctiva of a healthy dog with this purulent material. Guilmot observed that by placing dogs in a kennel which had been previously used by a dog affected with this disease that they soon became similarly affected. In many cases we see no ulceration, simply the development of the conjunctivitis. Fröhner states that he has observed purulent conjunctivitis, which he found to be due to the transmission of gonorrhœal secretion from the affected person placed on the conjunctiva of the dog. Guilmot says that gonorrhœal secretion of the dog itself is the cause of this disease, but this assertion is combated by Möller, whose experiments with secretions of preputial gonorrhœa in the dog have always given negative results.

THERAPEUTIC TREATMENT OF INFLAMMATION. If the disease is produced by foreign bodies, an eruption, etc., we have to remove the cause first. If we have to deal with dirt, coal-dust, or small bodies, it is sufficient to wash out the eye with a little syringe, such as a hypodermatic without a needle. If the bodies are adherent, such as iron fragments, sand, etc., accompanied by convulsive movements of the lids and intense secretion of tears, we must apply a certain amount of cocaine to the eye, remove the foreign bodies, or wipe them off by means of a blunt probe or sound, covered by a handkerchief. Then keep the animal away from strong light, smoke, etc.

In ophthalmic catarrh we must use astringents, such as sulphate of zinc, sulphate of copper, and nitrate of silver. These must be used in mild solutions, such as 0.2 to 0.75 per cent. These solutions may be applied by means of a camel's-hair pencil put between the lids and washed off in a short time with clean water; or we may apply nitrate of silver, following it up a few minutes afterward with a 2 per cent. solution of chloride of sodium. Alum solutions are also useful for washing or painting the inflamed membrane. In pronounced photophobia we may paint the conjunctiva with a solution of cocaine or tincture of opium and gum arabic. In chronic cases apply ointments of calomel, 10 to 20 per cent.; oxide of mercury, 3 to 5 per cent.; or iodoform, 20 per cent.

In chronic catarrh of the eyes a very effective method of reducing the irritation is to blow small quantities of calomel directly on the membrane. Follicular conjunctivitis may be removed by astringents, but in the acute forms which occur on the surface of the membrana nictitans we can only remove them by surgically removing the membrane. This is cut out in the following manner:

Removal of the Membrana Nictitans. We first place the eye under the influence of a few drops of a 4 per cent. solution of cocaine, then by means of a light suture needle we run a thread through the membrane and lift it up as far as possible from the eye. By means of a pair of scissors we then cut the enlarged membrane from the eye. The incision does not require any further treatment except to bathe it with cold water. The author has never seen any bad results from this operation, which has been especially recommended by Fröhner, Möller, and others.

The influence of cocaine upon the conjunctiva and cornea renders these parts insensitive and permits a number of small operations without producing any feeling of pain or convulsive irritation of the eyelid. We pour a little 5 per cent. solution of cocaine into the eye and obtain in this manner, from two to three minutes, an absolute insensibility to pain, both in the cornea and conjunctiva. This does not, as a rule, last more than ten minutes, and must therefore be renewed every five minutes if necessary. In order to reduce blepharospasm, as a consequence of violent conjunctivitis, we should apply solutions of cocaine every two or three hours.

THERAPEUTICS. In ophthalmic blennorrhœa we must endeavor to prevent it before it goes too far. We must treat it with antiseptic agents, and it is especially important to keep the conjunctiva clean with water or some non-irritating antiseptic fluid, such as boric acid, 3 per cent.; corrosive sublimate, 0.02 per cent.; permanganate of potassium, 0.05 per cent.; creolin, 1 per cent.; salicylic acid, 1 per cent. These must be introduced into the pouch of the lid by means of a syringe, brush, or sponge. When it is necessary we must irrigate the eye with strong solutions of nitrate of silver (1 to 3 per cent.), taking care to observe the rules mentioned on page 356. We may also use diluted alcohol (equal parts), covering the conjunctiva with calomel ointments or oxide of mercury, or blowing on it powder of iodoform or calomel. Aniline (pyoktanin) is also advised by some authors.

The treatment may also be materially altered by complications of the cornea, for which we would refer to page 359 for further details.

Besides the inflammatory condition which has just been described, we may have tumors of the conjunctiva, but, as a rule, these occur on the membrana nictitans. Their treatment depends on general rules which have been already described. It may be advisable to remove them in the manner described.

DISEASES OF THE SCLEROTIC COAT OF THE EYE.

Inflammation of the Sclerotic Coat.
(*Keratitis.*)

Notwithstanding the fact that the sclerotic coat does not contain any bloodvessels, it is frequently the seat of inflammatory processes which become present through a pericorneal injection due to intense irritation of the bloodvessels which surround the border of the sclerotic coat, and further by an opacity of the cornea forming an obstruction that prevents the admission of rays of light into the eye itself. This clouding or opacity may extend over the entire sclerotic coat, or it may only involve a small portion. It varies in color from a grayish-blue to a pure gray. It is yellowish-gray in some cases, but never pure white in coloration (cicatricial dulness). On careful examination it seems to be diffuse, forming spots or stripes. The lustre of the membrane is dull on its surface and a partial loss of the epithelium is noticed. The other symptoms are avoidance of light, convulsive movements of the eyelids, and discharge of thin water from the corner of the eyelids, visual deficiencies, and in some cases the animal may be partially or even totally blind. This is especially seen when the opacity of the sclerotic membrane is in the region of the visual line that is opposite the pupil.

PATHOLOGICAL ANATOMY. We have in other cases of keratitis the appearance of large quantities of round cells in the sclerotic membrane. These come from the bloodvessels of the neighboring membranes and conjunctiva. These are wandering cells which find their way into the sclerotic coat. As long as the round cells in the sclerotic membrane are not crowded together it remains unaltered in its true structure (infiltration of the sclerotic membrane), and complete recovery follows after the cells have disappeared. But as soon as the cells are packed too closely together the sclerotic tissue is partially destroyed by maceration and necrosis, followed by a loss of actual substance. If this is surrounded by intact tissue of the sclerotic membrane, it forms an abscess; if it is open externally, it is an ulcer. We consider as ulcers small superficial openings in the cornea which are always round in the early stages, and are caused by infiltrations located closely under the epithelium, forming little bags or sacs, and finally bursting through the epithelial covering. In the dog, as a rule, they heal without leaving any cicatrix. Still, many cases are seen where they finally close up, leaving a white cicatrix, or else they lead to perforation of the cornea or to a total destruction of the eye by extending into the anterior chamber.

We find the following forms of inflammation of the sclerotic membrane:

(1) **Keratitis Superficialis.** The cornea is clouded and opaque, being of a diffuse grayish-blue or grayish-white coloration, appearing with a slightly irregular surface, but under certain circumstances it may also be covered with small epithelial masses. In this affection the eyes are watery, and this may disappear in a few days or last for weeks. In the latter case we observe the formation of bloodvessels at the borders. These bloodvessels increase in size and the edges become very vascular. Möller found that during vascularization of the cornea it is not rare to see hemorrhages in that organ followed by a number of brownish-black pigment-spots.

ETIOLOGY. Superficial inflammation of the sclerotic membrane is caused by slight irritations of various kinds (superficial injuries, inversion of the eyeballs or entropium). It may also originate, secondarily, with acute conjunctivitis, the inflammation extending from the conjunctiva to the cornea.

THERAPEUTICS. The treatment is the same as in inflammation of the conjunctiva—that is, washing and painting with a solution of sulphate of zinc, corrosive sublimate, alum, or sulphate of copper. Avoid all use of lead solutions in such cases where there is any loss of substance of the cornea, as the lead is deposited in the cornea and produces black-colored spots. If there is any ulceration, we must apply the therapeutic treatment as indicated on page 362, and in cases where the spots on the sclerotic membrane remain use the treatment given on page 363.

(2) **Keratitis Profunda or Parenchymatosa.** The surface of the cornea has an opaque, dull, slightly grooved condition, the color bluish-gray or gray, rarely grayish-white, accompanied by watery eyes, sensitiveness to light (but only to a slight degree), and also the formation of new vessels, which extend from the borders of the cornea toward the centre. Abscesses and ulcerations, as a

rule, are rare. This form, however, must not be mistaken for ulcerative keratitis.

The course of this disease is generally favorable. After several weeks the dulness disappears and the new vessels become thinner, disappearing entirely in a short time.

THERAPEUTICS. We remove the irritation to a certain extent by applications of compresses. Also irrigate with warm water or boric acid, and drop atropia into the eyes. If the inflammatory symptoms are reduced, we then follow it up by stimulant irritants, such as calomel powder or ointments of red oxide of mercury.

(3) **Abscesses of the Sclerotic Membrane.** When there is intense dread of light and great increase of tears, and when we see a pericorneal injection and the cornea colored a gray, yellow, or straw yellow, and a certain spot on that part which is sharply defined from the tissue of the normal sclerotic membrane, or may be surrounded by a more or less dull zone, we then can safely conclude that it is the formation of an abscess. Its location varies; sometimes it is on the edge of the cornea, at other times in the centre; then, again, we may find it close to the surface of the membrane or deep in the centre of it. It may be very small in dimension, such as the size of a pin-head, or it may even include the whole sclerotic membrane.

The course varies also. In small abscesses it may disappear by simple absorption, while in large ones the acute inflammation subsides, frequently leaving an intensely white spot, or it may break out externally, forming an open ulcer. This latter conclusion, or termination, is the most common, and in rare instances it may break in a posterior direction toward the anterior chamber of the eye, causing an accumulation of pus in it, and producing further inflammatory processes in the internal part of the eyeball.

ETIOLOGY. Abscesses of the sclerotic membrane appear after some traumatism, especially contusions or bruises of the membrane, also after non-aseptic operations, in connection with blennorrhœa or conjunctivitis, or during distemper, and very frequently appear without any appreciable cause.

THERAPEUTICS. This is closely related to that of ulcerations of the sclerotic membrane—that is, to incise the abscess after using cocaine in the cornea, make a broad cut and turn up the borders of the wound. This has to be done to expose the bottom of the abscess. It is then dried with corrosive sublimate or iodoform-gauze and washed out with a solution of corrosive sublimate and dusted with iodoform or calomel until it dries up.

(4) **Ulceration of the Sclerotic Membrane.** In this condition we find a loss of substance in the cornea which varies in size and depth, showing a grayish-white or grayish-yellow ground, and, as a rule, has short, abrupt borders with a bluish-gray, gray, or grayish-yellow opacity in the immediate neighborhood of the ulceration. When the ulceration of the sclerotic membrane begins to heal it is indicated by a lessening of the infiltration in the immediate neighborhood of the ulcer, the dull circle surrounding it becomes clearer, the color shiny, and the pericorneal injection less. The dread of light begins to disappear. In rare instances the bloodvessel will shoot from the edge of the cornea toward the ulcer, and an epithelial covering is now formed over the pit-like ulcer, which resembles very much the normal tissue of the sclerotic membrane, but it is not as transparent in color as it was before. If the ulceration has not been very deep, we see the dulness gradually disappearing, leaving only a very thin white veil; or, if the ulceration is deep, we have as a result a distinct white spot which remains permanent (cicatrix of the sclerotic membrane, macular cornea). This cicatrix of the membrane may become clearer in the course of time, but, as a rule, it never disappears entirely. When the ulcer does not take a favorable termination we find the inflammation increases, the ulceration becomes deeper, and we have a perforation of the membrane in a few days. The contents of the anterior chamber escape through the opening, and in rare instances the iris and the lens push forward and may also escape if the opening is large enough. After perforation occurs the ulcer begins to heal, and we have an adhesion of the iris and lens to the posterior wall of the sclerotic membrane. In other cases where the opening of the ulcer is very narrow the anterior chamber fills up again, is forced forward, forming a clear bladder-like body, forming dropsy of the sclerotic membrane, or keratocele. If the ulceration is large, the whole ground of the ulcer becomes embossed —that is, it stands out from the surrounding membrane in a peculiarly distended manner. As a consequence of rupture we may have a series of ulcers of the membrane. The opening may close up quickly, the fluid of the anterior chamber may collect, and the

lens and iris may be pushed back into their normal position. In large ulcers the iris is generally forced into the orifice, filling up the opening and causing adhesions. When the fluid of the anterior chamber collects again the lens and iris may be pushed back from the cornea into their old position, but the section of the iris which has united at the orifice remains adherent, so that the pupil is pulled forward to the cicatrix of the sclerotic membrane, and the power of vision of the eye is greatly impaired. Externally the iris, which is drawn into the orifice, becomes covered with cicatricial tissue, and by its contraction it forms a lobule of the iris. This finally contracts into a peculiar club-shaped body over the anterior surface of the membrane (iris staphyloma). We must not confound this condition with staphyloma pellucidum. By it we mean a change of form in the sclerotic membrane, where it becomes more or less opaque, and is forced outward in the shape of a grape-like body by the dropsical condition of the anterior chamber. When there is great irritation of the sclerotic membrane in some cases we may have a prolapsus of the lens, and the eyeball subsequently collapses, forming an opening in the centre of the eye which finally becomes closed up by a whitish-gray cicatrix.

ETIOLOGY. Besides the causes already mentioned in the formation of abscesses, the following also produce them: cauterization, foreign bodies which adhere to the membrane, wounds in some cases, etc. This disease may appear in the epizootic form with or without distemper, and generally in connection with blennorrhœa of the connective tissue.

PROGNOSIS AND THERAPEUTIC TREATMENT. The prognosis depends to a large extent on the irritation of the ulcer and the rapidity of its progress. Ulcers which are small and located on the borders are easier to treat than those which are larger and located in the centre of the sclerotic membrane. In weak, badly fed young animals and in pugs the prognosis is more unfavorable than in healthy old animals.

The treatment requires cleanliness and strict antiseptic remedies. The use of a dressing is of great advantage, but few dogs can be made to submit to one. In canine hospitals, as a rule, they use a specially constructed leather cap (seen in Fig. 79). The various antiseptic agents which are used are corrosive sublimate, 0.1, or chlorine water (either pure or mixed with two or three parts of water), to be applied with a brush, and iodoform as a powder blown from a quill directly on the eye. The author has obtained very satisfactory results with hot fomentations of boric acid (3 parts to 100). These should be applied three times daily, ten minutes at a time. They are far better than cauterizations with nitrate of silver or painting with aniline.

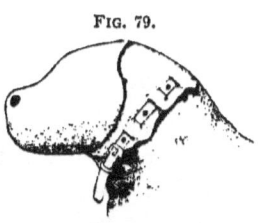

Fig. 79.

Eye-cap.

Besides the antiseptic treatment we can use atropine or eserine solution, of which a few drops are put in the eye. The first-named agent should be applied when the ulcer is located centrally, as it dilates the iris, and consequently the pupil is enlarged, and the latter when the ulceration is located on the borders, as it contracts the pupil and draws it away from the seat of irritation. The iris is dilated or contracted by these drugs and removed from the neighborhood of the ulcer, so that if the perforation does occur the iris will be drawn far enough out of the road to prevent any adhesion.

Good results have been obtained with cocaine, alternating with atropine:

  R.—Atropine sulphate 0.1
   Aqua destil. 10.0

  M. S.—In order to produce a dilatation of the pupil we must introduce five drops of this remedy into the conjunctiva, drop by drop, by means of a brush or a dropper.

  R.—Eserine salicylate 0.05
   Aqua destil. 10.0

  M. S.—To be used like the atropine solution.

When a keratocele is developed we may prevent rupture by puncturing the membrane with a needle and allowing the water in the chamber to escape. In prolapsus and adhesion of the iris we can do very little, as it is impossible to push back the iris into place.

We must dust it with iodoform; at the same time we may reduce the enlargement by means of nitrate of silver, sulphate of copper solutions, or a powder of oxide of mercury blown on the eyeball. If we have an iris staphyloma, it is best to remove it carefully by means of the scissors.

We must try to remove any spots on the sclerotic membrane by means of irritants, such as the mild chloride or oxide of mercury or massage. According to Bayer, massage of the cornea has to be performed in the following manner: The points of the fingers are placed on the closed-up eyelids and by a constant circular or centrifugal friction move the eyelid for some time. In some cases we may also apply the above-mentioned ointments and powders. The author has obtained far the best results from calomel than anything else. He placed daily a small amount of powder composed of equal parts of calomel and sugar (grape sugar) on the cornea, and applied it by massage for some time.

The following other alterations have been observed in the sclerotic membrane of the dog:

Dermoid of the Cornea. We occasionally find a peculiar abnormal collection of true membranous tissue on the cornea which is covered with hair and interferes with the direct action of light, and also produces irritation in the cornea and conjunctiva. The hair should be cut off by means of scissors. Thierry observed the same abnormality on the sclerotic membrane of both eyes in a three-months-old dog. There was a slight swelling and enlargement above the surface of the membrane, which was covered with fine hair. This trichiasis bulbus was removed with the scissors.

Pterygium. By this we mean a malformation of the connective tissues containing bloodvessels and branching over the cornea toward the centre. This growth can be removed by means of caustics or by an operation.

Injuries to the Cornea. It is not uncommon to observe injuries to the sclerotic membrane of dogs where the epithelium is removed slightly, or where they may have a deep penetration of the membrane, and in such cases, such as injuries from cats' claws, it is entirely perforated. Immediately after the injury we observe a great fear of light, closing of the eye, and copious tears. Wounds which have not entirely perforated the sclerotic membrane are rapidly followed by an opacity and swelling in the neighborhood of the injury. When the membrane is perforated the symptoms and results are very similar to ulceration. Superficial and very small wounds which penetrate deeply heal very quickly after a few days, leaving scarcely any opacity. This, of course, must be expected in wounds that have been caused by some object that was clean, while septic large wounds, caused by some unclean object, frequently produce great irritation, and penetrating ulceration results, ending in panophthalmia and destruction of the eye.

The therapeutic treatment of wounds of the sclerotic membrane is identical with that of ulcers.

DISEASES OF THE CRYSTALLINE LENS.

Cataract.

All diseases of the lens, either of its substance or of its capsule, as a rule, cause a certain amount of opacity, and may form one or more star-like gray bodies in the centre of the lens itself (cataract). It is not possible to enter into a description of the various forms of cataract and its pathological alterations, but we will only take up one form (gray) of cataract that can be subdivided into two forms—soft, which may be congenital; or traumatic and hard or contracted cataract, which is senile. The softening process generally begins in the equator of the lens, and becoming diffused soon causes a total opacity of light gray color. This may be streaked with darker lines or it may have a mother-of-pearl discoloration, with enlargement or distortion of the lens and a contraction of the anterior chamber. This is very often seen in young animals. The contracting process, on the contrary, begins in the shape of a number of small whitish striæ, or dull opacities, in the peripheric layers of the lenticular nucleus, and extend gradually over the cortical, giving the lens a yellowish-white or yellow aspect after some time. This is generally observed in old dogs (hard nuclear cataract, senile cataract). The so-called capsular cataract does not, as a rule, depend on true opacity of the capsule, but on an accumulation of products of the same, which have been developed from disease-processes which have gone on in its immediate neighborhood. For instance, in inflammation of the iris. In some cases they appear in small, star-like or streaked pigmented dull spots, which are distinctly marked.

ETIOLOGY. Gray cataract, as a rule, is a senile or old-age affection, but it appears quite frequently in young dogs, and now and then it is congenital. The author saw one case of hereditary star cataract in connection with microphthalmus. The development of cataract which occurs in advanced age—that is to say, after ten or twelve years—is what is known as senile cataract; this is slow in its development, while cases of opacity of the lens, which are observed in young animals, appear frequently without any marked cause. Haltenhoff was able to recognize traces of sugar in the urine of a dog which became very thin and anæmic in a short time, and developed cataract. The author has tested the urine of many dogs affected by blindness caused by cataract, but has never been able to find any sugar.

Inflammatory Process of the Eye. There is no doubt that cataract is also caused by inflammatory processes of the eye, and the nutritive supply of the lens becomes disturbed and its normal condition impaired, such as ulcerations of the cornea with central perforation, inflammation of the membrane of the veins and iris, and also bleeding into the anterior chamber. Injuries of the lens and concussions of the eye also cause a number of cases of cataract.

Certain conditions are developed as the result of concussion of the eye and appear quite frequently; they may be thus briefly described:

The lens either sinks downward with the capsule or becomes laterally displaced. It may lean against the iris or it may drop forward into the anterior chamber of the eye, and it may finally crowd into the vitreous humor. If the lens has undergone but slight displacement (subluxation), it may remain clear for some time, but the vision is much impaired. If it has fallen into the anterior chamber or has been forced into the vitreous humor, we see a rapid development of the cataract, and in the later stages considerable inflammation of the choroid membrane, of the iris, or of the whole eyeball.

CLINICAL SYMPTOMS. In cases where the disease is somewhat advanced, and the cataract is fully developed into one of the following forms: punctiform, streaked, spotted, or complete opacity of a whitish-blue, brownish-blue, or mother-of-pearl color, it is easily recognized; but, on the other hand, where there is a mere cloudy dimness and small spots of cataract, we must use candle-light or some illuminating power such as an ophthalmoscope and a strong light to see the action of the lens in the eye itself. Before doing so, however, we must dilate the pupil with atropia.

The prognosis is rather difficult to make, and, as a rule, it should be an unfavorable one. Hereditary cataract shows little inclination to enlargement, as is also the case in senile cataract. In soft cortical cataracts we may see a rapid opacity of the lens in a few days or weeks. The sight is entirely lost and medical treatment is of little use.

THERAPEUTIC TREATMENT. A cataract may be removed by an operation, and this is much more advisable in the dog because it is, as a rule, attended without any great danger, and its results are generally beneficial, producing a partial restoration of the vision. It is advisable to perform the operation of cataract after having first dilated the pupil by means of atropia, and then performing the operation under ether. The author has tried cocaine alone, but he finds it unsatisfactory. The animal must be tied up, placed on a table, and ether or chloroform administered. The operation is performed by one of the following methods:

Opening of the Capsule. The anterior capsule of the lens has to be opened in a transverse way with what is known as a discission needle. (Fig. 80, a.) The fluid in the anterior chamber causes a gradual breaking up and reabsorption of the lens. An assistant holds the eyelids open and the operator seizes a fold of the conjunctiva with a small tenaculum, holding the eye firmly with the left hand, while holding the needle in the right hand placed on the animal's head to steady it. The needle is then introduced into the cornea, in the middle of the lower external quadrant, in such a direction as to meet the ciliary insertion of the iris and as far as the upper internal quadrant. Before the point of the needle has reached this latter point, however, it is placed firmly on the capsule of the lens, and this is cut through in a transverse direction with a lever-like movement of the needle (Fig. 81). The instrument must then be removed in the same way that it was introduced in perforating the cornea. After the operation the animal must be placed for some time in a dark place and

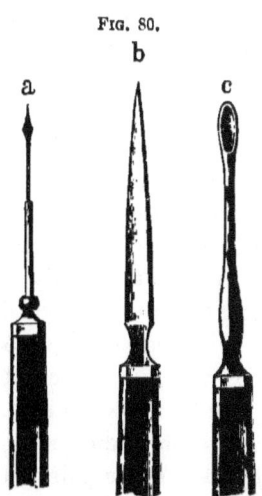

FIG. 80.

a, stop discission needle; b, Graefe's cataract knife; c, Daviel's cataract spoon.

the eye treated twice a day with atropine. We must treat all irritating symptoms of the eye by means of cold compresses, and sometimes we use purgatives. After six or eight weeks the reabsorption of the lens is complete. We generally perform discission in young

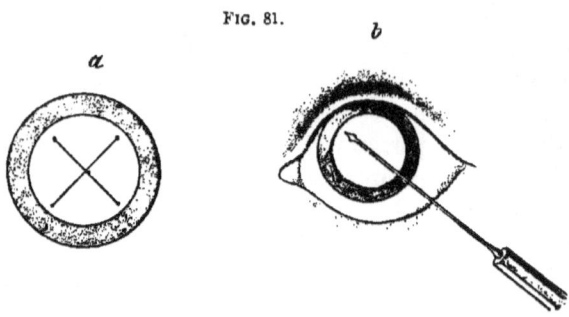

Fig. 81.

Discission of the lens: *a*, form and size of the cross-incisions; *b*, method of insertion of the needle.

animals affected with soft cataract. The result of this operation, however, is not always satisfactory, as reabsorption is slow and in many cases requires a second operation. Several months may also elapse before the cataract is absorbed. Schlampp advises in such cases puncturing the cornea, and by this means allowing the fluid of the anterior chamber to escape, leaving the lens untouched. Anterior displacement of the lens enlarges or ruptures the opening which has been made in the capsule. Reabsorption follows, as a rule, more quickly when this is performed, probably due to the fact that the fluid which contains the elements of the lens has been discharged and replaced by fresh fluid. The process is not dangerous, and may be repeated oftener than discission itself.

Linear Extraction. After having prepared the dog for this operation (indicated on page 367), we fix the membrana nictitans by means of a pair of forceps. With another forceps we seize the conjunctiva of the eyeball in the neighborhood of the median line of the eyeball, at the same time everting the upper eyelid. We then make an incision by means of Graefe's cataract knife (Fig. 80, *b*), about 5 mm. broad, through the cornea, about 2 or 3 mm. from the border of the sclerotic membrane. We then pass a discission needle through the wound, split the anterior capsule, as in discission, and empty the soft parts of the cataract by means of Daviel's spoon (Fig. 80, c). Any remnants of the cut capsule which may not be removed at the time are left to be reabsorbed. If during the operation we observe prolapsus of the iris, we must try to restore it to its position by means of Daviel's spoon (Fig. 80, c). If this is not possible, we may cut it off close to the wound of the cornea.

It is very evident that linear extraction is only to be performed in cases of complete softening of the lens. This may be recognized by total opacity of the lens and alteration of the iris, and also when the anterior capsule is pushed toward the cornea.

Lobular Extraction. Lobular extraction is indicated in shrunken cataract, which is generally senile, where the lens has prolapsed into the anterior chamber and where discission will only produce an imperfect result—that is to say, where reabsorption of the lens does not progress properly. It is performed in the following manner:

Make an incision into the cornea exactly as in linear extraction, by means of Graefe's cataract knife, but it must be enlarged to 8 or 10 mm. After that the capsule of the lens is split by the discission needle, the fluid of the anterior chamber is allowed to escape, and at the same time the lens must be detached by means of an even, but not too energetic, pressure upon the other side of the eye from the wound, and by means of the spoon the lens is scooped out of the opening. The consecutive treatment is the same as in linear extraction.

Dislocation of the Cataract. This operation, which has been abandoned lately on account of the impairment of the choroid membrane and retina, was performed in the following manner:

By means of a bent or straight needle pushed through the sclerotic membrane, and at other times through the cornea, steady pressure was made on the upper part of the lens, and it was pushed down into the lower posterior part of the vitreous chamber of the eye.

DISEASES OF THE SCLEROTIC MEMBRANE, OF THE NERVOUS PORTION OF THE EYE, AND ALSO THE VITREOUS HUMOR OF THE POSTERIOR CHAMBER.

These diseases are generally not of any great importance compared with the diseases before described, and therefore we will not go into minute details.

(1) **Inflammation of the Iris** (*Iritis*). This affection is very rare in the dog (Möller). It may be recognized by contraction and difficulty of movement of the iris, change in the color of the iris, fibrous accumulations in the shape of a gray veil-like coating, and dulness of the fluid of the anterior chamber, and slight dimness of the cornea. The cure for this disease consists in complete rest, keeping the animal in a dark place, and solutions of cocaine and atropine.

(2) **Purulent Inflammation of the Eye** (*Panophthalmitis*). This is produced by serious concussion of the eye itself. It may also be due to septic wounds of the cornea and sclerotic membrane, as well as to the large perforating ulcers of the cornea. We recognize the following acute symptoms:

The eyelids are constantly closed; great redness of the conjunctiva; total opacity of the cornea; purulent accumulations in the anterior chamber of the eye; myosis; great hardness and enlargement of the bulbus. After a short time we may have perforation through the cornea, and, in rare cases, through the sclerotic membrane. The lens and vitreous humor are ejected through the opening with the purulent mass; the eyeball collapses, becomes contracted, and forms a knob-shaped mass in the eye; the lids completely collapse and form a hollow in the face. The only thing to do in such a case is to perform *enucleation*, or removal of the eye.

Enucleation. Removal of the eyeball should be performed under a narcotic or ether. We pull out the eyeball by means of a tenaculum, cut through the conjunctiva with a pair of small, pointed scissors closely behind the cornea, snipping the scissors around the eye, keeping as close to the bulb of the eye as possible, and by this means separate the muscles and cut through the optic nerve. The author thinks it is advisable to remove the membrana nictitans at the same time (Fig. 82).

After enucleation, the cavity of the eye is washed out with an antiseptic fluid and the bleeding stopped by means of a tampon; it should be powdered with iodoform or sulphonal. Möller advises to pack the orbit

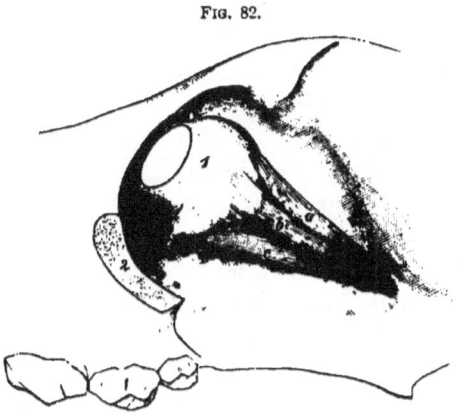

Fig. 82.

Muscles of the left eye: *a*, superior; *b*, external; *c*, inferior straight muscles of the eye; 1, eyeball; 2, orbital arch cut through.

with absorbent cotton and stitch the eyelids. Dogs are not badly disfigured by the loss of one eye, as the orbit becomes contracted and partially filled with granulations. It is not advisable to use artificial eyes, as the animal generally rubs them out.

(3) **Dropsy of the Anterior Chamber** (*Glaucoma*). Möller has observed this a number of times in the dog. The anterior chamber is very much enlarged, hard, and tense, so much so that the eyelids cannot be closed. The bloodvessels of the conjunctiva and the sclerotic membrane are injected, the cornea more or less opaque, the pupil much contracted and greenish in color. The animal cannot see. On post-mortem of one case Möller found total cataract and a partial luxation of the lens, liquefaction of the vitreous humor of the eye, swelling of the papilla, and injection of the vessels of the retina. He was inclined to consider this condition as identical with glaucoma in man. A number of authors have seen similar conditions in dogs.

(4) **Diseases of the Optic Nerve and the Retina.** These occur very frequently in the dog, and may be recognized at first by symptoms of what is known as "black cataract"—that is, impairment of visual power (amblyopia), or complete blindness (amaurosis). Total blindness in the dog may be recognized by anyone,

although it is difficult to detect blindness in one eye. The veterinarian may recognize blindness by the unaltered condition of the pupil when in contact with or close to light. It is necessary to cover up one eye of the animal in order to test the other, as the influence of light may act in a reflex way from the healthy organ.

We must especially point out that in very rare cases we may see a certain amount of reaction in the pupil under the influence of light, notwithstanding the fact that complete blindness exists. The author has observed this in a dog which had become blind from nervous distemper. Later symptoms, however, are not known; the author was unable to make any further observations. The brain of the animal had, however, probably undergone certain alterations in its hemispheres, although the patient did not seem to be affected with any cerebral complications. This is one of the so-called cases of "spiritual blindness."

Möller and Eversbusch have recognized pathological alterations in the visual nerve and retina in the form of small red spots and opacity of the retina (symptoms of retinitis), also a lifting or enlargement of the papilla. The author had two cases in which he observed papillo-retinitis from its beginning till it entirely disappeared. All these processes may be recognized by means of the ophthalmoscope.

For therapeutic treatment of inflammation of the eye, which is not given in this chapter, we refer you to the text-books on ophthalmology. It consists, as a rule, in rest, keeping the animal in the dark, the use of atropine or eserine, and an occasional laxative.

Prolapse of the Eyeball.
(*Exophthalmus; Prolapsus Bulbi Oculi.*)

There are a number of causes that produce prolapse of the eyeball; it may be crowded out of the cavity of the eye, or exposed in its external circumference by the swollen and distended eyelids which are closely adherent to its posterior surface. This condition occurs especially in bulldogs, although it may occur in any breed. The dog does not possess any bony arch of the eye (zygomaticus), the space being filled up by a ligament, and the muscles are also very weak. Occasionally, from any mechanical force, such as blows in the region of the eye, or bites in its neighborhood causing hemorrhage and a large amount of blood to collect in the posterior part of the orbit, it is pushed out of position; frequently the entire eyeball is crowded out, standing out on the face clear of the orbit (Hertwig). This condition has also been noticed in very rare instances to be due to inflammatory processes inside the eye, and by the formation of tumors in the orbits.

The prognosis of a prolapsed eyeball depends largely upon the circumstances and condition of the organ. If the prolapse is of recent origin, if the muscles of the eye and optic nerve are not torn, and if the eye itself has not been very much injured, we may expect complete recovery in a short time without any disturbance of sight. If the prolapse is recent and the muscles are not torn, or only partially so, but abnormally distended, we must expect there is some irritation of the optic nerve, and while the eye may be restored the animal may remain blind. If the muscles of the eye and optic nerve are lacerated and the eye proper is injured, or if any of the chambers of the eye are filled with blood, or if the prolapse has been sufficiently long that the irritating influence of the air is marked by an opacity and a dry look of the cornea, which has a horny appearance, the eye must be considered as lost.

The therapeutic treatment consists in returning the eyeball as soon as possible, especially when the organ appears to be in such a condition as would encourage you to think it can be saved; but if otherwise, it must be removed as soon as possible.

We try to return the eye to its position in the following manner:

First clean it thoroughly by means of an antiseptic that is not irritating, such as a 2 per cent. solution of boric acid or a 1 to 2000 solution of corrosive sublimate. Place the flat of the hand or the points of the fingers on the eyeball, at the same time an assistant distending the eyelids as much as possible, and by gentle pressure endeavor to push the eye back into the orbital cavity.

If it is impossible to return it by this means, the fissure of the eye must be distended by making a small incision in the external corner, or the anterior chamber of the eye may be perforated by means of a cataract-needle or pointed bistoury, so as to empty the eye to a certain extent and thus allow it to return to the chamber. After returning the eye we must try to prevent another prolapse by placing a bandage over the eye, taking care not to compress it too much. If the animal will not allow it to remain, we must join the fissure of the eye by one or two stitches. Hertwig says that after stitching the eye we generally see great inflammation of the lids and the eye itself, but the author has found that these bad effects may be easily prevented by taking care not to carry the stitch through the entire lid, but only through the external membrane. At the same time it is advisable to keep the animal without food for at least twenty-four hours, as the use of the jaw, and especially the pressure of the prolongation of the crown of the inferior maxillary, may push the injured eye out of position. Cold applications are useful if the eyeball cannot be saved, or if reduction is impracticable for some reason or other, on account of tumors in the orbit, etc., there is nothing left to do but enucleate the eyeball. (See page 37.)

DISEASES OF THE EAR.

Serous Cyst.
(*Othæmatoma; Hæmatoma.*)

By this term we mean a blood or lymphatic excretion lying between the skin and cartilage of the ear, and forming a tumor in the external or internal part of the lobe. It generally occurs on the inside. This swelling is fluctuating, and when the skin of the animal is white it may have a bluish coloration.

ETIOLOGY. This condition is probably due to some irritation or traumatic cause—for instance, by striking the ear against the collar or muzzle, pulling the ear, concussions, and injuries through biting. It is always seen in the lobe of the ear. If the sac is not emptied, after a few weeks the secretion is reabsorbed and it may leave quite a thickening and even malformation of the external ear. In some cases when the fluid suppurates it makes a perforation of the skin internally; this, however, is very rare.

CLINICAL SYMPTOMS AND PROGNOSIS. The swelling, as a rule, is on the internal part of the ear. The lobe, which generally hangs downward, is pushed upward in a peculiar manner. The swelling is hard, and in white animals it has a blue color. It is very sensitive to pressure and shows distinct fluctuation. The animal carries its head in an oblique manner, the affected ear being held downward, and the fact that it gives the dog more or less pain is indicated by the careful way that the animal shakes its head or scratches its ear.

The prognosis is favorable provided proper treatment is applied, although it may take some time before they are entirely cured.

In many cases where no dressing is applied, we may have as a sequence a slight thickening of the lobe of the ear. This, however, is of very little importance.

THERAPEUTIC TREATMENT. The methods of treatment which the author considers advisable are as follows:

1. We perforate the swelling with a large-sized hypodermatic

syringe or aspirator. The secretion is then removed and a solution of iodoform and ether (10 to 20 per cent. of iodoform) is injected. The needle must remain in the cavity for some time in order to allow the vapor of ether to escape. We then apply a compressing dressing in the following manner:

The ear is turned up and laid on the top of the head and covered with antiseptic wadding on both surfaces. It is then held in position by means of an ear-cap (Fig. 83). This dressing must not be displaced, but allowed to remain for eight days.

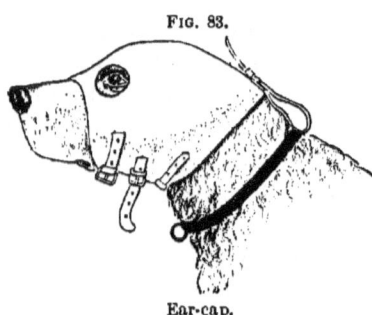

Fig. 83.

Ear-cap.

[Hobday has recently introduced a very practical method of treatment for this condition. He carefully removes the hair from the ear and renders it aseptic, and either paints the ear with cocaine or administers chloroform (the translator prefers ether). A longitudinal incision is made into the sac and it is completely emptied; sutures are then inserted, about one-third of an inch apart, directly through the ear and tied on the outer or hairy side, thus producing a firm pressure between the two surfaces of the sac and by that means get prompt union; the ear must then be irrigated with an antiseptic solution, carefully removing all blood, etc., and dressed with antiseptic wadding, and further covered with an ear-cap. It should be dressed every second day.]

2. The second method is to be resorted to if the first does not answer the requirements, or if we find pus in the swelling.

The swelling is opened at both ends—that is to say, at the base and inferior line of the lobe—and a drainage-tube placed in it, which must be kept in place by means of a tape or rubber fastening. The irritation caused by this seton is generally sufficient, and it is not necessary to inject any stimulating liquid like tincture of cantharides or nitrate of silver, but simply remove the seton twice daily, cleaning out the cavity and disinfecting it by means of antiseptic irrigations. After a certain time we replace the drainage-tube by a smaller one, and finally we remove it altogether.

3. The third method, which is generally the most successful, provided it is performed under antiseptic rules, is as follows:

Shave and thoroughly disinfect the lobe. A long incision in a longitudinal direction of the ear must be made, and the clots and remains of tissue removed. The cartilage must be scraped carefully, so that we see a fresh wound surface. Sew it up with catgut ligatures, keeping as close as possible to the cartilaginous surface. Place the drainage-tube in the ear, turn the ear up on the top of the head and dress it with antiseptic cotton. Examine the dressing every day to be certain that it is in its proper place. This, as a rule, cures the wound entirely in from three to six days, provided that the antiseptic rules are followed very carefully; but it is generally advisable to leave the dressing stay on from eight to ten days, as the union between the two surfaces is not strong enough to stand the energetic shaking of the head which every dog does for some time after the removal of an ear bandage which has been on for several days.

External Canker.

By this we mean a purulent or ulcerative process on the edge of the external ear. This, however, is not confined to the edge, but may spread over different parts of the lobe.

ETIOLOGY. The chief causes of this trouble are injuries and lacerations of the skin. Dogs are liable to scratch or shake the ears violently against the muzzle or collar, producing an inflammation. It may also be developed from the ear itself, as in cutaneous inflammations of the external auditory passages. We may also see this as a result of wounds or lacerations of the ear caused by bites of other dogs, which from neglect or improper treatment become ulcerated, and do not heal readily on account of constant shaking of the ear. This affection is almost entirely confined to animals with long ears.

CLINICAL SYMPTOMS. The animals hold their heads to one side, shaking the ear frequently, sometimes keeping it up so long that the ulcerated surface bleeds and the blood is thrown in all directions. They attempt to scratch the affected ear with their paws, and are very sensitive about having them touched. On making an examination we find at the edge of the external ear, generally its extreme end, an ulcer or a number of them which are covered with a blackish loose scab with turned-up edges, and the tissues of the immediate neighborhood are œdematous.

THERAPEUTIC TREATMENT. There is no doubt that the quickest results may be obtained by cutting off a portion of the diseased lobe of the ear; this, however, disfigures the animal very much. This is the easiest method of cure, and the operation is generally performed on animals under the influence of ether. First remove the hair and thoroughly disinfect the parts, and cut off a circular piece from the ear that will include the torn portion, being careful not to remove any more of the lobe than is actually necessary. Another method is to cut out of the edges of the slit ear a thin section about one-eighth of an inch in thickness, so as to insure two raw fresh surfaces; the two edges of the wound must then be drawn together by means of sutures; these should not be inserted too close to the edge of the wound, as they are apt to tear through. The stitched line is then powdered with iodoform or sulphonal. The external ear is covered with wadding, turned over the top of the head, and held in position by means of a bandage, as indicated on page 376 (Fig. 83).

If the animal is one that you cannot see and dress the part every day, instead of sewing the wound after the lobe has been cut, touch it up by means of the thermo-cautery, and by means of the consequent cicatricial contraction draw the edges together.

Hoffmann deviates from the above-described method, which was practised by Siedamgrotzky, by using cocaine and cutting a three-cornered piece out of the external integument, then stitching it together without any attempt to control the hemorrhage. The author has been able to obtain satisfactory results in slight cases of external ear-canker by covering the ulcer with oxide of mercury and tying the ear up. On the other hand, he was much disappointed by caustics, such as acids, nitrate of silver, and corrosive sublimate, as they gave only negative results.

Inflammation of the External Ear—Internal Canker.
(*Otitis Externa.*)

This consists of an inflammatory irritation of the external canal of the ear. It is generally of an eczematous nature and appears in a diffuse form, extending over a larger part of the lining of the ear. It is accompanied by redness, swelling of the membrane, and an exudation of a serous and, later, a purulent secretion, in the chronic course. We may also have the formation of abscesses and contraction of the meatus (caused by thickening of the cutis, by granulations, and by polypous malformations). Although we may have acute inflammation of the canal extending deep into the lining, it is very rare that the tympanic membrane becomes ulcerated and perforated.

ETIOLOGY. The causes are similar to those mentioned under eczema. It is due to an accumulation of cerumen, dirt, and cutaneous scabs. It is also recognized that otitis is produced by acari. (See Parasitic Otitis, page 381.) Hoffmann states that he has observed serious suppuration in cases where dogs' ears have been clipped too close to the head.

CLINICAL SYMPTOMS AND PROGNOSIS. The animals shake their head, and, as the disease is almost invariably located in one ear only, they hold their head in an oblique position, trying to scratch the head against the base of the ear or to rub it against some object. They avoid carefully any attempt which is made to touch the ear, and show great pain when the tube of a concha is touched. In examining the external ear we use a forceps-shaped speculum or ear-mirror (Fig. 84). If we distend the canal, we generally find it filled with a fetid, grayish-green, or reddish liquid consisting of glandular secretions, fungi, cutaneous scabs, pus, acari, etc. After the organ is cleaned out we find an intensely red, swollen, sometimes ulcerating surface of the skin. In advanced cases the meatus is almost entirely closed by thickening of the cutis. Numerous granulations appear quickly, and in some cases where both ears are affected we may have symptoms of impaired hearing or deafness. According to Hoffmann, in deep suppurating conditions we hear a characteristic smacking or sucking liquid sound, which is produced by side pressure or rapid compression on the base of the ear.

FIG. 84.

Kramer's ear speculum.

The general condition is very seldom affected. Vomiting is only observed in exceptional cases. Vertigo, spasms, and epileptiform symptoms sometimes follow where acari are present in enormous numbers.

THERAPEUTIC TREATMENT. The treatment which corresponds with that of eczema is generally followed. We must thoroughly clean the external ear. This is best performed by a syringe fitted with an acorn-shaped point so as to prevent injuring the ear (Fig. 85) [the translator finds the best ear syringe is one made entirely of soft rubber with a long flexible point that can be pushed into the meatus without any great danger of injuring the canal; the flexible point adapts itself to the turns of the canal], and by using applications of warm water injected into the meatus. The duct is then dried with absorbent cotton introduced into the ear on the end of a small pair of forceps. As the meatus is elongated, narrow, and slightly curved, there is not much danger of injuring the tympanic membrane. In very slight affections of this character, which may be recognized by a slight redness of the membrane, itching, and the presence of a certain amount of fluid, it is only necessary to clean the meatus several times, using solutions of lead-water, phosphate of lime, acetate of zinc, etc. The author has found that simply powdering with lycopodium, amylum or talcum, filling up the ear, is much preferable to any of the above-mentioned liquids.

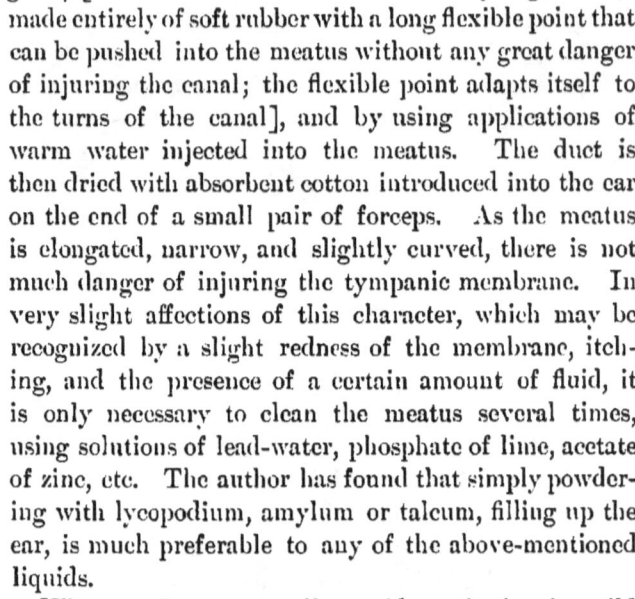

FIG. 85.

Ear syringe.

[The translator generally avoids syringing in mild cases. It causes a great deal of irritation, exciting the animal unduly. He generally cleans the ear with wood alcohol, filling in the cavity and working the alcohol into the canal by manipulation of the base of the ear. It is then to be dried thoroughly with absorbent cotton until all trace of brown coloration, characteristic of this condition, is removed. He then fills up the ear with powdered boric acid, working it thoroughly into the canal, and covering all the inflamed portions. This should be repeated every third day until the irritation is lessened, and then once a week. With this treatment he also prescribes a laxative, such as cascara sagrada. If there is eczema present, he adds to the treatment two drops of Donovan's solution, morning and evening.]

In serious diseased conditions where there is much ulceration, we may treat them in two different ways:

By syringing the ear with solutions of disinfecting and astringent agents, such as salol in alcohol (1 to 40), tannin in glycerin (1 to 30), nitrate of silver (1 to 100), carbolic acid in glycerin (1 to 10). This must be repeated several times, and we may also dry up the secretion by means of oxide of zinc or boric acid. Hoffmann advises us to use subnitrate of bismuth or sulphate of copper in starch. Imminger uses a 3 per cent. aqueous solution of chromic acid in auricular catarrh, cleans the ear with tepid water, and drops ten to twenty drops of the solution into the ear, and then massages the base for several minutes; this he repeats every second day. As a rule, the general treatment with powders is preferable to that with liquids, but the latter must be used when the meatus is much contracted and the ulcers located deeply. An ear-cap is only necessary when the animal is constantly shaking its head and the organ is very sensitive. We remove the numerous granular accumulations by means of nitrate of silver. If there are polypous enlargements, they may be touched with a thermo-cautery. Hoffmann states that in a very obstinate case he excised the entire lower region of the meatus, introduced a drainage-tube, and treated the wound with disinfecting powder.

External otitis may sometimes produce either partial or entire deafness. Both of these conditions are due to the entire closure of the external auditory canal, either by swelling and filling up with granulations or by polypous formations, etc., and more rarely by extension of the inflammatory process in the middle ear, destroying the tympanic membrane. Of course, any disturbance of the sense of hearing or entire deafness which comes from old age or is hereditary will not show any of the symptoms already described. When a dog is getting deaf he changes his manner very much: he seems strange, does not answer to the call of his master.

As a general rule, there is very little result from treatment. We have a contraction of the external meatus, and may try to dilate it by means of the introduction into the canal of cylindrical compressed tampon sponges.

[Parasitic Canker of the Ear.
(*Parasitic Otitis.*)

The symbiotes auricularis (canis) is a parasite that inhabits the ear of the dog, causing an aggravated form of canker (Nocard and

Sewell). The parasite which is common to the dog and cat is said to produce a peculiar form of vertigo.

The parasite differs from the common symbiot by the absence of abdominal lobes in the male, which are represented by a notch which has three bristles; the pubescent female has four pairs of legs which are simple knobs. The male is 30 mm. long and 23 mm. wide, and the female is 42 mm. long and 29 mm. wide (Neumann).

Hering found this parasite in an ulcer of the ear which was accompanied by a deep-seated otitis. Nocard describes minutely certain epileptiform fits in which the dog has a peculiar husky cry and rushes about violently, running into various obstacles, and finally falls insensible, and after a number of such attacks becomes totally deaf. Sewell describes the condition as finding a collection of brown or sooty-colored cerumen in the ear, or as looking dirty. If the inside of the ear is examined closely a number of tiny white specks, the size of the eye of a needle, are seen to be rapidly moving about the ear, and he believes that the tickling sensation caused by these movements and the biting of the parasite are what produce the irritation of the lining membranes of the ear.

SYMPTOMS. The ear is hot and slightly swollen, and on examination it is hardly distinguishable from ordinary otitis; there is, however, less discharge in this condition; the head is carried to one side, and the animal will scratch the base of the ear very gently with its paw and whine in a plaintive way. The translator has observed a number of animals infected with the parasite, and is inclined to think that the carrying of the head on one side and the gentle scratching of the ear are characteristic of the disease, although it is quite frequently seen in non-parasitic otitis. He has never observed the epileptiform symptoms described by Nocard, although he has made numerous examinations of animals that have presented similar symptoms.

TREATMENT. Nocard recommends naphthol 1 part, ether sulph. 3 parts, and olive oil 10 parts. This should be injected into the external auditory canal once daily, and the ear plugged up with cotton to prevent the escape of the ether. The translator does not think the latter procedure advisable, for if the ether is confined in the ear it causes great irritation, and has found from experience where he has followed this procedure that while he may not have observed epileptiform fits before the treatment, he has had symptoms simulating them very much after the ear was injected with ether and the cotton plug put into it.

Sewell advises the application of the following liniment:

  ℞.—Ung. hydrarg. nit. 4.0
    Oleum amygd. 32.0
  M. S.—Apply a small amount to the inner surface of the ear with a camel's-hair pencil.

The translator thinks it advisable to first clean the ear out with wood alcohol, and then inject the above.]

DISEASES OF THE SKIN.

INFLAMMATORY CONDITIONS OF THE CUTANEOUS MEMBRANE.

INFLAMMATORY symptoms of the skin vary according to their intensity, character, or location. The slightest irritation may produce redness, either with or without swelling—this is defined as erythematous inflammation; or we may have a formation of circumscribed, solid, firm protuberances, papillæ, fistules, boils, or granulations. These are ascribed to exudations originating partially in the papillary body, in the Malpighian membrane, and also in the neighborhood of the follicles.

The inflammatory exudation may become reabsorbed in certain cases, so that after the acute period of the disease has passed the epidermis, which has become loosened, is gradually desquamated in the form of scabs or crusts. We also occasionally see a dark pigmentation after the disease has run its course. This originates from the hæmoglobin of the extravasated red blood-corpuscles. If the inflammatory processes and exudations increase gradually in the cutaneous tissue, we may observe two different results. The inflamed location may become covered with a moist, liquid exudation, or the horny layer of the epidermis is raised up by the fluid, and we may have vesicles which raise the granular layer of the mucous strata, and also the deeper layer of the membrane becomes destroyed in the affected region. In the first case it is covered by the deep layers of the membrane; in the latter case the upper surface of the corium is exposed, having lost its vesicular covering.

The liquid which fills the small or large vesicles is deficient in cells in the early stages of its formation, and the liquid is clear or slightly yellow. Later it becomes turbid by the addition of leucocytes, and a number of whitish-yellow cells fill the fluid. In some cases it has this appearance from the very onset. When the liquid contained in the vesicle is yellow and filled with cells it is called a pustule. Sooner or later the covering of the pustules becomes ruptured, and the fluid dries up in a yellow, gray, or brown crust, under which the regeneration of the lost epidermic layer goes on rapidly.

Now and then the inflammatory process shows it is in the neighborhood of a follicle and its sebaceous glands, and we have the formation of a dark-red, very sensitive nodule, and finally suppuration of the same membrane and its adjacent tissues. As a consequence of that we find that the glands and canal of exit are filled with purulent or bloody matter. Soon the internal follicles become involved; the masses of matter can be easily pressed out of the orifice of the follicle, and we may have an elasticity of the purulent cavity surrounded by infiltrated cutis in which we find the hair has become entirely detached from the follicle and falls out. This condition is generally a rather serious affection in the dog, as in this animal there are always several follicles which are accumulated into one group with a common orifice, and in every case of cutaneous disease we find a group of affected sebaceous glands.

In very bad cases peri-glandular and peri-follicular inflammation may become so acute that we see the formation of an extended, nodule-shaped, dark-red swelling, forming a so-called "boil." This is marked after a certain period by a yellowish-green, necrotic thrombus, which becomes detached by purulent disintegration of the surrounding tissue, and is sloughed after the pus has been discharged. In such cases we find that not only is the external surface of the skin impaired, but the corium is affected, and as the follicles are destroyed the hair does not return. The formation of abscesses and ulcerations, also inflammations of the skin, will be discussed further on.

In chronic cutaneous inflammation we may see the formation of hypertrophic as well as atrophic conditions. In the former case we find as a consequence of the constant increase and congestion of blood to the part the formation of superfluous connective tissue, whereby the skin may be thickened several times its normal size, and may form large folds or callosities, and in rare cases club-shaped or warty elevations; in the latter case the corium becomes thinner. This is also the case with the epidermis. Its tissue is either greatly reduced or greatly increased in size, and in the latter case the epidermic cells which proceed from the deep part of the tissues do not undergo any horny degeneration, but rather a drying, mummifying process, covering the membrane in the shape of numerous whitish, or white-gray scabs.

We recognize the following inflammatory conditions:

Erythema.

Erythema is the mildest form of inflammation of the cutaneous membrane, and consists either of normal hyperæmia of the corium in its upper layers (erythema simplex), or it may be due to a slight sero-cellular infiltration of the membrane of Malpighi (dermatitis erythematosa).

ETIOLOGY. Erythema originates as the result of various cutaneous irritations which may be mechanical, chemical, or thermic—for instance, by friction of the collar upon the skin, by rubbing together two cutaneous surfaces, by ether, oils, chloroform, tar preparations applied to the skin, bites of insects, by ammoniacal urine (in catarrh of the bladder), and by slight burning or freezing. Erythema may also appear in connection with various cutaneous diseases, such as eczema, scab, and canine varioloid.

CLINICAL SYMPTOMS AND COURSE. The symptoms consist of a bright arterial redness of the cutaneous membrane, which disappears under pressure of the finger, but reappears immediately after, and may be complicated by slight swelling in a few cases. As a rule, the affected portion is reddened, but not irritable. The course is usually short, depending to a large extent on the cause. When this is suppressed erythema disappears, especially after the itching and rubbing have discontinued, and in certain conditions by consecutive desquamation of the upper membrane. There is, however, a more or less dark-red spot left after the acute symptoms of the disease have lessened. These finally disappear, but very slowly.

THERAPEUTIC TREATMENT. There is not, as a rule, any great irritation. It will be sufficient to remove the cause in order to remove the erythema. If there is a certain amount of irritation, we must lessen it by bathing the animal with cold water and sponging the parts with any of the following solutions: lead-water, ichthyol, or salicylic acid, soap, rubbing with salicylic oil (1 part of salicylic oil dissolved in 35 to 40 parts of olive oil and heated slightly), or a mixture of 1 part of glycerin and 5 of water; 1 part of carbolic acid, 10 of alcohol, 10 of water; 4 parts of creolin, 100 of water; 1 part of ichthyol, 10 of glycerin, 30 of water; 10 parts of nitrate of silver, 100 of water (Friedberger).

In very obstinate cases we may also use laxatives or purgatives (aloe, jalap, salines, etc.), also the internal administration of arsenic in the form of Fowler's or Donovan's solution.

Urticaria.
(*Nettlerash.*)

Nettlerash was only seen in three cases by the author. The subjects were all small, well-fed, middle-aged dogs, which were covered over the entire body with circumspect, flat, beet-like elevations, about one and one-half inch in diameter, only slightly red, and which had originated spontaneously. They were rapidly lessened by the administration of purgatives.

Eczema.
(*Red Mange.*)

By this we mean an inflammatory condition of the cutaneous membrane indicated by redness, swelling, nodules, pustules, vesicles, scabs, and crusts, which are generally accompanied with more or less itching. In the first stages development of a hyperæmia is seen, thus reddening the skin superficially, and accompanied by a serous exudation. If the inflammatory irritation stops, or if proper therapeutic measures are taken, recovery may occur at once, and we have a more or less prolonged desquamation of the epidermis. In the majority of cases, however, the irritation increases and we may have the formation of numerous pale red, tough, itching nodules, accompanied by serous swellings and slight cellular infiltration of the papillæ, but generally it is connected with the cutaneous follicles. This condition may become retrogressive; the nodules become depressed, forming scabs. In other cases the serous exudation increases constantly inside the papule, and, as a consequence, we have a rising of the horny layer in these locations; or, in other words, numerous vesicles are formed (eczema vesiculosum). If the horny covering is strong enough to resist the accumulated exudation for some time, the contents of the vesicles gradually become milky and pus-like, on account of the entrance of colorless blood-cells into the tissues (eczema pustulosum).

In other cases the vesicles burst or are scratched open; the skin is dark red in large blotches, and is marked by fine furrows which correspond with the location of the ruptured vesicles; the eczematous exudation oozes freely out of the upper surface (eczema rubrum). It is a common occurrence to see the detachment of small portions of tissue which are located between the numerous furrows in the epidermis. Thus the whole surface of the eczema is stripped of its horny layer and may become filled with pus. The oozing liquid dries rapidly and becomes a scab or crust (eczema impetiginosum), which is pushed away gradually by the consecutive exudation, and finally becomes hard, dry, and firm. Inflammation and swelling become gradually lessened under the crust, and we have the formation of a firm epidermic cover, from which the crusts gradually become detached. The diseased membrane, which is now exposed, is not swollen to any great extent, but very red (sometimes marked with dark, livid pigmentations), and covered with numerous loose scabs, which constantly fall off and are renewed from time to time (eczema squamosum).

ETIOLOGY. The etiology of eczema is of great importance for establishing the correct prognosis, as no cure can be obtained until after the cause of the trouble is removed. The first thing we must do is to lessen the mechanical irritations, such as appear under the collar and on the testicles. But the lesions which the patient inflicts upon himself are of very much more importance, for we see it in all forms of itching eruptions of the skin, in erythema, in cases of parasites of the cutaneous membrane—flies, lice, acari—in great accumulations of dirt, scabs, and falling out of the hair. We also have the appearance of eczema which extends very fast, and in some cases may go all over the body.

As regards the second group of agents which cause eczema, they are chemical irritants, especially those which have an influence upon the tissues, such as acids, alkalies, mixtures of mercury, also tar and carbolic salves, combinations of ether and oil of turpentine, of mustard, and also tar-soap.

The third group is formed by a number of thermic irritations, namely, excessively high temperature, but not high enough to produce vesicles.

Eczema appears more frequently in summer than in winter, and we have a great deal more difficulty in healing it during the summer weather. We also have a number of eczematous formations for which we can find no cause. In such cases the disease has been ascribed to acids in the blood or diseases of the nervous apparatus, and also to vegetable parasites.

CLINICAL SYMPTOMS AND COURSE. Eczema may appear in any breed of dogs, and in any region of the body without regard to age, sex, etc., but, as a rule, it affects old, well-fed dogs, such as terriers, Great Danes, and setters. It is usually seen on certain regions of the body (back, head, neck, and external surface of the extremities).

There are three general forms of eczema without taking into consideration the changes which may be produced by irritation, scratching, or rubbing.

The first type is restricted to small, irregularly circumscribed regions, but has a tendency to extend to the neighboring tissues. The eruption begins as eczema papulosum with close nodules. It is rapidly altered into the vesicular layer by change of the nodule, and finally we see the appearance of the median stage. This has a more or less extended surface without skin or hair, and shows a bright red, serous, sero-fibrinous, or purulent exudate, very painful to the touch, and having a great tendency to extend to the adjacent tissues. The stage of crustion follows very slowly.

The second type shows from the beginning an inclination to extend. In the early stages we see it as eczema erythematosum with formation of scattered papules. These are scratched open on account of the great itching they cause, or they become altered into pustules. Later we see the appearance of small scabs under which regeneration of the epidermis occurs. In the other regions desquamation of the epidermis follows.

The great tendency to scratching in dogs, notwithstanding the very slight alterations of the cutaneous tissue, may lead to what is classified under another form of skin affection called "prurigo." We must admit, however, with Friedberger and Fröhner, that true prurigo does not exist in the dog, and that all the cases mentioned in canine literature were simply modifications of papular eczema.

The third stage has a great tendency to become chronic. The skin is quite hot, a symptom which is not generally observed during the first stage of the disease; it is also much thickened and thickly covered with whitish-gray epidermic scabs. If these are removed, the affected region seems very red and shiny; the skin becomes tougher and more inflamed; the hair becomes erect, breaks off, or falls out to some extent. We see the formation of cracks and fissures, also certain dark pigmentations. A characteristic state of this chronic eczema in the dog which may also be developed from the other two forms is that of acute vesicular—that is to say, the moistened scab which forms later may be caused by the slightest irritation, rubbing, tar or carbolic soap, and this disease may reappear each summer, finally becoming chronic, reappearing each spring to dry up the following winter.

THERAPEUTIC TREATMENT. In the treatment of eczema we must consider the following facts:

1. That we have no specific drug that cures this disease; consequently it is very erroneous to treat all its forms with one agent only.

2. That in many cases the tar preparations which have been used almost exclusively are very harmful, as is also the method of systematically washing the animal with strong alkaline or carbolic soaps. The first thing to do is to give attention to the causes and find out from what cause the itching really occurs, as many cases of eczema disappear as soon as the irritation has been suppressed. The following treatment has given good results:

(*a*) We must first remove any cause of itching or irritation in the early stages of eczema erythematosum or eczema madidans. We dust the affected parts with a powder of oxide of zinc, cerussa, sulphur, or thiol mixed with cornstarch. If the affected parts are very moist, they may be dusted with lycopodium or smeared with vaseline.

℞.—Zinc. oxydat. 20.0
Lycopodium 80.0
S.—Dust on the parts several times daily.

℞.—Plumbi carbonas 10.0
Amylum pulv. 20.0
Talc. venet. pulv. 40.0
S.—Dust on the parts once daily.

In cases of extensive redness of the skin we must apply compresses of lead-water or thymol (1 per cent.), creolin (1 to 2 per cent.), carbolic-acid water, thiol water (20 per cent. thiol, liquid, 50 per cent. glycerin, and 50 per cent. water); but powdering is preferable, as every skin is not benefited by liquid applications. As soon as the marked symptoms of the disease have decreased we may replace the use of powder by ointments of zinc or lead, white precipitate ointment, or by mild ichthyol soaps.

(*b*) In very moist eczema with a prolonged course the use of powder is not always successful. In those cases we must apply drying fluids, such as corrosive sublimate solution (1 to 1000), nitrate of silver solution (2 per cent.), twice daily by means of a brush or a cotton tampon. Sublimate ointments (1 per cent.) or subiodide of mercury (2 per cent.) are beneficial, but strong solutions of blue-stone or crude sulphate of iron and tormentilla root are not to be recommended.

  R.—Hydrarg. bichlorid. 1.0
   Glycerinum 10.0
   Alcohol 90.0
  To apply upon eczematous surfaces.

  R.—Hydrarg. bichlorid. 1.0
   Alcohol }
   Glycerinum } . . . . . āā 5.0
   Adeps 90.0
  Ointment for chronic moist eczema.

(*c*) In cases of pustula we may use the same treatment as is indicated in *b*, after having pressed out and emptied the pustules. The author has also obtained good results with ichthyol liniment and salicylic ointment (see Acne).

(*d*) In eczema when it has reached the scaly stage we must first clean the skin thoroughly with some mild, non-irritating soap, but not carbolic or tar soap. The best kind to use is Castile, ivory, or a pure potash soap of the Pharmacopœia. The author has had good results from "Hebra's" alcoholic potash soap:

  R.—Saponis kalin. venal. 200.0
   Alcohol 100.0

Hebra's soap is poured or rubbed upon the surface which is thickly covered with crusts, and on the following day they are removed easily without subjecting the animal to much pain. After careful cleansing we use the same agents as are used in the moist forms of eczema—zinc powder, corrosive sublimate, or nitrate of silver.

(e) We use tar and ichthyol preparations with good results in the chronic forms of eczema where there is considerable cutaneous thickening with cracks, fissures, etc. Ichthyol is especially useful, and when used in concentrated form in ointments or liniments it is much more valuable than tar preparations, because it relieves the itching or irritation in a very short time.

Oil of tar in the treatment of eczema (Leistikow):

  R.—Oleum picis 3.0
    Spts. vini rect. 2.0
    Æther sulphuric. 1.0
  F. M. S.—Rub into the parts every third day.

  R.—Picis liquidæ ⎫
    Saponis kalin. venal. ⎬ . . . . . āā 100.0
    Spirit. dilut. ⎭
  Apply once daily.

  R.—Ammon. sulfo-ichthyolic. 15.0
    Aqua calcariæ ⎫
    Oleum olivarum ⎬ . . . āā 75.0
  Apply upon the thickened membrane once daily.

(f) If there is considerable thickening of the skin, and if the latter is covered at the same time with scabs, we can obtain good results by rubbing salicylic oil (1 part salicylic acid in 35 parts of warm olive oil) over it daily for a week. If this does not succeed, which, however, is very rare, we must first use tar or ichthyol preparations and follow it up by the other. Some authors advise friction with soft soap, chrysarobin ointment, iodoform, or naphthalin, and washing with potash.

Internal treatment, as a rule, has been abandoned. Formerly all used purgatives or laxatives, and administered arsenic, but this has lately fallen into disuse, and it is only in very obstinate or chronic cases that anyone uses them. [The translator can not entirely agree to this, as it is very evident that this disease is frequently caused by some disorder of the stomach or liver, and would advise slight laxatives, especially the salines, and small doses of arsenic in chronic cases, and also certain restrictions in the diet.]

Burning and Freezing.

In cases where a high degree of temperature acts upon the skin it causes hyperæmia, accompanied by a slight exudation, or an erythematous inflammation. This is called the first degree, or mild form of burning, and generally follows the same course as that described on page 384. When the skin is subjected to the action of a very high temperature we see violent serous exudation in the stratum mucosum. This lifts up the epidermis, forming large vesicles. The covering of the vesicles bursts, and healing proceeds very rapidly, also complete regeneration of the epidermis, provided there is no septic influence acting on the wound surface. If the burn is still more severe, the tissue of the skin becomes charred or burnt entirely, the whole skin being softened and healing by the formation of a cicatricial tissue underneath. In cases of burning in the first and second degrees the hair is only lost temporarily; in the third and fourth degrees of burn it is permanently lost.

THERAPEUTIC TREATMENT. The treatment of burns consists in mild cases of cooling agents, sugar of lead, lead ointments (1 part of lead plaster to 9 parts of olive oil); in burns accompanied by vesicles we use a powder of oxide of zinc and apply potash liniments (equal parts of linseed oil and lime-water), or boric-acid solution (20 per cent.). In cases where the burn is sufficiently deep to char and make the skin black we must wait for softening and detachment of the burnt portion and then proceed according to the ordinary antiseptic treatment of wounds.

Freezing has exactly the same effect as heat. In the first degree we find bluish-red, but not distinct, flat swellings. In more serious freezing we find serous vesicles somewhat bloody. This, however, is very rare in the dog. Complete loss of the skin after the freezing of a member has never been observed by the author in the dog. In such cases it is advisable to use the same treatment as is followed in human medicine—that is, friction with petroleum, spirit of camphor, injections of tincture of iodine, and in the severe forms strict antiseptic methods.

Gangrene of the Skin.

We may see necrotic withering of the skin from the effects of extremely high or low temperature, or it may be caused by traumatic influences, by disease-alterations of the mucous membrane or subcutaneous tissue—for instance, in phlegmone, acne, and in some cases from internal causes. Spontaneous gangrene belongs to this latter class. It is developed in some cases, according to Möller, on the cheeks, and corresponds with noma in the human species. The disease is recognized by salivation, poor appetite, fever, and necrosis of the corners of the mouth, which may extend gradually over the entire cheek.

The treatment is to follow strict antiseptic methods; to apply dressings of iodoform, sulphonal, or boric creolin (1 part of creolin to 50 of boric acid), and improve the general condition by means of tonics.

Acne.

Under the name of "acne" we mean an inflammation of the hair-follicles and sebaceous glands resulting in suppuration. This is not produced, however, by follicular acari. The anatomical processes which we recognize in this serious eruptive form have been already mentioned on page 385.

This condition generally appears on the nose, cheek, side of the face, and external fasciæ of the extremities, between the toes, and in some cases over the entire body.

ETIOLOGY. Very little is known of the actual cause of this disease. Local irritations have been thought to be the cause, such as constant pressure of the muzzle, rubbing the affected parts, and in certain cases to some hereditary predisposition in the character of the sebaceous glands. Vegetable irritants have also been said to cause this disease when the skin was in a certain irritable condition. It is not infectious.

CLINICAL SYMPTOMS AND PROGNOSIS. This disease develops very slowly, beginning with redness and loss of the skin and hair. These red spots are painful, irregular, swollen, and extend over the surface the size of a large dollar. They are caused by the formation of a large number of pea-like nodules which are hard and firm. In some cases we find the whole surface of the skin red, hard, and very painful to the touch. After a short time the nodules become soft, discharge spontaneously a more or less amount of bloody pus, and contain in some cases cores of necrotic tissue.

Occasionally we see the union of a number of these acne nodules, so that the skin presents a bluish-red discoloration and dies or becomes purulent, as if the skin was undermined by purulent collections; this may appear all over the body.

This "non-acarian" acne very often produces bad results. It has a great tendency to extend in almost all directions, and the cicatrices which appear after healing of the disease leave bare spots all over the body, pink in color, streaked with lines of black pigment deposits.

THERAPEUTIC TREATMENT. The treatment consists in the energetic local application of various preparations externally. If the acueous nodules are in the early part of their development, we must puncture them, or open the follicles by some strong antiseptic, such as salicylic or naphthalin ointment. In cases where purulent disintegration has gone on it is advisable to open the pustules. This is best performed by means of a small bistoury, and then fill in the opening with boric creolin, or paint it with disinfecting solutions, such as pyoktanin solution (1 to 10 of alcohol), or a 1 to 1000 solution of corrosive sublimate. This should be used once a day when the acne is developing.

R.—Acid. salicylic. 20.0
Oleum olivæ 40.0
Lanolin 80.0
S.—Put a small portion on the parts once daily.

The following should be used when the pustules have been emptied:

R.—Creolin 1.0
Acid. boraci. 40.0

Fröhner advises curetting the cavities and the use of the creolin ointment just mentioned, and in some cases cauterization with nitrate of silver, or powdering with iodoform and tannic acid. In cases of circumscribed acne it is advisable sometimes to cut out the diseased portion of the skin.

CUTANEOUS AFFECTIONS WHICH ARE CAUSED BY ANIMAL PARASITES.

The changes produced on the skin from disease caused by animal parasites are divided into two conditions—primary and secondary.

The primary appears as a superficial inflammatory process, produced directly by irritations of the parasites upon the skin, and this condition depends to a large extent upon the amount of irritation and the depth that the parasites have penetrated in the skin.

The secondary symptoms are the results of this penetration into the cutis, causing more or less itching and irritation, and, as a rule, scratching and rubbing on the part of the animal, producing heat, redness, papules, vesicles, pustules, hemorrhages, or excoriations. These irritated spots may not be restricted entirely to the affected region in which the parasites are located, but may spread to other localities. This form, which is nothing more or less than eczema, possesses two peculiarities which may distinguish it at once from the common form of eczema which is not produced by a parasite: .

1. It invariably appears in single, isolated eruptive spots, and it is only after the disease has been present for some time, or where there is extensive irritation, that we may find the surface connected together; and,

2. We see the appearance of these eczematous eruptions in certain locations which are especially preferred by the parasites, and showing their greatest development of the eruption in those regions, even when the whole body is affected.

A microscopical examination of the scales of the skin will furnish definite information as to the character of the cause of the eruption. We distinguish two groups of cutaneous parasites: First, those which live upon the external surface of the skin, and, second, those which enter the tissues of the membranes, puncturing deeply into the tissues. In the first group we have the following:

Ceratopsyllus (*Pulex*) Canis, the Dog Flea.

The true dog flea as well as the human flea (pulex irritans) is found in the dog. The former is distinguished from the latter by its size, by the different length of its tentacles, and by the presence of a number of sharp hairs arranged in a comb-like layer along the side of the head (Fig. 86). Coarse breeds of dogs are not particularly affected by the bites of fleas, but pet dogs and delicately bred animals scratch and rub to such an extent as to cause irritated splotches and redness over the entire body, and lead the owner to believe that the animal is affected with mange. If the fleas are removed from the skin by a bath or in some other manner, we may relieve the itching and irritation by the application of some soothing solution.

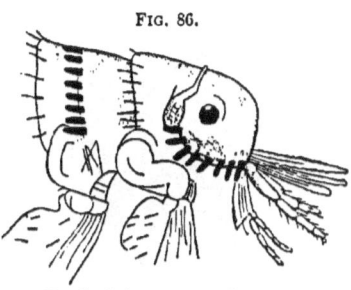

FIG. 86.

Head of the ceratopsyllus canis.
(MEGNIN.)

THERAPEUTIC TREATMENT. Fleas are best removed by means of Persian insect powder (Flores pyrethri). This must be moistened with alcohol and rubbed into the hair. Zurn recommends the placing of pine shavings in dogs' kennels.

Hæmatopinus Piliferus (*Dog Lice*) and Trichodectes Latus Canis (*Dog Parasites*).

Description of Hæmatopinus Piliferus. This parasite is distinguished by an egg-shaped head fitted with fine, short hairs and fleshy sheath-trunk with hooks at the edge. This when lifted shows a sucking tube and two movable knife-shaped stilettos. The thorax is wrinkled and possesses three pairs of scissor-like claws. The posterior portion of the body is large and possesses nine rudimentary legs. The length of the body is about 2 mm. (see Fig. 87).

Description of the Trichodectes. In this parasite the head is broad, quarter-shaped, with three manacle feelers and a tooth-shaped mouth. The thorax is contracted, the posterior part of the body has nine distinct members, and the length of the body is from 1 to 2 mm. (see Fig. 88).

The former parasites are the most disagreeable, as they suck the blood from the body, live particularly on those parts of the skin where the hair is thick and which are not exposed to the cold, such as the neck, flanks, and at the tail. The trichodectes feed, as a rule, upon the hair and epidermis, and are particularly found on the head and neck. Both skin parasites produce intense irritation

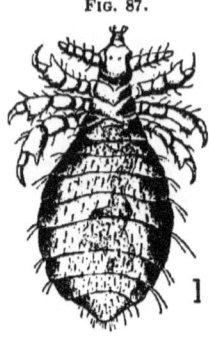

Fig. 87.

Haematopinus piliferus.

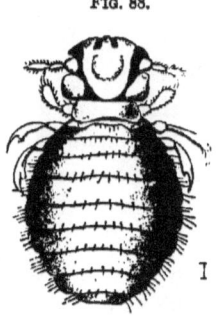

Fig. 88.

Trichodectes latus.

The accompanying small lines give the natural size of the parasite.

and rubbing, causing inflammatory efflorescences which look very much like squamous eczema, with partial loss of hair and formation of scabs. The diagnosis is usually easy, as we can see the parasites and their eggs by separating the hair.

THERAPEUTIC TREATMENT. This consists of destroying the parasites and their eggs. For that purpose it is often requisite to clip the animals. The safest and least harmful agents are decoctions of tobacco (5 to 10 per cent.), solutions of creolin (3 to 6 per cent.), petroleum (pure, or mixed with olive oil), and in small dogs anise-seed oil (1 to 10 per cent. of olive oil). Mercurial ointment may be rubbed in the neck around the collar, but we must not apply more than a piece the size of a bean. Washing with corrosive sublimate solution has been tried, but it must be very carefully done, and the animal not allowed to lick the body, as it is very apt to produce mercurial symptoms and salivation.

Fig. 89.

Ixodes ricinus. The accompanying line is the natural size of the parasite. (KUCHENMEISTER-ZURN.)

Ixodes Ricinus.

This parasite, which is about 2 mm. in length, and sometimes when full grown almost 3 mm., looks very much like an acari (Fig. 89). It penetrates into the skin and sucks the blood, and is generally seen in setters or pointers, and dogs when working through the woods and underbrush become filled with them. Turpentine and petroleum will destroy them instantly.

Leptus Autumnalis.

This is what is known as a "harvest bug," or acari. It is about 4 mm. in length, and is the red larva of thrombidium holosericeum. While human beings are quite frequently affected with this parasite, it is only rarely found in the dog. Defrance and Friedberger have seen pustular inflammations of the skin of the dog produced by this parasite. The rash was very prominent on the abdomen and the inner fascia of the legs, and was healed quickly by an application of carbolic acid and glycerin, or carbolated cosmoline.

Dermatophagus Canis. This is very rarely found in the dog, and is a parasite which affects the ear, producing otitis externa. For further details refer to Parasitic Otitis (page 381).

The following parasites belong to the second group:

Sarcoptes Scabiei Communis.
(Sarcoptic Mange; Scabies Sarcoptica.)

Description of the Sarcoptes. This parasite is about 0.25 to 0.30 mm. broad and from 0.20 to 0.50 mm. long. It has a rounded, turtle-like shape and a horseshoe-shaped head, with well-developed club-shaped scissor-like jaws. It has short rudimentary feet, and tulip-shaped suction cups which are attached to the first, second, and fourth pairs of feet in the male, while in the female they are found in the first and second pairs only. In the back we see a number of acorn-shaped scales or thorns, and four rows of lance-shaped scales on the upper surface of the back. The skin shows transverse folds and we find four elongated hairs on the posterior end of the body. (Fig. 90.)

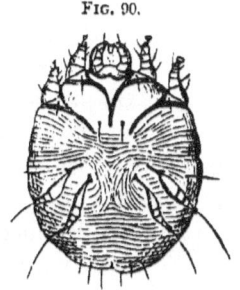

Fig. 90.

Female sarcoptes of the dog, magnified 75 times, giving the abdominal view. (SIEDAM-GROTZKY.)

The male acari and the young parasites generally inhabit cavities in the skin which they have made for themselves. These cavities are connected externally by short ducts, the entrances of which may be marked by small vesicles or pustules, while the females may move to different parts of the body when sexually ripe, burrowing ducts through the upper layers of the epidermis down as far as the membrana Malpighii, which contains a great deal of fluid. At the end of the duct—that is, the place of entrance of the acari—we see the development of a small, somewhat moist nodule—or a vesicle, which dries up ultimately, leaving a scar. This digging of the parasite may produce more or less detachment of the epidermis. We generally find that the parasite has a preference for certain parts of the body, such as the head, neck, abdomen, and chest, at the root of the tail, and the paws. It is very hard to detect it with the microscope. The best way is to remove some of the membrane with the scissors or scrape the upper portion of the skin to the corium. If parasites have been present for some time a secondary eczema is soon developed, which is produced by scratching and rubbing, also by itching of the scabs and scales. This "mange eczema" appears in various forms, according to the sensitiveness of the skin, and is either papular, vesicular, or pustular, and sooner or later produces decided thickness of the skin and leads to the formation of a number of folds, wrinkles, and ulcerated points between the clefts of the wrinkles. There is always a certain characteristic appearance about these affected localities which makes it easy to distinguish between the parasitic and simple eczema. The surfaces finally become confluent, forming large eczematous areas. It is very improbable that a mistake will be made in diagnosis, except in the early stages, when there is only a very small spot affected, because the parasitic eczema produces rapid characteristic changes, accompanied by scratching, twitching, rubbing, and licking, which are very much aggravated as soon as the animal is placed near any warm object—for instance, in the neighborhood of a stove or if covered up with a blanket, and also the evident pleasure which the animal gets if the affected part is rubbed or scratched; and finally, if the animal is kept with other dogs, the disease is carried to them and developed very quickly. The disease can also be produced in man by taking a mangy scab and applying it to the arm, holding it there by a bandage. As a rule, however, the parasite does not propagate rapidly in man.

THERAPEUTIC TREATMENT. In order to produce good results in mange we must kill or remove the parasites, as the itching and scratching cease as soon as they are destroyed, and on that account the artificial eczema disappears rapidly. A large number of antiparasitic agents are used—creosote, wood-tar, creolin, lysol, salicylic acid, and Peruvian balsam. They are all useful, and may be applied according to the following directions:

It is always necessary to make a general application of the agent, even in such cases where the disease seems to be restricted to one region of the body. The dog must be covered all over with a layer of soft soap or with Hebra's alcoholic potash soap (see page 391), which is to be shampooed into the skin with the hands or a stiff brush, and cleansed thoroughly in clear tepid water. The agent which is to be used is then applied with the hand or with a brush, covering only one-third of the body at a time [the translator thinks that the body can be covered entirely with the medicinal agent at each application, except in the creosote and carbolic acid combination], repeating this operation in two or three days. At the end of that period the application may be removed by soft soap and water. The best ointments for mange are:

1. Picis liquid., sapo potassii viridis, spiritus vini rect., āā q.s. Ft. linimentum.

2. Creolini, sapo potassii viridis, āā 1 part; spiritus vini rect., 10 parts.

3. Creosoti, 1 part; picis liquid., sapo viridis, spirit. vini rect., aqua, āā 7 parts.

4. Creolini (lysol), 1; petrolatum, 12.

5. Two to 5 per cent. oily solution of creosote or carbolic acid.

6. Peruvian balsam, pure or with a little alcohol, ether, glycerin, or oil.

The four agents which are mentioned first are very energetic, but more or less dangerous, so it is advisable to use them in healthy or not too young or delicate animals, and at the same time to administer small quantities of sulphate of sodium in their drinking-water in order to prevent carbolic poisoning. Peruvian balsam is harmless and very useful, but, unfortunately, it is expensive, and is only adapted to very fine pet dogs.

Prevention Methods. The owner of the dog must have his attention called to the fact that the sarcoptes are highly contagious, and may produce similar complications in other dogs and in man, and while this may be of a very mild character, it has been observed in the acute form in several cases (Siedamgrötzky, Friedberger, and others). The contact of mangy dogs with healthy animals must be prevented, and covers, blankets, bedding, etc., which have been used by the affected animals must be subjected to a thorough cleansing by washing with hot solutions of soda and a high degree of heat. The straw, of course, must be burned.

ACARUS DEMODEX FOLLICULORUM.
(*Follicular Mange.*)

Description of the Acarus This parasite is about 0.3 mm. in length and about 0.045 mm. in breadth. It has a broad, scissor-like masticatory apparatus, a mobile anterior trunk, and three jointed maxillary feet. It has a worm-shaped, wrinkled abdomen, with three jointed, clawy, thick, short feet attached to the thorax. The elongated oval larvæ have only six legs. (Fig. 91.)

FIG. 91.

Acarus folliculorum, magnified 250 diameters. (FRIEDBERGER.)

These parasites are found in the hair-follicles and sebaceous glands, and by their presence show a purulent disintegration of the peri-glandular and peri-follicular tissues. The sebaceous glands are also destroyed, causing acneous pustules (see pages 835 and 394). The demodex acne shows itself in certain preferred parts of the body, especially the head, throat, neck, and paws, but it may extend over the entire body. It is not very easily transmitted, as has been proven by the attempt made by Weiss, Martemucci, and others, who were unsuccessful.

CLINICAL SYMPTOMS AND COURSE. These are distinguished by a pustular and squamous form of eruption. The pustular form is the most common and may be recognized by the hair falling out, by hyperæmic and swollen skin, which becomes thickened and folded, forming nodules often the size of a millet-seed, which change from bluish-red to yellow pustules, and finally the purulent bloody contents escape, and in it and under the membrane we find hundreds of acari.

The itching, as a rule, is never very great, as in sarcoptes mange, and in some cases not even present. When the affected cutaneous regions are scratched or rubbed, the patients, as a rule, resent it and do not derive the pleasure that scratching gives in sarcoptes mange. The disease spreads very slowly, and only in very rare instances does it cover the whole body. The parts that are affected finally heal, but the skin remains thick, denuded of hair, marked in some places by scars or cicatrices, and also by cracks and wrinkles. In some cases we may have a dark pigmentation marked with warty projections. When there is any itching present the appearance of the cutis may be changed materially by secondary eczema. The appetite is very rarely affected, the animal eating well, although some cases, in spite of good food, have shown the animal to have an impoverished, unhealthy look.

The squamous form is seen in the neighborhood of the eyes, but it may show itself in other places of the body. It is a normal cutaneous inflammation accompanied by falling out of the hair and great accumulation of scabs. The hair drops from the affected places; the skin is only slightly reddened, but covered with thick scabs. If these places are squeezed, the parasites can be pushed out of the skin very rapidly. The easiest way to obtain the parasite is to rub the blunt end of a knife over the affected parts, and the microscope will aid you in distinguishing this disease from simple scaly eczema.

The prognosis is generally unfavorable, and it is almost impossible to reach the parasites. This is especially the case with the squamous form, which is always considered the worst form of parasitic mange.

THERAPEUTICS. (*a*) *Treatment of the Pustular Form.* When pustules are present they must be squeezed and emptied every day, and at the same time apply the antiparasitic agents already mentioned with a brush. The animals, as a rule, show great pain and object to it, but to obtain any good results this must be followed up patiently. Any of the solutions may be used, as one is as good as another, but we must remember that where we have an opening directly into the deep portions of the skin that reabsorption of poisons through the membrane is much easier, consequently it is better to select a non-poisonous remedy, such as Peruvian balsam or warm preparations of salicylic acid (1 part of salicylic acid to 40 parts of olive oil). Both agents may be replaced by styrax (in oil solution).

Another form of treatment which is advised by Friedberger is also recommended by Bruasco. In following this treatment we clip the dog carefully and put him in a bath of sulphate of potassium on the first day (100 grammes to 70 litres of water), and on the second, third, and fourth days rub the body with a thin ointment of cantharides (1 to 6 of lard). Then on the fifth or sixth day wash the animal thoroughly with soft potash soap. Allow a few days to intervene, then renew the treatment, going through the same course again. Megnin has obtained very good results from a sulphur bath. For this purpose he uses the bath-tub shown in Fig. 92.

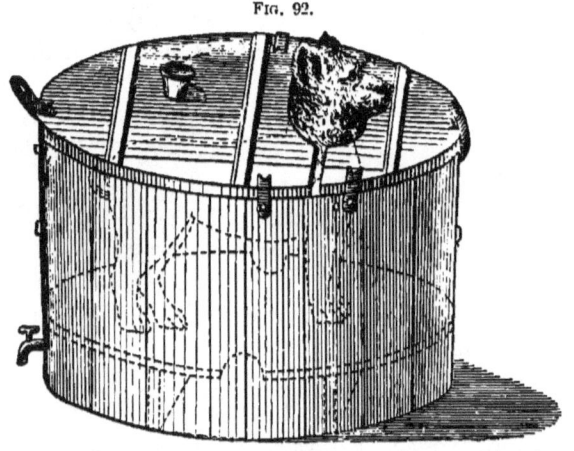

Fig. 92.

Bath-tub.

(b) *Treatment of the Squamous Form.* In this we must first try to reach the parasites, and this we do by systematic rubbing with acid ointments or strong concentrated salicylic ointments (1 to 5), and also with soft soap or lye. When we have removed the scabs and scales with this form of treatment we must apply the same treatment as prescribed in the pustular form.

The prophylactic measures must be the same as in sarcoptic mange. No transmission of this disease has ever been observed in man.

Filaria. Siedamgrotzky, Rivolta, and Griffith have seen pustular eruptions of the skin which were caused by thread-worms. The former saw upon the external surface of the legs red-bordered pustules which contained one or two round worms, which were 0.04 to 0.7 mm. long, and had awl-shaped tails. The parasites had probably entered the skin through the hair-follicles, and some were found measuring 1 mm. in length in the straw of the dog's kennel.

The treatment is simply cleanliness.

Cutaneous Affections which are Caused by Vegetable Parasites.

We know at present of but two skin diseases in the dog which are ascribed to the presence of vegetable parasites; these are favus and herpes, which belong to the fungi class, and may be simple or ramified, membranous or non-membranous, double contourated, cellular threads (hyphen), which become mixed in their growth and form a real fungous bed or fungous turf (mycelium). These fungous growths produce at their ends and at the point of their short side branches bead- or string-like spores, uniting and ligating each other, which are considered as sexual or multiplying organs (Fig.

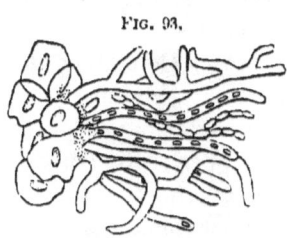

FIG. 93.

Favus spores, magnified 450 times. (VON DÜBEN.)

93). We cannot make a strong distinction between the fungi of favus and those of herpes, but there is a difference, as is seen in the disease in its local form, and we have given a description of both.

1. **Favus.** This fungus is called achorion Schonleinii, and is developed upon the skin, between the epidermic layers in the hair-follicles, and also in the hair itself. It may be transmitted to the cat, horse, rabbit, mouse, and human beings, causing a characteristic skin affection.

CLINICAL SYMPTOMS. Favus is found in special regions of the body, namely, upon the forehead, back of the nose, abdomen, and external surface of the hindlegs, as gray, gray-yellow or even saffron-yellow, dry, brittle crusts or eschars. These are about the size of the head of a needle in the beginning, but gradually by their growth cover the entire surface, and may finally become from 2 to 5 mm. in thickness. They appear in the shape of round or elliptical scutula, depressed in a saucer-like manner, generally perforated with a dull, lustreless hair, which drops out later on. If the escharious mass is removed we find a corresponding depression with exposed, very red epidermis. As a rule, this is followed by bleeding, and, according to St. Cyr, there is always great itching. This last, however, has not been the author's experience.

THERAPEUTIC TREATMENT. The treatment of this disease is easy, consisting of removal of the scutula and a daily application of antiparasitic agents, especially tincture of iodine, carbolic acid and creosote solution, sublimate solutions of red, white, or gray mercurial ointment, solution of salicylic acid (10 per cent. solution with alcohol), and tar soap. Chloride of sodium (common salt) has recently been advocated in the treatment of ringworm. It is either to be applied in saturated solution or else made into an ointment with vaseline.

Concerning the prophylaxis, we refer you to the indications which are given later in herpes.

2. **Herpes Tonsurans.** Depilating herpes, herpetic ring, herpetic eschar, bare herpes. This fungus which is said to be the cause of herpes, is called trichophyton tonsurans, and is found in large masses lying on the upper portion of the epidermis, and especially in the hair and its covering.

Trichophyton has a much more rapid growth than achorion. It not only grows from one centre, as in the other form, but it may make its appearance in a number of new centres scattered all over the body, until finally the whole is strewn with numerous, isolated, round-shaped bare spots. The parasite may be transmitted to dogs, man, cattle, goats, cats, pigs, and rabbits.

CLINICAL SYMPTOMS. The eruption is marked by small, round, or elongated herpes, which vary in shape and size between a lentil and a large bean. The spots are hairless and distinctly circumscribed; the blotches are arranged at intervals, and are generally very regular. They become confluent in some cases, and extend over the entire body. Affected regions show a peculiar grayish-white or dirty gray scab, and in old cases yellowish-brown crusts about 2 mm. in thickness. These crusts may have some hair adhering to them. The skin under the crust is copper-red in color and covered with numerous millet-like nodules (swollen hair-follicles). After a certain time, if the disease ceases to spread, the scab drops off gradually, and we see a bare, scaly herpes upon which the hair slowly returns. The animals are often affected with secondary eczema. This, however, is produced by constant scratching, due to the irritation of the disease.

THERAPEUTIC TREATMENT. The treatment of herpes depends on the removal of the favus. We must, therefore, clean the affected part, lift and remove all scabs and eschars by means of a thin knife, or shampoo with soft soap, following it up by a dressing of some of the agents mentioned under the head of mange.

Prophylaxis. The animals must be separated, as the danger of infection to both dog and man is very great. The kennels are to be cleaned and all straw, etc., burned, and the animals kept away from children.

ATROPHIC CONDITIONS OF THE CUTANEOUS MEMBRANE.

Alopecia.

(Falling out of the Hair.)

By this term we mean a falling out of the hair which is not caused by actual disease. We make a distinction, however, between general alopecia and alopecia areata. The former is an extensive falling out of the hair, often recognized after serious disease and during the period of convalescence. The latter is a symptom of bad nutritive condition (alopecia symptomatica), and is characterized in some cases by a circumscribed or rounded herpes; this may become confluent and is especially developed on the back, tail, and external fasciæ of the thighs. In both forms it is not rare to find the skin pigmented. Siedamgrotzky has proved that alopecia of the dog, if circumscribed or diffuse, depends on the atrophic condition of the hair and infiltration of the upper cutaneous layers, and it is especially seen in dogs with silky, white or grayish hair.

In some cases where the dog has black-tipped hair it is also noticeable.

THERAPEUTIC TREATMENT. The treatment consists of washing with alcoholic soap, and a diluted tincture of cantharides is also useful. It is advisable in alopecia areata to use antiparasitic agents, such as diluted tincture of iodine (Friedberger and Fröhner), or an alcoholic salicylic acid (10 per cent.). The principal therapeutic agents, however, are rubbing with a strong brush, increasing the nutrition of the skin, plenty of exercise, and, above all—patience.

INDEX.

ABDOMEN, fatty deposits in, 88
    puncture of, 90
Abdominal cavity, tumors of, 89
    dropsy, 86
Abscess of the kidneys, 167
    of the liver, 96
    of the sclerotic membrane, 360
Abscesses, perinephritic, 168
Acarus demodex folliculorum, 402
    mystax, 74
Acids, bile, 93
Acne, 394
Acute and chronic peritonitis, 88
    catarrh of the bowels, 59
      of the bronchia, 121
      of the stomach, 55
    diffuse peritonitis, 84
    inflammation of the kidneys, 162
    intestinal catarrh, 59
    laryngeal catarrh, 116
    laryngitis, 116
    nephritis, 162
    parenchymatous hepatitis, 95
    peritonitis, 8
    synovial inflammation of the joints, 272
Adenoma, 336
Affection of the eyelids, 350
Air-passages, diseases of, 120
Albumin, digestion of, 36
    in urine, 160
Alopecia, 407
Amaurosis, 371
Amblyopia, 371
Amount of urine, 156
Amputation, 298
    of the tail, 300
Amyloid kidney, 166
    liver, 97
Anæmia, 256
    of the brain, 204
Anæsthesia, 346
Anal glands, tumors of, 337
Anchylostomum, 81
Angina catarrhalis, 51

Angioma, 335
Animal parasites, affections caused by, 396
Anterior chamber, dropsy of, 371
    limbs, paralysis of, 200
Anthracosis pulmonum, 129
Anus, imperforate, 74
    prolapsus of, 71
    stitching of, 73
Aphthæ, 43
Apoplexia, 204
Areca nut, 80
Arsenical poisoning, 98
Arthritis deformans, 275
    rheumatic, 274
Articulations, diseases of, 268
Ascites, 86
Aseptic wound fever, 309
Asthma, 122
Ataxia, 201
Atresia ani, 74
Atrophic conditions of cutaneous membrane, 407
Auscultation of the thorax, 110

BACTERIA in the urine, 159, 172
    Bench-show distemper, 235
Bile acids, 93
    color in urine, 161
Bitch, castration of, 191, 193
    inguinal hernia in, 329
    menstruation of, 154
    passing the catheter in, 153
Black cataract, 371
Blackening of the lungs, 129
Bladder, catarrh of, 170
    cramp of, 175
    debility of, 173
    diseases of, 170
    examination of, 155
    stone in, 176
    urine in, 88
    worms, 76
Bleeding at the nose, 114
Blennorrhœa of the eyelids, 355

(409)

Blood-boils, 317
-corpuscles in urine, 158
filaria in, 149
Bloodvessels, inflammation of, 308
Boils, 385
Bones, diseases of, 268
fractures of, 291
tumors of, 334
union of fractured, 295
Bothriocephalus, 82
bubius, 82
cordatus, 82
fuscus, 82
latus, 82
reticulatus, 82
Bowels and peritoneum, physical examination of, 37
acute catarrh of, 59
chronic catarrh of, 62
distention of, with gas, 88
Brain, anæmia of, 204
diseases of, 202
hyperæmia of, 202
inflammation of, 206
Brom-ether, 348
Bronchia, acute catarrh of, 121
catarrh of, 120
chronic catarrh of, 121, 122
Bronchial breathing, 111
catarrh, infectious, 235
tubes, diseases of, 120
Bronchitis, 120
Broncho-pneumonia, 124
Bruises, 317
Buccal fungi, 43
Burning, 393
Bursa mucosa, diseases of, 287

CÆSAREAN operation, 192
Calculi, uric, 177
Cancerous tumor, 342
Cancer of glandular tissue, 342
of the prostate, 182
squamous, 342
Canker, external, 377
internal, 378
of the ear, parasitic, 381
Carbolic-acid poisoning, 98
Carcinoma, 342
Cartilaginous tumor, 333
Castration, 182, 191, 327
in the bitch, 191
Catarrh, acute, of bronchia, 121
laryngeal, 116
chronic, of bowels, 62
of bronchia, 122
of larynx, 118

Catarrh, infectious bronchial, 235
nasal, 113
of the bladder, 170
of the duodenum, 91
of the nose, 113
of the windpipe and bronchia, 120
Catarrhal fever, contagious, 223
inflammation of the lungs, 124
jaundice, 90
metritis, 188
ophthalmia, 354
pneumonia, 124
Catalepsy, 219
Cataract, 365
black, 371
Catheter, passing of, 152
Cauterization of tumors, 345
Cavity of the mouth, malformations of, 47
Ceratopsyllus canis, 396
Cerebral hemorrhage, 204
Cerebro-spinalis, 209
-spinal meningitis, 209
Cerebrum, inflammation of, 207
Cestodes, 75
Chest, dimensions of, 106
Chloroform, 348
Chlorosis, 256
Chorea, 217
Crystalline lens, diseases of, 365
extraction of, 368
Chronic catarrh of the bowels, 62
of the bronchia, 121, 122
of the larynx, 118
of the stomach, 57
dyspepsia, 57
induration of the lungs, 126
inflammation of the kidneys, 165
interstitial hepatitis, 95
nephritis, 165
irritable cough, 118
laryngitis, 118
nephritis, 165
parenchymatous nephritis, 165
peritonitis, 84, 85, 88
prostatitis, 182
serous inflammation of the joints, 273
Circumscribed peritonitis, 85
phlegmone, 307
Cirrhosis of the liver, 95
of the lungs, 126
Closure of the eyelids, 350
Coccidium, 82
perforans, 82
Cœnurus cerebralis, 78
Cold in the head, 113

Collections of urine in the bladder, 88
Color of urine, 156
Compression, 313
Condyloma, 336
Congestive hyperæmia of the liver, 94
Conjunctivitis, 234, 353, 354
  in distemper, 234
  purulent, 355
Conjunctiva, diseases of, 353
  inflammation of, 353
Connective tissue, tumors of, 333
Consciousness, disturbance of, 196
Constipation, 39
Constitutional diseases, 256
Contagious catarrhal fever, 223
Contraction of the intestines, 66
Controlling hemorrhage, 302, 313
Contusions, 317
  of the joints, 280
Convulsions, 200
Convulsive cough, 118
Cornea, dermoid of, 364
  injuries of, 364
Coryza, 113
Costiveness, 39
Cough, 102
  chronic irritable, 118
  convulsive, 118
Coverings of the brain, diseases of, 202
Cramp, cystic, 175
  of the bladder, 175
Croupal membranes, 52
  pneumonia, 129
Cruralis, hernia, 331
  paralysis of, 200
Cutaneous affections caused by animal parasites, 396
  caused by vegetable parasites, 405
  membrane, inflammatory conditions of, 384
  membranes, atrophic conditions of, 407
  tumors, 341
Cuterebro emasculator, 185
Cylindrical cell-tumor, 342
Cystic cramp, 175
Cysticercus pisiformis, 77
  tenuicollis, 78
Cystitis, 170
Cystotomy, 179
Cysts, 341
  dermoid, 341
  extravasation, 341
  glandular, 341
  honey, 51
  "honey-pouch," 341

Cysts of the kidneys, 169
  retention, 341
  serous, of the ear, 375

DEBILITY of the bladder, 173
  Deformans, arthritis, 275
Dentition, 47
Deposits in the abdomen, fatty, 88
Dermatitis, 386
Dermoid cysts, 341
  of the cornea, 364
Detrusor, paralysis of, 174
Diabetes insipidus, 260
  mellitus, 259
Diagnosis of the larynx and windpipe, 102
Diffuse peritonitis, 84
  phlegmone, 307
Digestive apparatus, diseases of, 27
  examination of, 27
Digestion of albumin, 36
  of hydrocarbonaceous food, 35
  of meat, 34
  of milk, 35
Dimensions of the thorax, 106
Discission, 367
Diseased malformations of the joints, 275
Diseases, constitutional, 256
  of the air-passages and bronchial tubes, 120
  of the articulations and the bones, 268
  of the bladder, 170
  of the brain and its coverings, 202
  of the bursa mucosa, 287
  of the conjunctiva, 353
  of the crystalline lens, 365
  of the digestive apparatus, 27
  of the ear, 375
  of the eyes, 350
  of the intestines, 59
  of the joints, 270
  of the kidneys, 162
  of the larynx, 116
  of the lens, 365
  of the liver, 90
  of the lungs, 124
  of the mouth, tongue, and salivary glands, 42
  of the nasal cavities, 113
  of the nervous portion of the eye, 370
  of the nervous system, 196
  of the œsophagus, 53
  of the optic nerve, 371
  of the penis and prepuce, 183

Diseases of the peritoneum, 83
    of the pleura, 130
    of the prostate, 181
    of the respiratory organs, 101
    of the retina, 371
    of the salivary glands, 49
    of the sclerotic coat of the eye, 358
    of the sclerotic membrane, 370
    of the sexual apparatus, 152
    of the skin, 384
    of the spinal cord and its coverings, 209
    of the stomach, 55
    of the teeth, 45
    of the testicle and its covering, 184
    of the urinary apparatus, 152
    of the vagina and the uterus, 185
    of the vitreous humor, 370
    of true infection, 223
Disinfection of wounds, 311
Dislocation of the elbow, 284
    of the lower jaw, 283
    of the patella, 285
Dislocations, 281
Distemper, 223
    bench-show, 235
    conjunctivitis in, 236
    false, 235
Distention of bowels with gas, 88
Distortions of the joints, 281
Disturbance of consciousness, 196
    of digestion, effect of, on gastric secretion, 35
    of motility, 197
    of sensitiveness, 196
Diuretics in dropsy, 89
Dochmius, 81
    duodenalis, 82
    stenocephalus, 82
    trigonocephalus, 82
Dog flea, 396
    lice, 397
    passing the catheter in the, 152
    parasites, 397
Dropsy, abdominal, 86
    of the anterior chamber, 371
Duodenum, catarrh of, 91
Dura mater, inflammation of, 206
Dyspepsia, 55
    chronic, 57
Dyspnœa, 107

EAR, diseases of, 375
    inflammation of external, 378
    parasitic canker, 381
Echinococcus polymorphus, 79

Eclampsia, 220
Ectropion, 352
Eczema, 387
    moist, 391
    parasitic, 396, 400, 402
Elbow, dislocation of, 284
Emasculating bot-fly, 185
Emphysema, 22
    of the lungs, 121, 129
Enchondroma, 333
Enteritis catarrhalis, 59
Enterotomy, 70
Entropion, 350
    operation for, 351
Enucleation, 370
Epilepsy, 214
Epistaxis, 214
Epithelial tumors, 335
Epithelium in the urine, 158
Erythema, 386
Ether, 348
Examination of the bladder, 155
    of the digestive apparatus, 27
    of the mouth and throat, 27
    of the nervous system, 196
    of the nose, 101
    of the œsophagus, 30
    of the prepuce and urethra, 152
    of the prostate, 154
    of the stomach, 31
    of the urinary apparatus, 152
    of the urine, 155
    physical, of the lungs, 103
Exarticulation, 300
Exophthalmus, 372
External canker, 377
Extravasation cysts, 341
Eyeball, prolapse of, 372
Eyes, diseases of the, 350
Eyelids, 350
    affections of, 350
    blennorrhœa of, 355
    closure of, 350
    inversion of, 350
    turning in of, 350
    turning out of, 352
Eye, dropsy of the anterior chamber, 371
    enucleation of, 369
    inflammatory processes of, 366
    opening the capsule of, 367
    purulent inflammation of, 370

FALLING out of the hair, 407
    False distemper, 235
Fat in urine, 158
Fatty deposits in the abdomen, 88

Fatty liver, 97
    tumors, 333
Favus, 405
Feces, 38
Femoral hernia, 331
Fever, 308
    aseptic wound, 309
    puerperal, 189
    purulent, 310
    septic wound, 309
Fibroma, hard, 333
    soft, 333
Filaria, 405
    immittis, 149
    in the blood, 149
Filix mas, 80
First intention, healing by, 304
Fistula, intestinal, 323
Flat condyloma, 336
Flea, dog, 396
Follicular mange, 402
    ophthalmia, 354
Forceps, 46
Foreign bodies in the œsophagus, 53
    substances in the urine, 158
Fractures, general classification of, 292
    of the bones, 291
    union of, 293
Freezing, 393

GALLSTONES, 97
Gangrene of the skin, 394
Gas in bowels, 88
Gastricismus, 55
Gastric secretion, disturbance of, 35
Gastritis catarrhalis, 55
Gastro-hysterotomy, 192
General classification of fractures, 292
    examination, 17
Gestation, 88
Glandular cysts, 341
Glands, cancer of, 342
    Lieberkühn's, 79
Glaucoma, 371
Goitre, 338
Gonorrhœa, 183
    of the prepuce, 183
    specific, 184

HÆMATOZOON subulatum, 151
Hair-follicles, inflammation of, 394
Hair, falling out of, 407
Hard fibroma, 333

Harvest bug, 399
Head, cold in, 113
Healing by first intention, 304
    by suppuration, 305
    process of a wound, 304
    under a moist scab, 305
Hebra's potash-soap, 391
Hæmatoma, 375
Hæmatopinus piliferus, 397
Hæmoglobinæmia, 264
Hæmoglobinuria, 264
Helminthiasis, 74
Hemorrhage, 302
    cerebral, 204
    controlling of, 313
Hemorrhoids, 63
Hepar adiposum, 97
Hepatitis, 95
    acute parenchymatous, 95
    interstitial, 95
Hepatogenous icterus, 91
Hernia, 320
    cruralis, 331
    femoral, 331
    inguinal, 327
        in the bitch, 329
    irreducible, 322
    perineal, 331
    reducible, 321
    scrotal, 327
    umbilical, 330
Herniotomy, 325
Herpes tonsurans, 406
Hobday apparatus, 348
Honey cysts, 51
"Honey-pouch" cyst, 341
Hydrobilirubin, 93
Hydrocarbonaceous food, digestion of, 35
Hydrocele, 329
Hydrocyanic-acid poisoning, 98
Hydronephrosis, 169
Hydrophobia, 237
Hydrops abdominalis, 86
    ascites, 86
    peritonii, 86
Hyperæmia of the brain, 202
    of the liver, 94
Hyperæsthesia, 197

ICTERUS catarrhalis, 90
    gastro-duodenalis, 90
    hepatogenous, 91
    of reabsorption, 91
    stagnating, 91
Imperforate anus, 74
Induration, chronic, of the lungs, 126

414 INDEX.

Infectious bronchial catarrh, 235
Inflammatory conditions of the cutaneous membrane, 384
Inguinal hernia, 327
   in the bitch, 329
Inflammation, mycotic, of the stomach and intestines, 64
  of the brain, 206, 207
  of the brain-mass, 207
  of the cerebral matter, 206
  of the cerebral membranes, 206
  of the conjunctiva, 353
  of the dura mater, 206
  of the external ear, 378
  of the hair-follicles, 394
  of the iris, 370
  of the joints, 270
    purulent, 273
    rheumatic, 274
  of the kidneys, 162
  of the liver, 95
  of the lungs, 124
  of the lymphatics, 308
  of the mammary gland, 343
  of the mucous membranes of the mouth, 42
  of the mucous membranes of the throat, 51
  of the pelvis of the kidney, 169
  of the peritoneum, 83
  of the pleura, 130
  of the prostate, 181
  of the salivary glands, 49
  of the sclerotic coat, 358
  of the spinal cord, 210
  of the testicle, 184
  of the uterus, 188
  of the vagina, 185
  of the walls of the bloodvessels, 308
  purulent, of the liver, 96
  toxic, of the stomach and intestines, 64
Inflammatory processes of the eye, 366
Injuries of the cornea, 364
  of the joints, 278
  to the testicles and scrotum, 184
Inoculation, Pasteur's method, 240
Internal canker, 378
  parasites, 74
Interstitial hepatitis, 95
  nephritis, chronic, 165
Intestinal fistula, 323
  catarrh, 59
Intestines, contraction of, 66
  diseases of, 59
  mycotic inflammation of, 64

Intestines, obstruction of, 68
  stenosis of, 66
  toxic inflammation of, 64
Inversion of the eyelid, 350
Iodoform-poisoning, 99
Iris, inflammation of, 370
Iritis, 370
Irreducible hernia, 322
Irritable cough, chronic, 118
Ixodes ricinus, 398

JAUNDICE, catarrhal, 90
  Jaw, dislocation of, 283
Joints, acute synovial inflammation of, 272
  chronic serous inflammation, 273
  contusions of, 280
  distortions of, 281
  diseases of, 270
  inflammation of, 270
  injuries of, 278
  luxations of, 281
  malformation of, 275
  puncturing of, 277
  purulent inflammation of, 273
  rheumatic inflammation of, 274
  suppuration of, 273
  wounds of, 278

KAMALA, 80
  Kennel distemper, 235
Keratitis, 358
  parenchymatosa, 359
  profunda, 359
  superficialis, 359
Kidneys, abscess of, 167
  acute inflammation of, 162
  amyloid, 166
  chronic inflammation of, 165
  cysts of, 169
  diseases of, 162
  inflammation of, 162
    of the pelvis, 169
Kusso, 80

LARDACEOUS liver, 97
  Laryngeal catarrh, acute, 116
Laryngitis, acute, 116
  chronic, 118
Laryngoscope, 28
Larynx, chronic catarrh of, 118
  diseases of, 116
  physical examination of, 102
Leptomeningitis, 216
Leptus autumnalis, 399

INDEX. 415

Leukæmia, 257
Lice, dog, 397
Lieberkühn's glands, 79
Ligation of tumors, 345
Linear extraction of the crystalline lens, 368
Linguatula tænoïdes, 114
Lipoma, 333
Lithiasis, 176
Liver, abscess of, 96
  amyloid, 97
  cirrhosis of, 95
  congestive hyperæmia of, 94
  diseases of, 90
  fatty, 97
  hyperæmia of, 94
  inflammation of, 95
  lardaceous, 97
  neoformations of, 97
  physical examination of, 41
  purulent inflammation of, 96
  stagnating hyperæmia of, 94
Lobular extraction of the crystalline lens, 369
  pneumonia, 124
Local temperature, 26
Lockjaw, 219
Lower jaw, dislocation of, 283
  paralysis of, 200
Lungs, blackening of the, 129
  catarrhal inflammation of, 125
  chronic induration of, 126
  cirrhosis of, 126
  diseases of, 124
  emphysema of, 121, 129
  œdema of, 110, 127
  physical examination of, 103
Lunguatula denticulata, 115
Luxations of the joints, 281
Lymphangitis, 308
Lymphatics, inflammation of, 308

MALE fern, 80
Malformation of the joints, 275
Malformations of the cavity of the mouth, 47
Mammary gland, inflammation of, 343
Mammitis, 343
Mange, follicular, 402
  red, 387
  sarcoptic, 399
Meat-diet, 34
  -digestion, 34
Melanotic sarcoma, 335
Membrana nictitans, removal of, 356
Meningitis, 209

Menstruation of bitch, 154
Mercury-poisoning, 100
Metritis, 188
  catarrhal, 188
  septic, 189
Milk-digestion, 35
Moist eczema, 391
  scab, healing under, 305
Motor symptoms of irritation, 211
  of paralysis, 211
Mouth and throat, examination of, 27
  diseases of, 42
  diseases of the mucous membrane of, 42
  malformations of, 47
  ulcerous inflammation of, 44
Mouth-gag, 28
Mucous membrane of the mouth, diseases of, 42
  membranes of the throat, inflammation of, 51
Mucus in urine, 158
Mumps, 50
Muscular rheumatism, 288
Mycotic inflammation of the stomach and intestines, 64
Myelitis, 210

NASAL catarrh, 113
  cavities, diseases of, 113
Neoformations of the glans penis and prepuce, 184
  of the liver, 97
Nephritic stones, 170
Nephritis, 162
  acute, 162
  chronic, 165
  interstitial, 165
  parenchymatous, 165
  suppurative, 167
Nephrolithiasis, 170
Nervous portion of the eye, diseases of, 370
  system, diseases of, 196
  examination of, 196
Nettlerash, 387
Nose, catarrh of, 113
  examination of, 101
Number and character of the respiratory movements, 106
Nux-vomica poisoning, 100

OBESITY, 262
Obstetrics, 191
Obstruction of the intestines, 68
Odor of urine, 157

Œdema, 22
  of the lungs, 110, 127
Œsophagotomy, 54
Œsophagus, diseases of, 53
  examination of, 30
  foreign bodies in, 53
Opening of the capsule of the eye, 367
Operation for entropion, 351
Ophthalmia, catarrhal, 354
  follicular, 354
  purulent, 355
Optic nerve, diseases of, 371
Orchitis, 184
Osteoma, 334
Othæmatoma, 375
Otitis externa, 378
  parasitic, 381
Ovariotomy, 193
Oxyuris vermicularis, 81

PACHYMENINGITIS, 206
Panophthalmitis, 370
Papilloma, 335
Paralysis, 197, 211
  of the anterior limbs, 200
  of the cruralis, 200
  of the detrusor, 174
  of the lower jaw, 200
  of the posterior limbs, 200
  of the sphincters, 212
  of the sphincter vesicæ, 174
Paraphimosis, 183
Parasites, 74
Parasitic canker of the ear, 381
  eczema, 396, 400, 402
  otitis, 381
Parasite, dog, 397
Parasites, internal, 74
  tapeworm, 75
Parenchymatous hepatitis, 95
  inflammation of the tongue, 43
  nephritis, chronic, 165
Parotitis, 50
Passing the catheter, 152
Pasteur's methods of inoculation, 240
Patella, dislocation of, 285
Pelvis of the kidney, inflammation of, 169
Penis, diseases of, 183
Pentastoma denticulatum, 115
  tænioides, 114
Percussion of the thorax, 109
Perineal hernia, 331
Perinephritic abscesses, 168
Peritoneum, physical examination of, 37

Peritonitis, 83, 88
  acute diffuse, 84
  chronic, 84
  circumscribed, 85
Peritoneum, diseases of, 83
  inflammation of, 83
Pharyngitis, 51
Phimosis, 183
Phlebitis, 308
Phlegmone, 307
Phosphorus-poisoning 99
Phthisis, 126
Physical diagnosis of the larynx and windpipe, 102
  examination, 17
  of the bowel and peritoneum, 37
  of the liver, 41
  of the lungs, 103
  of the respiratory apparatus, 101
Pilocarpine in dropsy, 89
Pleura, diseases of, 130
  inflammation of, 130
Pleurisy, 130
Pleuritis, 130
Pneumonia, 124
  broncho-, 124
  catarrhal, 124
  croupal, 129
  lobular, 124
  traumatic, 127
Poisoning by arsenic, 98
  by carbolic acid, 98
  by hydrocyanic acid, 98
  by iodoform, 99
  by mercury, 100
  by nux vomica, 100
  by phosphorus, 99
  by strychnine, 100
Poisons, 98
Pomegranate, 80
Posterior chamber of the eye, diseases of, 370
  limbs, paralysis of, 200
Potash-soap, Hebra's, 391
Prepuce, diseases of, 183
  examination of, 152
  gonorrhœa of, 183
  neoformations of, 184
Preventive inoculation, 240
Priessnitz's compress, 267
Probang, 30
Proglottides, 76
Prolapse of the eyeball, 372
  of the rectum, 71
  of the uterus, 186
  of the vagina, 186

INDEX.

Prolapsus bulbi, 372
   of rectum, reduction of, 73
   uteri, 186
   vaginæ, 186
Prostate, cancer of, 182
   diseases of, 181
   examination of, 154
   inflammation of, 181
Prostatitis, 181
   chronic, 182
Prurigo, 389
Prussic-acid poisoning, 98
Pseudo-leukæmia, 259
Puerperal fever, 189
Pulex, 396
Puncturing the abdomen, 90
   the joints, 277
Purgatives in dropsy, 89
Purulent conjunctivitis, 355
   fever, 310
   inflammation of the eye, 370
      of the joints, 273
      of the liver, 96
   ophthalmia, 355
Pyæmia, 310
Pyarthrosis, 273
Pyelitis, 169
Pyelonephritis, 167

RABIES, 237
   Rabific symptoms, 82
Ranula, 48
Reabsorption, icterus of, 91
Reaction of urine, 157
Rectum, preternatural, 323
   prolapsus of, 71
   stitching of, 73
Red mange, 387
Reducible hernia, 321
Removal of the membrana nictitans, 356
   of tumors, 346
Respiratory apparatus, physical examination of, 101
   organs, diseases of, 101
   movements, number and character of, 106
Retention cysts, 341
Retina, diseases of, 371
Rhachitis, 268
Rheumatic arthritis, 274
   inflammation of the joints, 274
Rheumatism, 288
Rhinitis, 113
Round worms, 74
Rupture, 320
   of the bladder, 88

SALIVARY glands, inflammation of, 49
Sarcocele, 328
Sarcoma, 334
   melanotic, 335
Sarcoptes scabiei communis, 399
Sarcoptic mange, 399
Sclerotic coat, diseases of, 358
   inflammation of, 358
   membrane, abscess of, 360
      diseases of, 370
      ulceration of, 361
Scrotum, injuries of, 184
Scurvy, 266
Sensitiveness, 211
   disturbance of, 196, 211
Septicæmia, 309
Septic infection of wounds, 305
   metritis, 189
   -wound fever, 309
Serous cyst, 375
   inflammation of the joints, chronic, 273
Sexual apparatus, diseases of, 152
Skin affections caused by animal parasites, 396
   caused by vegetable parasites, 405
   atrophic conditions of, 407
   diseases of, 384
   gangrene of, 394
   inflammatory conditions of, 384
Soft fibroma, 333
Sore-throat, 51
Specific gravity of urine, 157
   gonorrhœa, 184
Speculum, 38
Sphincter vesicæ, paralysis of, 174
Sphincters, paralysis of, 212
Spinal cord, inflammation of, 209
   membranes, inflammation of, 209
   myelitis, 210
Spine, nutritive disorders of, 212
Spiritual blindness, 372
Spiroptera sanguinolenta, 151
Spleen, 42
Sprains, 281
Squamous cancer, 342
Stagnating hyperæmia of the liver, 94
   icterus, 91
Staphyloma, 362
Stenosis of the intestines, 66
Stitches, 314
Stomacace, 44
Stomach, acute catarrh of, 55
   chronic catarrh of the, 57
   diseases of, 55
   examination of, 31

Stomach, mycotic inflammation of, 64
  -pump, 33
  toxic inflammation of, 64
  ulceration of, 58
Stomatitis, 42
Stone in the bladder, 176
Stones, nephritic, 170
Strongylus vasorum, 151
Struma, 338
Strychnine-poisoning, 100
St. Vitus's dance, 217
Sugar in urine, 161
Suppuration, healing by, 305
  of the joints, 273
Suppurative nephritis, 167
Syndesmitis, 353
Synovitis acuta serosa, 272
  chronica serosa, 273
Synovial inflammation of the joints, 272

TÆNIA, 74
  cœnurus, 78
  cucumerina, 78, 79
  echinococcus, 79, 80, 81
  marginata, 77
  serrata, 77, 80
Tæniafuge, preparation for, 81
Tæniafuges, 80
Tail, amputation of, 300
Tapeworms, 75
  natural history, 75
Tapping the abdomen, 90
Taxis, 325
Teeth, diseases of, 45
Temperature, 23
  -chart, 24
  increased, 23
  subnormal, 25
Testicles, diseases of, 184
  inflammation of, 184
  injuries of, 184
Tetanus, 219
Therapeutics of tumors, 344
Thermometer, 23
Thorax, auscultation of, 110
  dimensions of, 106
  percussion of, 109
Throat, inflammation of the mucous membranes, 51
Tobacco-bag stitch, 73
Tongue, diseases of, 43
  parenchymatous inflammation of, 43
Tooth-forceps, 46
Toxic inflammation of the stomach and intestines, 64
Trachea, physical examination of, 102

Transparency of urine, 157
Traumatic pneumonia, 127
Treatment of wounds, 301, 311
Trichocephalus, 82
Trichodectes latus canis, 397
True infection, diseases of, 223
Tumors, 333
  cancerous, 342
  cartilaginous, 333
  cauterization of, 345
  cutaneous, 341
  cylindrical cell, 342
  epithelial, 335
  fatty, 333
  ligation of, 345
  of the abdominal cavity, 89
  of the anal glands, 337
  of the bones, 334
  of the connective tissue, 333
  removal of, 346
  therapeutics of, 344
Turning in of the eyelid, 350
  out of the eyelid, 352

UMBILICAL hernia, 330
  Ulceration, 316
    of the sclerotic membrane, 361
    of the stomach, 58
Ulcers and ulceration, 316
Ulcerous inflammation of the mouth, 44
Ulcus ventriculi, 58
Union of fractured bones, 295
  of fractures, 293
Uræmia, 265
Urethra, examination of, 152
Uric calculi, 177
Urinary apparatus, examination of, 152
  diseases of, 152
Urine, albumin in, 160
  amount of, 156
  bacteria in, 159
  bile-coloring in, 161
  blood-corpuscles in, 158
  color of, 156
  epithelium in, 158
  examination of, 155
  fat in, 158
  foreign substances in, 158
  in the abdominal cavity, 88
  in the bladder, 88
  mucus in, 158
  odor of, 157
  reaction of, 157
  specific gravity of, 157

Urine, sugar in, 161
   transparency of, 157
Urethrotomy, 179
Urticaria, 387
Uterus, diseases of, 185
   inflammation of, 188
   prolapse of, 186

VAGINA, diseases of, 185
   inflammation of, 185

Vagina, prolapse of, 186
Vaginitis, 185
Vegetable parasites, cutaneous affections caused by, 405
Vermicularis, oxyuris, 81
Vitreous humor, diseases of, 370
Vomiting, 34, 36, 85

YELLOW mucous membranes, 92

www.ingramcontent.com/pod-product-compliance
Lightning Source LLC
Chambersburg PA
CBHW030547300426
44111CB00009B/888